African Americans in Sports

Volume 1

African Americans in Sports

Volume 1

Edited by David K. Wiggins

SHARPE REFERENCE
an imprint of M.E. Sharpe, Inc.

SHARPE REFERENCE

Sharpe Reference is an imprint of M.E. Sharpe INC.

M.E. Sharpe INC.
80 Business Park Drive
Armonk, NY 10504

© 2004 by M.E. Sharpe INC.

All rights reserved.

No part of this publication may be reproduced, stored in a retrieval system or transmitted in any form or by any means, electronic, mechanical, photocopying, recording, or otherwise, without the prior permission of the copyright holders.

Library of Congress Cataloging-in-Publication Data

African Americans in sports / David K. Wiggins, editor.
    p. cm.
    Includes bibliographical references and index.
    ISBN 0-7656-8055-6 (set : alk. paper)
      1. African Americans—Sports—Dictionaries. 2. African American athletes—Biography—Dictionaries. 3. African Americans—Societies, etc.—Dictionaries. 4. Sports—United States—Societies, etc.—Dictionaries. I. Wiggins, David Kenneth, 1951– II. Sharpe Reference (Firm)

GV583.A567 2003
796'.092'2—dc21
[B]

2002042799

Cover photo credits: Satchell Paige, David Robinson, and Serena Williams provided by AP/Wide World Photos; male runner (© ArtToday, Inc.); boxer (© Corbis Images/Picturequest)

Printed and bound in the United States of America

The paper used in this publication meets the minimum requirements of American National Standard for Information Sciences--Permanence of Paper for Printed Library Materials, ANSI Z 39.48.1984.

MV (c) 10 9 8 7 6 5 4 3 2 1

CONTENTS

VOLUME 1

Topic Finder xiii
Acknowledgments xxi
Contributors xxiii
Introduction xxvii
Hank Aaron 1
Cleveland Abbott 2
Kareem Abdul-Jabbar 3
Lucinda Adams 4
Herb Adderley 5
Agents 6
David Albritton 7
Muhammad Ali 8
Marcus Allen 9
American Tennis Association 10
Nate Archibald 11
Henry Armstrong 11
Arthur Ashe, Jr. 12
Emmett Ashford 13
Evelyn Ashford 15
Autobiographies 15
Ernie Banks 19
Charles Barkley 19
Don Barksdale 20
Baseball 21
Basketball 23
Dick Bass 26
Don Baylor 27
Elgin Baylor 28
Bob Beamon 28
Bill Bell 29
Bobby Bell 30

James "Cool Papa" Bell 31
Walter Bellamy 32
Dave Bing 33
Black Coaches Association 33
Black Sports Magazine 35
Black Women in Sports Foundation 35
Black World Championship Rodeo 36
Mel Blount 36
Edward Bolden 37
Barry Bonds 38
Bob Boozer 39
John Borican 40
Joseph Bostic 41
Ralph Boston 41
Bowling 42
Boxing 43
Valerie Brisco-Hooks 46
Louis Brock 48
Vivian Brown Reed 49
Jim Brown 49
Larry Brown 50
Roger Brown 51
Roosevelt Brown 52
Kobe Bryant 52
Matthew Bullock 53
Daniel Burley 54
Sol Butler 55
Lee Calhoun 57
Roy Campanella 57
Earl Campbell 58
Milt Campbell 59
John Carlos 60
Harold Carmichael 61

★ v ★

CONTENTS

J.C. Caroline 61
Cris Carter 62
Central Intercollegiate Athletic
  Association 63
Wilt Chamberlain 64
John Chaney 65
Ezzard Charles 66
Oscar Charleston 67
Civil Rights 67
Nat "Sweetwater" Clifton 71
Coaches and Managers 71
Alice Coachman 72
William Montague Cobb 74
Chuck Cooper 75
Ted Corbitt 75
Russ Cowans 76
Isabelle Daniels 77
Adrian Dantley 77
Ernie Davis 78
John Henry Davis 79
Dominique Dawes 80
Anita De Frantz 81
Gail Devers 82
Eric Dickerson 83
Harrison Dillard 84
George Dixon 85
Larry Doby 86
Arthur Dorrington 87
Charles Drew 87
Howard Drew 88
Walter Dukes 89
Eastern Colored League 91
Harry Edwards 91
Teresa Edwards 92
Lee Elder 93
Carl Eller 94
Jimmy Ellis 95

Wayne Embry 95
Julius Erving 96
Lee Evans 97
Patrick Ewing 97
Mae Faggs 99
Fencing 99
Films 100
George Flippin 102
Curt Flood 103
Tiger Flowers 104
Charles Follis 105
Football 105
Phil Ford 108
George Foreman 109
Bob Foster 110
Rube Foster 110
Joe Frazier 112
Walter Frazier, Jr. 112
Clarence Gaines 115
Jake Gaither 115
Willie Galimore 116
Joe Gans 117
Mike Garrett 117
Zina Garrison 118
Willie Gault 119
George Gervin 119
Althea Gibson 120
Bob Gibson 121
Josh Gibson 122
Artis Gilmore 122
Golf 123
Ed Gordon, Jr. 125
Ned Gourdin 126
Frank Grant 127
Edward Gray 127
Joe Greene 128
Gus Greenlee 129

Hal Greer	130
Ann Gregory	130
George Gregory, Jr.	131
Rosey Grier	132
Ken Griffey, Jr.	132
Florence Griffith-Joyner	133
Tony Gwynn	134
Gymnastics	134
Marvin Hagler	137
Harlem Globetrotters	137
Franco Harris	139
Frank Hart	139
Connie Hawkins	140
Bob Hayes	141
Elvin Hayes	142
Marques Haynes	142
Spencer Haywood	143
Thomas Hearns	144
Edwin Bancroft Henderson	145
Rickey Henderson	146
Stephanie Hightower	146
Calvin Hill	147
Grant Hill	148
Jim Hines	149
Historically Black Colleges and Universities	149
Historiography	153
Jerome Brud Holland	157
Steve Holman	157
Larry Holmes	158
Horse Racing	159
William Dehart Hubbard	161
Martha Hudson	161
Eddie Hurt	162
Lula Mae Hymes	162
Ice Hockey	165
International Afro-American Sports Hall of Fame and Gallery	167
International League of Baseball Clubs in America and Cuba	167
Interscholastic Athletic Association of Middle Atlantic States	168
Monte Irvin	169
"Rajo" Jack	171
Bo Jackson	171
Levi Jackson	172
Mannie Jackson	173
Peter Jackson	173
Reggie Jackson	175
Joe Jeannette	176
Bernie Jefferson	176
Cornelius Johnson	177
Jack Johnson	178
John Henry Johnson	179
Magic Johnson	180
Michael Johnson	181
Rafer Johnson	182
Robert L. Johnson	183
William "Judy" Johnson	184
Barbara Jones	185
David "Deacon" Jones	186
Hayes Jones	186
K.C. Jones	187
Marion Jones	188
Sam Jones	188
Wali Jones	189
Michael Jordan	190
Jackie Joyner-Kersee	191
Leroy Kelly	195
Ray Kemp	195
Leroy Keyes	196
Don King	196
William "Dolly" King	197
Lacrosse	199
Sam Lacy	199

CONTENTS

Betty Jean Lane 200
Dick Lane 201
Sam Langford 201
Bob Lanier 202
League of Colored Base Ball Clubs 203
Meadowlark Lemon 203
Buck Leonard 205
Sugar Ray Leonard 206
Lisa Leslie 207
Jerry LeVias 208
Carl Lewis 209
John Henry Lewis 210
Oliver Lewis 211
William Henry Lewis 211
Joe Lillard 212
Gene "Big Daddy" Lipscomb 213
Sonny Liston 213
Floyd Little 214
Earl Lloyd 214
John Henry Lloyd 215
Ronnie Lott 216
Joe Louis 217
James LuValle 218

VOLUME 2

Topic Finder xiii
Acknowledgments xxi
Contributors xxiii
Introduction xxvii
Biz Mackey 219
John Mackey 220
Karl Malone 221
Moses Malone 222
Effa Manley 223
Danny Manning 224
Madeline Manning-Mims 224
Bob Marshall 225
Jim Marshall 226

Ollie Matson 227
Margaret Matthews 227
William Clarence Matthews 228
Willie Mays 229
Willie McCovey 230
Mildred McDaniel 231
Pam McGee 231
Edith McGuire 232
John McLendon 233
Sam McVey 234
Ralph Metcalfe 235
Rod Milburn 235
Cheryl Miller 236
Bobby Mitchell 237
Tom Molineaux 237
Art Monk 238
Earl Monroe 239
Eleanor Montgomery 240
Warren Moon 240
Archie Moore 241
Lenny Moore 242
Joe Morgan 243
Edwin Moses 244
Marion Motley 245
Calvin Murphy 246
Isaac Murphy 247
Eddie Murray 248
National Association of Colored
    Base Ball Clubs of the United
    States and Cuba 251
National Bowling Association 252
Negro American League 252
Negro League Baseball Museum 253
Negro National League 254
Negro Southern League 255
Renaldo Nehemiah 256
New York Pioneer Club 256
New York Renaissance Five 257

Entry	Page
Don Newcombe	258
Ozzie Newsome	259
Ken Norton	260
William Nunn, Jr.	260
William Nunn, Sr.	261
Dan O'Brien	263
Hakeem Olajuwon	263
Olympic Games	264
Shaquille O'Neal	268
Buck O'Neil	269
Willie O'Ree	270
Jesse Owens	271
R.C. Owens	272
Satchel Paige	275
Jim Parker	276
Floyd Patterson	276
Mickey Patterson	277
Walter Payton	278
Drew Pearson	279
Calvin Peete	280
Don Perkins	281
Joe Perry	282
Tidye Pickett	282
George Poage	283
Fritz Pollard	283
Fritz Pollard, Jr.	284
Cum Posey	285
Kirby Puckett	286
Pythian Base Ball Club (Philadelphia)	287
Racial Theories	289
Ted Radcliffe	292
Rainbow Coalition for Fairness in Athletics	293
Ahmad Rashad	293
George Raveling	295
Dwight Reed	296
Willis Reed	297
Mel Renfro	297
Butch Reynolds	298
Ray Rhodes	298
Ted Rhodes	299
Willy T. Ribbs	300
Jerry Rice	301
Nolan Richardson	301
Bill Richmond	302
Ric Roberts	303
Oscar Robertson	303
Paul Robeson	305
David Robinson	306
Eddie Robinson	307
Frank Robinson	308
Jackie Robinson	309
Mack Robinson	310
Sugar Ray Robinson	311
Rodeo	312
Johnny Rodgers	313
Wilbur Rogan	315
George Rogers	315
Mike Rozier	316
Wilma Rudolph	317
Bill Russell	318
Cazzie Russell	319
Ralph Sampson	321
Barry Sanders	321
Deion Sanders	322
Gale Sayers	323
Charlie Scott	324
Wendell Scott	324
Shady Rest Golf and Country Club	325
Art Shell	326
John Shippen, Jr.	327
Wilmeth Sidat-Singh	327
Charlie Sifford	328
Paul Silas	329
Ozzie Simmons	330

CONTENTS

Willie Simms 330
O.J. Simpson 331
Mike Singletary 332
"Duke" Slater 332
Slavery 333
Lucy Diggs Slowe 334
Bruce Smith 335
"Bubba" Smith 336
Emmitt Smith 337
John Smith 338
Ozzie Smith 339
Tommie Smith 340
Wendell Smith 341
Fred Snowden 341
Bill Spiller 342
Leon Spinks 343
Michael Spinks 343
Sportswriters 344
Dave Stallworth 346
Willie Stargell 346
Norman "Turkey" Stearnes 347
Louise Stokes 348
Toni Stone 348
George Stovey 349
Vivian Stringer 350
Woody Strode 351
Lynn Swann 352
Swimming 353
Sheryl Swoopes 354
George Taliaferro 357
Jack Tatum 357
Reece "Goose" Tatum 358
Charley Taylor 359
John Baxter Taylor 359
Lawrence Taylor 360
Marshall "Major" Taylor 361
Ed Temple 362
Tennis 363

Debra Thomas 364
Frank Thomas 365
Isiah Thomas 366
John Thomas 367
David Thompson 367
John Thompson 368
Eddie Tolan 369
Gwen Torrence 370
Track and Field 371
Emlen Tunnell 374
Mike Tyson 374
Wyomia Tyus 375
United Golfers Association 377
Wes Unseld 378
Gene Upshaw 378
Volleyball 381
Wake-Robin Golf Club 383
Joe Walcott 383
Herschel Walker 384
Leroy Walker 385
Mel Walker 386
Moses Fleetwood Walker 386
Charlie Ward 387
Paul Warfield 388
Chester Washington 389
Gene Washington 389
Kenny Washington 390
Ora Washington 391
Quincy Watts 391
Weightlifting and Bodybuilding 392
Reginald Weir 394
Willie Wells 395
Charlie West 396
Howard Wheeler 397
Bill White 397
Jo Jo White 398
Reggie White 399

Sherman White	400
Sol White	400
Willye White	401
Mal Whitfield	402
Sydney Wicks	403
Archie Williams	403
Doug Williams	404
Ike Williams	404
Joseph "Smokey" Williams	405
Serena Williams	406
Venus Williams	407
Bill Willis	407
Harry Wills	408
Maury Wills	409
Rollo Wilson	410
Dave Winfield	410
Jimmy Winkfield	411
Kellen Winslow	412
Women	413
Lynette Woodard	415
John Woodruff	416
Eldrick "Tiger" Woods	416
James Worthy	418
Wrestling	418
Andrew S. "Doc" Young	421
Buddy Young	421
Fay Young	422
Paul "Tank" Younger	423
Chronology	425
Bibliography	431
General Index	I-1
Sports Index	I-21

TOPIC FINDER

INDIVIDUALS

Hank Aaron 1
Cleveland Abbott 2
Kareem Abdul-Jabbar 3
Lucinda Adams 4
Herb Adderley 5
David Albritton 7
Muhammad Ali 8
Marcus Allen 9
Nate Archibald 11
Henry Armstrong 11
Arthur Ashe, Jr. 12
Emmett Ashford 13
Evelyn Ashford 15
Ernie Banks 19
Charles Barkley 19
Don Barksdale 20
Dick Bass 26
Don Baylor 27
Elgin Baylor 28
Bob Beamon 28
Bill Bell 29
Bobby Bell 30
James "Cool Papa" Bell 31
Walter Bellamy 32
Dave Bing 33
Mel Blount 36
Edward Bolden 37
Barry Bonds 38
Bob Boozer 39
John Borican 40
Joseph Bostic 41

Ralph Boston 41
Valerie Brisco-Hooks 46
Louis Brock 48
Vivian Brown Reed 49
Jim Brown 49
Larry Brown 50
Roger Brown 51
Roosevelt Brown 52
Kobe Bryant 52
Matthew Bullock 53
Daniel Burley 54
Sol Butler 55
Lee Calhoun 57
Roy Campanella 57
Earl Campbell 58
Milt Campbell 59
John Carlos 60
Harold Carmichael 61
J.C. Caroline 61
Cris Carter 62
Wilt Chamberlain 64
John Chaney 65
Ezzard Charles 66
Oscar Charleston 67
Nat "Sweetwater" Clifton 71
Alice Coachman 72
William Montague Cobb 74
Chuck Cooper 75
Ted Corbitt 75
Russ Cowans 76
Isabelle Daniels 77
Adrian Dantley 77

TOPIC FINDER

Ernie Davis	78
John Henry Davis	79
Dominique Dawes	80
Anita De Frantz	81
Gail Devers	82
Eric Dickerson	83
Harrison Dillard	84
George Dixon	85
Larry Doby	86
Arthur Dorrington	87
Charles Drew	87
Howard Drew	88
Walter Dukes	89
Harry Edwards	91
Teresa Edwards	92
Lee Elder	93
Carl Eller	94
Jimmy Ellis	95
Wayne Embry	95
Julius Erving	96
Lee Evans	97
Patrick Ewing	97
Mae Faggs	99
George Flippin	102
Curt Flood	103
Tiger Flowers	104
Charles Follis	105
Phil Ford	108
George Foreman	109
Bob Foster	110
Rube Foster	110
Joe Frazier	112
Walter Frazier, Jr.	112
Clarence Gaines	115
Jake Gaither	115
Willie Galimore	116
Joe Gans	117
Mike Garrett	117
Zina Garrison	118
Willie Gault	119
George Gervin	119
Althea Gibson	120
Bob Gibson	121
Josh Gibson	122
Artis Gilmore	122
Ed Gordon, Jr.	125
Ned Gourdin	126
Frank Grant	127
Edward Gray	127
Joe Greene	128
Gus Greenlee	129
Hal Greer	130
Ann Gregory	130
George Gregory, Jr.	131
Rosey Grier	132
Ken Griffey, Jr.	132
Florence Griffith-Joyner	133
Tony Gwynn	134
Marvin Hagler	137
Franco Harris	139
Frank Hart	139
Connie Hawkins	140
Bob Hayes	141
Elvin Hayes	142
Marques Haynes	142
Spencer Haywood	143
Thomas Hearns	144
Edwin Bancroft Henderson	145
Rickey Henderson	146
Stephanie Hightower	146
Calvin Hill	147
Grant Hill	148
Jim Hines	149
Jerome Brud Holland	157

TOPIC FINDER

Steve Holman 157	Sam Lacy 199
Larry Holmes 158	Betty Jean Lane 200
William Dehart Hubbard 161	Dick Lane 201
Martha Hudson 161	Sam Langford 201
Eddie Hurt 162	Bob Lanier 202
Lula Mae Hymes 162	Meadowlark Lemon 203
Monte Irvin 169	Buck Leonard 205
"Rajo" Jack 171	Sugar Ray Leonard 206
Bo Jackson 171	Lisa Leslie 207
Levi Jackson 172	Jerry LeVias 208
Mannie Jackson 173	Carl Lewis 209
Peter Jackson 173	John Henry Lewis 210
Reggie Jackson 175	Oliver Lewis 211
Joe Jeannette 176	William Henry Lewis 211
Bernie Jefferson 176	Joe Lillard 212
Cornelius Johnson 177	Gene "Big Daddy" Lipscomb 213
Jack Johnson 178	Sonny Liston 213
John Henry Johnson 179	Floyd Little 214
Magic Johnson 180	Earl Lloyd 214
Michael Johnson 181	John Henry Lloyd 215
Rafer Johnson 182	Ronnie Lott 216
Robert L. Johnson 183	Joe Louis 217
William "Judy" Johnson 184	James LuValle 218
Barbara Jones 185	Biz Mackey 219
David "Deacon" Jones 186	John Mackey 220
Hayes Jones 186	Karl Malone 221
K.C. Jones 187	Moses Malone 222
Marion Jones 188	Effa Manley 223
Sam Jones 188	Danny Manning 224
Wali Jones 189	Madeline Manning-Mims 224
Michael Jordan 190	Bob Marshall 225
Jackie Joyner-Kersee 191	Jim Marshall 226
Leroy Kelly 195	Ollie Matson 227
Ray Kemp 195	Margaret Matthews 227
Leroy Keyes 196	William Clarence Matthews 228
Don King 196	Willie Mays 229
William "Dolly" King 197	Willie McCovey 230

TOPIC FINDER

Mildred McDaniel 231	Mickey Patterson 277
Pam McGee 231	Walter Payton 278
Edith McGuire 232	Drew Pearson 279
John McLendon 233	Calvin Peete 280
Sam McVey 234	Don Perkins 281
Ralph Metcalfe 235	Joe Perry 282
Rod Milburn 235	Tidye Pickett 282
Cheryl Miller 236	George Poage 283
Bobby Mitchell 237	Fritz Pollard 283
Tom Molineaux 237	Fritz Pollard, Jr. 284
Art Monk 238	Cum Posey 285
Earl Monroe 239	Kirby Puckett 286
Eleanor Montgomery 240	Ted Radcliffe 292
Warren Moon 240	Ahmad Rashad 293
Archie Moore 241	George Raveling 295
Lenny Moore 242	Dwight Reed 296
Joe Morgan 243	Willis Reed 297
Edwin Moses 244	Mel Renfro 297
Marion Motley 245	Butch Reynolds 298
Calvin Murphy 246	Ray Rhodes 298
Isaac Murphy 247	Ted Rhodes 299
Eddie Murray 248	Willy T. Ribbs 300
Renaldo Nehemiah 256	Jerry Rice 301
Don Newcombe 258	Nolan Richardson 301
Ozzie Newsome 259	Bill Richmond 302
Ken Norton 260	Ric Roberts 303
William Nunn, Jr. 260	Oscar Robertson 303
William Nunn, Sr. 261	Paul Robeson 305
Dan O'Brien 263	David Robinson 306
Hakeem Olajuwon 263	Eddie Robinson 307
Shaquille O'Neal 268	Frank Robinson 308
Buck O'Neil 269	Jackie Robinson 309
Willie O'Ree 270	Mack Robinson 310
Jesse Owens 271	Sugar Ray Robinson 311
R.C. Owens 272	Johnny Rodgers 313
Satchel Paige 275	Wilbur Rogan 315
Jim Parker 276	George Rogers 315
Floyd Patterson 276	Mike Rozier 316

TOPIC FINDER

Wilma Rudolph 317
Bill Russell 318
Cazzie Russell 319
Ralph Sampson 321
Barry Sanders 321
Deion Sanders 322
Gale Sayers 323
Charlie Scott 324
Wendell Scott 324
Art Shell 326
John Shippen, Jr. 327
Wilmeth Sidat-Singh 327
Charlie Sifford 328
Paul Silas 329
Ozzie Simmons 330
Willie Simms 330
O.J. Simpson 331
Mike Singletary 332
"Duke" Slater 332
Lucy Diggs Slowe 334
Bruce Smith 335
"Bubba" Smith 336
Emmitt Smith 337
John Smith 338
Ozzie Smith 339
Tommie Smith 340
Wendell Smith 341
Fred Snowden 341
Bill Spiller 342
Leon Spinks 343
Michael Spinks 343
Dave Stallworth 346
Willie Stargell 346
Norman "Turkey" Stearnes 347
Louise Stokes 348
Toni Stone 348
George Stovey 349

Vivian Stringer 350
Woody Strode 351
Lynn Swann 352
Sheryl Swoopes 354
George Taliaferro 357
Jack Tatum 357
Reece "Goose" Tatum 358
Charley Taylor 359
John Baxter Taylor 359
Lawrence Taylor 360
Marshall "Major" Taylor 361
Ed Temple 362
Debra Thomas 364
Frank Thomas 365
Isiah Thomas 366
John Thomas 367
David Thompson 367
John Thompson 368
Eddie Tolan 369
Gwen Torrence 370
Emlen Tunnell 374
Mike Tyson 374
Wyomia Tyus 375
Wes Unseld 378
Gene Upshaw 378
Joe Walcott 383
Herschel Walker 384
Leroy Walker 385
Mel Walker 386
Moses Fleetwood Walker 386
Charlie Ward 387
Paul Warfield 388
Chester Washington 389
Gene Washington 389
Kenny Washington 390
Ora Washington 391
Quincy Watts 391
Reginald Weir 394

Willie Wells 395
Charlie West 396
Howard Wheeler 397
Bill White 397
Jo Jo White 398
Reggie White 399
Sherman White 400
Sol White 400
Willye White 401
Mal Whitfield 402
Sydney Wicks 403
Archie Williams 403
Doug Williams 404
Ike Williams 404
Joseph "Smokey" Williams 405
Serena Williams 406
Venus Williams 407
Bill Willis 407
Harry Wills 408
Maury Wills 409
Rollo Wilson 410
Dave Winfield 410
Jimmy Winkfield 411
Kellen Winslow 412
Lynette Woodard 415
John Woodruff 416
Eldrick "Tiger" Woods 416
James Worthy 418
Andrew S. "Doc" Young 421
Buddy Young 421
Fay Young 422
Paul "Tank" Younger 423

SPORTS

Baseball 21
Basketball 23
Bowling 42
Boxing 43
Fencing 99
Football 105
Golf 123
Gymnastics 134
Horse Racing 159
Ice Hockey 165
Lacrosse 199
Olympic Games 264
Rodeo 312
Swimming 353
Tennis 363
Track and Field 371
Volleyball 381
Weightlifting and Bodybuilding 392
Wrestling 418

TEAMS

Harlem Globetrotters 137
New York Pioneer Club 256
New York Renaissance Five 257
Pythian Base Ball Club
  (Philadelphia) 287

INSTITUTIONS AND ORGANIZATIONS

American Tennis Association 10
Black Coaches Association 33
Black Sports Magazine 35
Black Women in Sports Foundation 35
Black World Championship Rodeo 36
Central Intercollegiate Athletic
  Association 63
Eastern Colored League 91
Historically Black Colleges and
  Universities 149

International Afro-American Sports Hall of Fame and Gallery 167
International League of Baseball Clubs in America and Cuba 167
Interscholastic Athletic Association of Middle Atlantic States 168
League of Colored Base Ball Clubs 203
National Association of Colored Base Ball Clubs of the United States and Cuba 251
National Bowling Association 252
Negro American League 252
Negro League Baseball Museum 253
Negro National League 254
Negro Southern League 255
Rainbow Coalition for Fairness in Athletics 293
Shady Rest Golf and Country Club 325
United Golfers Association 377
Wake-Robin Golf Club 383

KEY PERSONNEL, CULTURAL THEMES, AND SOCIAL ISSUES

Agents 6
Autobiographies 15
Civil Rights 67
Coaches and Managers 71
Films 100
Historiography 153
Racial Theories 289
Slavery 333
Sportswriters 344
Women 413

ACKNOWLEDGMENTS

I would like to express my deepest appreciation to all the contributors for their time, patience, and hard work. Their commitment to this project has been unwavering. Ellen Drogin Rodgers was indispensable during the final days of rewrites and was selfless, as usual. I would also like to thank my wife, Brenda, and two boys, Jordan and Spencer, for their constant support and understanding. Lastly, I would like to thank Lisa Reeves for her editorial assistance. This project could not have been completed without her help and expertise.

EDITOR
David K. Wiggins
George Mason University

CONTRIBUTORS

Donna Abruzzese
George Mason University

Ronald Althouse
West Virginia University

Logan Bailey-Perkins
University of Miami

C. Robert Barnett
Marshall University

Gai Ingham Berlage
Iona College

Jack W. Berryman
University of Washington

Mary Jo Binker
George Mason University

Gregory Bond
University of Wisconsin, Madison

Larry S. Bonura

Ron Briley
Sandia Preparatory School

Dana D. Brooks
West Virginia University

John M. Carroll
Lamar University

Amy M. Cawley
Salem Academy, Winston-Salem

Nicholas P. Ciotola
Senator John Heinz Pittsburgh Regional History Center

James R. Coates, Jr.
University of Wisconsin, Green Bay

Eddie Comeaux
University of California, Los Angeles

Doris R. Corbett
Howard University

Scott A.G.M. Crawford
Eastern Illinois University

Richard O. Davies
University of Nevada, Reno

Robert Davis
Yale University

Gregory H. Duquette
University of Alberta

Sara A. Elliott

Robert Epling
Reinhardt College

John D. Fair
Georgia College & State University

Albert J. Figone
Humboldt State University

John E. Findling
Indiana University Southeast

Rob Fink
McMurry University

Michael T. Friedman
University of Maryland

Alison M. Gavin
George Mason University

Gerald R. Gems
North Central College

Larry R. Gerlach
University of Utah

Steven P. Gietschier
The Sporting News

Dennis Gildea
Springfield College

Gregory S. Goodale
University of Illinois at Urbana-Champaign

Adolph H. Grundman
Metropolitan State College, Denver

Pamela Grundy

Susan Hamburger
Pennsylvania State University

CONTRIBUTORS

C. Keith Harrison
University of Michigan

Clay E. Harshaw
Guilford College

Billy Hawkins
University of Georgia

Leslie A. Heaphy
Kent State University

Debra A. Henderson
Ohio University

Adam R. Hornbuckle

Trisha M. Hothorn

Cecile Houry
University of Miami

David W. Hunter
Hampton University

J. Thomas Jable
William Paterson University

Rick Knott
St. Bonaventure University

Deane A. Lamont
Saint Mary's College

Rita Liberti
California State University, Hayward

Alar Lipping
Northern Kentucky University

Michael E. Lomax
University of Georgia

Richard D. Loosbrock
Adams State College

Stephen R. Lowe
Olivet Nazarene University

Angela Lumpkin
The University of Kansas

Bill Mallon
Duke University

Michael Marsh
Chicago Reader

Daniel S. Mason
University of Alberta

Keith McClellan

Daniel A. Nathan
Skidmore College

Murry R. Nelson
Pennsylvania State University

James E. Odenkirk
Arizona State University

Michael Oriard
Oregon State University

Steven J. Overman
Jackson State University

Troy D. Paino
Winona State University

Clyde Partin
Emory University

Adam Phillips
George Mason University

Robert Pruter
Lewis University

Danny Rosenberg
Brock University

Gary A. Sailes
Indiana University

Tracey M. Salisbury
University of North Carolina at Greensboro

Sue Scaffidi
Lenoir-Rhyne College

John R. Schleppi
University of Dayton

Raymond Schmidt

Kenneth L. Shropshire
University of Pennsylvania

Calvin H. Sinnette

David C. Skinner

Earl Smith
Wake Forest University

Maureen M. Smith
California State University, Sacramento

Donald Spivey
University of Miami

CONTRIBUTORS

Jim L. Sumner
North Carolina Museum of History

Richard A. Swanson
University of North Carolina at Greensboro

John A. Vernon
National Archives and Records Administration

Sara B. Washington
Michigan State University

John S. Watterson
James Madison University

Danielle A. Mincey White
George Mason University

Audrey A. Wiggins
University of North Carolina at Greensboro

Brenda P. Wiggins
George Mason University

Suzanne Wise
Appalachian State University

Jerry J. Wright
Pennsylvania State University at Altoona

Alison M. Wrynn
California State University, Long Beach

Susan G. Zieff
San Francisco State University

INTRODUCTION

African-American athletes have made extraordinary contributions to sport at both the national and international levels of competition. Since the nineteenth century, African-American athletes have achieved enormous success in interscholastic, college, Olympic, and professional sport. Although experiencing racial injustice and discrimination, such athletes as Tom Molineaux, Jack Johnson, Jesse Owens, Satchel Paige, Jackie Robinson, Althea Gibson, Muhammad Ali, Michael Jordan, Eldrick "Tiger" Woods, and Serena Williams have garnered fame and fortune and mesmerized people of all races for their athletic exploits. Perhaps more than anything else, the great performances of African-American athletes have served as examples of achievement and symbols of possibility for the African-American community and helped in the process of assimilation.

Over the last two decades an increasing number of scholars have recounted the story of African-American involvement in sport. These studies have included examinations of such topics as Negro league baseball, the role of sport in historically black universities, involvement of African-American athletes in predominantly white university sport, and biographies of notable African-American athletes and the racial inequities still existing in sport. Although varying in quality, these studies have all combined to provide a more complete picture of the experiences of African-American athletes and how the racial realities of this country have impacted sport at all levels of competition.

Included among these studies are several biographical encyclopedias that furnish good information on the individual accomplishments of some of this country's most famous African-American athletes. Perhaps the best known of these works are David L. Porter's *Biographical Dictionary of American Sports* (1988) and *African-American Sports Greats* (1995). This encyclopedia complements Porter's fine work and that of others by incorporating biographical entries, but it makes advances by also including topical and organizational entries. In addition, this encyclopedia stands apart from other reference works in that it includes large numbers of entries that deal with various aspects of sport behind segregated walls. Readers will find coverage of such notable all-black institutions as the Negro National League as well as such lesser-known parallel sport organizations as the American Tennis Association, the Central Intercollegiate Athletic Association, the National Bowling Association, the United Golfers Association, and the Black Coaches Association. This encyclopedia is unique, moreover, by virtue of the fact that it includes many entries on African-American coaches, managers, executives, entrepreneurs, and sportswriters. Only by including these individuals in the encyclopedia can a full understanding of sport in the African-American community be realized.

This encyclopedia is certainly not exhaustive in scope. The selection of entries was based on judgments about their significance to the African-American experience in sport and potential appeal to both the lay public and academic audience. Those entries that are included are written in a clear and concise fashion by contrib-

INTRODUCTION

utors who have expertise in some aspect of the African-American experience in sport. All of the contributors have either written about or shown a passion for the study of African-American athletes, race relations, or sport history. In each of the more than four hundred entries a great deal of attention is devoted to essential facts and details as well as to historical context and changes over time. Every effort has been made to provide more than a mere recounting of accomplishments and list of records and career statistics. Each entry also includes biographical references to the most important sources on the particular topic. Readers can turn to these sources as they pursue their own studies and seek additional information.

Hank AARON

Born February 5, 1934, Mobile, Alabama
Baseball player

Aaron was one of seven children born to Estelle (Pritchen) and Herbert Aaron, who worked as a rivet bucker for a shipbuilding company. A member of major league baseball's All-Century team, Aaron shattered Babe Ruth's record of 714 home runs, finishing his distinguished career with 755 home runs. After his playing days, Aaron served as a baseball executive and established several successful business enterprises.

Aaron attended Central High School in Mobile and graduated from Josephine Allen Institute in 1951. After playing semi-professional baseball with the Mobile Black Barons, he was signed by the Indianapolis Clowns of the Negro leagues. However, on June 12, 1952, Aaron was purchased by the Milwaukee Braves and dispatched to their Class C farm club in Eau Claire, Wisconsin. In 1953, Aaron was promoted to the Jacksonville, Florida, team in the Class A South Atlantic ("Sally") League. Although he led the league in batting, the African-American player was subjected to racial taunts by many white Jacksonville fans. Aaron started his career as an infielder, but he opened the 1954 baseball season for the Braves in right field, where he would remain a fixture for twenty-one years. In 1956, Aaron led the National League in batting (.328) and was selected as the league's Most Valuable Player in 1957, when the Braves achieved a world championship.

After pennant-winning seasons in 1957 and 1958, the business fortunes of the Braves in Milwaukee declined. Following the 1965 season, the franchise was transferred to Atlanta. Aaron expressed reser-

Hank Aaron, the great outfielder and home run king, posing for the cameras in 1975 following his signing with the Milwaukee Brewers. *(AP/Wide World Photos)*

vations about accompanying the team to the South, but he made a successful transition and continued his assault upon the sport's all-time home run mark. On April 8, 1974, Aaron homered off the Dodgers' Al Downing, surpassing Ruth's record. However, the historic occasion was marred by racist threats and slurs.

Aaron played his final two seasons with the Milwaukee Brewers of the American League, retiring from the game in 1976. Aaron was then hired by the Braves as vice president in charge of player development, building Atlanta's farm system into one of the most productive in baseball. Since 1990, he has served the Braves as senior vice president and assistant to the president.

Aaron has also been involved in lucrative business ventures, working in community relations for Ted Turner's media empire and owning numerous franchise restaurants.

In addition to his home run record, Aaron attained a .305 batting average in twenty-three major league seasons and established the career runs batted in mark of 2,297. In 1982, he was inducted into the National Baseball Hall of Fame. While some criticized him for not being more assertive during his playing days, as a baseball executive Aaron has been a vocal critic of the baseball establishment's hiring practices.

Ron Briley

See also: Autobiographies; Baseball; Willie Mays.

FURTHER READING
Aaron, Hank, with Furman Bisher. *Aaron*. New York: T.Y. Crowell, 1974.
Aaron, Hank, with Lonnie Wheeler. *I Had a Hammer: The Hank Aaron Story*. New York: HarperCollins, 1991.
Hank Aaron file. National Baseball Hall of Fame Museum and Library. Cooperstown, New York.
Capuzzo, Mike. "A Prisoner of Memory." *Sports Illustrated*, March–April 1997, 80–84, 86, 89–92.
Caruso, Gary. *The Braves Encyclopedia*. Philadelphia: Temple University Press, 1995.

Cleveland ABBOTT

Born December 19, 1894, Yankton, South Dakota
Died April 14, 1955, Tuskegee, Alabama
Coach

Abbott, born to Mollie Brown and Everet B. Abbott, grew up in Watertown, South Dakota. A solid academic student, he was also an all-around star athlete in high school. He earned fourteen varsity awards in track, football, baseball, and basketball at South Dakota State College before graduating in 1916.

During his college years, young Abbott was offered a faculty and coaching position by Booker T. Washington, founding president of Tuskegee Institute, to begin following his graduation. Washington died in 1915; Abbott accepted the position as an agricultural chemist and assistant football, basketball, and baseball coach in 1916. After his first year, he entered the U.S. Army and saw action in World War I. He left the military as a major in 1919 and accepted a position as director of physical education and athletics at Kansas Industrial and Educational Institute in Topeka. In 1923 he returned to Tuskegee as director of physical education and athletics; he would remain there until his death in 1955.

Abbott experienced great success as Tuskegee's head coach of football from 1923 through 1945, winning eleven Southern Intercollegiate Athletic Conference (SIAC) titles, seven Black College national championships, enjoying six undefeated seasons and once in the mid-1920s winning forty-six consecutive games. He also instituted women's track and field at the school and contributed a number of athletes to American Olympic teams in the 1930s and 1940s. He is enshrined in the South Dakota State University Athletic Hall of Fame.

Richard A. Swanson

See also: Track and Field.

FURTHER READING
Ashe, Arthur R., Jr. *A Hard Road to Glory: A History of the African-American Athlete*. 3 vols. New York: Amistad, 1993.
Cahn, Susan K. *Coming On Strong: Gender and Sexuality in Twentieth-Century Women's Sport*. New York: Free Press, 1994.
Thaxton, Nolan A. "Tuskegee Institute: Pioneer in Women's Track & Field." *Physical Educator* 29 (May 1972): 77–79.
Welch, Paula. "Tuskegee Institute: Pioneer in Women's Olympic Track and Field." *Delta Psi Kappa Foil* (Spring 1988): 10–13.

Kareem ABDUL-JABBAR

Born April 16, 1947, New York, New York
Basketball player

The son of professional parents, Abdul-Jabbar attended and graduated from Power Memorial High School in 1965. His father was a Juilliard-trained musician and a police officer. When he was in grade school, he played Catholic Youth Organization basketball in New York City. Abdul-Jabbar was born Ferdinand Lewis Alcindor, Jr., but changed his name when he converted from Catholicism to Islam in 1971.

A seven-foot, two-inch African American, Abdul-Jabbar chose coach John Wooden's UCLA as his college school, leading the Bruins to three consecutive National Collegiate Athletic Association (NCAA) titles (1963–1965). He is the first and only player to be named the NCAA basketball tournament's Most Outstanding Player three times. He was the College Player of the Year from 1967 to 1969. He majored in history.

His professional debut in the National Basketball Association (NBA) began with the Milwaukee Bucks in 1969. He played for the Bucks until 1975, when he was traded to the Los Angeles Lakers. He played for the Lakers until 1989.

While in the NBA Abdul-Jabbar compiled a legendary record of accomplishments. He won six NBA titles with the Bucks and the Lakers. He won a record six Most Valuable Player awards. He played a total of 1,560 games in his career. He played a total of 57,446 minutes, averaging sixty-five games a season. He holds the top nine NBA statistical categories: points scored (38,387), seasons played (twenty),

Kareem Abdul-Jabbar, the great center of the Los Angeles Lakers, shooting his classic skyhook over James Donaldson of the Dallas Mavericks in a 1988 NBA playoff game at The Forum in Inglewood, California. *(AP/Wide World Photos)*

playoff scoring (5,762), MVP awards (six), minutes played (57,446), games played (1,560), field goals made and attempted (15,837 of 28,307), and blocked shots (3,189). Abdul-Jabbar retired in 1989 at the age of forty-two as one of the oldest players ever to play professional basketball; he was inducted into the Basketball Hall of Fame on May 15, 1995. He was named one of the NBA's 50 greatest players in 1997.

In 1998 he was an assistant basketball coach at Alchesay High School in Whiteriver, Arizona, on the White Mountain Apache Reservation.

He has also been an actor and a film and television producer. He has written several books, including a memoir of his coaching days on the Apache reservation.

Earl Smith

See also: Autobiographies; Basketball; Films; Elvin Hayes; Oscar Robertson.

FURTHER READING
Abdul-Jabbar, Kareem. *Giant Steps: The Autobiography of Kareem Abdul-Jabbar.* New York: Bantam Books, 1983.
"Basketball Hall of Famers Kareem Abdul-Jabbar, Cheryl Miller Savor Their Inductions." *Jet*, June 5, 1995, 48.
Berkow, Ira. "When Some Wondered If Lew Had It." *New York Times*, April 22, 1989.
Bradley, John Ed. "Buffalo Soldier." *Sports Illustrated*, November 30, 1998, 72–85.
Lipsyte, Robert. "A Towering Presence and a Complex Figure." *New York Times*, May 14, 1995.
"NBA's 50 Greatest Players." *Jet*, February 24, 1997, 54–55.
Nolan, Timothy. "The Kareem of the Crop." *Coach and Athletic Director* 67 (September 1997): 50–58.

Lucinda Williams (Adams), the outstanding Tennessee State sprinter who was a member of several great women's sprint relay teams. *(Tennessee State University Special Collection)*

★ ★ ★

Lucinda ADAMS

Born August 10, 1937, Savannah, Georgia
Sprinter

Adams's parents were David and Willie Mae Williams. She graduated in 1954 from Woodville/Thompkin High School in Savannah, Georgia, where she played on the basketball team and ran track and field, excelling in sprints. After participating in the Tuskegee Relays, Adams was recruited for Tennessee A & I (now Tennessee State University) by its renowned coach Ed Temple. She studied there from 1955 to 1961, including work for a master's degree. With few colleges sponsoring women's teams in the 1950s, Tennessee A & I competed in national indoor and outdoor track competitions sponsored by the Amateur Athletic Union (AAU).

Adams's rapid progress led to her selection to the U.S. Olympic team in 1956. She was eliminated in the early rounds of the 200 meters that year. However, her ability placed her on the first United States–Soviet Union women's track and field exchange competition in Moscow in 1957, where she won the 200-meter dash. In 1958 she was on the exchange team that met the Soviet women in Philadelphia's Franklin Field. At the Pan American games in Chicago in 1959, Adams won the 100- and 200-meter dash and was a member of the 4 x 100 relay team. These accomplishments led her to third place in the balloting for the coveted Sullivan Award in 1959. As an Olympian in Rome in 1960, she advanced to the 200-meter semifinals and was a member of the gold medal 4 x 100 relay team.

Following college, where she was on the dean's list, she taught physical education at Roosevelt High School in Dayton, Ohio, from 1962 to 1974. She was then supervisor of physical education for the Dayton school system until her retirement in 1996. Adams served as president of the Ohio, Midwest, and National American Alliance for Health, Physical Education, Recreation and Dance (2000–2001). The University of Dayton awarded her an honorary doctorate in education in 1997. She continues to be involved in professional organizations and civic groups in Dayton and other parts of Ohio.

John R. Schleppi

FURTHER READING
Killanin, Lord, and John Rodda. *The Olympic Games.* New York: Macmillan, 1976.
Personal interview with Lucinda Williams Adams, August 7, 2001, Dayton, Ohio.
Wallechinsky, David. *The Complete Book of the Summer Olympics.* Sydney 2000 ed. Woodstock, NY: Overlook Press, 2000.

Herb ADDERLEY

Born June 8, 1939, Philadelphia, Pennsylvania
Football player

Adderley was born and brought up in Philadelphia, Pennsylvania. He graduated from Northeast High School in Philadelphia and attended Michigan State University in the class of 1961. An All-American at Michigan State, he was primarily a running back, playing only briefly as a safety. Herb earned a bachelor of science degree in education in 1961 and was drafted by the Green Bay Packers in the first round. During the College All-Star Game against the Philadelphia Eagles, coach Otto Graham put Herb on defense in an effort to neutralize the Eagles' outstanding receivers.

Slowed down by a training camp injury during his rookie season with the Packers, Adderley was unable to crack the starting lineup until the Thanksgiving Day game at Detroit, where he was used as a cornerback. Herb quickly became committed to becoming a great defensive back. Adderley was named to the All-NFL team as a defensive back in 1962 through 1966, and again in 1969—seven times in all. He played in five College All-Star Games and five Pro Bowls. During his pro career, he was credited with forty-eight interceptions and 120 kickoff returns. Over the course of his pro career, he averaged 25.7 yards per return. Adderley played for the Green Bay Packers from 1961 to 1969 and the Dallas Cowboys from 1970 to 1972. He also served in the National Guard, from 1962 through 1966.

Adderley played in eight NFL Championship games, including four Super Bowls, and was on the winning team seven times. On January 14, 1968, in Super Bowl II, Adderley intercepted a pass early in the fourth quarter and returned it for a touchdown to clinch the game. It was the only interception returned for a TD in the first ten years of the Super Bowl. Green Bay quarterback Bart Starr later remarked, "I'm just thankful he's playing for the Packers. He's the best cornerback I've ever seen." Adderley was also on five Pro Bowl teams. He was inducted into the Professional Football Hall of Fame in 1980.

Keith McClellan

FURTHER READING
Carroll, Bob, Mike Gershman, David Neft, and John Thorn, eds. *Total Football II: The Official Encyclopedia of the National Football League.* New York: HarperCollins, 1999.
Phelps, Shirelle, ed. *Who's Who Among Black Americans,* 1994/5. 8th ed. Detroit: Gale Research, 1994.

AGENTS

The sports-agent profession is not a new one. There was no notable African-American presence in the business, however, until the 1970s, and it was really not until the 1980s and 1990s that significant numbers of African Americans had even moderate degrees of success in the business.

Most attribute the genesis of the athletic-agent industry to the theatrical promoter, impresario, and showman Charles C. "Cash and Carry" Pyle. Pyle was the agent for many athletes in the early part of the twentieth century, most notably the legendary football star Harold "Red" Grange—the "Galloping Ghost," a charter member of the National Football League Hall of Fame. It was Pyle who negotiated a $3,000-per-game contract for Grange to play professional football with the Chicago Bears in 1925. In addition, he negotiated for Grange to receive over $300,000 in movie rights and endorsements, including a Red Grange doll, a candy bar, and a cap. Other Pyle sports clients included tennis stars Mary K. Brown and Suzanne Lenglen. Lenglen was the Wimbledon singles champion from 1919 to 1923. She signed with Pyle in 1926 for $50,000 and became the first professional tennis player. Another example of an early sports agent was cartoonist Christy Walsh. Walsh, according to *Sports Illustrated*, advised baseball Hall-of-Famer Babe Ruth to invest in annuities prior to the stock market crash of 1929.

The agent concept in sports is similar to that which has long existed in the motion picture, theatrical, television, and music sectors of the entertainment industry, as exemplified by the influential William Morris Agency. The duties that agents undertake in the entertainment industry, however, are often more specific than those of agents in sports. In the entertainment industry, it is traditional for a performer to employ a group of advisers, including an agent, a personal manager, a business manager, and an attorney, where an athlete may employ *an* agent. The combined fees for the entertainer's group of advisers have been estimated to equal 30–40 percent of the entertainer's gross income. The "agent" in the entertainment industry is loosely defined as the person who finds employment for the entertainer.

Increasingly, sports agents provide services beyond the negotiation of professional contracts. These additional services may include: providing advice regarding such financial matters as tax, investment, insurance, and money management; obtaining and negotiating endorsement contracts; medical and physical health and training consultations; legal (including criminal) consultation; post–playing career counseling; and counseling regarding a particular sport, media image, and everyday life. All of these services and more are certainly required, in varying degrees, by today's professional athletes. Some agents are finished once the player contract is negotiated; at that point they simply receive their fees. Others, depending on the athlete/agent contract, maintain ongoing relationships, performing some or all of the functions described above, particularly financial, endorsement, and counseling services.

The first African-American sports agent of any prominence was Los Angeles-based Fred Slaughter. Slaughter is an attorney who began representing athletes in the NBA following a successful career playing for UCLA and a law degree from Columbia University School of Law.

In recent years a number of successful African-American agents have emerged, but fewer than many consider there should be. The question that reverberates was prominently stated in the subtitle to a *Howard Library Journal* article, "A Search into Why Black Athletes Do Not Hire Black Agents." At the heart of this question is a belief that there would be a natural affinity between the world of black athletes, who numerically dominate certain sports (e.g., basketball and football), and well-qualified black agents. The fostering of these relationships, however, has been impeded by stereotypes and the longtime dominance of white agents, to the exclusion of black agents. At the heart of the stereotypical belief that it is more advantageous for athletes to secure white representation is what some black agents allege is being said by some white agents. According to Fred Slaughter, "'Only a white man can make that deal for you,' they have actually said that. And some kids, kids who are sitting in a well-furnished office with computers clicking and listening to a guy with gold teeth say that, they'll think, 'Wait a minute: if he's saying that, he must be right.' There are a lot of problems. It's been rough."

Successful African-American agents in recent years have included Bill Strickland with NBA clients, C. Lamont Smith and Eugene Parker with NFL clients, and Raymond Anderson with coaches.

Kenneth L. Shropshire

FURTHER READING
Hoose, Phillip N. *Necessities: Racial Barriers in American Sports*. New York: Random House, 1989.
Ruxin, Robert H. *An Athlete's Guide to Agents*. Bloomington: Indiana University Press, 1983.
Sammataro, James G. "Business and Brotherhood, Can They Coincide? A Search into Why Black Athletes Do Not Hire Black Agents." *Howard Library Journal* 42 (Spring 1999): 535.
Shropshire, Kenneth L. *Agents of Opportunity: Sports Agents and Corruption in Collegiate Sports*. Philadelphia: University of Pennsylvania Press, 1990.
Shropshire, Kenneth L. *In Black and White: Race and Sports in America*. New York: New York University Press, 1995.

★ ★ ★

David ALBRITTON

Born April 13, 1913, Danville, Alabama
Died May 14, 1994, Dayton, Ohio
High jumper

David Albritton's career as a world-class high jumper spanned fifteen years. One of the earliest jumpers to use the straddle style, Albritton finished second in the high jump competition at the 1936 Olympic Games in Berlin, behind teammate Cornelius Johnson. Albritton was among a group of African-American track and field athletes who dominated the Berlin Games. In addition to Albritton and Johnson, the group included 400-meter champ Archie Williams; 800-meter winner John Woodruff; sprinters Ralph Metcalfe, Fritz Pollard, Jr., and Mack Robinson; and most famously, the legendary Jesse Owens.

Albritton and Owens had other similarities as well. Both were born in Danville, Alabama, both moved to Ohio and attended East Technical High School in Cleveland, both attended Ohio State University, both competed in the 1936 Olympics, and both are members of the USA Track and Field Hall of Fame.

Albritton had an unusually long career as a world-class high jumper. He lettered at Ohio State from 1935 to 1937. At the Olympic Trials in 1936, he and the aforementioned Cornelius Johnson both jumped 6 feet, 9¾ inches to set a world record, becoming the first black athletes to hold the record in that event. Albritton won or tied seven AAU outdoor titles from 1936 to 1950 and tied three national collegiate titles from 1936 to 1938. He later became a politician and served in the Ohio House of Representatives.

Robert Epling

See also: Track and Field.

FURTHER READING
Baker, William J. *Jesse Owens: An American Life*. New York: Free Press, 1986.
Baltimore Afro American, August 8, 1936.
Bennett, Lerone, Jr. "Jesse Owens' Olympic Triumph over Time and Hitlerism." *Ebony*, April 1996, 68.
Henderson, Edwin B. *The Black Athlete: Emergence and Arrival*. Cornwell Heights, PA: Publisher's Agency, 1978.
Hickok Sports (www.hickoksports.com/biograph/albrittn.shtml).
The USA Track and Field Hall of Fame (www.usaft.org/athletes/hof/albritton.shtml).

★ ★ ★

Muhammad ALI

Born January 17, 1942, Louisville, Kentucky
Boxer

Muhammad Ali following his last training session prior to his 1974 title bout against George Foreman in Zaire. *(AP/Wide World Photos)*

Muhammad Ali was born to Odessa and Cassius Marcellus Clay, Sr. Clay Senior owned a shop where commercial trucks were painted with logos. When he was twelve, Clay Junior's bicycle was stolen, and he turned to boxing in order to defend himself. At the age of eighteen, he won a gold medal during the 1960 Olympics, after which he reportedly threw the medal into the Ohio River in disgust at racism in America.

In 1964 he became the world heavyweight champion, a title he successfully defended until 1967. Ali held the title again from 1974 to February 1978 and from September 1978 to 1979, when he briefly retired. After mounting an unsuccessful comeback, he retired permanently in 1981. His charismatic bravado and self-effacing manner earned him both popularity and notoriety during the 1960s and 1970s. Along with sportscaster Howard Cosell, Ali is credited with making boxing one of America's most popular sports during this period.

Recruited by Malcolm X, Ali became a minister of the Nation of Islam and in that capacity was a vocal proponent of African-

American rights and antiwar views, stands that increasingly reduced his popularity with white Americans. In 1967, Ali was stripped of his title as a result of his refusal to submit to the draft, on the ground that he had become a Black Muslim (in 1964). This resulted in a conviction that was not overturned until 1971. In that year the U.S. Supreme Court unanimously found that the Justice Department had improperly advised Ali's draft board that his beliefs were not genuine, a position that had swayed the all-white jury and, by extension, American public opinion. After the Vietnam War, Ali's popularity returned, in part because he distanced himself from the Nation of Islam, embracing traditional Islam instead, and because of his charitable efforts on behalf of many causes. His redemption before the American public was made complete by his appearance at the 1996 Olympics in Atlanta, where he lit the flame. Though hampered by Parkinson's disease, Ali continues his involvement in charitable activities and, guided by the management skills of his fourth wife, Lonnie Williams, continues to grow in popularity.

Gregory S. Goodale

See also: Autobiographies; Boxing; Civil Rights; Jimmy Ellis; Films; Joe Frazier; Historiography; Larry Holmes; Don King; Sonny Liston; Ken Norton; Olympic Games; Floyd Patterson; Leon Spinks.

FURTHER READING
Ali, Muhammad, with Richard Durham. *The Greatest: My Own Story.* New York: Ballantine Books, 1975.
Early, Gerald, ed. *The Muhammad Ali Reader.* New York: Ecco Press, 1998.
Gorn, Elliott J., ed. *Muhammad Ali: The People's Champ.* Urbana: University of Illinois Press, 1995.
"The Making of a Champ." *Louisville (KY) Courier-Journal* (www.courier-journal.com/ali/).
Remnick, David. *King of the World: Muhammad Ali and the Rise of an American Hero.* New York: Random House, 1998.

★ ★ ★

Marcus ALLEN

Born March 26, 1960, San Diego, California
Football player

Allen attended Abraham Lincoln High School in San Diego, where he was a *Parade Magazine* scholastic All-American. During his first two seasons at the University of Southern California, he was primarily a blocking back for Heisman tailback Charles White. He was returned to the tailback position his junior year and over the next two years set twelve NCAA records, including the NCAA single-season rushing record (2,342 yards) and the record for the most 200-yard rushing games (eleven), and tied another. He played in the Hula Bowl and the Olympic Gold Bowl; won the Walter Camp, Maxwell Cup, and Football News awards as College Player of the Year; and was the 1981 Heisman Trophy winner.

He played professionally with the Los Angeles Raiders, 1982–1992, and the Kansas City Chiefs, 1993–1997, as a running back. In 1982, his rookie season, Allen led the NFL in scoring, with eighty-four points in nine games, and was Rookie of the Year. In 1985 he led the NFL in rushing, with 1,759 yards in 380 tries. He averaged 4.6 yards per carry that season and was the American Football Conference player of the year. Allen was the top receiver among AFC backs for three straight seasons, 1982–1984. In 1983 he was the Most Valuable Player (MVP) in the Super Bowl, when he set the Super Bowl rushing record with 191 yards. In 1984 he was the league's highest non-kicking scorer. He was All-AFC four times and a member of the Pro Bowl five times. He was named the NFL's MVP in 1985. At the turn of the twenty-first century, he was the sixth-leading NFL rusher of all time and the fifth-leading player in playoff rushes. He is married and lives in Kansas City.

Keith McClellan

FURTHER READING

Carroll, Bob, Mike Gershman, David Neft, and John Thorn, eds. *Total Football II: The Official Encyclopedia of the National Football League.* New York: HarperCollins, 1999.

Phelps, Shirelle, ed. *Who's Who Among Black Americans,* 1994/5. 8th ed. Detroit: Gale Research, 1994.

Rust, Edna, and Art Rust, Jr. *Art Rust's Illustrated History of the Black Athlete.* Garden City, NY: Doubleday, 1985.

★ ★ ★

AMERICAN TENNIS ASSOCIATION

The American Tennis Association (ATA) was founded on November 30, 1916, in Washington, DC, by H.S. McCard, William H. Wright, B.M. Rhetta, Ralph V. Cook, Henry Freeman, John F.N. Wilkinson, and Talley Holmes, at the invitation of the Association Tennis Club of Washington. The ATA was intended as an outlet for competition by members of the black professional classes and black collegians. Its four primary goals were to develop tennis among black people in the United States, to encourage the formation of clubs and the building of courts, to encourage the formation of local associations, and to encourage and develop junior players. The first ATA Nationals were held at Baltimore's Druid Hill Park Courts in 1917, the same year that the United States Lawn Tennis Association (USLTA) women's singles championships were introduced. By 1949, ATA membership had grown to fifteen associations, with 134 individual clubs. The ATA was instrumental in introducing tennis to black college campuses. The growth experienced by ATA caused several policies to be effected, such as limitation of tournament entrants to two events and prohibition of juniors under sixteen entering senior events.

Although the USLTA did not set aside its policy against African Americans' participating in its sanctioned events, Dwight Davis (donor of the Davis Cup, former secretary of defense, and former president of the USLTA) served as an umpire during the 1921 ATA National semifinals matches.

One of the most widely known ATA alumni is Althea Gibson, the first black Wimbledon champion. Ms. Gibson's participation in ATA was representative of the purpose of the ATA itself—to interest boys and girls in tennis as a major sport regardless of socioeconomic background. After World War II, the quality of the play of such notables as Ms. Gibson and Oscar Johnson of Los Angeles forced the USLTA to admit blacks to its sanctioned tournaments.

Today, integration and grassroots programs offered by the USTA have diminished membership in the ATA. However, the ATA remains active in pursuit of the goals set by its founders. The organization remains committed to complementing national developmental tennis programs in areas where African Americans await the introduction of tennis to their communities.

Danielle A. Mincey White

See also: Arthur Ashe, Jr.; Zina Garrison; Lucy Diggs Slowe; Tennis; Reginald Weir.

FURTHER READING

Ashe, Arthur R., Jr. *A Hard Road to Glory: A History of the African-American Athlete Since 1946.* New York: Amistad, 1988.

Henderson, Edwin B. *The Negro in Sports.* Washington, DC: Associated, 1949.

Edwin B. Henderson Papers. Box 44–1, folder 14, Manuscript Division, Moorland-Spingarn Research Center, Howard University.

William A. Joiner Papers. Box 148–4, folder 8, Manuscript Division, Moorland-Spingarn Research Center, Howard University.

★ ★ ★

Nate ARCHIBALD

Born September 2, 1948, Bronx, New York
Basketball player

Nate "Tiny" Archibald grew up in the tough South Bronx section of New York City, graduating from DeWitt Clinton High School in 1966. He spent one year at Arizona Western Junior College before transferring to the University of Texas at El Paso in 1967, where on the basketball team he averaged twenty points per game the next three years. Archibald began a fourteen-year professional career in 1970, when he was selected in the second round of the NBA draft by the Cincinnati Royals.

Archibald holds the distinction of being the only player in NBA history to lead the league in scoring and assists the same season, a feat he accomplished in 1972–1973 by averaging thirty-four points and 11.4 assists as a member of the Kansas City–Omaha Kings (previously the Cincinnati Royals). A six-time NBA All-Star and MVP of the 1981 All-Star game, Archibald was known early in his career for dazzling quickness and ball-handling ability. Later, after injuries diminished his quickness, he displayed tremendous leadership and court awareness. In addition to playing with the Royals/Kings from 1970 to 1975, Archibald played with the New York Nets, the Boston Celtics, and the Milwaukee Bucks before retiring in 1984. He helped lead the Boston Celtics to an NBA championship in 1981.

After retiring as a player, Archibald became a college coach, then a teacher and community activist and leader in his native New York. He was enshrined in the Basketball Hall of Fame in 1991 and was named one of the 50 greatest players in NBA history in 1996.

Robert Epling

FURTHER READING
Athlon Sports (www.athlonsports.com/article389).
Basketball Hall of Fame (www.hoopball.com/halloffamers/Archibald.html).
Hickok Sports.com (www.hickoksports.com/biograph/archbald/shtlm).
Nance, Roscoe. "Archibald Takes the NBA to Asia." *USA Today*, June 2, 2000.
O'Keefe, John. "Tiny Archibald, Basketball Hall of Famer." *Sports Illustrated*, November 9, 1998, 22.
Wolff, Alexander. "All Points Bulletin." *Sports Illustrated*, November 20, 2000, 128–40.

★ ★ ★

Henry ARMSTRONG

Born December 12, 1912, Columbus, Mississippi
Died October 24, 1988, Los Angeles, California
Boxer

Henry Armstrong was the first and only boxer to hold three championship titles in three different weight classes at the same time. Born Henry Jackson, his mother died when he was very young. Raised by his grandmother, Armstrong graduated as a honor student at Vashon High School.

Armstrong started fighting at the Colored YMCA and fought professionally under the name Melody Jackson. Wanting to fight as an amateur again, he moved to California and changed his name to Henry Armstrong. When Armstrong failed to make the 1932 Olympic team, he decided to turn pro again. Armstrong beat Petey Sarron in six rounds for the featherweight title on October 29, 1937. Armstrong's second title was in the welterweight division, which he won on May 31, 1938, beating Barney Ross. Armstrong defeated Lou Am-

Featherweight Henry Armstrong being fitted with his championship belt by *Ring Magazine* editor Nat Fleicher in 1938 at Pompton Lakes, New Jersey. Armstrong's manager, Eddie Meade, is on the right. (AP/Wide World Photos)

bers for the lightweight title on August 17, 1938. Over a ten-month span, Armstrong had become the first and only fighter to hold titles in three weight classes. Armstrong was unsuccessful in his bid to win a fourth weight-division title when he lost to Ceferino Garcia in the middleweight division. Armstrong retired in 1945.

Armstrong battled alcoholism and won that fight as well. He was ordained as a Baptist minister in 1951. He founded the Henry Armstrong Youth Foundation and became the director of the Herbert Hoover Boys Club in his hometown of St. Louis.

ESPN, in its list of the 100 greatest North American athletes of the twentieth century, listed Armstrong as number eighty-seven, one of only a handful of boxers. He was elected to the Boxing Hall of Fame in 1954.

Maureen M. Smith

See also: Boxing.

FURTHER READING
Ashe, Arthur R., Jr. *A Hard Road to Glory: A History of the African-American Athlete Since 1946.* New York: Warner Books, 1988.
Jackson, George. *Soul Brother Superfighter.* Placerville, CA: Green Valley Graphics, 1985.
Schwartz, Larry. "He Was 'Homocide Hank' for a Reason" (www.Hespn.go.com/classic/biography/s/armstrong_henry.html).

★ ★ ★

Arthur ASHE, JR.

Born July 10, 1943, Richmond, Virginia
Died February 16, 1993, New York, New York
Tennis player

Son of Arthur Ashe, Sr., a policeman, and Matte Cordell (Cunningham), Ashe was one of the world's great tennis players. He first learned the game from Ron Charity, a well-known African-American tennis player from Richmond, and Dr. Walter Johnson, a legendary instructor of young African-American players, most notably Althea Gibson. Under the tutelage of Johnson, Ashe captured several American Tennis Association (ATA) championships, including the national boys' twelve-and-under singles title in 1955; the national boys' sixteen-and-under singles titles in 1957, 1958, and 1959; the national boys' 18-and-under singles title in 1960; and the national men's singles titles in 1960, 1961, 1962, and 1963. He captured the NCAA singles title in 1965 while a student at UCLA; three years later he won the prestigious U.S. Open singles title; and in 1975 he won the coveted Wimbledon singles title. In addition to his many individual titles, Ashe was captain and a member of several Davis Cup teams.

Ashe was always more than simply a tennis player. His life off the court was

Arthur Ashe, Jr., executing a backhand return against Harold Solomon at the Grand Prix Masters Tennis Tournament in New York. *(AP/Wide World Photos)*

filled with purpose, activity, and accomplishment. He was a strong advocate for the education of African-American youth, fought valiantly against apartheid in South Africa, and became a leading spokesman for education about AIDS after he was stricken with the illness. He was a prolific author, penning autobiographical accounts of his life and career—with coauthors Neil Amdur, *Off the Court* (1981); with Frank Deford, *Portrait in Motion* (1975); and with Arnold Rampersad, *Days of Grace* (1993). He also published a three-volume history of the African-American athlete, *A Hard Road to Glory* (1988).

Ashe was honored for his extraordinary tennis accomplishments by being inducted into the International Tennis Hall of Fame in 1985. In 1994, *Sports Illustrated* ranked Ashe twenty-seventh on its "40 for the Ages" list. His legacy lives on, most notably through the efforts of his wife, Jeanne-Marie Moutousammy, and daughter, Camera.

David K. Wiggins

See also: American Tennis Association; Autobiographies; Tennis.

FURTHER READING
Ashe, Arthur, Jr., with Neil Amdur. *Off the Court*. New York: New American Library, 1981.
Ashe, Arthur, Jr., with Frank Deford. *Portrait in Motion*. Boston: Houghton Mifflin, 1975.
Ashe, Arthur, Jr., with Arnold Rampersad, *Days of Grace*. New York: Alfred A. Knopf, 1993.
Berkow, Ira. "The Changing Faces of Arthur Ashe." *New York Times*, October 25, 1992.
Heldman, Julius. "The Ashe Game." *World Tennis*, December 1968, 36–37.

★ ★ ★

Emmett ASHFORD

Born November 23, 1914, Los Angeles, California
Died March 1, 1980, Marina Del Rey, California
Baseball umpire

Born to Adele Bain and Littleton Ashford, Emmett and his brother were raised by their mother. He graduated from Chapman College, where he was a utility player on the baseball team and also played with a

Emmett Ashford, Major League Baseball's first African-American umpire, conferring with California Angels manager Bill Rigney and his fellow umpires prior to a 1966 spring training game in Palm Springs, California. (AP/Wide World Photos)

semiprofessional baseball club. Pressed into umpiring duty when the regular umpire failed to appear, he found that he enjoyed the role. While working in the Payroll and Finance Department in the post office, he continued to umpire in city recreation leagues until enlisting in the U.S. Navy during World War II. Following the war he resumed umpiring, first in high schools, then junior colleges, and finally for Pacific Coast Conference universities.

In July 1951, Ashford became the first African-American umpire in "organized baseball," with the Class C Southwest International League. Two years later he was promoted to the Class A Western International League, and in 1954 he began a twelve-year tenure in the AAA Pacific Coast League. In 1966 he began a five-year American League career as the first African-American umpire in the major leagues. Known for his exuberant style, he worked the 1967 All-Star Game and the 1970 World Series, retiring one year beyond the mandatory age of fifty-five. In retirement, he served for a time as the West Coast representative of the commissioner of baseball and also conducted umpiring clinics around the world.

Richard A. Swanson

FURTHER READING
Ashe, Arthur R., Jr. *A Hard Road to Glory: A History of the African-American Athlete Since 1946.* New York: Amistad, 1993.
Gerlach, Larry R. *The Men in Blue: Conversations with Umpires.* New York: Viking Press, 1980.
Salzman, Jack, David Lionel Smith, and Cornel West. *Encyclopedia of African-American Culture and History.* New York: Simon and Schuster, 1996.

Evelyn ASHFORD

Born April 15, 1957, Shreveport, Louisiana
Sprinter

The daughter of Samuel Ashford, a sergeant in the U.S. Air Force, and Vietta Ashford, Evelyn Ashford attended the University of California at Los Angeles (UCLA) and currently works as a speaker, encouraging young people in sports.

Ashford began her athletic career as the only girl on her high school track and field team in Roseville, California. In 1975, she was one of the first women to receive a track and field scholarship from UCLA. She competed in the 1976 Montreal Olympic Games, coming in an unexpected fifth in the 100 meters. After two years as an All-American and victories in the Association of Intercollegiate Athletics for Women (AIAW) championships, she left UCLA to train full-time for the 1980 Olympics. Despite her disappointment over the U.S. boycott of the Moscow Games, she continued to train and in the 1984 Los Angeles Olympics ran the 100 meters in an Olympic record time of 10.97, earning her an Olympic gold medal. She won another in the 4 x 100 relay that same year.

Ashford had to combat the stereotypes that confronted successful women athletes in the latter half of the twentieth century. She chose to combine motherhood and an athletic career, and in 1985 her daughter Raina Ashly Washington was born. Ashford returned to top form over the next few years and in the 1988 Seoul Olympics won another gold in the 400-meter relay and a silver in the 100-meter race. In 1992 at Barcelona she did it again—winning gold in the 400-meter relay.

Ashford is a role model for young women in track and field today. She is an active promoter of youth sports and works with the USA Track and Field Junior Olympics program. Her persistence and longevity are legendary.

Alison M. Wrynn

See also: Olympic Games; Track and Field.

FURTHER READING
Davis, Michael D. *Black American Women in Track and Field. A Complete Illustrated Reference.* Jefferson, NC: McFarland, 1992.
Kort, Michael. "Evelyn Ashford, Olympic Sprinter." *MS*, May 1984, 40, 42–43.
Woolum, Janet. *Outstanding Women Athletes: Who They Are and How They Influenced Sports in America.* Phoenix, AZ: Oryx Press, 1992.

AUTOBIOGRAPHIES

On the face of it, the autobiography of a black athlete is simply an account of that individual's experiences in and out of sport, but each of the three terms in the phrase "African-American sports autobiography" complicates this straightforward understanding. An *autobiography*, whether St. Augustine's, Benjamin Franklin's, or Maya Angelou's, is not the transparent record of a lived life but the consciously crafted self-presentation of an individual framed by certain social, economic, and political contexts and guided by any number of personal motives. From Frederick Douglass to Malcolm X, *African-American* autobiographers have developed a tremendously rich and important literary genre. The *sports* autobiography, in contrast, is a commercial product arising from and contributing to American celebrity culture, rarely written by the athlete alone but

AUTOBIOGRAPHIES

"with" or "as told to" a professional writer. The conflicting demands of these literary forms make African-American sports autobiographies anything but straightforward accounts of black athletes' experiences.

Although the first ghostwritten sports autobiographies appeared in the nineteenth century, the life story of the celebrity athlete did not become commonplace until after the Second World War. Even when men such as John N. Wheeler and Christy Walsh in the 1910s and 1920s made careers out of ghostwriting for athletes and coaches, the books they wrote were "inside" accounts of the sports themselves rather than of the athletes' lives. The paucity of African-American sports autobiographies before the 1950s is thus a consequence of more than racism. The earliest appear to be Jack Johnson's *In the Ring and Out* (1927) and "Major" Taylor's *The Fastest Bicycle Rider in the World* (1928), neither of which received mainstream publication. Johnson's florid style makes a modern reader wonder if he was indeed the author; Taylor's artless and tedious yet fascinating self-published chronicle of prejudice is clearly his own. The first conventional coauthored autobiography of a black celebrity athlete appeared in 1947, Joe Louis's *My Life Story*, followed a year later by Satchel Paige's *Pitchin' Man* (originally published in the *Cleveland News* during Paige's belated rookie season in major league baseball). Willie Mays and Roy Campanella published autobiographies in the 1950s, but Jackie Robinson's did not appear until 1972. In the 1960s and 1970s, great black athletes such as Sugar Ray Robinson, Floyd Patterson, and Muhammad Ali in boxing; Emlen Tunnell and Jim Brown in football; Bill Russell and Wilt Chamberlain in basketball; Jesse Owens (belatedly) and Wilma Rudolph in track and field; and Althea Gibson and Arthur Ashe in tennis fully established the genre.

Several of the autobiographies from this period adopted the same formula: early poverty; strong parental influence (whether from one parent or two); escape through sport, usually with the guidance of black or white mentors; hard work, setbacks, and triumphs. This is the pattern of the American success story since Ben Franklin, its appeal to readers lying in its utter familiarity, as well as its reassurances that talent and hard work can defeat all obstacles, even racial ones. Many of these author-athletes—Louis, Mays, Campanella, Tunnell, Gibson, Moore, Chamberlain, Patterson, Sugar Ray Robinson—conspicuously downplayed race or relegated it to a single brief section, most plausibly so as not to alienate a predominantly white readership. An evasion of racial issues, for altogether different reasons, also marks the autobiographies of the 1980s and 1990s, when blacks thoroughly dominated the major sports. There is a telling anecdote in Magic Johnson's 1983 autobiography about teammate Michael Cooper's joke to a reporter after missing a layup: "It makes me feel like a white dude." In defending Cooper against the subsequent accusations of racism, Johnson dismissed the remark as part of the "different language" spoken by basketball players, a language "that's neither black nor white." For NBA players, Johnson insisted, "the color of a man's skin is as incidental as the color of a man's shorts." No knowledgeable sports fan could believe this, but for millionaire "crossover" stars like Magic Johnson the illusion of color-blindness had become essential to sports marketing. Sports autobiographies of the 1990s, when black athletes were least constrained from speaking out, are much more striking for their sexual than their racial candor.

The best African-American sports autobiographies tend to come from the civil rights and Black Power eras, from that transitional period between segregation and integration when competing at the highest level was most obviously a political act. Arnold Rampersad, the prize-winning biographer of Langston Hughes as well as one of tennis star Arthur Ashe's several coauthors, has suggested that great autobiographies, such as St. Augustine's *Confessions* and Cardinal Newman's *Apologia Pro Vita Sua*, do not celebrate but examine the self; their mode is confessional rather than promotional. Much of the most powerful African-American autobiographical writing has this quality, grappling with what W.E.B. DuBois called "double consciousness," the collision of the writer's sense of self with the dominant culture's racist assumptions. However, the best sports autobiographies—those by activist athletes, such as Jackie Robinson, Bill Russell, and Arthur Ashe—are not particularly introspective in this way; rather, they openly address the racial and racist conditions that have faced minority athletes. Vincent Matthews was a minor figure, but his *My Race Be Won* is the only participant account of the black-power protests at the 1968 and 1972 Olympics. Football player Bernie Parrish says little about race, but his *They Call It a Game* is an important document from that brief period of political activism in sport in the late 1960s and early 1970s. To this list must be added Muhammad Ali, whose 1972 autobiography lacks any sense of Ali's own voice but remains a crucial record of an important historical figure.

Athletes' autobiographies are generally regarded as slight amusements, no more consequential than newspaper gossip columns. When the athlete is black, however, his or her story has an inescapable political dimension, whether or not the author chooses to acknowledge that reality. Not simply documentary records of the African-American sporting experience, autobiographies are accounts of the self-fashioning of black athletes, as dictated by current racial politics as well as by more narrowly personal intentions. (Because they tell the same story at different times, reading multiple autobiographies—such as those by Joe Louis, Jesse Owens, Jim Brown, Hank Aaron, Wilt Chamberlain, and Kareem Abdul Jabbar—can be particularly revealing in terms of shifting historical contexts and authorial motives.) What even the most conventional stories collectively reveal is the range of acceptable definitions of blackness within sport over time.

Michael Oriard

See also: Kareem Abdul-Jabbar; Arthur Ashe, Jr.; Marshall "Major" Taylor.

FURTHER READING
Andrews, William L., ed. *African American Autobiography: A Collection of Critical Essays*. Englewood Cliffs, NJ: Prentice Hall, 1993.
Mostern, Kenneth. *Autobiography and Black Identity Politics: Racialization in Twentieth-Century America*. New York: Cambridge University Press, 1999.
Rampersad, Arnold. "Biography, Autobiography, and Afro-American Culture." *Yale Review* 73 (1983): 1–16.

Ernie BANKS

Born January 31, 1931, Dallas, Texas
Baseball player

Known as "Mr. Cub," Ernie Banks began his baseball career on the sandlots of Dallas, where at the age of eighteen he joined the Dallas Black Eagles, a local semiprofessional black team. His play attracted the attention of the Kansas City Monarchs. After a short stint with that team in 1950, Banks joined the army. In 1953, he rejoined the Monarchs.

Before the 1953 season ended, Banks's ability as a shortstop attracted the attention of the Chicago Cubs, who signed him to a contract. Only twenty-two years old, Banks reported immediately to Chicago, becoming the franchise's first African-American baseball player. He remained with the Cubs until his retirement in 1971, playing shortstop, third base, first base, and the outfield.

Banks proved to be one of the greatest players in the major leagues and helped pave the way for further integration on his team. In 1955, Banks hit forty-four home runs, the most ever up to that time by a shortstop. From 1957 to 1960, he hit over forty home runs and amassed 100 runs batted in a year. Also, between 1955 and 1960, Banks hit more home runs than any other player in major league baseball. Banks's individual accomplishments during this period won him back-to-back National League Most Valuable Player awards, in 1958 and 1959.

Banks finished his nineteen-year career with a .274 lifetime batting average, 2,583 hits, 512 home runs, twelve All-Star Game appearances, and a Gold Glove Award in 1960. In 1971, the Cubs retired Banks's number. He was inducted into the National Baseball Hall of Fame in 1977.

Rob Fink

See also: Baseball.

FURTHER READING
Banks, Ernie, and Jim Enright. *Mr. Cub*. Chicago: Follett, 1971.
Baseball Encyclopedia: The Complete and Definitive Record of Major League Baseball. 10th ed. New York: Macmillan, 1996.
Holtzman, Jerome, and George Vass. *The Chicago Cubs Encyclopedia*. Philadelphia: Temple University Press, 1997.
Libby, Bill. *Ernie Banks: Mr. Cub*. New York: Putnam, 1971.
Riley, James A. *The Biographical Encyclopedia of the Negro Baseball Leagues*. New York: Carroll and Graf, 1994.

★ ★ ★

Charles BARKLEY

Born February 20, 1963, Leeds, Alabama
Basketball player

Barkley attended Auburn University on a basketball scholarship. Listed at six feet, six inches in height, during his college days Barkley often weighed over three hundred pounds. Noted as an outstanding rebounder and defender with a weight problem, Charles was referred to as the "Round Mound of Rebound." He was drafted fifth overall by the National Basketball Association's Philadelphia 76ers in the first round of the 1984 draft.

Barkley made the all-rookie team his first year but was often criticized by even his own teammates for inconsistent play and temper tantrums on the basketball court. By the 1987–1988 season Barkley had learned how to keep his weight down and was named to the first of four straight All-NBA teams. He had become a well-rounded player on the court, but off the court Charles became outspoken. One well-known sport sociologist has noted that what Barkley had to say depended on what he had had to eat that day and whether or not it agreed with him. In 1991, criticism of Barkley intensified when he was accused of spitting on a young fan sitting courtside at a game.

Barkley's play and outspokenness increased during the 1990s. He created a great deal of attention and controversy with a commercial for Nike. In the televised spot Barkley solemnly states to the viewing audience, "I am not a role model. . . . Parents should be role models." He was selected to the 1992 U.S. Olympic basketball team. He was traded to the Houston Rockets in 1996 and retired from the NBA with that team in 1998. Barkley was named one of the fifty greatest NBA players of all time in 1996. Today he is a color commentator for TNT broadcasts of NBA games, and an avid golfer.

James R. Coates, Jr.

See also: Olympic Games.

FURTHER READING
Barkley, Charles, and Roy S. Johnson. *Outrageous!* New York: Avon Books, 1993 (www.nba.com/playerfile/charles_barley.html).
Barkley, Charles, and Rick Reilly. *Sir Charles: The Wit and Wisdom of Charles Barkley.* New York: Warner Books, 1994.

Don BARKSDALE

Born March 31, 1923, Oakland, California
Died March 8, 1993, Oakland, California
Basketball player

A graduate of Berkeley High School in Berkeley, California, and the University of California at Los Angeles (UCLA) (BA), Don Barksdale ranks among the pioneer African-American basketball players. Barksdale was cut from his high school basketball team but starred at Marin County Junior College before enrolling at UCLA in 1943. His career was interrupted by World War II, but Barksdale returned after the war to UCLA and in 1947 led the Bruins in scoring with 368 points, a 14.7 average. He made the All-Conference team and several All-American teams.

After graduation Barksdale joined the Oakland Bittners, one of the top AAU teams of the late 1940s. During the 1947–1948 season, the six-foot six-inch, two-hundred-pound Barksdale led the American Basketball League in scoring with a 16.7-point scoring average. In January 1948 Barksdale became the first African American to play in an integrated basketball game in Oklahoma when the Bittners traveled to Bartlesville to play the powerful Phillips 66ers, led by Bob Kurland, two-time All-American at Oklahoma A & M. The 66ers had not lost on their home floor since 1944, but on January 7, 1948, before a standing-room-only crowd, Barksdale scored seventeen points to lead the Bittners to a 45–41 victory. In March Barksdale led the Bittners to a third-place finish in the national AAU tournament in Denver, which put his team in the Olympic Tournament in New York City. There Barksdale earned a spot on the U.S. Olympic team, making him the first African American to win this honor. Barksdale joined a team dominated by the Phillips 66ers and the University of Kentucky Wildcats, and he helped the United States win its second gold medal in basketball.

For the next three years, Barksdale remained one of the dominant AAU basketball players. At the 1949 national AAU tournament in Oklahoma City, he scored seventeen points to lead the Bittners to a 55-51 victory over the Phillips 66ers and break their string of six consecutive national AAU championships. In 1950, Barksdale led the Oakland Blue 'n Gold to the AAU tournament finals before losing to Phillips. The Oakland Blue 'n Gold joined the National Industrial Basketball League during Barksdale's last year there, 1950–1951. Barksdale led the NIBL in scoring and was named its MVP. In early March 1951 he led the United States to a gold medal in the first Pan American Games, held in Buenos Aires, Argentina. In six games Barksdale averaged 22.5 points, which is still a record. Although injured during the national AAU tournament, Barksdale was selected to the AAU All-American Team for the fourth successive year.

In 1951 the Baltimore Bullets (NBA) made Barksdale the fourth black NBA player. During his third NBA season, he joined the Boston Celtics and on January 13, 1953, became the first black player to perform in an NBA All-Star Game. By his retirement after the 1954–1955 season, Barksdale had scored 2,895 points and averaged eleven points per game in four NBA seasons.

After retiring, Barksdale owned several Oakland, California, nightclubs, hosted a television show, scouted for the Golden State Warriors of the NBA, and worked as a disc jockey at several black radio stations. In 1982 he created the Save High School Sport Foundation to fund financially strapped athletic programs in the San Francisco Bay area. Upon his death, the foundation had raised over $1 million to help high school sports. In July 2001 Oakland honored Don Barksdale posthumously by inducting him into the African-American/Ethnic Sports Hall of Fame.

Adolph H. Grundman

See also: Basketball; Olympic Games.

FURTHER READING
Carlson, Lewis H., and John J. Fogarty. *Tales of Gold: An Oral History of the Summer Olympic Games Told by America's Gold Medal Winners*. New York: Contemporary Books, 1987.
Dickey, Glenn. "Remembering a Local Visionary." *San Francisco Chronicle*, March 10, 1993.
Porter, David L., ed. *Biographical Dictionary of American Sports: 1992–1995, Supplement for Baseball, Football, Basketball and Other Sports*. Westport, CT: Greenwood Press, 1995.

★ ★ ★

BASEBALL

African Americans have participated in baseball since at least the second half of the nineteenth century. In those years they competed in the sport on an informal basis, organized their own amateur and professional teams, and were represented in the white minor and major leagues. Seemingly every large town and city in the post–Civil War period had African-American teams that competed against both all-black and integrated amateur nines on a fairly regular basis. Perhaps the most famous of these teams was the Philadelphia Pythians, a club founded in 1867 by members of Philadelphia's African-American elite. There were also a number of African-American teams at the professional level during this period that competed in white leagues as well as against other black nines.

The Cuban Giants, initially recruited from waiters at the Argyle Hotel in Babylon, New York, in 1885, was the most no-

BASEBALL

table of the black professional teams. Typical of other black baseball teams of this era (and other black teams in other sports, for that matter), the Cuban Giants were not affiliated with any league but traveled the country seeking competition with any team willing to pay the price to play a game. In addition to all-black amateur and professional teams, a number of African-American players found their way into white professional baseball leagues. Between 1883 and 1898 a total of fifty-five African-American players participated in white organized baseball. Among these players were Bud Fowler, a native of Cooperstown, New York, who is considered the first black professional player; and Moses Fleetwood Walker, who became the first black major leaguer, playing in 1884 with Toledo in the American Association.

By the last decade of the nineteenth century, Jim Crow laws and a host of other societal factors resulted in the exclusion of Walker and other African Americans from white professional baseball. This forced African Americans to organize their own teams and leagues behind segregated walls. The most famous of these leagues were the Negro National League (NNL) established in 1920 by Rube Foster, and the Negro American League (NAL), organized in 1937. These two leagues, with franchises in such cities as Kansas City, Pittsburgh, Indianapolis, Chicago, and Detroit, were extremely important to the African-American community. Although suffering from instability, including the continual movement of players from team to team and on junkets to Latin America and Mexico to earn extra money, the two leagues were symbols of possibility for an African-American community suffering from the worst racial indignities and prejudices. African Americans took enormous pride in the success of such teams as the Homestead Grays and Pittsburgh Crawfords, and in the exploits of players like Satchel Paige, Josh Gibson, "Cool Papa" Bell, Ray Dandridge, and Oscar Charleston.

The unquestioned highlight of Negro league baseball was the East-West All-Star Game. Founded by Pittsburgh gambler and entrepreneur Gus Greenlee in 1933, the game quickly became perhaps the single most important sporting event in the African-American community. Held each year in Chicago, the game drew literally thousands of African Americans from across the country; they came to watch the greatest players in Negro league baseball, as chosen by voting through the *Chicago Defender* and *Pittsburgh Courier*. Tellingly, the game, which far outdistanced Negro league baseball's annual World Series in popularity, provided an ideal opportunity for black players to showcase their talents to white sportswriters and fans in attendance, and it helped convince the larger public that these players belonged in major league baseball. Black sportswriters like Wendell Smith, Sam Lacy, and Joe Bostic all used the performances in the East-West Game to persuade white owners that black players had the requisite talent to play major league baseball.

The reintegration of major league baseball finally took place in 1947, when Jackie Robinson joined the Brooklyn Dodgers. This event was of enormous symbolic significance to the African-American community; the fact that a black man was participating in the sport considered America's national pastime and the great social leveler was perhaps a sign that the rhetoric about freedom of opportunity and racial equality was about to come true. Unfortunately, Robinson's entry into major league baseball did not result in a steady influx of African-American players into the game. While four other African-American players would appear on major league rosters the same year as Robinson, the conservative and cautious white owners made racial integration a painfully slow and uneven process that would not be realized by all teams until 1959, when the Boston Red Sox signed outfielder Pumpsie Green.

The last few decades have witnessed great performances by many African-American major leaguers. Willie Mays, Hank Aaron, Frank Robinson, Bob Gibson, Tony Gwynn, Joe Morgan, Ernie Banks, Barry Bonds, and Derek Jeter are just several of the great African-American players who have achieved lasting fame for their exploits on the diamond. As in virtually every other sport, however, African Americans have continued to be underrepresented in coaching, managerial, and administrative positions. Only a few African Americans have been able to transcend continual prejudices and deep-seated racial stereotypes to assume these positions of power in the major leagues. There has been an apparent decline, moreover, in the number of African Americans pursuing careers in the national game. As a result of the increasing popularity of other sports, urban decay, and other factors, fewer African Americans are striving to enter a sport they spent years trying to integrate. The sport has experienced an influx of players from Cuba, the Dominican Republic, and other Latin American countries. The popularity of baseball in their native countries and the promise of financial rewards has lured enormously gifted players to the United States from the city of San Pedro de Macoris and other faraway places.

David K. Wiggins

See also: Joseph Bostic; Rube Foster; Gus Greenlee; Sam Lacy; Negro American League; Negro National League; Wendell Smith; Sportswriters.

FURTHER READING
Rader, Benjamin G. *Baseball: A History of America's Game*. Urbana: University of Illinois Press, 1992.
Rogosin, Donn. *Invisible Men: Life In Baseball's Negro Leagues*. New York: Athenaeum, 1987.
Tygiel, Jules. *Baseball's Great Experiment: Jackie Robinson and His Legacy*. New York: Oxford University Press, 1983.
White, G. Edward. *Creating the National Pastime: Baseball Transforms Itself, 1903–1953*. Princeton, NJ: Princeton University Press, 1996.

★ ★ ★

BASKETBALL

Unlike in many other sports, it is fairly easy to trace the spread of basketball after its invention at the YMCA Training College in Springfield, Massachusetts, in December 1891. Clients and users of settlement houses and YMCAs were soon exposed to the game, and many of those people would certainly have been African Americans, though there is no record of African-American involvement in the sport until 1902. In that year Harry "Bucky" Lew played for the Lowell, Massachusetts, and later Haverhill, teams of the New England League, a professional league that existed briefly in the early 1900s. Lew gained a reputation as a tenacious defensive player in a game that was largely dominated by defense and rough play.

In that same year, Edwin Bancroft Henderson, a well known physical educator and historian of African Americans in sport, first learned the game and taught it to boys in Washington, DC. "By 1906 a league of teams had developed in Washington," according to Henderson, and his 1909–1910 Washington YMCA team (Henderson was its organizer and captain) was the national "Y" champion. From 1904 through 1910 there are records of a number of African-American college basketball players: Samuel Ransom at Beloit College, Wilbur Wood at Nebraska, Cumberland

Posey at Penn State, and Fenwich Watkins at Vermont.

Over the next five years (1911–1916), one of the greatest African-American basketball teams, the Loendi Big Five, from Pittsburgh, was formed by Cum Posey, and many black colleges developed teams. This growth led to the formation in 1912 of the Colored Intercollegiate Athletic Association (later renamed the Central Intercollegiate Athletic Association), which established academic standards for its athletes. In 1923 Bob Douglas formed the New York Renaissance team in Harlem; over the next twenty-five years it won over 2,300 games, including a record eighty-eight straight. Led by great players like Hilton Slocum, "Fats" Jenkins, George Fiall, "Pappy" Ricks, "Bruiser" Saitch, "Tarzan" Cooper, Bill Yancey, "Wee Willie" Smith, Johnny Holt, and later "Pop" Gates, John Isaacs, and "Puggy" Bell, the Rens were the dominant team of the 1930s. The Rens are one of four teams enshrined in the Basketball Hall of Fame in Springfield, Massachusetts. In 1939 the Rens won the first world championship tournament for professional basketball; many of those Rens players were on the Washington Bears team that won the 1943 tournament championship. The Rens were also the first all-black team to be a member of a regular, established (white) professional league. In 1948 the Rens took over the franchise of the Detroit Vagabond Kings in the National Basketball League (NBL); the franchise disbanded as a league entity that December. The Rens finished the season as the Dayton Rens in the NBL before they also disbanded.

Though the Rens were the first team to play in an organized league, there were individual African-American players in the NBL before 1948. In 1935 Hank Williams played briefly for the Buffalo entry in the Midwest Conference, the predecessor of the NBL, which officially began operations in the 1937–1938 season. For the 1942–1943 NBL season the Toledo franchise had five African-American players (including Bill Jones, a University of Toledo graduate), but the team folded after four games as players left for the war. The players on the Chicago Studebakers, sponsored by the United Auto Workers, were exempt from the draft, because they worked in a war industry. Led by former Harlem Globetrotters Sonny Boswell, Duke Cumberland, and Bernie Price, the team started strong but ran into difficulty as the season progressed. The next year (1943–1944) "Wee" Willie Smith, a former Ren, was signed by the Cleveland Chase Brass in February and finished the season as the only African American in the four-team league.

The best-known African-American team in the world, the Harlem Globetrotters, was originally formed by Abe Saperstein, who changed the name of a Chicago team, the Savoy Big Five, and then promoted it over a forty-year period. In 1940 the Globetrotters defeated the Chicago Bruins and in 1948 the Minneapolis Lakers, led by George Mikan, for the world professional championship. This was proof of the tremendous abilities of the Globetrotters, though they have been best known for their showmanship on the court.

In the 1920s African Americans began participating in basketball at largely white universities and colleges. Paul Robeson had been a star at Rutgers from 1915 to 1918. Ralph Bunche, later Nobel Peace Prize recipient, starred at UCLA in the mid-1920s. Dr. Charles Drew played at Amherst and won that school's award as best all-around athlete. George Gregory of Columbia was named to the Helms Foundation All-American team in 1931. Wilmeth Sidat-Singh played at Syracuse before beginning an outstanding professional career that was cut short in 1943 when he was killed in a military plane crash. Jackie

Robinson was a star at UCLA, winning the Pacific Coast Conference-Southern Division scoring title two years in a row, 1939 and 1940. Don Barksdale, also from UCLA, became the first consensus African-American All-American in 1946–1947. William "Dolly" King was the leader of the Long Island University squad beginning in 1937. The Big Ten conference was notable for its unwritten agreement to remain segregated, but the first blacks began play in the league in the 1940s.

Until 1950 not a single black appeared on the roster of any of NCAA championship team. In that year, however, the City College of New York, coached by Nat Holman, a former Original Celtic and member of the Basketball Hall of Fame, won both the NCAA and the National Invitational Tournament titles with three African-American starters: Floyd Lane, Joe Galiber, and Ed Warner. The next season (1950–1951), the National Basketball Association, which had been formed through a merger of the NBL and the Basketball Association of America (BAA) the prior year, began the year with three African Americans on team rosters. Chuck Cooper, an All-American at Duquesne, was drafted by the Boston Celtics. Clifton Nathaniel, who played as Nat "Sweetwater" Clifton, was signed by the New York Knicks from the Harlem Globetrotters. Earl Lloyd was signed by the Washington Capitols and was actually the first African American to play in a regular-season NBA game. Later that year, Hank De Zonie, a former Ren who had appeared in the NBL, was signed by the Tri-Cities Blackhawks and played in five games.

African Americans became more and more prominent on NBA rosters, though it was not until 1958 that at least one African American appeared on each of the NBA's eight team rosters. By 1962 every team in the NBA was starting at least two African Americans. In 1959 a man who was to become the most heralded basketball player up to that time, Wilt Chamberlain, entered the NBA. After smashing all records at Overbrook High in West Philadelphia, Wilt had played two years at the University of Kansas (freshmen were ineligible for varsity play) before leaving school after his junior year to play with the Globetrotters. He had been the first NBA territorial (professional teams at this time had the first rights to players from their local area) draft pick out of high school, signing with the Philadelphia Warriors in 1959. His impact was immediate and long lasting. Chamberlain was the most dominant player of his time, if not ever, and some of the records he holds may never be broken. In his most amazing year, 1961–1962, he averaged 50.4 points and 25.7 rebounds per game; he scored 100 points in a game against the Knicks in March. Despite Chamberlain's dominance, his teams often finished second to the Boston Celtics, with their defensive stalwart Bill Russell. More than anything else, Russell was a winner; he exemplified the sacrifice and tenacity necessary to achieve greatness. With Russell the Celtics won eleven NBA titles, the greatest run of any team ever.

Oscar Robertson also must be noted, as possibly the greatest all-around player in history. In 1955 his high school, Crispus Attucks, became the first all-black school to win the Indiana state championship; the next year it won the championship again, going undefeated. The significance of this championship was great, since Indiana is seen as a citadel both of high school basketball and of the Ku Klux Klan. When the Klan was at its peak in the 1930s, Indiana had the largest number of active members of any state. Robertson refused to back down in the face of racial intimidation, on or off the court. He later left the state to attend the University of Cincinnati, where he led the nation in scoring three straight years and was a territorial draft pick of the Cincinnati Royals. In 1971 he teamed with Lew Alcindor (who later changed his name to Kareem Abdul-Jabbar) to lead the Milwaukee Bucks to the NBA championship.

One of the most significant events in college basketball was the victory in 1966 of Texas Western University (now the University of Texas at El Paso) with five black starters over a heavily favored University of Kentucky team, from the segregated Southeastern Conference (SEC). No longer were there remarks about what blacks could *not* do in basketball; instead, the ability of blacks to excel at all aspects of the game was thereafter widely recognized.

Since then, change has been rapid. In 1972 a number of teams had all-black starting fives. Similar developments transpired in the 1980s in the Big Ten, the Atlantic Coast Conference (ACC) and the SEC, conferences that had been segregated up until the 1940s, 1960s, and the 1960s, respectively. In 1979 Earvin "Magic" Johnson led his Michigan State team to the NCAA title and then proceeded to do the same as a rookie with the Los Angeles Lakers. He was acknowledged as the best all-around player of the 1980s, followed closely by Michael Jordan, possibly the most recognizable figure in the world, who led the Chicago Bulls to six NBA championships before retiring and later returning to play for the Washington Wizards in 2001 after serving as the president of the team. He is now set to retire again following the 2003 season.

African Americans have been participants since the early years of the game of basketball. Their success at the high school, college, and professional levels has been steady despite setbacks related to ethnic discrimination, not ability. Despite such discrimination, basketball has been a dramatic success story for African Americans in sport in the century since the invention of the game.

Murry R. Nelson

See also: Central Intercollegiate Athletic Association; Harlem Globetrotters; Edwin Bancroft Henderson; New York Renaissance Five; Cum Posey.

FURTHER READING
Fitzgerald, Frank. *And the Walls Came Tumbling Down.* Lincoln: University of Nebraska Press, 2000.
Henderson, Edwin B. *The Negro in Sports.* Washington, DC: Associated Publishers, 1949.
Neft, David, Roland Johnson, Richard Cohen, and Jordan Deutsch, eds. *The Sports Encyclopedia: Basketball.* New York: Grosset and Dunlap, 1975.
Peterson, Robert. *Cages to Jump Shots: Pro Basketball's Early Years.* New York: Oxford University Press, 1990.
Rayl, Susan J. "The New York Renaissance Professional Black Basketball Team, 1923–1950." Ph.D. diss., Pennsylvania State University, 1996.
Roberts, Randy. "But They Can't Beat Us: Oscar Robertson and the Crispus Attucks Tigers." Indianapolis: Indiana Historical Society, 1999.

★ ★ ★

Dick BASS

Born April 15, 1937, George, Mississippi
Football player

Bass played interscholastic sports at Vallejo High School in Vallejo, California. His collegiate football play took place at the University of the Pacific, where he was a three-year letter winner. In 1958, Bass led the nation in total offense, rushing, and scoring; he also was named to the All-American team, as a running back. In 1959, Bass was named the team MVP and played in the East-West Shrine Game. The following year he played in the College All-Star Game. At the University of the Pacific, Bass ranks third in all-time rushing (2,714 yards) and second in all-time scoring (thirty-three touchdowns and 208 points). He was the first college player in twelve years to gain more yards by carrying the football than by throwing. He culminated his collegiate career by finishing eighth in the balloting for the Heisman Trophy.

In 1959, after his collegiate career, Bass was drafted by the Los Angeles Rams in the first round. With the Rams, he was named Most Valuable Player three years, made the Pro Bowl five years, and was an All-Pro player for three years. In 1967, because of a trip to Vietnam to visit combat-zone hospitals and entertain troops, the Defense Department conferred upon Bass an honorary rank.

Billy Hawkins

FURTHER READING
Courtesy of Erin Thompson, Sport Information Office at the University of the Pacific.
Ashe, Arthur R., Jr. *A Hard Road to Glory: A History of the African-American Athlete Since 1946.* New York: Amistad, 1988.
Henderson, Edwin B., with the editors of *Sport* Magazine. *The Black Athlete: Emergence and Arrival.* Cornwall Heights, PA: Pennsylvania Publishers, 1968.

★ ★ ★

Don BAYLOR

Born June 28, 1949, Austin, Texas
Baseball player

Don Baylor, a graduate of Stephen F. Austin High School in Austin, Texas, broke into major league baseball with the Baltimore Orioles in 1970. Considered a leadership presence in the locker room, Baylor played for six teams over his nineteen-year career: Baltimore, Oakland, Boston, Minnesota, California, and the New York Yankees. With these teams he participated in seven league championship series and three World Series. His three World Series appearances took place between 1986 and 1988 with Boston, Minnesota, and Oakland. In 1987, he batted .385 for the world-champion Minnesota Twins.

In 1979 Baylor won the American League Most Valuable Player award as a member of the California Angels. He batted .296 with thirty-six home runs and led the Angels to the American League Western Division title. He also led the league in runs with 120 and runs batted in, with 139. Baylor retired after the 1988 season, finishing his career with a .260 lifetime batting average and 338 home runs. He also set the major league record for most times hit by pitches, with 244.

In 1993, Baylor became the first manager of the expansion Colorado Rockies, a position he held until 1998. In 1995 he led the Rockies to the National League wild card and earned himself the Manager of the Year award. Under Baylor's leadership the Rockies compiled a record of 280 wins and 308 losses from 1993 to 1996, the best-ever four-year record for an expansion team.

Rob Fink

FURTHER READING
Baseball Encyclopedia: The Complete and Definitive Record of Major League Baseball. 10th ed. New York: Macmillan, 1996.
Baylor, Don, and Claire Smith. *Don Baylor: Nothing but the Truth: A Baseball Life.* New York: St. Martin's Press, 1989.
Hall, Michael. "I'm Not Loveable, and I'm Not a Loser." *Texas Monthly*, June 2000, 128–31, 179–80.
Leavy, Walter. "Don Baylor: On Top of the World in Colorado. The National League's Manager of the Year Has Become a Favorite Son in Denver." *Ebony*, August 1, 1996, 44.

★ ★ ★

Elgin BAYLOR

Born September 16, 1934, Washington, DC
Basketball player

Baylor, a basketball player, first attended Phelps Vocational, then Spingarn High School (DC), graduating in 1954. He attended the College of Idaho in 1954–1955, averaging 31.3 points per game. He transferred to Seattle University in 1955. Because of his transfer, he forfeited one year of competition. During his year of ineligibility, he played for an AAU team, Westside Ford in Seattle, averaging thirty-four points per game. Baylor averaged over thirty points per game in his two years at Seattle University and was a first-team All-American selection by the *Sporting News*.

Drafted by the Minneapolis Lakers of the National Basketball Association in 1958, he played his entire career (1958–1972) there and in Los Angeles, where the Lakers moved in 1960. Baylor was the NBA Rookie of the Year in 1959 and a ten-time first-team All-NBA selection in the period 1958–1969. He averaged twenty-seven points per game for his career and holds the NBA record of sixty-one points in a playoff game versus Boston on April 14, 1962.

Baylor's fluid play and floor generalship were the hallmarks of his career. He remained in the game as assistant and head coach of the NBA's New Orleans Jazz from 1975 to 1979. He became one of the few black vice president/general managers in professional sport when he assumed that position with the Los Angeles Clippers in 1986.

Baylor was voted into the Naismith Basketball Hall of Fame in 1976 and to the NBA's Fiftieth Anniversary All-Star Team in 1996.

John R. Schleppi

FURTHER READING
Hubbard, Jan, ed. *The Official NBA Encyclopedia*. 3d ed. New York: Doubleday, 2000.
Los Angeles Times, June 25, 1995.
New York Post, April 13, 1979.
New York Times, November 10, 1971.
Walton, David, and John Hareas, eds. *The Sporting News Official NBA Register, 2000–2001*. St. Louis: Sporting News, 2000.

★ ★ ★

Bob BEAMON

Born August 6, 1946, Jamaica, New York
Track and field

Orphaned before he was a year old and raised by his stepfather, James, and grandmother Minnie, Beamon grew up to become one of track and field's greatest stars. His early childhood was marred by much difficulty, and at the age of fourteen he was sent to Public School 622, a New York City school for juvenile delinquents. He distinguished himself athletically at the school, starring on the basketball team and reaching a mark of twenty-four feet in the long jump. He continued his athletic career at Jamaica High School, where he excelled in basketball and achieved national rankings in both the long jump and triple jump. In 1965 he ranked second nationally in the long jump with a leap of 25 feet, 3½ inches and set a national mark in the triple jump with a mark of 50 feet, 3¾ inches.

In 1965 Beamon took his athletic talents to North Carolina Agricultural and Technical University, where over a two-year period he established personal bests in the long jump, triple jump, and 100-meter dash. In 1967 Beamon transferred to Texas Western University, choosing to compete for coach Wayne Vandenberg, who had assembled an outstanding team of track ath-

inches at the Mexico City Olympic Games. Although overshadowed somewhat by the black protests of Tommie Smith, John Carlos, and other African-American athletes, Beamon's jump was one of the greatest single achievements in Olympic history and would not be surpassed until 1991, when Michael Powell leaped 29 feet, 4½ inches at the world championships in Tokyo, Japan. Beamon retired from track and field in 1972. That year he earned a bachelor's degree in sociology and physical education from Adelphi University; he eventually earned a master's degree in psychology from San Diego State University. He operated for a time a center for ghetto children and since 1982 has worked in the Sports Development Office of the County Parks and Recreation Department in Miami, Florida. He was elected to the National Track and Field Hall of Fame in 1977 and the United States Olympic Hall of Fame in 1983.

David K. Wiggins

Bob Beamon, the renowned long jumper who had shattered the world record in the event at the Mexico City Olympic games, finishes a jump in 1975 in a comeback attempt at the Salt Palace in Salt Lake City, Utah. *(AP/Wide World Photos)*

letes. His career at Texas Western was marked by many successes, including indoor world records in the long jump at the 1968 National Association of Intercollegiate Athletics (NAIA) championships and NCAA championships. Beamon's career at Texas Western, however, was also marked by controversy. In April 1968 he joined seven of his teammates in boycotting a track and field meet against Brigham Young University to protest that institution's treatment of African Americans. Beamon lost his scholarship because of his participation in the boycott.

Just a few months after the Brigham Young University boycott, Beamon shocked the international sporting community and garnered lasting fame by shattering the world record in the long jump with a remarkable leap of 29 feet, 2½

See also: Ralph Boston; Track and Field.

FURTHER READING
Moore, Kenny. "Great Leap Forward." *Sports Illustrated*, September 9, 1991, 14–19.
Phinizy, Koles. "The Unbelievable Moment." *Sports Illustrated*, December 23, 1968, 53–56.
Schapp, Dick. *The Perfect Jump*. New York: New American Library, 1976.
Smith, Red. "To Reach the Unreachable Star." *New York Times*, December 24, 1971.

★ ★ ★

Bill BELL

Born June 10, 1909, Polk County, Georgia
Coach, athletic director

Dr. William "Big Bill" Bell was an outstanding African-American football player at Ohio State University who went on to great success in administration, coaching, and education. Bell lettered in football from 1929 to 1931, earning all-conference honors and honorable-mention All-American. Academically, he earned three degrees—a B.A. (1932), M.A. (1937), and Ph.D. (1960)—all from Ohio State University.

Bell's professional life included stints at several historically black colleges. He was an assistant football coach at Howard University, then head football coach and athletic director at Claflin College, South Carolina, in the early 1930s. In 1936, Bell became head coach as well as athletic director and director of physical education at Florida A & M University. From 1936 to 1942, his Rattler teams would win three national titles and compile an overall record of 45–9–6.

In 1943, Bell resigned his position to enlist in the military to serve in World War II. He was director of physical training and coach at the famed Tuskegee Army Air Field from 1943 to 1945. After the war, Bell began a long tenure in the Athletic Department at North Carolina A & T; it lasted from 1946 to 1968. In 1970, he was named athletic director and physical education chair at Fayetteville State University. Dr. Bell is a member of the Hall of Fame of the National Association of Collegiate Directors of Athletics, and he holds the American National Red Cross 25-Year Service Award. He published an autobiography, *Black Without Malice*, in 1983.

Robert Epling

FURTHER READING

"Bell Brilliant as State Sinks Navy." *Pittsburgh Courier Journal*, November 14, 1931.

Bell, William M. *Black Without Malice: The Bill Bell Story*. Fayetteville, NC: William McNeil Bell, Sr., 1983.

Davis, Howard. *Contributions of Blacks to the Physical Education Profession*. Birmingham, AL: Center for Higher Education, 1978.

"Dr. William M. Bell." *Ohio State Monthly* 72 (September 1980): 15.

Florida A & M University Rattler Football (www.famu.edu/athletics/football/news/footballhistory.htm).

"Former Ohio State Grid Great Rates Bell Among Best in Game." *Pittsburgh Courier Journal*, November 7, 1931.

"Private Bill Bell." *Ohio State Monthly* 35 (June 1943): 32.

★ ★ ★

Bobby BELL

Born June 17, 1940, Shelby, North Carolina
Football player

Bell played twelve seasons (1963–1974) as a linebacker for the Kansas City Chiefs and is considered by many as the finest defensive player of his era. In 1983 he was the first outside linebacker and fifth player from the American Football League (AFL) to be inducted into the National Football League (NFL) Hall of Fame. Bell is also a member of the College Football Hall of Fame for his play at the University of Minnesota.

At Cleveland High School in Shelby, North Carolina, Bell was an all-around athlete, earning All-State honors at quarterback. At Minnesota, Bell was a three-year starter, and as a senior (1962) won the Outland Trophy as college football's outstanding lineman.

Bell's signing with the Chiefs was considered a significant victory for the AFL in its competition with the NFL. In twelve seasons, Bell played in two Super Bowls, made twenty-six interceptions, scored eight touchdowns, and was selected for nine All-Star and Pro Bowl games. In 1969, he was named to the All-Time AFL team.

In 1965, Bell was among twenty-one African-American players selected for the AFL All-Star Game in New Orleans. Due to discriminatory conditions in New Orleans, the African-American players chose to boycott the game, which was then relocated to Houston.

Since his retirement, Bell has remained in Kansas City, where he has owned three restaurants, become a motivational speaker, and devoted much of his time to helping local charities, including the Special Olympics and the YMCA.

Michael T. Friedman

FURTHER READING
Dorna Sports Promotions. "Bobby Bell" (www.dornausa.com/speaker/nfl/nfl_index/bell.html).
Porter, David L., ed. *Biographical Dictionary of American Sports: Football.* Westport, CT: Greenwood Press, 1987.
Pro Football Hall of Fame. "Bobby Bell" (www.profootballhof.com/players/enshrinees/bobell.cfm).
Pro Football Hall of Fame. "Gladiator: Bobby Bell Excelled at Many Positions on the Gridiron, EspeciallyLinebacker" (www.profootballhof.com/history/mainpage.cfm?cont_id 3620).
Sherrington, Kevin. "Walk, Don't Run." *Denver Post,* February 22, 1999.

★ ★ ★

James "Cool Papa" BELL

Born May 17, 1903, Starkville, Mississippi
Died March 7, 1991, St. Louis, Missouri
Baseball player

James "Cool Papa" Bell capitalized on his incredible speed in a career as an outfielder for at least seven Negro league teams and in 1974 won election to the National Baseball Hall of Fame. Bell grew up on a farm in rural Mississippi, playing pickup baseball games and helping out in the fields. In 1920 he moved to St. Louis to live with two of his older brothers and go to high school. While attending school Bell also worked in a local packing plant and started playing ball with the Compton Hill Cubs.

Bell finally got his chance in 1922, when the St. Louis Stars signed him to a contract as a pitcher. Manager Bill Gatewood gave him his nickname after watching how calm Bell stayed in pressure situations. He moved to the outfield in 1924 because of an injury to his pitching arm. Bell was a switch-hitter and used his great speed to keep his batting average consistently over .300. Fans loved to watch him play, electing him to the East-West All-Star Game from 1933 through 1944, except when he was playing in Mexico. Bell also spent over twenty winter seasons playing throughout Latin America and in California.

Bell retired from active playing in 1950. He worked for four years as a scout for the St. Louis Browns before leaving the game and taking work as a custodian and security officer at City Hall in St. Louis.

Leslie A. Heaphy

See also: Baseball; Negro National League.

FURTHER READING
Bankes, James. "Flying Feet: The Life and Times of Cool Papa Bell, the Fastest Runner BB Has." *Baseball History* (Fall 1986): 39–58.
Clark, Dick, and Larry Lester. *The Negro Leagues Book.* Cleveland: SABR, 1994.
Holway, John. "How to Score from First on a Sacrifice." *American Heritage,* August 1970, 30–36.
Kram, Mark. "No Place in the Shade: Cool Papa Bell of the Old Negro Leagues." *Sports Illustrated,* August 1973, 68–73, 77–78.
Riley, James A. *The Biographical Encyclopedia of the Negro Baseball Leagues.* New York: Carroll and Graf, 1994.

★ ★ ★

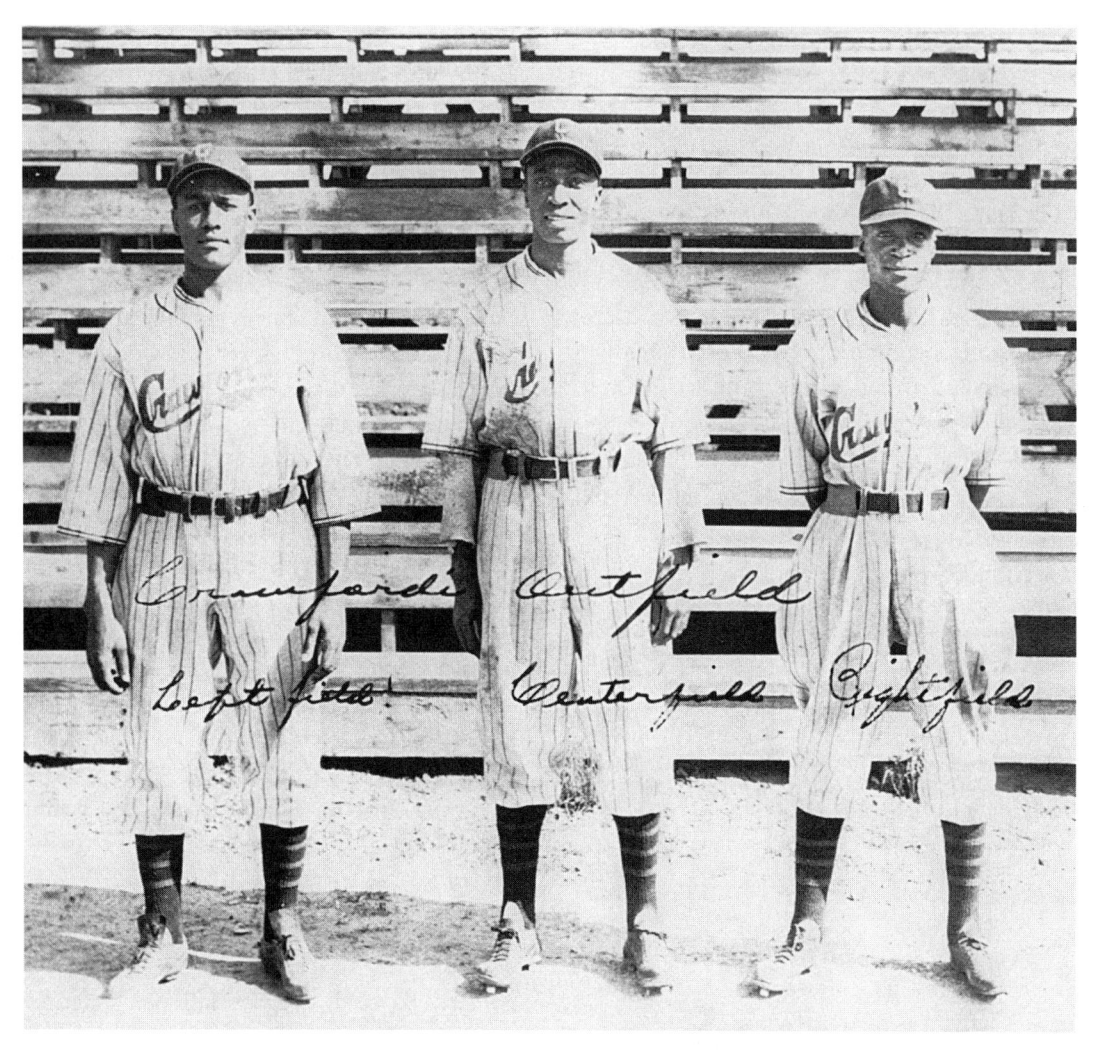

Pittsburgh Crawfords outfielder James "Cool Papa" Bell with teammates Sam Bankhead (left) and Jimmie Crutchfield (right). *(National Baseball Hall of Fame Library, Cooperstown, NY)*

Walter BELLAMY

Born July 24, 1939, New Bern, North Carolina
Basketball player

Bellamy attended J.T. Barber High School in New Bern, North Carolina, where he was a three-year letter winner in basketball, named two times to both the All-State Team and All-Conference Team. He continued his academic and athletic pursuits at Indiana University in Bloomington. At Indiana, Bellamy averaged 20.6 points per game, was selected two times to the All-Big-Ten team and twice to the All-American team, and was named to the *Sporting News* All-America second team. In 1960, Bellamy was a member of the gold medal-winning U.S. Olympic Team.

At six feet, eleven inches and 245 pounds, Bellamy was the first player chosen in the 1961 college draft by the Chicago Packers, for whom he became the NBA Rookie of the Year by averaging 31.6 points per game and nineteen rebounds per game.

Bellamy was a four-time NBA All-Star, was named to the All-NBA first team in 1962, and played in 1,043 of 1,055 games during his fourteen-year pro career. In 1974, Bellamy retired from the NBA. He was ranked sixth in scoring (20,941 points) and third in rebounding (14,241) and field goal percentage (.516). He was inducted into the Pro Basketball Hall of Fame on May 10, 1993.

Billy Hawkins

FURTHER READING

Ashe, Arthur, Jr. *A Hard Road to Glory: A History of the African-American Athlete Since 1946.* New York: Amistad, 1988.

Henderson, Edwin B., with the editors of Sport Magazine. *The Black Athlete: Emergence and Arrival.* Cornwall Heights, PA: Pennsylvania Publishers, 1968.

Pro Basketball Hall of Fame (www.hoophall.com/index.htm).

★ ★ ★

Dave BING

Born November 29, 1943, Washington, DC
Basketball player

Dave Bing's parents moved to Washington, DC, from South Carolina before he was born. His father was a bricklayer and his mother a domestic. Though their combined income left them on the edge of poverty, Bing's parents instilled in him a strong work ethic. At the age of five, a nail pierced his left eye, an injury that would leave him with permanently blurred vision.

A gifted athlete, Bing was forced to choose between baseball and basketball. After choosing the latter, he attended Syracuse University, where he became an All-American. The Detroit Pistons selected him second overall in the 1966 draft, and he became the NBA's Rookie of the Year. A detached right retina in 1971 nearly ended his NBA career; however, he recovered and enjoyed seven more years of play in the NBA, the final two with the Washington Bullets.

After spending summers working at the National Bank of Detroit and with the Chrysler Corporation, Bing used his dual degree in economics and marketing to found Bing Steel in 1980. The corporation, engaged primarily in the auto parts industry, began with $230,000 in capital; it is now one of the largest black-owned corporations in the United States, with 1,500 employees and a gross income of almost $400 million in 2000. He has also been a community leader in Detroit, heading a campaign to save Detroit public schools' athletic programs, supporting such charities as Boys and Girls Clubs and the Urban League, and developing a partnership with Ford Motor Company to train African Americans for jobs.

Gregory S. Goodale

FURTHER READING

"Athlon's No. 36 NBA Greatest: Dave Bing." *Athlon Sports* (www.athlonsports.com/article/463).

Bing, Dave. "Acceptance Speech for Outstanding Business Leader 2001." Norwood University, January 26, 2001, Palm Beach, Florida (www.northwood.edu/obl/2001/Dave percent20Bing percent202001.htm).

Henning, Lynn. "Bing Made Pistons Glad They Chose Him." *Detroit News*, July 23, 2001.

Oprea, Terrence. "Tough as Steel." *Detroiter,* May 2000.

★ ★ ★

BLACK COACHES ASSOCIATION

Founded in 1988, thirty-four years after the end of segregation in public schools, the Black Coaches Association (BCA) was formed by a group of African-American Division I assistant basketball coaches, who were concerned about the lack of head-coaching opportunities available to minorities, and African-American football coaches, who had joined together to discuss their concerns. Eventually, the BCA extended membership to all coaches. The early concerns and the national debate over the National Collegiate Athletic Association's adoption of initial-eligibility standards and disparaging remarks about the readiness and qualifications of minorities in decision-making roles in professional and collegiate sport sparked a civil rights movement within the sport industry. The formation of the BCA brought national attention to the existence of institutional barriers that had blocked the paths of all minorities at one time or another within sport.

The mission of the BCA is two-pronged: to address significant issues pertaining to the participation and employment of minorities in sport in general and intercollegiate athletics in particular; and to assist minorities aspiring to careers in athletics either as coaches or as administrators at the high school, collegiate, or professional levels. The BCA has five specific goals: to strengthen commitment to diversity within the membership of the NCAA; to create professional development seminars and workshops for BCA members; to encourage and solicit support for the enhancement of opportunities for minorities in athletics to form other sport and nonsport organizations; to assist members in their career development strategies; and to keep the membership and the general public informed of relevant BCA activities.

Under the direction of Rudy Washington, the organization's first executive director, the BCA evolved into an activist group. Early activities brought to the forefront the hiring practices within sport and spearheaded the NCAA's formation of the Minority Opportunities and Interests Committee, dedicated to increasing opportunities for minorities. Information is disseminated through the *BCA Journal*, a vehicle for furthering diversity within the ranks of coaching and athletic administration via the publication of articles on research, coaching, and career networking techniques.

In 1996 the BCA entered the arena of event management and marketing by production of the BCA Football Classic preseason football game and the BCA Basketball Classic. These events feature top-ranked predominantly white and historically black institutions of higher education. Fan support of the teams and total return for corporate sponsors have earned national television coverage on ESPN2. Such events enable the organization to award ten $5,000 ethnic-minority postgraduate scholarships to students pursuing careers in athletics administration.

To fulfill its commitment to removing barriers, the BCA moved its executive offices from Georgia to Indianapolis, Indiana, home of the NCAA. This move and the hiring of a new executive director, Floyd Keith, in early 2001 are evidence of the organization's continuing effort to confront challenges facing minorities at all levels of sport.

Danielle A. Mincey White

See also: Coaches and Managers.

FURTHER READING
Black Coaches Association (www.bcasports.org).
Brooks, Dana, and Ronald Althouse. "African American Head Coaches and Administrators: Progress But . . . ?" In *Racism in College Athletics: The African American Athlete's Experience*, eds. Dana Brooks and Ronald Althouse, 85–117. Morgantown, WV: Fitness Information Technology, 2000.
Wiggins, David K. "Black Coaches Association." In *Encyclopedia of Ethnicity and Sports in the United States*, ed. George B. Kirsch, et al. Westport, CT: Greenwood Press, 2000.

BLACK SPORTS MAGAZINE

Black Sports magazine was published monthly from 1971 to 1978. The New York–based magazine was primarily dedicated to covering African-American athletes. The first issue, published in April 1971, featured a cover story on Oscar Robertson and Kareem Abdul-Jabbar, then known as Lew Alcindor. *Black Sports* provided cover-story opportunities for African-American athletes who were traditionally overlooked by such mainstream sport magazines as *Sport Illustrated*. Athletes ranging from basketball legend Julius Erving to soccer hero Pele graced the cover of *Black Sports*.

The sole owner and publisher of *Black Sports* magazine was Allan P. Barron. He had earned degrees in anthropology and psychology from the University of London and was the founder of a computer software company named Computer Deductions. Barron raised all the capital to create Black Sports, Inc., which published *Black Sports* and *Discovery* magazines.

During its publication history, *Black Sports* magazine was a limited success with a small circulation. The last issue was published in June 1978.

Tracey M. Salisbury

FURTHER READING
New York Times, January 12, 1971.
New York Times, December 8, 1971.
Staff of the Hallie Q. Brown Memorial Library Central State University, Wilberforce, Ohio, comps. *Index to Periodical Articles by and about Blacks*. Boston: G.K. Hall, 1977.
Who's Who in the East. 14th ed. Chicago: Marquis Who's Who, 1974–1975.

BLACK WOMEN IN SPORTS FOUNDATION

The Black Women in Sports Foundation (BWSF), located at 712 North Twenty-third Street, Philadelphia, Pennsylvania, was founded in 1992 by Tina Sloan Green, Nikki Franke, and Dr. Alpha Alexander. Building on alliances between Temple University and the greater Philadelphia community, Green and Franke, Temple University faculty members who had notable careers in sports, combined with Alpha Alexander, an earlier Temple University associate who had become director of health and sports advocacy for the YWCA in New York, to convene a national assembly of women who could use their experience and knowledge to explore and exploit the many opportunities in sports for black women.

The BWSF established Project Challenge (based in Philadelphia) in 1995 to provide resources necessary to train fourteen outstanding African-American female tennis players (ages eight through twelve) and facilitate competitive experiences for them. The BWSF's first conference, in 1997, included speakers such as Wendy Halliard (national team captain of Rhythmic Gymnastics) and Sara Lomax Reese (editor, publisher, and founder of *Health Quest Magazine*). Although still dedicated to "hands-on," grassroots outreach programs, by 1998 BWSFs mission was to establish a national foundation to increase involvement of black women in all aspects of the multimillion-dollar sports industry, a goal that is to be accomplished through seven strategic objectives—governance, strategic/corporate financial partnering, greater public relations awareness, mentoring partnerships to serve black girls and women, media, brokering information, and charting careers for black women in sports.

Dana D. Brooks and Ronald Althouse

FURTHER READING

BWSF Newsletter, P.O. Box 2610, Philadelphia, PA, 19130.

Corbett, Doris, and William Johnson. "The African American Female in Collegiate Sports: Sexism and Racism." In *Racism in College Athletics: The African American Athlete's Experience*, eds. Dana Brooks and Ronald Althouse, 200–25. Morgantown, WV: Fitness Information Technology, 2000 (www.blackwomen in sport.org).

FURTHER READING

Geist, William E. "New Home on the Range." *New York Times*, July 27, 1985.

Newman, Andy. "Deep in the Heart of Brooklyn, Cowboys & Kosher Food." *New York Times*, September 1, 1997.

Reyes, Damaso. "On the Open Range in Harlem." *New York Amsterdam News*, May 21, 1998.

Sullivan, Robert. "Each Year in Harlem the Old West Meets the Inner City." *Sports Illustrated*, August 8, 1988, 6–7.

★ ★ ★

BLACK WORLD CHAMPIONSHIP RODEO

Founded by Dr. George E. Blair, the first annual Black World Championship Rodeo (BWCR) was held in 1984 in the streets of Harlem, in New York City. Blair's major objective is to bring western black history and modern-day black cowboys and cowgirls to the attention of black and white Americans. Many are not aware that during the days of slavery, black cowboys and cowgirls in the West established an important part of our heritage by forming the first rodeos.

Competitors in the event consist of world-class riders from the West and individuals from Harlem who complete tryouts. A typical event consists of bull and bronco riding, calf roping, bareback riding, and steer wrestling. The BWCR expanded to Brooklyn and Queens and, in 1988, traveled to Bridgeport, CT, Newark, NJ, and Philadelphia. When first held, the rodeo drew one or two thousand spectators, but it has grown to host over 150,000 spectators of varying racial backgrounds. People, both young and old, come out to enjoy this event, which has been described as "one of the two most outstanding outdoor events in New York City."

Audrey A. Wiggins and Amy M. Cawley

Mel BLOUNT

Born April 10, 1948, Vidalia, Georgia
Football player

Blount was a premiere cornerback of his era. He starred at Lyons High School in Georgia and at Southern University before being drafted in the third round (fifty-third overall) by the Pittsburgh Steelers in 1970. He demonstrated superior strength, speed, and intelligence as an NFL cornerback. The following accomplishments highlight his abilities: All-Pro three years, five Pro Bowls, four Super Bowls, NFL defensive MVP in 1975, and played in 200 of 201 regular-season games. At six feet, three inches and 205 pounds, Blount in his career made fifty-seven interceptions, which he returned for a total of 736 yards; recovered thirteen fumbles; and scored three touchdowns. Blount played a major role in the Pittsburgh "Steel Curtain" defense that led the team to four Super Bowl championships (1974, 1975, 1978, and 1979).

Blount retired after the 1983 season, later becoming the NFL's director of player relations. He was enshrined into the Pro Football Hall of Fame in 1989. In addition to his outstanding NFL career and accomplishments, Blount has had considerable impact on the lives of troubled youth. He has two youth homes, one in Pennsylvania and one in Georgia, places where young boys can find a refuge of love, discipline, and renewed hope. His courageous community activism for youth has been documented in the book *The Cross Burns Brightly*.

Billy Hawkins

FURTHER READING

Ashe, Arthur, Jr. *A Hard Road to Glory: A History of the African-American Athlete Since 1946.* New York: Amistad, 1988.

Blount, Mel, and Charles Sterling. *The Cross Burns Brightly: A Hall-of-Famer Tackles Racism and Adversity to Help Troubled Boys.* Grand Rapids, MI: Zondervan, 1993.

Pro Football Hall of Fame (www.profootballhof.com).

★ ★ ★

Edward BOLDEN

Born January 17, 1881, Concordsville, Pennsylvania
Died September 27, 1950, Philadelphia, Pennsylvania
Baseball team owner

Edward Bolden was not originally a baseball player but a butler and a postal clerk for the Central Post Office in Philadelphia. He exemplifies the African-American professionals who emerged in the early twentieth century thanks to a willingness to work within the parameters of a biracial society, emphasizing self-reliance and racial cooperation rather than protest against mounting injustices.

Bolden began his career in baseball as a scorekeeper for the Hilldale Field Club and eventually assumed control of the team. Renaming it the Hilldale Athletic Club, Bolden transformed the club into one of the top black independent baseball teams in the East. He promoted the club around the notion of "clean baseball" and required his players to be "gentlemen in uniform as well as off the ballfield." In 1923, Bolden formed the Eastern Colored League, in which his Hilldale Athletic Club won the first three League championships. In 1925, Hilldale defeated the Kansas City Monarchs in the Colored World Series. He suffered a nervous breakdown in 1927, and without his leadership the league disbanded the following year.

In 1933, after he recovered his health, Bolden organized the Philadelphia Stars with the financial support of Eddie Gottlieb. The following year the Stars entered the Negro National League, winning the pennant in their first season. The Stars defeated the Chicago American Giants in the championship playoff.

Bolden was also active in black community affairs. He participated in several black fraternal organizations as an Elk, a thirty-second-degree Mason, and a Shriner. He was also a member of the Citizen's Republican Club, a local black business and professional group. The Hilldale Corporation of Philadelphia gave generously to black causes, and the team participated in annual benefit and charity functions.

Michael E. Lomax

See also: Eastern Colored League.

FURTHER READING

Lanctot, Neil. *Fair Dealing and Clean Playing: The Hilldale Club and the Development of Black Professional Baseball, 1910–1932.* Jefferson, NC: McFarland, 1994.

———. "Fair Dealing and Clean Playing: Ed Bolden and the Hilldale Club, 1910–1932." *Pennsylvania Magazine of History and Biography* 67 (January/April 1993): 3–49.

Lomax, Michael E. "Black Baseball, Black Community, Black Entrepreneurs: The History of the Negro National and Eastern Colored Leagues, 1880–1930." Ph.D. diss., Ohio State University, 1996.

Riley, James A. *The Biographical Encyclopedia of the Negro Baseball Leagues.* New York: Carroll and Graf, 1994.

Edward Bolden (in top hat and coat far left), long-time and influential owner of the Hilldale Baseball Club of Philadelphia, standing with his players prior to the first Negro World Series in 1924. *(National Baseball Hall of Fame Library, Cooperstown, NY)*

★ ★ ★

Barry BONDS

Born July 24, 1964, Riverside, California
Baseball player

His father (Bobby) was an outstanding major league baseball player, his mother (Pat) is a housewife. Bonds was drafted by the Pittsburgh Pirates in 1985 after playing at Arizona State and reached the big leagues the following year. Moving on to his hometown San Francisco Giants in 1993, he would be named Player of the Decade and win three MVP awards in the 1990s. His one disappointment as a player was his lack of postseason success, including losing to the California Angels in the 2002 World Series.

Bonds was reviled by media and fans alike for his aloofness. It took a 2001 season in which the left-handed slugger hit his 500th home run and broke season records held by Mark McGwire (seventy-three home runs) and Babe Ruth (.863 slugging percentage) to gain widespread recognition as one of the greatest players of all time. By the end of his record-shattering season, the fans, media, and Bonds himself had been caught up in the events and had come to terms with each other.

During 2001 he moved ahead of Reggie Jackson into sixth place on the career home run list (567) and could lay claim to being the best left fielder ever; perhaps only his godfather, Willie Mays, could challenge him as the greatest African-American major leaguer. Bonds remained the only player to hit 400 home runs and steal 400 bases. A fine fielder with an accurate arm, the nine-time All-Star has also won eight Gold Gloves.

David C. Skinner

FURTHER READING
Gammons, Peter. "Bonds Reputation Continues to Take a Beating." *Baseball America*, April 10, 1991, 5.
———. "Taking Stock of Bonds: Barry Bonds Has Never Tried to Play Mr. Good." *ESPN Magazine*, May 15, 2000, 106.
Keown, Tim. "BFD: Barry Feels Determined to Win the Giants a Championship—and That's All." *ESPN Magazine*, September 17, 2001, 42–48.
Verducci, Tom. "Pushing 70." *Sports Illustrated*, October 8, 2001, 38–43.
White, Paul. "Approaching the Magic Number 500: Barry Bonds Is Shooting for a Pair of Milestones." *USA Today Baseball Weekly*, April 18, 2001, 22–23.

San Francisco Giants' Barry Bonds celebrates with his son Nikolai after hitting his 73rd home run against the Los Angeles Dodgers in 2001. (AP/Wide World Photos)

★ ★ ★

Bob BOOZER

Born April 26, 1937, Omaha, Nebraska
Basketball player

The son of John and Viola Boozer and a graduate of Kansas State University, Boozer was part of the first wave of outstanding African-American basketball players of the 1950s who made a profound impact on the game by integrating college basketball. He played eleven years in the NBA before embarking on a successful career in business and public service.

Boozer's basketball education began at Omaha Technical High School, a predominantly African-American school in inner-city Omaha. After earning All-State honors and leading his team to a second-place finish in 1955, Boozer chose to play college basketball at Kansas State University, where Tex Winter, the master of the triple-post offense, was building a formidable team. Between 1957 and 1959 the six-foot eight-inch, 220-pound Boozer would lead the Wildcats to two conference titles, two NCAA appearances, and a "Final Four" appearance (1958). In three years Boozer scored 1,685 points, a 21.6 average, which established new KSU records. In 1958 he was the Big Eight "Player of the Year," and he earned All-American honors in 1958 and 1959.

In 1959 the Cincinnati Royals made Boozer the first pick of the 1959 NBA draft. Rather than signing a contract with the Royals, Boozer chose to play for the Peoria Caterpillars in the National Industrial Basketball League so that he could pursue his dream of representing the United States in the 1960 Olympics in Rome. In 1960, Peoria, coached by Warren Womble, won its fifth AAU national tournament, and Boozer was the tournament's MVP. Although Peoria lost to the University All-Stars in the championship game of the Olympic Trials, Boozer joined Oscar Robertson, Jerry West, Jerry Lucas, and Walt Bellamy on what some have called the first U.S. Olympic basketball "Dream Team." Coached by Pete Newell, who had led the University of California to a 1958 NCAA title, the United States posted a perfect 8–0 record, and Boozer earned a gold medal.

After the Olympics Boozer signed with the Royals; in his eleven NBA years he played for six teams. He scored 12,964 points for a career average of 14.8. His most productive years were with the Chicago Bulls between 1966 and 1969. With Chicago he averaged in two seasons over twenty points, played in the 1967 All-Star Game, and helped to establish the city's first successful professional basketball franchise. In 1970–1971 Boozer ended his career with the Milwaukee Bucks, after helping Oscar Robertson and Kareem Abdul-Jabbar bring that city its only NBA title.

Following his career in basketball, Boozer held a variety of management positions for Northwestern Bell (1971–1977) and U.S. West (1977–1997). After retiring from U.S. West, Boozer became a member of the Nebraska Parole Board. In 1992 Kansas State made Boozer a charter member of its Athletic Hall of Fame. In 1994 Governor Ben Nelson of Nebraska presented Boozer with the state's "Trailblazer" award for his contributions. In 1996 Governor William Graves inducted Boozer into the Kansas Sports Hall of Fame.

Adolph H. Grundman

FURTHER READING
Biographical Sketch, Kansas Sports Hall of Fame.
Biographical Sketch, Kansas State Hall of Fame.
Phone interviews, July 25, 2001, and October 25, 2001.

★ ★ ★

John BORICAN

Born April 4, 1913, Bridgeton, New Jersey
Died December 22, 1942, Bridgeton, New Jersey
Runner

John Borican attended Temple University and earned his undergraduate degree from Virginia State University; he received a master's of arts from Columbia University and was a candidate for a doctorate when he died. Professionally, Borican was a portrait artist, specializing in oil painting, and had worked as the assistant director of the Boys Club of Newark.

As a track and field competitor, Borican was arguably one of the most talented African-American athletes between 1936 and 1942. He held numerous running records, including the American record for 660 yards-yard (1:10.2, 1941), 880 yards-yard (1:50.5, 1940), 800 meters-meter (1:50, 1942), and 1,000 yards-yard (2:08.8, 1939). Borican was the AAU pentathlon winner in 1938, 1939, and 1941, and he was the first to win the pentathlon and decathlon in the same year (1941). Additionally, Borican set the world record in the three-quarter-mile race (3:02.6, 1940) and was selected to the 1939 and 1941 All-American Track and Field Team for the 1000-yard-yard run. Borican did not qualify for the 1936 Olympics and was unable to compete in the 1940 Olympics due to World War II.

In 1929, Borican assisted a Chicago police detective in capturing a murderer and became interested in police and intelligence work. Borican wanted to join an intelligence staff in the armed forces and passed the entrance exam for the New York Police Department.

Borican died of a mysterious form of pernicious anemia. In 2000, he was inducted into the National Track and Field Hall of Fame.

Sara A. Elliott

FURTHER READING
Ashe, Arthur R., Jr. *A Hard Road to Glory: A History of the African-American Athlete, 1919–1945*. New York: Warner Books, 1988.
"John Borican, 29, Champion Runner." *New York Times*, December 23, 1942.
Murray, Florence. *The Negro Handbook*. New York: Wendell Malliet, 1942.
———. *The Negro Handbook: 1944*. New York: Current Reference, 1944.
Rose, Lester. "Artful Athlete." *Negro Digest* 3 (May 1945): 37–40.
"World Record Trio Picked for Hall of Fame." *USA Track and Field*, October 23, 2000 (www.usatf.org/news/hallvets2000.html).

★ ★ ★

Joseph BOSTIC

Born March 24, 1908, Mount Holly, New Jersey
Died May 29, 1988, Long Island, New York
Journalist, promoter

The son of Lawrence and Lillian Eldridge Bostic, Bostic attended Mount Holly High School, Atlantic City High School, and Morgan State College (later University). He started graduate studies at Columbia University but did not earn a degree. Bostic was a journalist, stadium announcer, broadcaster, educator, and concert and theatrical promoter.

A fearless advocate for black athletes, Bostic crusaded for the integration of major league baseball. While he was sports editor for the *New York People's Voice*, he helped arrange a tryout for two black players with the Brooklyn Dodgers. He also criticized blacks, complaining that the Negro leagues did not treat their fans well and denouncing Satchell Paige for making what he considered outrageous demands.

Bostic achieved several firsts. He was the first black to announce boxing matches at Madison Square Garden and join the boxing writers and track writers associations. He served as stadium announcer for Negro National League games at Yankee Stadium. For four consecutive years, he announced the annual East-West All-Star Game in Chicago. Bostic also worked for the *Baltimore Afro-American* and the *New York Amsterdam News*.

Bostic found success away from the field of sports. He became the first black broadcaster at WCBM in Baltimore. During his career as a promoter, he organized the first all-black gospel program at Carnegie Hall. Bostic and his wife Dorothy also founded a private school in Brooklyn.

Michael Marsh

See also: Sportswriters.

FURTHER READING
Evans, Howie. "Bostic: Sports Pioneer Dies." *New York Amsterdam News*, June 4, 1988.
"Newsman Joseph Bostic Eulogized." *Los Angeles Sentinel*, June 9, 1988.
Orodenker, Richard, ed. *Dictionary of Literary Biography: American Sportswriters and Writers on Sport*. Farmington Hills, MI: Bruccoli Clark Layman, 2001.
Reisler, Jim. *Black Writers/Black Baseball: An Anthology of Articles from Black Sportswriters Who Covered the Negro Leagues*. Jefferson, NC: McFarland, 1993.

★ ★ ★

Ralph BOSTON

Born May 9, 1939, Laurel, Mississippi
Jumper

An outstanding competitor in the long jump, Ralph Boston was raised as the tenth child in a poor Mississippi family. He became a high school track star and attended Tennessee A & I University (now Tennessee State University), where he was the NCAA long-jump champion in 1960 and 1961. In 1960, he won the gold medal in the long jump at the Rome Olympic Games and became the first athlete to break Jesse Owens's Olympic long-jump record with a leap of 26 feet 7¾ inches. He was also undefeated in high-hurdle competition in 1961, but he soon abandoned that event to concentrate on the long jump.

As a long jumper, he won the AAU outdoor championship every year from 1961 to 1966 and the AAU indoor championships in 1961 and 1965. In May 1961, he became the first to break twenty-seven feet in the long jump, and he held the world record on several other occasions during the 1960s. In the 1964 Tokyo Olympic Games, he finished second by an inch and a half to Lynn Davies. A knee injury in 1967 threatened to keep him out of the Mexico City Olympic Games of 1968, but he competed anyway, finishing third behind Bob Beamon, who jumped 29 feet 2½ inches, and Klaus Beer from East Germany.

Since retiring from competition in 1969, he has worked as a television commentator and an administrator at Tennessee State University. He was elected to the National Track and Field Hall of Fame in 1974.

John E. Findling

See also: Track and Field.

FURTHER READING
Henderson, Edwin B., with the editors of *Sport* Magazine. *The Black Athlete: Emergence and Arrival.* Cornwall Heights, PA: Pennsylvania Publishers, 1968.
Page, James A. *Black Olympian Medalists.* Englewood, CO: Libraries Unlimited, 1991.
Porter, David L., ed. *Biographical Dictionary of American Sports: Outdoor Sports.* Westport, CT: Greenwood Press, 1988.

★ ★ ★

BOWLING

Bowling has been an enormously popular sport among African Americans, just as it has been for white Americans. For much of our history, however, African Americans were forced to participate in the sport on a segregated basis because of racially discriminatory practices. Throughout the first half of the twentieth century African-American bowlers competed on separate teams and in separate leagues because of the "Caucasians only" clauses in the constitutions of the white American Bowling Congress (ABC) and the Women's International Bowling Congress (WIBC). In 1939 these separate black teams and leagues would be organized into the National Bowling Association (NBA), a group that is still in existence today, although the "Caucasians only" clauses were taken out of the constitutions of the ABC and WIBC in 1951. The NBA has been an important institution in the African-American community, with a large membership base, sponsorship of important national tournaments, and strong leadership. Included among its many presidents was William Dehart Hubbard, the first African-American gold medalist in the long jump in the 1924 Olympic Games.

A number of outstanding African-American men and women have distinguished themselves in the sport, particularly in NBA-sponsored tournaments. Included among these bowlers are Hazel Lyman, Ben Harding, Ruth Coburn, Alphonso Harris, Clyde Wilson, and Laura Jones. In addition to participation in NBA tournaments, African Americans have competed on the Professional Bowlers Association (PBA) tour. The first to participate on the tour was Fuller Gordy, a Detroit, Michigan, bowler whose family started Motown Records. Following Gordy into the PBA have been such outstanding African-American bowlers as Charlie Venable of Brooklyn, New York; George Branham of Indianapolis; Willie Willis of New Haven, Connecticut; Kim Terrell of Daly City, California; and Cheryl Daniels of Detroit.

David K. Wiggins

See also: National Bowling Association.

FURTHER READING
Ashe, Arthur R., Jr. *A Hard Road to Glory.* New York: Amistad, 1993.
Dent, David J. *In Search of Black America: Discovering the African-American Dream.* New York: Simon & Schuster, 2000.
"Negroes in Bowling: Maurice Kilgore Is Negro America's First TV Bowler." *Ebony* 13 (April 1958): 95–98.
Pezzano, Chuck. "Charlie Venable." *Black Sports,* February 1974, 60.
Pozenal, John. "Black Bowling Pros." *Black Sports,* April 1974, 39.

BOXING

Boxing has a long history. Originally a brutal sport practiced by the ancient Greeks, in the eighteenth century it was popular in England and appeared in the American colonies. Frontiersmen practiced a no-holds-barred form of fighting to settle disputes and test their mettle, while slaves were probably pitted against one another for their owners' entertainment.

Jack Broughton, a British fighter, developed a set of rules in 1743, and the earliest African Americans to win renown did so in England. Bill Richmond, born in New York in 1763, traveled there as the servant of a British lord and general. He took up boxing in 1804, winning several matches before losing to the champion, Tom Cribb, in 1805. Richmond continued to fight into his sixth decade but spent most of his time as a tavern keeper and boxing instructor. One of his charges, Tom Molineaux, proved even better than he had been. Reputed to be a former Virginia slave, Molineaux arrived in England illiterate and uneducated but possessing great courage, stamina, and punching power, at five feet, nine inches and nearly 200 pounds. Under Richmond's tutelage, he began boxing in 1810, and his decisive wins earned him a bout with Cribb in December of that year, his first (albeit disputed) loss. An 1811 rematch drew a crowd estimated as high as 25,000, mostly hostile and nationalistic, fearing the loss of the British crown to an American; Cribb prevailed convincingly. Molineaux continued to defeat lesser fighters for years before lapsing into alcoholism and destitution.

In 1838, the London Prize Ring Rules revised Broughton's earlier regulations by eliminating kicking, gouging, and biting. Under these conditions, a number of Irish-American fighters emerged to challenge the British by mid-century. The rules underwent further revision in 1865 under the auspices of the London Athletic Club and the sponsorship of the Marquis of Queensberry. The new regulations allowed for padded gloves, three-minute rounds with an intervening rest periods of a minute, and a knockout victory after a ten-second count. The Queensberry rules gained slow and limited acceptance, and a bare-knuckle championship, won by John L. Sullivan, occurred as late as 1889 in America.

Having gained the heavyweight championship, Sullivan declared a color ban, refusing to fight black boxers and thereby denying Peter Jackson a legitimate chance for the title. Jackson had been born in St. Croix in the Virgin Islands; his family had soon moved to Australia, where he grew to formidable size at 6 feet, 1½ inches and over 190 pounds. Jackson won the Australian heavyweight championship in 1886 and arrived in the United States in 1888, where he fought a sixty-one-round draw with Jim Corbett in 1891. When Corbett subsequently defeated Sullivan for the championship, he too enforced a color line, despite the fact that Jackson gained the British Empire championship in 1892. Jackson died at age forty of tuberculosis, denied an opportunity to fulfill his world championship dream.

George Dixon, born in Halifax, Nova Scotia, began his twenty-year boxing career at age sixteen and reputedly appeared in more than 800 fights. He garnered the world bantamweight title in 1890 and ruled the featherweight division from 1891 to 1900, but his most famous fight occurred in the New Orleans Carnival of Champions in 1892. Dixon's bloody thrashing of the white Jack Skelly challenged the survival of the fittest mentality of the period and notions of white superiority. It produced a racist backlash in the southern city and a move to ban interracial fights. Only Joe Gans, who held the lightweight title twice between 1902 and 1908, gained distinction. Racism thus stunted the careers of black fighters, particularly at the heavyweight level, the ultimate prize, where such top fighters as Sam McVey, Sam Langford, Joe Jeannette, and Harry Wills repeatedly fought each other for purses at the turn of the century. It remained for Jack Johnson to break the deadlock.

Born the son of a slave, Johnson learned to fight as a boy in Galveston, Texas. Like many young African Americans, he was thrown for the amusement of white spectators into "battle royals," group free-for-alls from which one victor emerged. His pugilistic proficiency earned him professional status and the dominant position among his African-American peers. In 1908, unable to gain a championship match in America, he pursued champion Tommy Burns to Australia; he punished and taunted the white man in the ring and became the first black heavyweight champion of the world. Johnson used his acquired status as a social prod, tormenting white sensibilities and challenging social mores by defeating subsequent challengers and taking white wives; the response was a search for the "Great White Hope" who might salvage white pride. The previous champion, undefeated Jim Jeffries, came out of retirement to resurrect racist hopes, only to suffer another demoralizing beating. Johnson did, however, succumb to the Mann Act, a federal law that prohibited interstate traffic for immoral purposes, which affected his entourage of white prostitutes. Forced to flee the country, he eventually lost a controversial 1915 bout in Havana, Cuba, to Jess Willard, permitting his return to the United States, but he soon encountered another color ban.

While black heavyweights languished for more than 20 years, blacks in other divisions gained short-lived successes. Louis Phal, a Senegalese who fought as "Battling Siki," held the light heavyweight title in 1922–1923 but was shot and killed in a New York riot in 1925. "Tiger" Flowers, the first African-American middleweight champ in 1926, died a year later in surgery. Panama Al Brown, born in the Canal Zone, turned pro at twenty and held the bantamweight crown from 1929 to 1935.

During the 1920s, boxing was legalized in some states where it had been illegal, and a proliferation of amateur tournaments ensued. National competitions, like the Golden Gloves, fueled the aspirations of poverty-stricken or working-class youths and trained fighters for the professional ranks; among them was Joe Louis. Born the seventh child of an Alabama sharecropper family that sought refuge in Detroit, Louis emerged as a top amateur. In order to pursue the lucrative possibilities at the professional level, his managers carefully crafted a more docile, compliant image, unlike Jack Johnson. As America's most promising heavyweight, Louis fought his most significant battle before gaining the championship. He was matched against Max Schmeling, the German champion, in 1936, as Hitler spread his Nazi message; the fight assumed international political proportions, portrayed as fascism versus democracy; Schmeling delivered Louis's first defeat. After gaining the championship with a victory over James J. Braddock the next year, Louis avenged his loss with a first-round knockout of Schmeling in 1938. Louis held the title through twenty-five defenses over the next eleven years, grossing more than $4 million; nonetheless, he was later forced out of retirement by tax debts and suffered bankruptcy and humiliation.

Other African Americans gained distinction in the ring during Louis's reign, though none won his hero status. John

Henry Lewis, great-great-nephew of Tom Molineaux, held the light-heavyweight championship from 1935 to 1939. Henry Armstrong, a nonstop aggressor in the ring, won the featherweight crown in 1937 and added the welterweight then lightweight titles in 1938, becoming the first to hold three championships simultaneously. Armstrong fought in at least 175 bouts, including twenty defenses of the welterweight throne.

A series of African-American fighters emerged in the late 1940s. Ike Williams defeated Beau Jack for the lightweight championship, which Williams held from 1947 to 1951. Sandy Saddler, a slugging featherweight, took that title in 1948 and bested Willie Pep in a memorable series, winning four of their five bouts. Upon Joe Louis's initial retirement, Ezzard Charles, another product of the Golden Gloves program, defeated "Jersey Joe" Walcott for the heavyweight championship; Walcott won the next two rematches before both succumbed to Rocky Marciano. Archie Moore fought over 200 fights and finally in 1952 won the light-heavyweight crown, which he held through nine defenses until the age of forty-eight.

In 1949, the founding of the International Boxing Club (IBC) brought monopolization of the sport by a small group, which controlled boxers, boxing venues, and television rights. It signaled a more overt role by organized crime, a role that was somewhat lessened by the Supreme Court in a federal antitrust case in 1960. In these years African-American boxers won recognition, acclaim, and titles but often lost their purses to unscrupulous business partners and criminals.

Lightweight Joe Brown successfully defended his title eleven times between 1956 and 1961, and Davey Moore assumed the featherweight crown relinquished by Saddler. Archie Moore ruled the light heavyweights, but the most spectacular boxer of the era, and perhaps of any era, proved to be "Sugar Ray" Robinson. Walker Smith, Jr., took the name Robinson to box as an underage teenager. He won the national Golden Gloves championship in 1939 and 1940 before engaging in a pro career that covered more than 200 bouts over twenty-five years. Fast, immensely skilled, and aesthetic in his performances, Robinson won the welterweight title in 1946 and then the middleweight championship, which he recovered four times thereafter. His four victories in five fights with Jake LaMotta, and his less favorable battles with Carmen Basilio and Gene Fullmer, remain among boxing's highlights.

Floyd Patterson became the youngest heavyweight champion at age twenty-one in 1956 and the first to regain that title, in his return match with Ingemar Johansson in 1960. Managed by Cus D'Amato, who refused to be ruled by the IBC, Patterson helped to break the club's stranglehold by ignoring its dictates while he held the title. Patterson lost the title when he suffered two bitter defeats at the big hands of Charles "Sonny" Liston, a devastating puncher, intimidating presence, and an ex-convict beholden to criminal elements.

Though seemingly indestructible, the menacing Liston fell to the brash, young Cassius Clay in a famous 1964 encounter. Clay then announced that he had renamed himself Muhammed Ali and converted to Islam. Using the world as his stage, the colorful, flamboyant, and rebellious champion questioned race relations and the U.S. involvement in the Vietnam War, earning the enmity of many citizens. Although unbeaten in the ring, his refusal to submit to the draft cost him his title and a three-year suspension from boxing.

A Supreme Court reversal and a lifting of the suspension allowed Ali's return, initially marred by a loss to then champion

Joe Frazier in 1971; Frazier's relentless style and Ali's speed, grace, and footwork interacted to produce some of the most memorable bouts in boxing history. Ali regained the title in a dramatic eight-round knockout of George Foreman, a lumbering slugger who had conquered Frazier in 1973; the fight set the stage for two Frazier rematches, both of which Ali won in dramatic fashion. Ali then lost the world title to Leon Spinks in 1978, only to regain it that same year to become the first three-time heavyweight champion.

Although Ali held center stage for nearly twenty years, Bob Foster dominated the light-heavyweight division from 1968 to 1974, making fourteen title defenses in that time. At the lighter weights, Asian and Hispanic fighters came to the fore in the 1960s and would remain prominent for the remainder of the century.

Larry Holmes owned the heavyweight mantle for much of the 1980s, but the most excitement emanated from an array of stellar performances at the middle and welterweight classes. "Sugar Ray" Leonard emulated his namesake's, as well as Ali's, styles in the ring, winning popular support and the World Boxing Council's (WBC) welterweight title in 1979. A loss to Roberto Duran, avenged in a rematch, and a dramatic come-from-behind technical knockout against the devastating puncher Thomas Hearns made Leonard a favorite by 1981. In 1987, Leonard won a split decision over Marvelous Marvin Hagler, who then had his own victorious, but brutal, encounter with Hearns. Hagler, a devastating puncher, ruled the middleweights with a dozen successful title defenses during the decade. Aaron Pryor proved nearly as dominant among junior welterweights with eight victories in title matches, including memorable knockouts over Alexis Arguello. Michael Spinks held the light-heavyweight title from 1981 to 1985 before taking Holmes's heavyweight crown, which he surrendered three years later to Mike Tyson.

Under the tutelage of Cus D'Amato, Tyson seemed an invincible knockout machine, becoming the youngest heavyweight champ (WBC) at age twenty. His victory over Spinks gave him undisputed claim to the title, but D'Amato's death, a 1990 upset by unheralded Buster Douglas, and a 1992 rape conviction derailed Tyson's meteoric rise and left boxing in a shambles.

Fractured by the proliferation of sanctioning bodies, and incomprehensible ranking systems and weight classes, boxing championships have lost much of their significance, and African-American fighters have been left to pursue a futile chase to achieve the American dream in the ring.

Gerald R. Gems

FURTHER READING
Brailsford, Dennis. *Bareknuckles: A Social History of Prizefighting.* Cambridge, MA: Lutterworth Press, 1988.
Carpenter, Harry. *Boxing: An Illustrated History.* New York: Crescent Books, 1982.
Odd, Gilbert. *Boxing: The Great Champions.* London: Hamlyn, 1974.
Roberts, James B., and Alexander G. Skutt. *Boxing Register.* Ithaca, NY: McBooks, 1997.
Roberts, Randy. *Papa Jack: Jack Johnson and the Era of White Hopes.* Riverside, NY: Free Press, 1983.
Sammons, Jeffrey T. *Beyond the Ring: The Role of Boxing in American Society.* Urbana: University of Illinois Press, 1988.

★ ★ ★

Valerie BRISCO-HOOKS

Born July 6, 1960, Greenwood, Mississippi
Sprinter

The daughter of Arguster and Guitherea Brisco, she was the sixth of ten children. The family moved to Los Angeles when Brisco-Hooks (her married name) was five.

An ecstatic Valerie Brisco-Hooks following her victory in the 200-meters in the 1984 Los Angeles Olympic games. *(AP/Wide World Photos)*

She attended Locke High School, near the Watts section of the city, where she began her track career as a sprinter. Brisco-Hooks was to become the second American female athlete to win three gold medals at an Olympiad, the 1984 Los Angeles Olympic Games, a feat first achieved by Wilma Rudolph in the 1960 Rome Olympics.

Brisco-Hooks was first noticed in high school in 1977, when she ran 400 meters in a time of 54.19 seconds. She also excelled in the 100 and 200-meter events. In 1978 she was a high school All-American and held national records for 100 yards (10.5 seconds), 100 meters (11.57 seconds), and 200 meters (23.77 seconds). In the same year, she lowered her 400-meter time to 53.70 seconds, and the following year lowered it further to 52.08 seconds, her best performance until she bettered this time at the Olympic trials five years later. In 1979 Brisco-Hooks became a member of the track team at California State University, Northridge. She improved her 200-meter time to 23.16 seconds. In the same distance she captured the Association of Intercollegiate Athletics for Women title, placed second at the Amateur Athletics Union championships, and placed fourth in the Pan American Games in San Juan, Puerto Rico. She won a gold medal at the Pan-Am Games as a member of the 400-meter relay team.

In 1979 Valerie Brisco met Alvin Hooks, who was also on the track team at California State. The two married in 1981. She then competed for Long Beach City College, where she ran 200 meters in 23.49 seconds. She did not run in 1982, having given birth to a son, Alvin, Jr. In 1983 Brisco-Hooks resumed sprinting and was coached by Bob Kersee (her coach at Northridge) as part of his world-class track team. Kersee saw an Olympic-caliber athlete in Brisco-Hooks and convinced her to train seriously, especially at 400 meters. In 1984, a week before the Olympic trials, she competed in the 400-meter race at a track meet of The Athletic Congress (TAC), an event many Olympic hopefuls stayed away from due to fear of injury. She not only captured the title but broke, with her time of 49.83 seconds, an Olympic record and became the first American woman to run under fifty seconds at that distance. At the Los Angeles Games, however, Brisco-Hooks exceeded all expectations by setting U.S. and Olympic records in the 200 meters (21.81 seconds), 400 meters (48.83 seconds), and the 1,600-meter relay (3:18.29 seconds).

Soon after the Olympics, Brisco-Hooks competed in Europe and was defeated by East German sprinters. Still, she continued to dominate the indoor track season in early 1985 by winning seven of eight races and setting five American records. In August 1985, at a meet in Switzerland, she upset the best East German runners in the

100-, 200- and 400-meter events to avenge her earlier losses and reaffirm her world-class stature. She ranked third in the world at 200 and 400 meters and fifth at 100 meters in 1986. In June 1987, she placed fourth in the 400-meter race at the USA/Mobil (TAC) Outdoor Track and Field Championships. A month later she captured three gold medals at the Olympic Festival in Durham, North Carolina, in the 200- and 400-meter races, and the 1,600-meter relay event. At the World Track and Field Championships in Rome that same year, Brisco-Hooks won a bronze medal as a member of the 4 x 400 relay team. She won a silver medal running the third leg in the same event at the 1988 Seoul Olympics in South Korea.

Danny Rosenberg

See also: Track and Field.

FURTHER READING
Davis, Michael D. *Black American Women in Olympic Track and Field: A Complete Illustrated Reference*. Jefferson, NC: McFarland, 1992.
Page, James A. *Black Olympian Medalists*. Englewood, CO: Libraries Unlimited, 1991.
Porter, David L., ed. *Biographical Dictionary of American Sports: Outdoor Sports*. Westport, CT: Greenwood Press, 1988.
Salem, Dorothy C. *African American Women: A Biographical Dictionary*. New York: Garland, 1993.

★ ★ ★

Louis BROCK

Born June 18, 1939, El Dorado, Arkansas
Baseball player

Brock, the seventh of nine children of Maud and Paralee Brock, graduated from Union High School in Mer Rouge, Louisiana, where he starred on both the basketball and baseball teams. He continued his baseball career at Southern University, earning All-Southwestern Athletic Conference (SAC) honors and leading his team to the National Association of Intercollegiate Athletics (NAIA) championship his junior year.

In 1961 Brock was signed to a contract by the Chicago Cubs. After playing for three years with the Cubs, both their minor league affiliate in St. Cloud, Minnesota, and the parent club, Brock was traded to the St. Louis Cardinals for pitcher Ernie Broglio. The trade was a godsend for Brock; his baseball career blossomed after joining the Cardinals. In each of his first ten years with the club, Brock accumulated over 180 hits and in twelve consecutive seasons stole over fifty bases. In the Cardinals defeat of the Red Sox in the 1967 World Series, Brock batted .414 and stole a record seven bases. In 1974 Brock broke Maury Wills's stolen-base record with 118 steals. For his entire major league career, Brock had 3,023 hits, 486 doubles, 141 triples, and 149 home runs; he scored 1,610 runs and stole a national league record 928 bases. These achievements earned him induction into Baseball's Hall of Fame in 1985.

Brock's postbaseball career has included involvement in many charitable organizations. This service has garnered Brock such honors as the B'nai B'rith Brotherhood Award, the Roberto Clemente Award, the St. Louis Jaycees' Man of the Year Award, and the St. Louis Award for Distinguished Service to the Community. He has spent much of his post-baseball career in business ventures.

David K. Wiggins

FURTHER READING
Ashe, Arthur R., Jr. *A Hard Road to Glory*. New York: Amistad, 1988.
Brock, Lou, and Franz Schulze. *Stealing Is My Game*. Englewood Cliffs, NJ: Prentice Hall, 1976.
Fortus, Bob. "Success Story: Lou Brock's Climb to the

Hall of Fame." *Baseball Digest*, November 1985, 39–44.

★ ★ ★

Vivian BROWN REED

Born December 17, 1941, Detroit, Michigan
Sprinter

Born into a family of fourteen, Brown showed an interest in sports at an early age. Raised in Cleveland, Ohio, Brown began her track and field career at nine by joining a Junior Olympics program supported by the local Board of Education. She specialized in sprints and was named the Outstanding Girl in the Junior Olympics program during her elementary and junior high school years. Because her high school did not have a track and field program, she trained under Alex Ferenczy of the Cleveland Recreation Department track team. She participated in national competitions before graduating from East Technical High School.

With encouragement from her family, Brown decided to pursue a degree in physical education. In 1960, she received a work-aid scholarship to join the Tigerbelles of Tennessee State University. She gained initial recognition by beating her teammate, Wilma Rudolph, in the 220-yard dash at the 1961 National Amateur Athletics Union meet. She set a championship record the following year in the same event. For two years in a row, Brown was named to the All-America Women's Track and Field Teams. In 1963, Brown set a record in the 200-meter event in the Pan American Games in Sao Paulo, Brazil. Brown became a member of the U.S. Women's Olympic track and field team that competed in the 1964 Olympics in Tokyo, Japan. In 1965, she graduated and married Lawrence Reed. Since then, she has coached track and field and taught physical education.

Sara B. Washington

FURTHER READING
Adkins, Vivian B.L. "The Development of Negro Female Olympic Talent." Ph.D. diss., Indiana University, 1967.
Thaxton, Nolan A. "A Documentary Analysis of Competitive Track and Field for Women at Tuskegee Institute and Tennessee State University." Ph.D. diss., Springfield College, 1970.
Tricard, Louise M. *American Women's Track and Field: A History, 1895 Through 1980.* Jefferson, NC: McFarland, 1985.

★ ★ ★

Jim BROWN

Born February 17, 1936, St. Simon's Island, Georgia
Football player

Jim Brown was raised by his grandmother early in his life. His mother moved from the South to New York City. He did not know his father. At the age of eight he went to live with his mother in Manhasset, Long Island, New York.

Brown attended Manhasset High School, where he was a star athlete in football and basketball. In one high school basketball game he scored fifty-five points. He attended Syracuse University in 1953 starting the trend there that saw several African-American offensive football players coming to Syracuse in the late 1950s and 1960s. During that time the football team was run by legendary coach Ben Schwartzwalder, whom Brown would later call a racist. At Syracuse Brown would become a star player in football and lacrosse and a letterman in basketball.

At six feet, two inches and weighing just over 200 pounds Brown entered the Na-

Jim Brown, the outstanding all-around athlete, is considered by many to be the greatest running back in football history. (AP/Wide World Photos)

tional Football League (NFL) in 1957 and became the Rookie of the Year. When he walked away from the game, Brown was the consensus All-Pro running back. His style was to run over defensive players instead of trying to run around them. He piled up in his career almost nine miles on NFL gridirons, averaging 1,368 yards a season. Brown played in the Pro Bowl nine straight years. He won the Jim Thorpe trophy for the Pro Bowl's MVP in 1958 and 1965, and was chosen All-NFL eight times. In 1963 he became the first player ever to rush for more than a mile. In 1964 he won the Hickok award as the outstanding pro athlete, having scored 126 touchdowns, 109 of them rushing. He stayed in the league just nine years, all of them on the Cleveland Browns, retiring at the then unheard of age of thirty in 1966; he was inducted into the Pro Football Hall of Fame in 1971.

After retiring from football Brown entered into a lucrative movie career. He became as famous on the movie screen as he was on the football field. He was "drafted" by Hollywood in the 1960s and appeared in a number of movies. His biggest movie was the 1966 film *The Dirty Dozen*, with Lee Marvin. When his movie career faded, Brown became involved in community service, which he continues today.

Brown was recognized for his great playing days when he was named the grand marshal at the 49ers versus Bengals Super Bowl XVI in 1982. He was inducted into the Lacrosse Hall of Fame in 1983, making him the only man to be inducted into three sports halls of fame: pro football, college football and college lacrosse.

Earl Smith

See also: Autobiographies; Films; Lacrosse; Floyd Little; Bobby Mitchell.

FURTHER READING
Brown, Jim. *Off My Chest*. New York: Doubleday, 1964.
Brown, Jim, with Steve Delsohn. *Out of Bounds*. New York: Kensington, 1989.
Neft, David, et al. *The Sports Encyclopedia: Pro Football*. New York: Grossett and Dunlap, 1974.
Ross, Charles K. *Outside the Lines: African Americans and the Integration of the National Football League*. New York: New York University Press, 1999.

★ ★ ★

Larry BROWN

Born September 19, 1947, Clairton, Pennsylvania
Football player

Larry Brown was unanimously named the 1972 National Football League's (NFL) Most Valuable Player (MVP) for the Washington Redskins. Despite deafness in his right ear that forced him to use a hearing aid, Brown played eight seasons (1969–1976) with Washington and was a three-time NFL All-Pro at running back and twice National Football Conference (NFC) rushing leader.

In college, Brown was unheralded at Kansas State University, where he was used primarily as a blocking back. An eighth-round draft pick by the Redskins in 1969, Brown impressed coach Vince Lombardi, who started Brown as a running back during his rookie season. In 1969, Brown gained 888 yards rushing and an additional 302 yards receiving. Brown improved upon his performance in 1970 and led the NFC in rushing.

During his MVP season in 1972, Brown led the Redskins to Super Bowl VII. Despite missing two games with an injury, Brown led the NFC in rushing yards (1,216), gained another 473 yards receiving, and scored twelve touchdowns.

In 1974, Brown suffered a knee injury that ultimately led to his retirement from football during the 1977 preseason. In his eight seasons, he gained 5,875 yards rushing and scored fifty-five touchdowns and played in four Pro Bowl games in his first five seasons. Brown has been honored by the Redskins as an inaugural member of the team's Ring of Fame at FedEx Field.

Since retirement, Brown has remained in the Washington area, where he sells real estate.

Michael T. Friedman

FURTHER READING
The Locker Room. "Larry Brown" (www.thelocker-room.com/larrybrown.htm).
Shapiro, Leonard. "Larry Brown Retires, Cites Damaged Knees." *Washington Post*, July 27, 1977.
———. "In Allen's Form, Shades of Brown." *Washington Post*, November 15, 1996.
A Who's Who of Sports Champions: Their Stories and Records. Boston: Houghton Mifflin, 1995.

★ ★ ★

Roger BROWN

Born May 22, 1942, Brooklyn, New York
Died March 4, 1997, Indianapolis, Indiana
Basketball player

A renowned basketball star at Wingate High School in Brooklyn, New York, Brown, a six-foot, five-inch forward, won a scholarship to the University of Dayton in Ohio and led his freshman team to victory. Despite his diverse abilities, Brown never played a varsity game and was placed on the ineligible list of the NBA. This disruption in Brown's career was the result of his association with a sports gambler, Jack Molinas. Though Brown was never personally accused of any wrongdoing, the questions surrounding the issue cost Brown his scholarship and his NBA dreams.

Following his 1964 graduation, Brown settled in Dayton, married, worked in a General Motors plant, and reestablished his reputation as a basketball phenomenon, this time in the Amateur Athletic Union leagues in Dayton. In 1967 Brown became the first player drafted by the Indiana Pacers to play in the newly formed American Basketball Association. Brown led the Pacers to three ABA championships and remains the third-highest scorer in the history of the franchise. His jersey, number 35, is one of three retired by the Pacers; he was nominated for the Basketball Hall of Fame. Brown eventually cleared his name with the NBA but chose to remain with the Pacers until he retired two years before the team joined the NBA in 1976. Brown died of cancer in 1997.

Trisha M. Hothorn

FURTHER READING
Bock, Hal. "Roger Brown: Remembering a Rivalry." Nando and Associated Press, March 16, 1997.

Rhoden, William. "A Pacer Hero Facing His Hardest Challenge." *New York Times*, February 16, 1997.

Thomas, Robert McG., Jr. "Roger Brown, Basketball Star from Brooklyn, Is Dead at 54." *New York Times*, March 6, 1997.

FURTHER READING

Ashe, Arthur R., Jr. *A Hard Road to Glory: A History of the African-American Athlete Since 1946.* New York: Amistad, 1988.

Henderson, Edwin B., with the Editors of Sport Magazine. *The Black Athlete: Emergence and Arrival.* Cornwall Heights, PA: Pennsylvania Publishers, 1968.

Pro Football Hall of Fame (www.profootballhof.com).

★ ★ ★

Roosevelt BROWN

Born October 20, 1932, Charlottesville, Virginia
Football player

Brown played football at Jefferson High School in Charlottesville, Virginia, and his collegiate years at Morgan State. In 1953 he was drafted by the New York Giants in the twenty-seventh round and was a starting tackle for the team for thirteen straight years. He developed the reputation of being a big, fast blocker who was mobile enough to make blocks downfield. Because of his size and blocking ability, he was used along the defensive front on goal-line stands.

During those thirteen years, Brown achieved several astounding accomplishments. He was named to the Pro Bowl nine times and was an All-NFL eight straight seasons. In 1956, when the Giants won the Championship game, the Associated Press named Brown Lineman of the Year. Brown also helped the Giants advance to the NFL Championship games in 1958, 1959, 1961, 1962, and 1963.

He was forced to retire in 1966 because of a phlebitis condition. After his playing career in the NFL ended, Brown continued with the Giants as a coach and later as a scout. He has served in this position since the 1971 season. In 1975, Brown was inducted into the NFL Hall of Fame.

Billy Hawkins

★ ★ ★

Kobe BRYANT

Born August 23, 1978, Philadelphia, Pennsylvania
Basketball player

Bryant, son of former professional basketball player Joe "Butter Bean" Bryant, is one of the most famous and recognizable players in the game today. He is fluent in Italian, having spent part of his childhood living in Italy. He was elected by *USA Today* and *Parade Magazine* as the National High School Player of the Year while a senior at Lower Merion High School. After deciding not to attend college, in favor of playing professional basketball, he was drafted by the Charlotte Hornets and shortly thereafter traded to the Los Angeles Lakers.

In November 1996 at the age of 18, Bryant became the youngest player to appear in a National Basketball Association (NBA) game when the Los Angeles Lakers played the Minnesota Timberwolves. Since his debut, Bryant has established himself as one of professional basketball's greatest all-around players and helped lead the Lakers to three NBA championships. He became the youngest All-Star player ever, when he was voted a starter in the 1998 All-Star game. His career highlights include selection to the 1999–2000 NBA All-Defensive first team, recipient of the most valuable

Los Angeles Lakers' Kobe Bryant, center, goes to the basket as teammate Robert Horry, left, and Utah Jazz forward Karl Malone look on during a game between the two teams. (AP/Wide World Photos)

player award in the 2002 NBA All-Star Game, and being named to the 2001–2002 All-NBA first team. In addition Bryant, teamed with Shaquille O'Neal and a collection of other great players, guided the Lakers to NBA championships in 2000, 2001, and 2002.

The force of Bryant's personality and excellent communication skills were evident by his selection to the 1999–2000 NBA All-Interview second team. He is also one of the most influential people in all of sport, ranking 31st among *Forbes* Top 100 Most Powerful Celebrities. Among his many business dealings are endorsement contracts with Spalding, McDonald's, and Sprite.

David K. Wiggins

FURTHER READING
"Changing the Game." *Sports Illustrated*, May 5, 2003, 32–47.
Hubbard, Jan, ed. *The Official NBA Encyclopedia.* 3d ed. New York: Doubleday, 2000.
Postman, Andrew, and Larry Stone. *The Ultimate Book of Sports Lists.* New York: Black Dog & Leventhal, 2003.

★ ★ ★

Matthew BULLOCK

Born September 11, 1881, Dabney, North Carolina
Died December 17, 1972, Detroit, Michigan
Football coach

Matthew Bullock was the son of Jesse and Amanda (Sneed) Bullock, both former slaves who fled the South and moved to Massachusetts when Matthew was eight years old. A graduate of Everett High School, Everett, MA, Dartmouth College in 1904 (B.A.), and Harvard Law School in 1907 (LL.B.), Bullock spent his professional career as a college football coach, college professor, college dean, attorney, and assistant attorney general.

Bullock coached the football teams at Massachusetts Agricultural College (now University of Massachusetts, Amherst) for the 1904, 1907, and 1908 seasons to help finance his law school education. He coached football at Malden (MA) High School for the 1905 and 1906 seasons. In so doing, Bullock became one of the first salaried college coaches in America and the first African American to hold the position of head football coach at a predominantly white college. Noted sport historian Edwin Henderson writes, "Bullock was one of the brainiest men of football ability the game has had."

Bullock joined the faculty of Atlanta Baptist (later Morehouse) College after completing law school and served as athletic director. It was here that he and Edwin Henderson began the annual selection of All-College Negro teams. In 1915, Bullock became dean of the faculty at the Agricultural and Mechanical College in Normal, AL. He was admitted to the Massachusetts bar in 1917 and moved back to that state. During World War I, Bullock served as a YMCA war work physical director with the American Expeditionary Force in Europe.

His long career lasted from 1919 to 1965, during which time he served as executive secretary of the Boston Urban League (1919–1921), a Massachusetts special assistant attorney general (1925–1926), and as a member and later chairman of the Massachusetts Board of Parole (1927–1948). After he retired, Bullock devoted much of his time and money to the Baha'i faith. Dartmouth awarded him an honorary doctor of laws degree at its 1971 commencement in recognition of his distinguished career.

Jack W. Berryman

FURTHER READING
Berryman, Jack W. "Early Black Leadership in Collegiate Football." Paper read at the Second Canadian Symposium on the History of Sport and Physical Education, University of Windsor, Windsor, Ontario, Canada, May 1972.
———. "Early Black Leadership in Collegiate Football: Massachusetts as a Pioneer." *Historical Journal of Massachusetts* 9 (June 1981): 17–28.
Berryman, Jack W., and John W. Loy. "Historically Speaking: Matthew Bullock." *Black Sports* 2 (February 1973): 18–19.

★ ★ ★

Daniel BURLEY

Born November 7, 1907, Lexington, Kentucky
Died October 30, 1962, Chicago, Illinois
Journalist

The son of a former slave and Baptist evangelist (James) and a teacher at Tuskegee Institute (Anna Seymour), Burley attended Wendell Phillips High School in Chicago. After graduating from high school, he joined the *Chicago Defender* as a reporter. He was a journalist, musician, author, and disk jockey.

Sports journalism was a small part of his career but a memorable one. While Burley was sports editor and columnist at the *New York Amsterdam News*, he campaigned for the integration of major league baseball and argued that Joe Louis should not serve in the U.S. Navy because it was a racist institution. He advised the Negro National League to give its umpires better pay and wrote a sympathetic article about Joe DiMaggio's father, an Italian immigrant who was detained by U.S. authorities during World War II.

Burley also was editor of the *Amsterdam News*, assistant editor at Johnson Publishing Company (which produces *Ebony* and *Jet*), editor of the *New York Age*, contributing editor for *Sepia*, and founder and editor of *The Owl*, a community newspaper in Chicago. Burley also worked at the *Chicago Bee* and the Associated Negro Press.

Burley had interests away from the press box. He was a student of black life in Chicago and New York. He wrote *Dan Burley's Original Handbook of Jive*, a classic work about the speech of Harlem musicians and many of the residents there. A self-taught pianist, Burley often performed at parties. He also established the famous *Amsterdam News* midnight shows at the Apollo Theater.

Michael Marsh

See also: Sportswriters.

FURTHER READING
"Dan Burley Dies in Chicago at 55." *New York Amsterdam News*, November 3, 1962.
Orodenker, Richard, ed. *Dictionary of Literary Biography: American Sportswriters and Writers on Sport.*

Farmington Hills, MI: Bruccoli Clark Layman, 2001.

Reisler, Jim. *Black Writers/Black Baseball: An Anthology of Articles from Black Sportswriters Who Covered the Negro Leagues.* Jefferson, NC: McFarland, 1993.

★ ★ ★

Sol BUTLER

Born March 3, 1895, Wichita, Kansas
Died December 1, 1954, Chicago, Illinois
Sprinter

Sol Butler was the son of Benjamin, an emancipated slave and laborer, and Mary Butler, a housewife. An outstanding athlete, Butler first displayed his physical skills at Hutchinson High School (KS) and later at Rock Island High School (IL).

Reverend Benjamin Lindamen persuaded Butler and his brother Benny to attend Dubuque (IA) German College and Seminary (later renamed University of Dubuque) in 1915, where Lindamen had graduated. Butler gained national attention in 1914 when he broke the national interscholastic record for the sixty-yard dash. In 1915 the young competitor won the National Amateur Athletic Union (AAU) junior championship in the broad jump.

Arguably the greatest athlete to ever don a uniform at the University of Dubuque, Butler excelled in four sports. Track and field, in particular, became his vehicle to athletic fame.

After World War I, Butler was acknowledged as the best broad jumper in the United States. Invited to the Inter-Allied Games in Paris in 1919, the barrel-chested trackster leaped 24 feet, 9½ inches to win the broad jump and set an American record. King Nicholas of Montenegro, reigning dignitary at the games, bestowed upon Butler the Medal of the Fourth Class of the Order of Danillo. While still in Europe, Butler competed in the Tuilleries Games. He defeated the renowned American speedster Charlie Paddock in the ninety-yard dash.

In 1920 Butler was one of three African-American athletes to qualify for the U.S. Olympic track and field team. Butler was favored to win the broad jump at the games in Antwerp, Belgium. On his first jump in the qualification round he pulled a tendon; after another attempt, the distraught Butler withdrew, finishing seventh in the competition. He continued to compete in track and field events with an eye toward the 1924 Olympic Games. He was unable to jump more than twenty-three feet, six inches and in 1923 turned in his AAU card to its headquarters in New York.

Butler had short stints with several teams in the fledgling National Football League during the 1920s. The versatile athlete also played professional basketball and had bit parts in several Tarzan movies. Butler settled in Chicago in the 1930s and worked as a recreation instructor for the Chicago Parks and Recreation Department. He enjoyed helping young black athletes improve their skills. In the 1950s Butler managed Pappy's Lounge on the tough South Side of Chicago. On December 1, 1954, he escorted Jimmy Hill out of the bar for molesting a female patron. Hill returned shortly, and in an exchange of gunfire both men died. Butler, fifty-nine, was buried in Wichita (KS).

James E. Odenkirk

FURTHER READING

Ashe, Arthur R., Jr. *A Hard Road to Glory: A History of the African-American Athlete, 1619–1918.* New York: Warner Books, 1988.

Carroll, John. *Fritz Pollard, Pioneer in Racial Advancement.* Urbana: University of Illinois Press, 1992.

Chalk, Ocania. *Black College Sport.* New York: Dodd Mead, 1976.

The Key. University of Dubuque (IA) Annual, 1917–1920.

Quercentani, Robert L. *A World History of Track Athletics, 1864–1964.* London: Oxford University Press, 1964.

Lee CALHOUN

Born February 23, 1933, Laurel, Mississippi
Hurdler

An outstanding track competitor in the 110-meter high hurdles, Lee Calhoun graduated from Roosevelt High School in Gary, IN, and from North Carolina Central State College (now North Carolina Central University). In 1956, he won the Amateur Athletic Union (AAU) indoor and outdoor, National Association of Intercollegiate Athletics (NAIA), and the NCAA high hurdles championships. At the 1956 Melbourne Olympic Games, he won a gold medal in the high hurdles in a photo finish over Jack Davis, then the world record holder.

He successfully defended his American championships in 1957 but was suspended for the entire 1958 season amid allegations that he had received gifts as a consequence of his being married on the *Bride and Groom* television show. During his year of competitive inactivity, he assisted the juvenile bureau of the Cleveland Police Department. Reinstated in 1959, he won another AAU championship and a gold medal at the Pan American Games but lost several other major events and finished the year ranked only third in the world. He redeemed himself, however, by winning a gold medal in the high hurdles at the Rome Olympic Games in 1960, becoming the first man to win that event in two consecutive Olympiads.

Following his retirement from competition, Calhoun coached at Grambling, Yale, and Western Illinois Universities, and was an assistant coach for the U.S. team at the Pan American Games in 1971 and 1979 and at the Montreal Olympic Games in 1976. In 1974, he was elected to the National Track and Field Hall of Fame.

John E. Findling

FURTHER READING
Carlson, Lewis H., and John J. Fogarty. *Tales of Gold: An Oral History of the Summer Olympic Games Told by America's Gold Medal Winners*. Chicago: Contemporary Books, 1987.
Page, James A. *Black Olympian Medalists*. Englewood, CO: Libraries Unlimited, 1991.
Porter, David L., ed. *Biographical Dictionary of American Sports: Outdoor Sports*. Westport, CT: Greenwood Press, 1988.

★ ★ ★

Roy CAMPANELLA

Born November 19, 1921, Philadelphia, Pennsylvania
Died June 26, 1993, Los Angeles, California
Baseball player

Before Ivan Rodriguez, Mike Piazza, and Johnny Bench, there was Roy Campanella. The first black catcher in the majors combined remarkable defensive ability with unusual hitting prowess to help propel the Brooklyn Dodgers to five pennants and one triumphant World Series during the years he played, 1948–1957.

The longtime Negro league veteran impressed Dodgers scouts so much that his signing shortly followed Jackie Robinson's own in 1945. In 1948 the roly-poly receiver became the Dodgers regular catcher, and the next year a league All-Star. The latter honor was bestowed on him every year subsequently. Physically and temperamentally unlike the high-strung Robinson, the racially easy-going fireplug proved his equal in courage, leadership, and clutch performance.

Campanella batted over .300 three times, hit twenty or more home runs six times, slugged forty-one home runs in 1953 to set a catcher's record (since broken), led in put-outs six times, threw out nearly two

Roy Campanella (right) with Baltimore Elite Giants' teammate Sammy Hughes in 1942. Campanella eventually became one of Major League Baseball's best catchers before having his career ended by a tragic car accident. *(AP/Wide World Photos)*

out of three would-be base stealers, and, like Yogi Berra, won his league's Most Valuable Player award three times. In 1963 the ever-popular Dodger was voted into the Baseball Hall of Fame five years after a car accident left him crippled permanently. His transcendent optimism and zest for life remained. When a 1959 appreciation night was held for him, the largest crowd in baseball history, 93,103 fans, showed up.

John A. Vernon

See also: Autobiographies; Films.

FURTHER READING
Campanella, Roy. *It's Good to Be Alive*. New York: Signet Books, 1974.
Golenbock, Peter. *Bums: An Oral History of the Brooklyn Dodgers*. New York: G.P. Putnam's Sons, 1984.
Honig, Donald. *The Greatest Catchers of All Time*. Dubuque, IA: William C. Brown, 1991.
Prince, Carl E. *Brooklyn's Dodgers: The Bums, the Borough, and the Best of Baseball, 1947–1957*. New York: Oxford University Press, 1996.

★   ★   ★

Earl CAMPBELL

Born March 29, 1955, Tyler, Texas
Football player

Earl Campbell was the sixth of eleven children born to B.C. and Ann Campbell. Nicknamed "the Tyler Rose," Campbell led John Tyler High School to the Texas Football State Championship in 1973, rushing for 2,224 yards. He attended the University of Texas at Austin as one of the most sought-after running backs in the country. Campbell's outstanding career at Texas gained him many accolades, including the Southwest Conference Newcomer of the Year his freshman year; he was named to several All-Southwest Conference and All-American teams over his four-year collegiate career. Campbell was selected as the Southwest Conference Athlete of the Decade. The highlight of his distinguished collegiate career came in December 1977, when the Downtown Athletic Club of New York selected him as the Heisman Trophy Award winner, recognizing the best collegiate football player in the country. Campbell rushed for 4,443 yards and forty-one touchdowns in his career.

The Houston Oilers selected the five-foot, eleven-inch, 232-pound Campbell as the first pick of the 1978 National Football League draft. Campbell's outstanding performance continued in the professional ranks. As a rookie, he finished the season with an unprecedented 1,450 yards rushing; he was named the National Football League Rookie of the Year and Most Valuable Player. He repeated as league Most Valuable Player in 1979, rushing for 1,697 yards and nineteen touchdowns. Campbell's best season came in 1980, when he rushed for 1,934 yards and thirteen touchdowns. He was picked for the Pro Bowl five of his first six NFL seasons. In eight professional seasons with the Houston Oilers and New Orleans Saints, Campbell rushed for 9,407 yards and seventy-four touchdowns. He appeared on the cover of *Sports Illustrated* six times. In 1981 Campbell was proclaimed an Official State Hero of Texas, one of only four men bestowed this honor. Campbell was inducted into the Pro Football Hall of Fame in 1991.

David W. Hunter

FURTHER READING
Campbell, Earl. *The Official Earl Campbell Website* (www.earlcampbell.com/index2.html).
Campbell, Earl, and John Ruane. *The Earl Campbell Story: A Football Great's Battle with Panic Disorder.* Toronto: ECW Press, 1999.
Devaney, John. *Winners of the Heisman Trophy.* New York: Walker, 1990.
Miller, Paddy Joe. *The Tyler Rose: The Earl Campbell Story.* Houston: Schuromil, 1997.

★ ★ ★

Milt CAMPBELL

Born December 9, 1933, Plainfield, New Jersey
Decathlete, hurdler

The second son of Edith and Thomas Campbell, a merchant mariner and taxicab driver, Campbell graduated from Emerson Elementary and Plainfield High School, attended Indiana University, and served in the U.S. Navy, 1955–1956.

A superb all-around athlete, Campbell excelled in football, swimming, and track and field. He was the national high school hurdles champion in 1951, 1952, and 1953; the AAU national decathlon champion in 1953; and the AAU and NCAA high hurdles champion in 1955, setting a new world record in the 120-yard high hurdles. He was a national all-American swimmer in 1951, and in 1952 he was named the world's greatest high school athlete. His athletic prowess and versatility were evident in his performances in the decathlon at the 1952 and 1956 Olympic Games. He outscored Rafer Johnson for the gold medal in 1956 and won the silver medal in 1952, losing the gold by a slim margin to Bob Mathias. He won the decathlon over Mathias (later a congressman from California) and Johnson, two household names, but Campbell never received the recognition he deserved as the world's greatest athlete of his time. At Indiana University he played football and ran track. He went on to play professional football for the Cleveland Browns, Hamilton Tiger-Cats, and Toronto Argonauts.

Following his career in the professional ranks, Campbell turned his attention to youth programs. He served as board chair of the Black Youth Organization, Newark, established the Milt Campbell Community Center in Newark, cofounded Chad School in Newark, and founded Olympic Experience for youth. He is founder of Milt Campbell Enterprises, a personal development and motivational company. Currently, he is a lecturer and motivational speaker.

Campbell's accolades and recognition include New Jersey Athlete of the Century, 2000; State of New Jersey Assembly proclamation, Best Track and Field Athlete in New Jersey History; and U.S. Postal Service, 1988 Summer Olympic Games stamp and commemorative replica. He is a member of the U.S. Olympic Hall of Fame, National Track and Field Hall of Fame (1989), New Jersey Sports Hall of Fame, International Swimming Hall of Fame (1995), Black Athlete's Hall of Fame, New Jersey Interscholastic Hall of Fame, and the Indiana University Hall of Fame.

J. Thomas Jable

See also: Track and Field.

FURTHER READING

BlackAthlete.Com. Williams, Charles. "The Greatest and Most Forgotten" (www.blackathlete.com/trackf527.htm).

Izenberg, Jerry. *New Jersey Online.* "Athlete of the Century—Milt Campbell." *Newark Star-Ledger* (www.nj.com/varsity/ledger/index.ssf?/varsity/stories/1203_century.html).

Murray, Jim. "Forgotten Decathlete Speaks Out." *Los Angeles Times*, July 16, 1991.

★ ★ ★

John CARLOS

Born June 5, 1945, New York, New York
Sprinter

John Carlos did not do very well in school while growing up in Harlem and frequently was involved with the police for fighting in public. He did, however, break a record in his first relay race in high school, and that led to a track scholarship to East Texas State in Commerce, Texas. He found racial injustice in the South unbearable, and he did not get along with East Texas State coach, Delmar Brown. In January 1968 he transferred to San Jose State College in California and became a member of one of the best track teams in the country. He also got involved with a black athlete protest movement, headed by sociologist Harry Edwards, which threatened to boycott important track and field meets, including the Olympics.

Carlos went on to become an Olympic sprinter and world-record holder. He and teammate Tommie Smith are best known for their protest at the 1968 Mexico City Olympic Games. On the victory podium following the 200-meter final they wore protest buttons, black gloves and socks, and no shoes; they lowered their heads and extended their arms in a black-power salute. The demonstration resulted in their expulsion from the U.S. team and the Olympic Village.

Carlos's best performance was at the 1968 pre-Olympic trials, where he clocked a 19.7-second time in the 200-meter final. The time was not an official world record, because the spikes he was wearing were illegal. At the Olympics he earned a bronze medal in the same event, with a time of 20.1 seconds. In 1969 he won the Amateur Athletic Union (AAU) and National Collegiate Athletic Association (NCAA) championships in the 200-meter and 220-yard events, and he equaled the world record for the indoor sixty-yard and 100-yard dashes. For a short period after college, Carlos pursued a career in professional football. Between 1973 and 1975 he participated in the professional International Track Association. He founded the Los Angeles-based John Carlos Youth Development Program in 1977 to encourage youth to remain in school rather than participate in elite competitive sports. Throughout the 1970s he spoke out against racial discrimination in sport; most notably, he appeared at a rally to protest the treatment of black athletes at Oregon State University. Carlos was a member of the 1984 Los Angeles Olympic Organizing Committee and served as a liaison between the community and the games organizers.

Danny Rosenberg

See also: Civil Rights; Lee Evans; Olympic Games; Tommie Smith; Track and Field.

FURTHER READING

Axthelm, Pete. "The Angry Black Athlete." *Newsweek*, July 15, 1968, 56–60.

Edwards, Harry. *The Revolt of the Black Athlete*. New York: Free Press, 1969.

Kirsch, George B., Othello Harris, and Claire E. Nolte, eds. *Encyclopedia of Ethnicity and Sports in the United States*. Westport, CT: Greenwood Press, 2000.

Matney, William C., ed. "John Carlos." *Who's Who Among Black Americans*. 5th ed. Lake Forest, IL: Educational Communications, 1988.

"The Olympics' Extra Heat." *Newsweek*, October 28, 1968, 74, 79–80.

"2 Accept Medals Wearing Black Gloves." *New York Times*, October 17, 1968.

Wiggins, David K. *Glory Bound: Black Athletes in a White America.* Syracuse, NY: Syracuse University Press, 1997.

★ ★ ★

Harold CARMICHAEL

Born September 22, 1949, Jacksonville, Florida
Football player

Harold Carmichael spent almost his entire professional career, 1971–1983, with the Philadelphia Eagles, where at six feet, eight inches he was one of the tallest and most successful wide receivers to ever play the game.

Carmichael grew up in the Jacksonville, Florida, area. He attended Northwestern (1963–1965) and Raines (1966–1967) high schools, where he starred in basketball and football. He went to Southern University in Louisiana and won the wide receiver job as a walk-on his freshman year. He completed his collegiate career with eighty-nine receptions and sixteen touchdowns.

Philadelphia drafted Carmichael in the seventh round. He sat on the bench his first two years, but after he won the first-string wide receiver position in 1973 his career took off. Fully exploiting his large hands, thirty-six-inch vertical leap, and six-foot, eight-inch height, he made himself the clutch receiver on the team. Carmichael was elected to the Pro Bowl in the 1973 season, and again three years consecutively from 1979 to 1981. In 1981, Carmichael saw his record-setting pass-reception streak in consecutive games broken at 127. In that season he had sixty-one catches for 1,601 yards and six touchdowns.

Age and injuries slowed Carmichael's productivity his last two seasons in Philadelphia. When the Eagles waived him after the 1983 season, he held team records for most receptions (589), most yards gained receiving (8,978), and most touchdown receptions (seventy-nine). The 1984 season with the Dallas Cowboys was his last. In 1998, Carmichael was named director of player relations for the Philadelphia Eagles.

Carmichael was a late bloomer in football, but his remarkable emergence as one of the premier wide receivers in the pro ranks changed the game. His size advantage combined with agility and good hands led the NFL thereafter to recruit tall men as wide receivers.

Robert Pruter

FURTHER READING

Banks, Don. "Consistency Was Key to Carmichael's Football Success." *St. Petersburg Times*, August 20, 1987.

Frenette, Gene. "Carmichael's Career More than a Tall Tale." *Florida Times-Union*, December 23, 1999.

Porter, David L., ed. *Biographical Dictionary of American Sports: Football*. Westport, CT: Greenwood Press, 1987.

★ ★ ★

J.C. CAROLINE

Born January 17, 1933, Warrenton, Georgia
Football player

Caroline is best known for a brief but spectacular college football career at Illinois and a ten-year career with the Chicago Bears in the National Football League (NFL). The son of African-American parents Benny Gordon and Eugenia (Caroline) Gordon, J.C. was named for his grandfather, James Caroline. His grandmother, Minnie Pearl Yarber, raised Caroline in Columbia, SC, where he graduated from

Booker T. Washington High School. Caroline grew up in extreme poverty in segregated Columbia, but he led Booker T. Washington to the South Carolina Athletic Conference football championship.

In 1952 he chose to attend the University of Illinois, because southern colleges were segregated and Illinois had a history of recruiting African-American athletes. The six-foot, one-inch, 185-pound Caroline was an immediate success as a halfback, running for 102 yards and two touchdowns against Ohio State in his first Big Ten conference game. He proceeded to lead the nation in rushing with 1,256 yards. Illinois finished the season with a 7–1–1 record and tied for the Big Ten championship. Caroline was named to most All-American teams. That season was the high point of Caroline's career. The following season Illinois had a weak team, winning only one game, and Caroline gained only 440 yards. He was declared academically ineligible and could not play his senior season; instead he played a season in the Canadian Football League. He graduated from Florida A & M University with a teaching degree in 1966.

Caroline joined the Chicago Bears in 1957. During his ten-year NFL career he was an outstanding defensive back and was named to the All-Pro team. Following his retirement from the NFL, Caroline was an assistant coach at Illinois and later the head coach at Urbana High School. He was named to the College Football Hall of Fame in 1981.

C. Robert Barnett

FURTHER READING
Caroline, J.C., file. Pro Football Hall of Fame Archives.
———. University of Illinois Archives
Carroll, Bob, et al., eds. *Total Football II: The Official Encyclopedia of the National Football League.* New York: HarperCollins, 1999.
Kroner, Fred. "Caroline Resigns as Urbana Grid Coach." *Champaign-Urbana News-Gazette*, November 18, 1982.
"Men in the Middle: University of Illinois Football Stars J.C. Caroline and Mickey Bates." *Sports Illustrated*, October 18, 1954, 64–68.

★ ★ ★

Cris CARTER

Born November 25, 1965, Troy, Ohio
Football player

Cris Carter attended high school in Middletown, Ohio, and college at Ohio State University before becoming in the 1990s a premier wide receiver in the National Football League, playing for the Philadelphia Eagles and then starring for the Minnesota Vikings.

Carter was one of seven children and a brother of pro basketball star Clarence "Butch" Carter. He was heavily recruited when he graduated from Middletown High School. He chose Ohio State and by the end of his junior year had established himself as the Buckeyes' all-time leading receiver, with 168 receptions and twenty-seven touchdown catches. His sixty-eight catches his junior year helped him garner first-team All-American honors in 1986.

Carter lost his senior year of eligibility for signing with an agent and was drafted by the Philadelphia Eagles in 1987. While showing flashes of brilliance, Carter failed to live up to his promise in Philadelphia, becoming out of shape and beset by alcohol and drug addiction problems.

Minnesota picked Carter up on waivers in 1990, and his career began to flourish as he reformed himself. He was named to the Pro Bowl six times (1993–1998). In 1994 he set a NFL single-season record with 122 receptions. In the 2000 season, Carter caught his 1,000th regular-season pass, the second player after Jerry Rice of San Francisco to achieve that goal.

Collaborating with his brother Butch,

Carter, who was ordained a minister in 1996, came out with an inspirational memoir, *Born to Believe* (2000). In 1999, Carter was named 1999 Man of the Year by the NFL. He retired at the end of the 2001 season with a lifetime record of 129 touchdowns and 1,093 pass receptions.

Robert Pruter

FURTHER READING

Bell, James. "Viking Star Carter Saving Best for Last Receiver Working Harder than Ever for Final Season." *USA Today*, July 3, 2001.

Carter, Butch, and Cris Carter, with Cynthia Martin. *Born to Believe*. Upper Tantallon, Nova Scotia: Full Wits Publishing, 2000.

Chadiha, Jeffri. "Time Trial." *Sports Illustrated*, July 3, 2000, 60–63.

Phelps, Shirelle, ed. *Contemporary Black Biography*. Detroit: Gale Group, 1999.

★ ★ ★

CENTRAL INTERCOLLEGIATE ATHLETIC ASSOCIATION

The Central Intercollegiate Athletic Association was founded February 1912 by Allen Washington and Charles H. Williams of Hampton University; George Johnson of Lincoln University (Pennsylvania); W.E. Atkins, Charles R. Frazier, and H.P. Hargrave of Shaw University (North Carolina); and J.W. Barco and J.W. Pierce of Virginia Union University. The CIAA's original members consisted of Hampton Institute (now University), Howard University, Lincoln University, Shaw University (North Carolina), and Virginia Union University. The CIAA was first named the Colored Intercollegiate Athletic Association; its purposes were to organize the original five institutions for mutual advantage, enforce rules and regulations, and raise athletic standards to the academic standards of each of the historically black institutions.

The first black athletic conference, the CIAA's constitution was published in the *Official Handbook: Interscholastic Athletic Association of Middle Atlantic States.* As more white colleges began allowing African Americans to participate in sports, the CIAA changed its name in 1950 to Central Intercollegiate Athletic Association, in order to integrate its athletic teams and attract white athletes. In 1971, the larger institutions—Howard, Lincoln, and Hampton—withdrew from the conference to capitalize on the National Collegiate Athletic Association (NCAA)'s television contracts. Today, the conference consists of twelve historically African-American institutions of higher education: Bowie State University, Elizabeth City State University, Fayetteville State University, Johnson C. Smith University, Livingstone University, North Carolina Central University, St. Augustine's College, St. Paul's College, Shaw University, Virginia State University, Virginia Union University, and Winston-Salem State University. These institutions compete in NCAA Division II.

The conference is divided into Eastern and Western Divisions in all sports except football and baseball. The CIAA sponsors thirteen men and women's championships. The seven men's championships include cross-country; indoor and outdoor track and field, basketball, golf, tennis, and baseball. The six women's championships include, cross-country, volleyball, indoor and outdoor track and field, basketball, and softball. The football champion is determined by standings as determined by regular season records. Expansion of television broadcasts has resulted in nationwide coverage of football and basketball contests, as well as the annual CIAA Basketball Tournament. Increasing competitiveness in other sports is leading to continued success and recognition of CIAA member schools as athletic powerhouses.

Danielle A. Mincey White

See also: Historically Black Colleges and Universities.

FURTHER READING
"About the CIAA" (www.theciaa.com/about/excellence.htm).
Ashe, Arthur R., Jr. *A Hard Road to Glory.* Vol. 1. Amistad: New York, 1988.
"CIAA Celebrates Golden Anniversary." *Ebony*, December 1962, 93–94.
Duval, Earl H. "An Historical Analysis of the Central Intercollegiate Athletic Association and Its Influence on the Development of Black Intercollegiate Athletics, 1912–1984." Ph.D. diss., Kent State University, 1985.
Francis Harris and Edwin B. Henderson Papers; box 44–1, folder 14. Manuscript Division, Moorland-Springarn Research Center, Howard University.
Henderson, Edwin B. *The Negro in Sports.* Washington, DC: Associated Publishers, 1949.
Williams, Charles H. "Twenty Years Work of the C.I.A.A." *Southern Workman* 61 (February 1932): 65–76.

★ ★ ★

Wilt CHAMBERLAIN

Born August 21, 1936, Philadelphia, Pennsylvania
Died August 12, 1999, Bel Air, California
Basketball player

Wilt Chamberlain, the great scorer and dominating center of the Los Angeles Lakers, overpowering the Philadelphia 76ers rookie Dennis Awtrey in 1970. *(AP/Wide World Photos)*

Wilt Chamberlain was born in the Hoddington section of Philadelphia into a family of nine brothers and sisters. His mother, Olivia, was a maid, and his father, William, worked as a welder, handyman, and janitor. His parents instilled a work ethic in him at an early age, and at five he was working odd jobs in his neighborhood.

Though he was first attracted to track and field, he found that his height (he eventually grew to seven feet, one inch) marked him for basketball. He went in 1955 to the University of Kansas, where he experienced racial discrimination that was more severe than he had seen in Philadelphia. Because he played only three years he was ineligible to play in the NBA during what would have been his fourth year of college eligibility. Unable to join the NBA, he played one year for the Harlem Globetrotters. His first year with the Philadelphia Warriors, 1959–1960, produced both Rookie of the Year and Player of the Year honors. His thirteen-year NBA career was marked by two championships, a 100-point game against the New York Knicks, and NBA records for most points (since eclipsed by

Kareem Abdul-Jabbar and Michael Jordan) and most rebounds.

After retiring from the Los Angeles Lakers in 1973, Chamberlain coached the San Diego Conquistadors (ABA). Next came movie roles, including a part in *Conan the Barbarian*, and involvement in many different sports. However, Chamberlain reserved his greatest interest for professional and Olympic volleyball, and for marathon running. Chamberlain also supported charities, including the Sunny Hill League in his hometown of Philadelphia and Operation Smile in his adopted town of Los Angeles. Before the end of his life, Chamberlain reconciled with the press, which he believed had unfairly focused attention on his claim that he had slept with 20,000 women, and with the University of Kansas. He also owned and operated a restaurant, wrote three books, and remained active with the National Basketball Association. His election to the Hall of Fame in 1979 was a formality, as he had enjoyed the greatest career in the history of basketball until that time.

Gregory S. Goodale

See also: Autobiographies; Basketball; Films; Harlem Globetrotters.

FURTHER READING
Chamberlain, Wilt. *A View from Above.* New York: Villard Books, 1991.
Libby, Bill. *Goliath: The Wilt Chamberlain Story.* New York: Dodd, Mead, 1977.
Schwartz, Larry. "Wilt Battled 'Loser' Label." ESPN.com (http://espn.go.com/sportscentury/features/00014133.html).
"Wilt Chamberlain." NBA.com (www.nba.com/history/chamberlain_bio.html).
"Wilt Chamberlain." *SLAM! Basketball* (www.canoe.ca/BasketballChamberlain/oct13_cha2.html).

★ ★ ★

John CHANEY

Born January 21, 1932, Jacksonville, Florida
Basketball coach

A star basketball player at Franklin High in Philadelphia and at Bethune-Cookman College in Daytona Beach, Florida, John Chaney went on to become one of the most respected and successful college basketball coaches in history.

Chaney came from a poor working-class family—his stepfather, Sylvester, was a shipyard worker, and his mother, Earley, was a seamstress. His family settled in Philadelphia, where he played at Franklin High, being selected the city league's Most Valuable Player in 1950. At Bethune-Cookman, he was named the Most Valuable Player in the 1953 National Association of Intercollegiate Athletics tournament. He graduated with a B.S. degree (1953) and earned a M.S. degree from Antioch College (1974).

An exceptional ball handler, Chaney found his entry into the National Basketball Association (NBA) barred by unwritten quota on the number of blacks. He played for ten seasons (1957–1966) in the semiprofessional Eastern Professional Basketball League.

Chaney coached at Simon Gratz High (1966–1972) in Philadelphia, where he built a 84–6 record. In 1973 he joined Cheyney State College in Cheyney, PA, as head coach. There he compiled a 225–59 record, leading the Wolves to five National Collegiate Athletic Association (NCAA) Division II regional titles and a Division II national championship in 1978.

Chaney became head coach at Temple University in Philadelphia in 1983. He guided the Owls to a 32–2 record in 1988 and a number-one ranking by both AP and UPI at the end of the regular season, winning Coach of the Year honors. In 2001,

Chaney was elected to the Naismith Memorial Basketball Hall of Fame. At the time, he had led the Owls to seventeen NCAA tournaments, including final-eight berths in 1988, 1991, 1993, and 1999.

Chaney, a fiery and cantankerous coach who fought hard for his players, was one of the strongest opponents of Proposition 48 (which raised academic requirements to compete), feeling that the rule limited career opportunities for athletes, African-American students in particular.

Robert Pruter

See also: Coaches and Managers.

FURTHER READING
Macnow, Glen. "John Chaney." In *Newsmakers, 1989 Cumulation*, ed. Peter M. Gareffa, 73–76. Detroit: Gale Research, 1990.
Porter, David L., ed. *Biographical Dictionary of American Sports. 1989–1992 Supplement for Baseball, Football, Basketball, and Other Sports.* Westport, CT: Greenwood Press, 1992.
Russell, Don. "He's a Legend: Temple Coach John Chaney May Be Most Recognized Philadelphian." *Philadelphia Daily News*, March 17, 2000 (www.phillynews.com/daily_news/2000/Mar/17/local/JOHN17.htm).

★ ★ ★

Ezzard CHARLES

Born July 7, 1921, Lawrenceville, Georgia
Died May 27, 1975, Chicago, Illinois
Boxer

Ezzard Charles was born in Lawrenceville, Georgia, in 1921 and attended high school in Cincinnati, at Harriet Beecher Stowe and Woodward High Schools. He married Gladys Gartell in 1949, and together they had three children.

Charles enjoyed boxing, and while living in Cincinnati began his career in the sport. As an amateur boxer, Charles won forty-two consecutive bouts from 1937 to 1940. Just after turning professional, he served two years in the U.S. Army. In 1949, soon after Joe Louis's retirement, Charles fought "Jersey Joe" Walcott for the heavyweight championship. Charles won on points but was never really accepted by the public, in part because of his boxing style. He lacked a true knockout punch, winning many of his bouts on points.

Charles was a quiet, unassuming individual, but he certainly had some attention-filled moments while fighting professionally. Before turning heavyweight he fought Archie Moore, one of the all-time great middleweights. After stepping up to heavyweight, Charles was in the spotlight, with bouts against both Joe Louis and Rocky Marciano. He defeated Louis in 1950 but lost twice to Marciano in 1954. Charles retired in 1954 but came out of retirement in 1956, finally retiring for good that same year. His final professional record was 122 bouts, ninety-six wins, twenty-five losses, and one draw. In 1966 Charles was diagnosed with Lou Gehrig's disease and died nine years later.

James R. Coates, Jr.

See also: Boxing; Joe Louis; Joe Walcott.

FURTHER READING
Charles, Ezzard. "I Was Jinxed by Joe Louis." *Ebony*, October 1951, 114–16.
"Ezzard Charles: Winner and Old Champion." *Life*, July 30, 1951, 66–67.
Lardner, John. "Bloodshed, Overdue." *Newsweek*, June 14, 1954, 64.
Sports Biography, Charles, Ezzard M. *Boxing* (www.hickoksports.com/biograph/charleez.shtml).
"Twice Is Once Too Often." *Life*, September 27, 1954, 32.

★ ★ ★

Oscar CHARLESTON

Born October 14, 1896, Indianapolis, Indiana
Died October 6, 1954, Philadelphia, Pennsylvania
Baseball player

Born the son of an Indianapolis construction worker, Oscar Charleston embarked on a life in baseball while still a child. His career began as a batboy for the all-black Indianapolis ABCs. Throughout his own playing career, Oscar Charleston was to dominate Negro league baseball.

At the age of fifteen, Charleston left Indianapolis and joined the army. Stationed in the Philippines, Charleston blossomed into an outstanding athlete. He competed in track and baseball as a member of the Twenty-Fourth Infantry Regiment team. Upon returning to the United States and leaving the army in 1915, he joined the ABCs as a pitcher and outfielder.

Gifted with speed, power, and a quick eye, Charleston hit for both power and average. He was considered by many to be the greatest Negro league player of all-time; his hitting and aggressive base running earned him the nickname "the Black Ty Cobb." Charleston's best season came in 1921, when he batted .434 and led the Negro National League with thirty-five stolen bases, fourteen doubles, eleven triples, and fifteen home runs. He was able to maintain this level of excellence throughout his thirty-eight-year career. Playing for and managing fourteen different teams, Charleston posted a lifetime batting average of .357 and hit 151 home runs.

In 1932, Charleston agreed to manage Gus Greenlee's Pittsburgh Crawfords, a team that consisted of Josh Gibson, Judy Johnson, and Satchel Paige. Charleston continued to manage various black teams until his death in 1954. In 1974, Charleston was inducted into the National Baseball Hall of Fame.

Rob Fink

Oscar Charleston (second from left), Satchel Paige (second from right) and Josh Gibson (far right), three of the greatest stars in Negro league baseball, standing in front of the Pittsburgh Crawfords' team bus. *(National Baseball Hall of Fame Library, Cooperstown, NY)*

See also: Negro National League.

FURTHER READING
Holway, John. *Blackball Stars: Negro League Pioneers.* New York: Carroll and Graf, 1988.
Peterson, Robert. *Only the Ball Was White: A History of Legendary Black Players and All-Black Professional Teams.* New York: Oxford University Press, 1970.
Ribowsky, Mark. *A Complete History of the Negro Leagues: 1884 to 1955.* Secaucus: Citadel Press, 1995.
Riley, James A. *The Biographical Encyclopedia of the Negro Baseball Leagues.* New York: Carroll and Graf, 1994.
Rogosin, Donn. *Invisible Men: Life in Baseball's Negro Leagues.* New York: Kodansha International, 1983.

★ ★ ★

CIVIL RIGHTS

Racial discrimination has always been a part of sport, just as it has been for American society in general. From the days of boxer Tom Molineaux in the early nineteenth century to the present, African-American athletes have experienced various forms of racial discrimination and injustice. This racial discrimination has been met with resistance by African-American athletes themselves, sportswriters, and regional and national civil rights organizations. Although not eliminating all vestiges of racial discrimination in sport, this resistance, along with the racial advancements in society at large, has generally contributed to more freedom of opportunity and better treatment of African-American athletes. Rather than experiencing racial slurs, segregated housing, and other forms of overt racial prejudice, African-American athletes of today are faced with slanted media portrayals and other types of more subtle forms of racial discrimination.

African-American athletes experienced their first significant forms of success in highly organized sport in the years immediately following reconstruction. Talented athletes like Marshall "Major" Taylor in bicycling, Isaac Murphy in horse racing, and Moses Fleetwood Walker in baseball garnered national and sometimes even international notoriety for their outstanding sports performances. Unfortunately, these athletes and many others were eliminated from the large majority of highly organized sports at the turn of the century because of Jim Crow laws and general hardening of racial lines in all aspects of American life. With the notable exception of a select number of African-American athletes continuing to participate in Olympic competition, the sport of boxing, and predominantly white college sports, the large majority of African-American athletes were forced to organize their own teams and leagues operating with little white interference. The most famous of these separate institutions was Negro league baseball, but there were also vibrant and culturally significant parallel institutions in football and basketball as well as amateur sport in historically black colleges and universities.

The forced transition from predominantly white organized sport to parallel black sporting institutions for the majority of African-American athletes was not accompanied by any immediate groundswell of protest from individuals or groups within the African-American community. The racial hatred in American culture at the time, combined with the lack of formal civil rights organizations, precluded any substantial protest against racial segregation in sport. This slowly began to change, however, as the twentieth century progressed and the African-American community was instilled with a new sense of political activism and racial pride. By the late 1920s, for instance, a decided increase in the number of protests against northern and southern universities for their "gentlemen's agreements" barring African-American players from intersectional athletic contests had become more evident. One highly publicized protest took place in 1929 against coach Chuck Meehan and New York University (NYU), which had acceded to southern racial tradition by benching its outstanding black player, Dave Myers, in a football game with the University of Georgia. The black press, along with the NAACP and other civil rights groups, renounced NYU and other northern institutions for acquiescing to the exclusionary policies of southern schools.

The protests lodged against racial exclusion in intercollegiate athletic contests between southern and northern institutions would be duplicated at the professional level. Black newspapers in particular led campaigns throughout the first half of the twentieth century to reintegrate professional sport. One of the most important campaigns was lodged by *Pittsburgh Cour-*

ier sportswriter Wendell Smith against the racially exclusionary policies of major league baseball. In 1938 Smith began attacking, through his column in the *Courier,* the bureaucrats in major league baseball for their racist policies. Smith's campaign, which recognized the symbolic importance of baseball because of its supposed status as America's national pastime and great leveler in society, was remarkably aggressive and took many forms. He conducted interviews with eight managers and forty players in the National League, producing a series of articles in the *Courier* entitled "What Big Leaguers Think of Negro Baseball Players." He also interviewed National League president Ford Frick; admonished Washington Senators owner Clark Griffith for his racist views of black ballplayers; called upon President Franklin D. Roosevelt to adopt a "fair employment policy" in baseball, as he had done in war industries and governmental agencies; helped arrange a meeting between baseball commissioner Judge Kenesaw Mountain Landis and the Black Newspaper Publishers Association; assisted in arranging a tryout for three African-American players with the Boston Red Sox; and suggested to Branch Rickey that Jackie Robinson would be the ideal player to integrate the national game.

Smith's campaign, along with those waged by other sportswriters and various civil rights organizations, would finally pay dividends in 1945, when Rickey signed Robinson to a contract with the Brooklyn Dodgers. After a year with the Montreal Royals, Robinson joined the parent club, an event that was received with unabated enthusiasm by the African-American community and paved the way for other black athletes to integrate various amateur and professional sports. In 1949, for instance, the American Bowling Congress allowed African Americans to use its lanes for the first time. A year later, Althea Gibson became the first African American to play in the United States Tennis Championships at Forest Hills. The color line was broken in the National Basketball Association when the Harlem Globetrotters' Nat "Sweetwater" Clifton signed with the New York Knicks and Chuck Cooper of Duquesne University inked a contract with the Boston Celtics. In 1952, Art Dorrington became the first black hockey player in America when he signed with the Johnstown Jets.

By and large, the African-American athletes who integrated sport in the 1950s and early 1960s did not become involved in civil rights issues or actively protest racial discrimination within American society. African-American athletes of this period were seemingly content with honing their skills and avoiding activities that would jeopardize their careers. This attitude began to change by the late 1960s, as more African-American athletes became involved in the civil rights struggle and black power movement. Inspired by more outspoken athletes, such as Muhammad Ali and Bill Russell, and instilled with a new sense of racial consciousness, African-American athletes of this period protested racial discrimination in both sport and the larger American society. The most celebrated and internationally known protest of African-American athletes involved the proposed boycott of the 1968 Olympic games in Mexico City. Under the leadership of Professor Harry Edwards, a number of African-American athletes threatened to withdraw from the games unless certain demands were met, including the restoration of Muhammad Ali's heavyweight championship, barring of South Africa and Rhodesia from Olympic competition because of their apartheid policies, and the ousting of Avery Brundage as president of the International Olympic Committee because of his racist policies.

Ultimately, the athletes decided, in spite of the fact their demands were not realized, to participate in the games and make some form of protest there in order to point to the racial discrimination in the United States and around the world. The most famous of these protests was the black-gloved power salute of Tommie Smith and John Carlos on the victory stand following their first and third place finishes in the two-hundred-meter dash.

The protests at the Mexico City games were followed over the next few years by literally hundreds of revolts by African-American athletes at predominantly white universities. Taking their cues from many other students on campuses across the country, African-American athletes at such institutions as the University of California, Berkeley, Syracuse University, University of Michigan, and the University of Texas at El Paso risked their careers by insisting on more African-American coaches, more African-American studies courses in the curriculum, better housing, and more humane treatment on the part of the athletic department officials and university administrators. Although not able to realize all their demands, African-American athletes were able to effect on predominantly white university campuses changes that are still in evidence today.

By the early 1970s the more visible protests of African-American athletes declined in number. Desegregation resulting from civil rights legislation, combined with the women's rights movement and concerns with unemployment and inflation, took some steam out of the black athletic revolts. African-American athletes continued to fight racial discrimination, but they increasingly became the topic of discussion among people of both races who had become sensitized to racial issues emanating from the athletic protests. The result was an outpouring of research studies and popular essays dealing with the various forms of discrimination committed against African-American athletes themselves. During the last three decades, much of the attention has shifted from the racial discrimination experienced by African-American athletes to the lack of opportunities for African Americans in coaching, managerial, and upper-level administrative positions in sport. In essence, because of the changing racial climate in contemporary American society, the struggle for civil rights on the part of African Americans has moved from the playing fields to the board rooms.

David K. Wiggins

See also: Muhammad Ali; Arthur Ashe, Jr.; Black Coaches Association; John Carlos; Harry Edwards; Edwin Henderson; Historiography; New York Pioneer Club; Rainbow Coalition for Fairness in Athletics; Jackie Robinson; Bill Russell; Tommie Smith; Wendell Smith.

FURTHER READING
Gorn, Elliott J. *Muhammad Ali: The People's Champ*. Urbana: University of Illinois Press, 1995.
Shropshire, Kenneth L. *In Black and White: Race and Sports in America*. New York: New York University Press, 1996.
Spivey, Donald. "Black Consciousness and Olympic Protest Movement, 1964–1980." In *Sport in America: New Historical Perspectives,* ed. Donald Spivey. Westport, CT: Greenwood, 1985.
Tygiel, Jules. *Baseball's Great Experiment: Jackie Robinson and His Legacy*. New York: Oxford University Press, 1983.
Wiggins, David K. *Glory Bound: Black Athletes in a White America*. New York: Syracuse University Press, 1997.

Nat "Sweetwater" CLIFTON

Born October 13, 1932, Chicago, Illinois
Died August 30, 1990, Chicago, Illinois
Basketball player

Nathaniel Clifton, nicknamed "Sweetwater" by childhood friends because he drank great quantities of flavored soda, was a standout basketball player at DuSable High School in Chicago. He then attended Xavier University of Louisiana in New Orleans.

From Xavier he went on to play with the Harlem Globetrotters for three seasons. Signed by Ned Irish of the New York Knicks, Clifton was one of the first three blacks to join the National Basketball Association in 1950. He played for seven years, 1950–1957, with New York, participating in three NBA finals and one All-Star Game. Clifton was well ahead of his time for position play; he was a forward who handled the ball as a guard would in the 1990s, and he ran to his position to press offensive action, as one would see today. He finished his NBA career with Detroit in 1958 with a ten-point-per-game average. He also appeared on the roster of the Chicago Majors of the short-lived American Basketball League in 1961–1962. Abe Saperstein, owner of the Harlem Globetrotters, directed the Majors. In addition to basketball, Clifton played professional baseball briefly in the Cleveland Indians farm system in the late 1940s.

Clifton was selected for the Black Athletes Hall of Fame in 1978. He was an often-recognized and popular cab driver in Chicago after his professional basketball career.

John R. Schleppi

See also: Basketball; Harlem Globetrotters.

FURTHER READING
Boston Herald, January 24, 1988.
Chicago Majors Media Guide 1961–62. Colorado Springs (CO) Gazette-Telegraph, September 2, 1990.
Hubbard, Jan, ed. *The Official NBA Encyclopedia*. 3d ed. New York: Doubleday, 2000.
New York Times, September 2, 1990.
Salzberg, Charles. *From Set Shot to Slam Dunk: The Glory Days of Basketball in the Words of Those Who Played It*. New York: E.P. Sutton, 1987.

★ ★ ★

COACHES AND MANAGERS

Over the past sixty years, African-American men and women made a significant contribution as coaches and administrators at the college and professional sports levels. Legendary African-American head coaches include John B. McLendon (former advisee of basketball's inventor, Dr. Naismith, the first African-American professional head basketball coach, and coach at Tennessee State University), Ed Temple (head track and field coach at Tennessee State University, coach of the U.S. women's Olympic track squad in 1960 and 1964 and Pan American teams in 1959 and 1975), and Eddie Robinson (record-setting head football coach at Grambling).

An overview of American sports suggests that significant progress has been made to hire African-American head and assistant basketball coaches in NCAA Division I. Basketball coaches include John Chaney (Temple University), C. Vivian Stringer (Rutgers University), and Mike Jarvis (St. Johns, New York). Unfortunately, college football head coaches remain a white male domain. A report in the August 3, 2001, *Chronicle of Higher Education* concluded that colleges continue to do a poor job of hiring minorities for coaching and other leadership positions. Similarly, the

1999 NCAA Minority Opportunities and Interest Committee's race report reflected few increases, over a four-year period, in the percentage of ethnic minority coaches or administrators. In 1996, Brooks and Althouse reviewed the "African American in Sport" literature and found a recurring theme, a lack of African Americans occupying college sport leadership positions—coaches, athletic directors, or managers. In January 2001, there were 115 Division I-A head football coaches, of whom only five were African American: Bobby Williams (Michigan State University), Tyrone Willingham (Stanford University), Fitz Hill (San Jose State University), Tony Samuel (New Mexico State University), and Jerry Baldwin (Louisiana-LaFayette).

Turning to professional baseball, basketball, and football, the 1998 *Sport in Society Racial and Gender Report Card* listed the total number of black managers and head coaches (as of July 1999) as twelve. The list of 1998 African-American major league baseball managers included Dusty Baker (San Francisco Giants), Jerry Manuel (Chicago White Sox), and Don Baylor (Colorado Rockies). The close of the 1999 NBA basketball season witnessed the following head coaches: Butch Carter (Toronto Raptors), Alvin Gentry (Detroit Pistons), Lenny Wilkins (Atlanta Hawks), and Paul Silas (Charlotte Hornets). Presently, there are ten African-American head coaches in the NBA and six African-American managers in major league baseball.

Overall, African-American male and female coaches have not attained parity and remain underrepresented in college and professional sports.

Dana D. Brooks and Ronald Althouse

See also: Black Coaches Association; John Chaney; John McLendon; Nolan Richardson; Eddie Robinson; Vivian Stringer; Ed Temple.

FURTHER READING
"Black Coaches Still Looking to Make Mark" (www.usatoday.com/sports/Football/sfc/2001-01-22-coaches.htm).
Brooks, Dana, and Ronald Althouse. *The African American Resource Directory*. Morgantown, WV: Fitness Information Technology, 1996.
———. "African American Head Coaches and Administrators: Progress but...?" In *The African American Athlete's Experience: Racism in College Athletics*, eds. Dana Brooks and Ronald Althouse, 85–117. Morgantown, WV: Fitness Information Technology, 2000.
Brooks, Dana, Ronald Althouse, and Delano Tucker. "African American Male Head Coaches: 'In the Red Zone, But Can They Score?'" *Journal of African American Men* 2 (1997): 93–112.
Lapchick, Richard E., and Kevin J. Matthews. *1998 Racial and Gender Report Card. Sport in Society: The Center for the Study of Sport in Society*. Boston: Northeastern University Press, 1998.
Suggs, Welch. "Top Jobs in College Sports Still Go Largely to White Men, Study Finds." *Chronicle of Higher Education*, August 3, 2001, A42.

★ ★ ★

Alice COACHMAN

Born November 9, 1923, Albany, Georgia
Sprinter, high jumper

The daughter of Fred and Evelyn Jackson Coachman and graduate of Tuskegee Institute and Albany State University, Alice Coachman spent her career teaching physical education and coaching high school athletics.

Coachman began her running career without shoes. Her family's financial circumstances and racial segregation in the South made it difficult at times for Coachman to compete, but she persevered and became an elite track and field athlete. In 1939, at the age of sixteen, she began a string of ten consecutive years as the national outdoor high jump champion. In ad-

Alice Coachman of Tuskegee University capturing the 100-meters in the Women's 1946 National A.A.U. Track and Field Championship in Buffalo, New York. To the left of Coachman is Stella Walsh, running for Cleveland's Polish-Olympic Women's Athletic Club. *(AP/Wide World Photos)*

dition, she was an outstanding sprinter, winning AAU championships in the fifty-meter dash and participating on national championship teams in the 4 x 100 meter relay at Tuskegee Institute.

Her career would have undoubtedly included more than one Olympic gold medal if the 1940 and 1944 Olympic Games had not been canceled because of World War II. Coachman had only one chance at Olympic glory—in 1948 in London—and she made it count. Despite the lack of success on the part of her track and field teammates, Coachman secured a gold medal in the high jump, defeating the home-country favorite, Dorothy Tyler, with a jump of 5 feet, 6½ inches. She won the first gold medal for the American women's team that year and became the first African-American woman to win a gold medal in Olympic competition.

Coachman's accomplishments were celebrated upon her return to the United States, including a visit to the White House to meet President Harry S Truman. However, celebrations in her home state were tainted by the racist attitudes of the time. At one ceremony blacks and whites sat on separate sides of the stage and auditorium. Coachman retired from athletics at the top and spent her life teaching and coaching others. She gave back to her sport by forming the Alice Coachman Foundation to help other athletes whose postathletic lives had not been as successful as her own.

Alison M. Wrynn

See also: Olympic Games; Track and Field.

FURTHER READING
Ashe, Arthur R., Jr. *A Hard Road to Glory.* Vol. 2. New York: Warner Books, 1988.
Cahn, Susan K. *Coming on Strong: Gender and Sexuality in Twentieth-Century Women's Sport.* New York: Free Press, 1994.
Davis, Michael D. *Black American Women in Track and Field: A Complete Illustrated Reference.* Jefferson, NC: McFarland, 1992.
Lansbury, Jennifer H. "'The Tuskegee Flash' and the 'Slender Harlem Stroker': Black Women Athletes on the Margin." *Journal of Sport History* 28 (Summer 2001): 233–52.

★ ★ ★

William Montague COBB

Born October 12, 1904, Washington, DC
Died November 20, 1990, Washington, DC
Track and field athlete, scholar

The son of Alexzine, a housewife, and William, a printer, Cobb was an outstanding student-athlete at both the high school and college levels who became well known as an educator, physical anthropologist, civil rights activist, and historian of African Americans in medicine.

Cobb distinguished himself academically and as an athlete in track and field while a student at Dunbar High School and later at Amherst College. A holder of a medical degree from Howard University (1929) and a Ph.D. in anatomy and physical anthropology from Case Western Reserve University (1932), Cobb was a professor of anatomy and physical anthropology in the Howard University College of Medicine for forty years (1932–1973). He was a prolific writer, publishing hundreds of articles on an assortment of topics in some of academia's most highly respected journals. He became well known for his work on the history of African Americans in medicine, but he also wrote extensively about variation in human anatomy, including the supposed physiological differences between the races and their effects on sport performance. His article "Race and Runners," based on anthropometric measurements of Jesse Owens and other athletes, is one of the classic refutations of biological determinism as an explanation of athletic superiority. In addition to his publications, Cobb was the longtime editor of the *Journal of the National Medical Association* (1949–1977) and president of such important organizations as the National Association for the Advancement of Colored People (1976–1982), the American Association of Physical Anthropologists (1957–1959), the National Medical Association (1964–1965), and the Anthropological Society of Washington (1949–1951).

Cobb was honored for his many accomplishments with a number of awards and tributes. Included among these were honorary degrees from ten universities, a "Living Legacy" award presented by President Jimmy Carter in 1979, and the Henry Gray award, conferred in 1980 by the American Association of Anatomists for significant contributions to the field of anatomy.

David K. Wiggins

See also: Jesse Owens; Racial Theories.

FURTHER READING
Baker, Lee D. *From Savage to Negro: Anthropology and the Construction of Race, 1896–1954.* Berkeley: University of California Press, 1998.
Dyreson, Mark. "American Ideas About Race and Olympic Races from the 1890s to the 1950s: Shattering Myths or Reinforcing Scientific Racism?" *Journal of Sport History* 28 (Summer 2001): 173–215.
Miller, Patrick B. "The Anatomy of Scientific Racism:

Racialist Responses to Black Athletic Achievement." *Journal of Sport History* 25 (Spring 1998): 119–51.

Rankin-Hill, Leslie M., and Michael L. Blakey. "W. Montague Cobb: Physical Anthropologist, Anatomist, and Activist." In *African-American Pioneers in Anthropology*, eds. Ira E. Harrison and Faye V. Harrison, 101–36. Urbana: University of Illinois Press, 1999.

Scarupa, Harriet Jackson, "W. Montague Cobb: His Long, Storied, Battle-Scarred Life." *New Directions* (April 1988): 6–17.

★ ★ ★

Chuck COOPER

Born September 29, 1926, Pittsburgh, Pennsylvania
Died February 5, 1984, Pittsburgh, Pennsylvania
Basketball player

Charles Cooper graduated from Westinghouse High School in Pittsburgh, PA, in 1944. He was twice selected to the All-City basketball team from Westinghouse. He served in the navy late in World War II before entering West Virginia State University and then Duquesne University. At Duquesne he played in two National Invitational Tournaments, was an All-American, and captained the team his senior year.

Cooper is most remembered as the first black player drafted by the National Basketball Association (NBA). Walter Brown, founder and owner of the Boston Celtics, made history by selecting Cooper on April 25, 1950, and signing him to a contract. Cooper spent four years with the Celtics (1950–1954) before moving to the Milwaukee Hawks in 1954–1955. He finished his NBA career in the 1955–1956 season, first with St. Louis and then the Fort Wayne Zollner Pistons.

After his NBA career he worked for the U.S. Post Office and returned to professional basketball with the touring Harlem Magicians. A year of traveling convinced him that further education was needed to advance in a profession. He then obtained a master's degree in social work from the University of Minnesota. Returning to Pittsburgh, Cooper served on the city's school board. Then, as director of parks and recreation, he became the first African American to head a municipal department in Pittsburgh. Before his death he also served as an official with a Pittsburgh bank.

John R. Schleppi

See also: Basketball.

FURTHER READING
Boston Sunday Globe, April 3, 1977.
Hubbard, Jan, ed. *The Official NBA Encyclopedia*. New York: Doubleday, 2000.
New York Times, April 27, 1980.
Pittsburgh Post Gazette, April 25, 2000.

★ ★ ★

Ted CORBITT

Born January 31, 1919, near Dunbarton, South Carolina
Distance runner

Ted Corbitt, considered the "Father of Distance Running," pioneered ultramarathoning in the United States and was a leader in measurement criteria and course certification. Corbitt's father (John Henry) worked as a part-time preacher and farmer, and his mother (Alma Bing) worked on the family farm. He graduated with honors from Woodward High School and the University of Cincinnati, earned an M.S. in physical therapy from New York University (1950), and worked as a physical therapist at the International Centre for the Disabled for over forty-three years. Additionally, he taught at Columbia University,

New York University, and other colleges. During high school and college, Corbitt faced segregation and was excluded from certain interstate and local AAU meets during his first two years in college. In 1947, he joined the New York Pioneer Club, which had no color barrier.

Corbitt did not become serious about distance running until age thirty. Corbitt ran in his first marathon in 1951 and made the 1952 Olympic team in Helsinki. In 1954, he won Amateur Athletic Union (AAU) marathons in Philadelphia and Detroit. During his career, which ended in 1974 due to bronchial asthma, Corbitt ran in 199 marathons and ultramarathons and set American records for the fifty-mile (5:54, 1966), the hundred-mile (13:33.06, 1969), and the twenty-four-hour event (134.7 miles, 1973). He was inducted into the Road Runner Hall of Fame (1972) and was one of the first five inductees into the National Distance Running Hall of Fame (1998).

Sara A. Elliott

FURTHER READING

Blaikie, David. *Ted Corbitt at 80: Still a Humble Pioneer*. Ultramarathon World (www.fox.nstn.ca/dblaikie/n02fe98d.html).

Chodes, John. *Corbitt: The Story of Ted Corbitt, Long Distance Runner*. Los Altos, CA: Tafnews Press, 1974.

Distance Running Hall of Fame: Ted Corbitt. Distance Running (www.distancerunning.com/induccorbitt.html).

Road Runners Club of America Hall of Fame, Road Runners Club of America (www.rrca.org/publicat/rrcahof.htm).

Russ COWANS

Born July 29, 1899, Chicago, Illinois
Died December 27, 1978, Detroit, Michigan
Sports reporter

Russell Cowans had a notable career while working in Detroit and Chicago. He was a sports reporter for the *Detroit Tribune* (also known as the *Tribune Independent*). One of the athletes he covered was future journalist Wendell Smith, who was then a basketball star. Cowans also was a city reporter for the Detroit edition of the *Chicago Defender*. He helped found the *Michigan Chronicle* and became a sportswriter for the publication. He once led a brief boycott against the Detroit Stars of the Negro National League because the team's owner allegedly mistreated players and fans. A secretary for Joe Louis, Cowans answered fan mail, compiled scrapbooks, and sent pictures.

When he traveled to London for the 1948 Olympics, he became one of the first African Americans to cover the event. Later, he succeeded Frank A. "Fay" Young as the *Chicago Defender*'s sports editor. He returned to Detroit and worked as managing editor of the *Chronicle*.

Cowans often listened to the radio while composing stories in his office. Although he did not get the same notoriety as several of his peers, he was a respected journalist. In 1962, Cowans was honored by Brewster Old Timers, a charitable organization based in Detroit.

Michael Marsh

FURTHER READING

Bak, Richard. *Turkey Stearnes and the Detroit Stars: The Negro Leagues in Detroit, 1919–1933*. Detroit: Wayne State University Press, 1994.

Cabell, Terry. "Friends Remember Russ . . . and the Way It Was." *Michigan Chronicle*, October 21, 1978.

Cowans, Russell. "Detroit Team Defeats West Virginia 28–19." *Tribune Independent*, December 30, 1933.

Saunders, Frank H. "Russell Cowans, Noted Journalist, Mourned." *Michigan Chronicle*, December 30, 1978.

Isabelle DANIELS

Born July 31, 1937, Jakin, Georgia
Sprinter, coach

The daughter of Fred Daniels, a farmer and bus driver, and his wife Vera, a schoolteacher, Daniels was the youngest of nine siblings. A graduate of Carver High School and Tennessee State University, Daniels shared the bronze medal for the 4 x 100 relay in the 1956 Olympics in Melbourne, Australia.

The dirt, back roads of Fred Daniel's farm served as a training ground for Daniels and her athletic brothers. Receiving a scholarship to Tennessee State University, she trained under Coach Ed Temple and with his lady athletes, the Tigerbelles. Daniels made the Olympic track and field team in 1956 and won bronze at the games in Melbourne with teammates Mae Faggs, Margaret Matthews, and Wilma Rudolph. Daniels collected many national and international medals, including a gold for the 200-meter race in the Goodwill Games in 1958.

As a career track and basketball coach, Daniels has won seven county, ten regional, and four state titles. Daniels was inducted into the Tennessee State University Hall of Fame in 1984 and the Georgia State Hall of Fame in 1987. She was named All-State Role Model in 1992 and was given the key to her hometown of Jakin, Georgia, during its 1995 Centennial Celebration.

Daniels, now a mother of four, is secretary to Church Twinnings, her missionary husband Rev. Sidney R. Holston's organization, which pairs up churches in America with churches in Africa. An autobiography is in progress.

Alison M. Gavin

Tennessee State University's Isabelle Daniels shortly after capturing the 50-yard dash at the 1958 Women's National A.A.U. Track and Field Championship in Morristown, New Jersey. *(AP/Wide World Photos)*

FURTHER READING
Ashe, Arthur R., Jr. *A Hard Road to Glory.* Vol. 3. New York: Amistad, 1988.
South Central Bell, official sponsor of the 1986 Olympic Games in Atlanta, *Isabelle Daniels Holston*, "Spirit of Legends" calendar 1995–1996.
Telephone interview, August 24, 2001.

★ ★ ★

Adrian DANTLEY

Born February 26, 1955, Washington, DC
Basketball player

Adrian Dantley was raised by his mother Virginia and her aunt Mariel after his parents divorced when he was three. In high school, he was named a basketball All-

American while leading DeMatha Catholic Prep School in Hyattsville, Maryland, to a 57–2 record in three years. He matriculated in 1973 at Notre Dame, where he became a two-time All-America (1975–1976) and the second-leading scorer in Irish history. He left school after his junior year, leading the 1976 U.S. Olympic Basketball team in scoring en route to a gold medal before signing with the Buffalo Braves of the National Basketball Association.

Dantley averaged 20.3 points per game and earned NBA Rookie of the Year honors but was traded in 1977 to the Indiana Pacers and again in midseason to the Los Angeles Lakers. In 1979 he joined the Utah Jazz and immediately established himself as one of the NBA's most prolific scorers. Despite his lack of height, the six-foot five-inch, 210-pound Dantley was a low-post forward who used fakes and footwork to get to the basket and the free-throw line. During seven seasons with the Jazz he averaged from 26.6 to 30.7 points per game, led the league in scoring in 1980–1981 (30.7 points) and 1983–1984 (30.6), was a six-time NBA All-Star (1980–1982, 1984–1986), was twice named second team All-NBA (1980–1981, 1983–1984), and was the NBA Comeback Player of the Year in 1983–1984 (a wrist injury had limited him to twenty-two games the previous season). A contract dispute and clashes with the head coach led to his trade to Detroit in 1986. He played with Dallas 1989–1990 and Milwaukee 1990–1991 before ending his pro career in 1991–1992 with Milan of the Italian League.

Over fifteen NBA seasons Dantley scored 23,177 points for a 24.3-point average. He was elected to the Utah Basketball Hall of Fame in 1999.

Larry R. Gerlach

FURTHER READING
Hubbard, Jan, ed. *The Official NBA Encyclopedia*. 3d ed. New York: Doubleday, 2000.

Neely, Tim. *Hooping It Up: The Complete History of Notre Dame Basketball*. South Bend, IN: Notre Dame University, 1985.
Porter, David L., ed. *Biographical Dictionary of American Sports: Basketball and Other Indoor Sports*. Westport, CT: Greenwood Press, 1989.
Salt Lake City Deseret News, February 23, 1988, and October 27, 1999.
Salt Lake Tribune, November 15, 1982; August 22, 1986; and November 14, 1999.
Utah Jazz Media Guide and Record Book. Salt Lake City: Utah Jazz, 2001.

★ ★ ★

Ernie DAVIS

Born December 14, 1939, New Salem, Pennsylvania
Died May 18, 1963, Cleveland, Ohio
Football player

Son of Mrs. Arthur Radford (his father died when he was an infant), Davis was an outstanding all-around athlete in both high school and college. He earned eleven varsity letters in football, basketball, and baseball at Elmira Free Academy in Elmira, New York. He was selected as a high school All-American in football and basketball in both his junior and senior years. After being courted by thirty colleges and universities, Davis decided to take his talents to Syracuse University, where he continued to display his extraordinary athletic skills. He competed on the school's basketball and track and field teams. It was as a running back in football, however, that he realized lasting fame. In thirty-one games for the Orangemen, Davis rushed for 2,836 yards, scored thirty-five touchdowns, and accounted for 220 points. His exploits on the gridiron garnered Davis many accolades and awards. He was recipient of the Walter Camp Trophy and *Sport* magazine's Player of the Year in 1961, was a consensus All-American in 1960 and 1961, and in 1961 became the first African American to win the prestigious Heisman Trophy as college football's best player.

Davis was taken by the Washington Redskins as the first choice of the 1961 NFL draft. He was then dealt to the Cleveland Browns for Bobby Mitchell—a famous trade, in that Mitchell became thereby the first African American to play for the Redskins. Davis ultimately signed a $80,000 contract with the Browns but would never play a down of professional football. As he was training for the college All-Star Game in the summer of 1962, Davis became ill. He was initially diagnosed with mononucleosis, but later tests determined that he suffered from monocytic leukemia, a fatal condition that took his life on May 18, 1963.

David K. Wiggins

See also: Football; Floyd Little.

FURTHER READING
Davis, Ernie, and Bob August. "I'm Not Unlucky." *Saturday Evening Post*, March 30, 1963, 60–62.
"Ernie Davis, Everybody's All American." *Ebony*, December 1961, 73–79.
"Pro Patient." *Newsweek*, October 22, 1962, 76.
Wright, Alfred. "Ernie Davis, a Man of Courage." *Sports Illustrated*, May 27, 1963, 25.

★ ★ ★

John Henry DAVIS

Born January 12, 1921, Smithtown, New York
Died July 25, 1984, Albuquerque, New Mexico
Weight lifter

Named after the mythical black strongman John Henry, he was the son of Margaret Davis and attended public schools in Brooklyn. He never knew his father. Davis was to become an Olympic and world champion, the world's premier heavyweight lifter from 1940 to 1953.

He was an all-around athlete and started weightlifting in 1937 with a friend's barbell. Displaying great pulling power, Davis quickly reached the heights of national and international competition. In 1938 he won the world light heavyweight title in Vienna at age seventeen. His 258.5-pound press and 854-pound (three-lift) total were world records. As a heavyweight he became the first man in history to exceed a 1,000-pound total, with a 320 press, 315 snatch, and 370 clean and jerk at the 1941 national championships. His lifting career was interrupted by service in World War II and a bout of haemolytic jaundice, but Davis returned to win five more world championships and Olympic gold medals in 1948 (London) and 1952 (Helsinki). In 1951, at the first Pan American Games in Buenos Aires, he made his best lifts—a 330 pound press, 330 pound snatch, and 402 pound clean and jerk—for a world record 1,062 total. His feats of strength include a 500-pound squat for ten repetitions and a 705 pound deadlift at 193 body weight. Davis also lifted the unwieldy Apollon Railway Wheels in Paris in 1949, with his famous thumbless grip.

By Hoffman Formula body-weight calculations, Davis often was rated the world's best lifter. For most of his competitive career, he was regarded as invincible. John Davis is a member of the U.S. Olympic Hall of Fame and is one of three African-American athletes in the Weightlifting Hall of Fame.

John D. Fair

See also: Olympic Games; Weightlifting and Bodybuilding.

FURTHER READING
Drechsler, Arthur. "John Davis: Hero & Legend." *Weightlifting USA* (Winter 2000/2001): 14–15.
Hoffman, Bob. "John Davis, World's Greatest Weightlifter." *Strength & Health* (October 1951): 9, 45, 48.

Kiiha, Osmo. "John Henry Davis, Jr." *Iron Master*, April 1993, 6–35.

Murray, Jim. "John Davis, Iron Game Immortal." *Iron Master*, June 1954, 9–11, 37–39.

Shields, Charlie. "John Davis, Portrait of a Champion." *Iron Master*, January 1974, 50–55, 85.

★ ★ ★

Dominique DAWES

Born November 20, 1976, Silver Spring, Maryland
Gymnast

The daughter of Don and Loretta, Dawes became not only one of the first African Americans to make the U.S. Olympic gymnastics team but also the first African-American woman to win a national gymnastics championship.

With her parents' encouragement, Dawes began training and competing at the age of six. Her skills emerged through countless hours of training at Hill's Gymnastic Training Center in Gaithersburg, Maryland. In 1992, Dawes placed first in the uneven bars and fourth in the all-around U.S. National Championship competition. These accomplishments secured the fifteen-year-old a spot on the 1992 Olympic Team. In the Olympic Summer Games in Barcelona, Dawes won the bronze medal in team competition. One year later Dawes won two silver medals in the uneven bars and the balance beam at the World Championships. Dawes was the first woman in twenty-five years to win each event, including vault, uneven bars, balance beam, and floor exercise, in the 1994 U.S. National Championships. That same year brought Dawes a silver medal for team competition at the World Championships. By winning the bronze medal in the floor exercise, Dawes became the first African-American woman to win a medal in an individual event. She also won a gold in team competition at the 1996 Olympic Games in Atlanta, where she earned, and lived up to, her nickname—"Awesome Dawesome." Dawes's talent and leadership qualities guaranteed her a position on the 2000 U.S. Olympic team as well.

After graduating from Gaithersburg High School in 1994, Dawes was offered an athletic scholarship to Stanford University.

Sara B. Washington

Dominique Dawes competing in the vaulting competition at the 1994 National Gymnastics Championships in Nashville, Tennessee. *(AP/Wide World Photos)*

See also: Gymnastics; Olympic Games.

FURTHER READING
Hine, Darlene Clark. *Facts On File Encyclopedia of Black Women in America: Dance, Sport, & Visual Arts.* New York: Facts On File, 1997.

Johnson, Anne Janette. *Great Women in Sports.* Detroit: Visible Ink Press, 1996.

Sherrow, Victoria. *Encyclopedia of Women and Sports.* Santa Barbara, CA: ABC-CLIO, 1996.

★ ★ ★

Anita DE FRANTZ

Born October 4, 1952, Philadelphia, Pennsylvania
Rower, IOC member

Anita De Frantz, who was to become an Olympic competitor in rowing and a member of the International Olympic Committee, graduated from Shortridge High School in Indianapolis, from Connecticut College (1974), and from the University of Pennsylvania Law School (1977). While an undergraduate, she took up rowing and became a member of her college rowing team. She moved on to the U.S. women's national rowing team, won a bronze medal in the eights at the Montreal Games (1976), and rowed in five world championship finals between 1976 and 1980, winning a silver medal in 1978. Her team was unable to participate in the Moscow Games (1980) because of the U.S. boycott; she sued unsuccessfully for her team to be allowed to compete. For her efforts in opposing the U.S. boycott, the International Olympic Committee (IOC) awarded her the Medal of the Olympic Order.

De Frantz was appointed a vice presi-

Anita De Frantz, at the time, spokeswoman for the United States Olympic Committee's Athletes Advisory Council, answering questions for reporters outside the White House concerning the boycott of the 1980 Moscow Olympic games. *(AP/Wide World Photos)*

dent of the Los Angeles Olympic Organizing Committee (LAOOC) for the 1984 Summer Games and became president of the Amateur Athletic Foundation, an organization created with the profits from the games. In 1986, she was the first woman and the first African American appointed as a U.S. representative to the International Olympic Committee, where she has been influential in increasing the participation of women at the games. For example, she was instrumental in adding women's soccer and softball to the program of the Atlanta games in 1996. The following year, she was elected a vice president of the IOC, the first woman accorded that honor. In recent years, she has been active in the efforts to develop stricter drug testing protocols for the IOC and in increasing the number of women serving on the IOC. In 1999, however, members of the Senate Commerce Committee, investigating allegations of bribery and other illegal activities in connection with the Salt Lake City bid for the 2002 Winter Games, criticized her and James Easton, the other U.S. representative on the IOC, for helping to create a "culture of corruption" in the Olympic movement.

Apart from her work in the IOC, De Frantz has been vice president of the International Rowing Federation and has been active in other organizations devoted to promoting sport opportunities for girls and women.

John E. Findling

See also: Olympic Games.

FURTHER READING
Christensen, Karen, Allan Guttmann, and Gertrud Pfister, eds. *International Encyclopedia of Woman in Sports.* New York: Macmillan, 2001.
Collier, Aldene. "Olympic Power." *Ebony,* July 1992, 76–80.
New York Times, April 15, 1999.
Page, James A. *Black Olympian Medalists.* Englewood, CO: Libraries Unlimited, 1991.

★ ★ ★

Gail DEVERS

Born November 19, 1966, Seattle, Washington
Sprinter, hurdler

Gail Devers's parents—her father was a Baptist minister and her mother a teacher's aide—raised her in San Diego, California. Devers's running career exploded in college. She had been recruited by a number of universities, but chose the strong track program at the University of California at Los Angeles (UCLA). For two years she was the PAC-Ten athlete of the year, and in 1988 she set an American record in the 100-meter hurdles. This was also the year that Devers faced her greatest challenge, a thyroid condition known as Graves' disease. Doctors thought they would have to amputate her feet, but she overcame the disease, and less than a year and a half later she arrived at the 1992 Olympic Games in Barcelona, where she won the gold medal in the 100-meter dash.

Over the next four years she continued to set American records and win national and world championships in both the 100-meter dash and the 100-meter hurdles. In Atlanta in 1996 she repeated her Olympic victory in the 100 meters and added a gold in the 4 x 100 relay. It appeared that her dominance would continue four years later in Sydney, but an injury forced her from the games.

Today, Devers is a successful businesswoman and motivational speaker. The Gail Devers Foundation and Gail Force, Inc., are organizations she has established to provide assistance to people in need as well as to spread her message of overcoming life's challenges through hard work and faith.

Alison M. Wrynn

Eric DICKERSON

Born September 2, 1960, Sealy, Texas
Football player

A native of Sealy, Texas, Eric Dickerson was a *Parade* magazine high school All-American and led his school to the state championship in 1978. The six-foot three-inch, 220-pound Dickerson ran the 100-yard dash in 9.4 seconds for Sealy High. Dickerson attended Southern Methodist University, where he and Craig James constituted one of the most prolific football backfields in collegiate history. At Southern Methodist, Dickerson was a two-time All-America selection. He amassed 4,450 yards rushing and forty-seven touchdowns in four seasons.

In 1983 he became a first-round draft choice of the National Football League's Los Angeles Rams. During his rookie year he rushed for 1,808 yards to lead the league, and he was selected as the Rookie of the Year, All-Pro, Pro Bowl, and National Football Conference Player of the Year. In his second season, 1984, Dickerson ran for a league-record 2,105 yards and rushed for 100 or more yards in twelve games. Dickerson gained more than 1,000 yards in each of his first four years with the Rams. In three of those four seasons he gained more than 1,800 yards. In 1985 he ran for a league-playoff-record 248 yards versus the Dallas Cowboys. In 1987 Dickerson was traded to the Indianapolis Colts. As a Colt his prolific performance continued; he led the league in rushing for the fourth time in 1988. In 1989 he became the first player in National Football League history to gain more than 1,000 yards in seven consecutive seasons.

He finished his career in 1993 after one-

Gail Devers reacting to the crowd following her victory in the 100-meters at the 1992 Barcelona Olympic games. *(AP/Wide World Photos)*

FURTHER READING
"Gail Devers" (www.gaildevers.com/biography.htm).
Johnson, Dave. "A Truly Amazing Comeback." *Track and Field News*, December 1991, 11.
Laney, Ruth. "Controversy Dogs Devers." *Track and Field News*, November 1993, 49.
Moore, Kenny. "Gail Force." *Sports Illustrated*, May 10, 1993, 41–43.
Porter, David L., ed. *African-American Sports Greats: A Biographical Dictionary.* Westport, CT: Greenwood Press, 1995.

Indianapolis Colts running back Eric Dickerson warding off New England Patriot defenders in a 1987 contest in Foxboro, Massachusetts. *(AP/Wide World Photos)*

year stints with the Los Angeles Raiders and the Atlanta Falcons. Dickerson was the seventh back in National Football League history to gain more than 10,000 yards rushing and did so the soonest, in just ninety-one games. Eric Dickerson played a total of eleven seasons in the National Football League, totaling 13,259 yards rushing, 2,137 yards receiving, and ninety-six touchdowns. He was enshrined into the Pro Football Hall of Fame in 1999.

David W. Hunter

FURTHER READING
Carroll, Bob, Michael Gershman, David Neft, and John Thorn. *Total Football II: The Official Encyclopedia of the National Football League.* New York: HarperCollins, 1999.
Pro Football Hall of Fame, *Eric Dickerson* (www.profootballhof.com/players/enshrinees/edickerson.cfm).

★ ★ ★

Harrison DILLARD

Born July 8, 1923, Cleveland, Ohio
Sprinter, hurdler

Harrison Dillard was raised in Cleveland, where his father (William) lost the family's small business during the Depression; his mother (Terah) was forced to become a maid. Dillard's thin build as a child led to his nickname, "Bones." He attended East Technical High School and earned a B.A.

in business from Baldwin-Wallace College. He spent his professional life as a businessman in public relations and education.

A prominent athlete in high and low hurdles, Dillard was a state champion in high school, won four NCAA titles in college, and earned fourteen AAU championships. A world record holder in both events, Dillard won eighty-two consecutive hurdle competitions and developed two hurdling techniques that are still popular today. In 1948 he won Olympic gold medals (400-meter relay, 100-meter sprint) and captured gold again in 1952 (400-meter relay and 110-meter hurdles). Dillard is the only man ever to win gold medals in both the 100-meter sprint and the high hurdles. He received the Sullivan Award as the outstanding amateur athlete (1953) and was inducted into the National Track and Field (1974) and Olympic (1983) Halls of Fame.

Upon retirement from competition, Dillard continued his involvement with sport, working for the Cleveland Indians and officiating at local track events. He later became an administrator for the Cleveland Public Schools, committing himself to educational and community service. Because of his Olympic fame and his civic duty, he received an honorary doctorate of humane letters from his alma mater, Baldwin-Wallace.

Debra A. Henderson

See also: Track and Field.

FURTHER READING
Dawson, D.P., R.K. Rasmussen, A. Miller, and E. Slocum, eds. *Great Athletes*. Pasadena, CA: Salem Press. 2002.
Page, James A., ed. *Black Olympian Medalists*. Englewood, CO: Libraries Unlimited, 1991.
Porter, David L., ed. *Biographical Dictionary of American Sports*. Westport, CT: Greenwood Press. 1988.
———. *African American Sports Greats: A Biographical Dictionary*. Westport, CT: Greenwood Press. 1995.
Staff Writer. "Harrison Dillard." *USA Track and Field Official Site* (www.usatf.org), 2001.

★ ★ ★

George DIXON

Born July 29, 1870, Halifax, Nova Scotia, Canada
Died January 6, 1909, New York, New York
Boxer

Descended from blacks who had migrated from the United States to Canada during the Revolutionary War period, Dixon was one of the world's great boxers. Only five feet, three inches in height and weighing approximately 100 pounds, Dixon dominated the lower weight divisions from the time he turned professional at the age of sixteen. He first garnered international acclaim when he defeated Nunc Wallace for the bantamweight title in London on June 27, 1890. His most famous fight, however, was against the white featherweight boxer Jack Skelly on September 6, 1892, at the Olympic Club in New Orleans. The fight, which was part of a three-day boxing festival that included the lightweight title bout between Jack McAuliffe and Billy Myer as well as the famous heavyweight championship match between John L. Sullivan and James J. Corbett, was viewed with great interest, since it pitted black and white boxers in the deep South.

Dixon scored a decisive victory over Skelly in front of a packed house, including a number of black fans, who had been provided separate seating arrangements by club officials. Although no skirmishes broke out immediately following the fight, Dixon's victory ignited local prejudices and contributed to growing racial separatism in the sport in New Orleans and throughout the South. Dixon, for his part, realized mixed success following his celebrated bout against Skelly, relinquishing his crown in 1900 and then fighting for another six years before retiring. Unfortunately, as was true of so many boxers of

Larry DOBY

Born December 13, 1924, Camden, South Carolina
Died June 18, 2003, Montclair, New Jersey
Baseball player

The son of David Doby, a horse groomer, and Etta Brooks, a domestic, Doby spent his early youth in South Carolina living with his grandmother and then an aunt and uncle. He attended Browning Home-Maher Academy, in Camden, through the eighth grade, and then moved to Paterson, New Jersey, to join his mother, who had migrated there a decade earlier. Doby graduated from Eastside High School, where he lettered in four sports. He attended Long Island University and Virginia Union University prior to entering the U.S. Navy in 1943.

Doby played baseball two seasons with the Newark Eagles, leading them to the Negro League World Championship in 1946. The following year, Bill Veeck of the Cleveland Indians purchased his contract from the Eagles and made Doby the first black player in the American League; he joined the team on July 4, 1947. He helped the Indians win the 1948 World Series and the American League crown in 1954. Doby led the American League in home runs with thirty-two in 1952 and again in 1954, to become the first black to win a major league home-run crown. He played in nine All-Star Games (seven with the Indians and two with the Eagles). He also played for the White Sox, Tigers, Orioles, and in Japan. He became the major leagues' second black manager when he took over the White Sox during the last half of the 1978 season. He was elected to the Baseball Hall of Fame by the Veterans Committee in 1998.

J. Thomas Jable

Larry Doby, shown here in a Chicago White Sox uniform, gained lasting fame by becoming the first African American to play in the American League with the 1947 Cleveland Indians. *(AP/Wide World Photos)*

FURTHER READING

Moore, Joseph Thomas. *Pride Against Prejudice: The Biography of Larry Doby*. New York: Greenwood Press, 1988.

Porter, David L., ed. *Biographical Dictionary of American Sports: Baseball*. Westport, CT: Greenwood Press, 2000.

Sports Illustrated. "Perseverance Pays, Sutton, Doby Used Toughness, Guile, Ability to Earn Hall Status" (http://sportsillustrated.cnn.com/baseball/mlb/1998/07/23/halloffame/).

★ ★ ★

Arthur DORRINGTON

Born 1930, Truro, Nova Scotia, Canada
Hockey player

Dorrington was signed by the New York Rangers of the National Hockey League (NHL) to play in that team's minor-league system. However, Dorrington elected to play instead for the Atlantic City team in the Eastern Hockey League (EHL), where he played his first game on November 15, 1950, becoming the first black player to play hockey professionally. His career ended in 1960–1961 after an unsuccessful attempt to return from a broken femur. Dorrington was known for his fast, fluid skating style and led EHL's Washington Lions in goals, assists, and points during the 1954–1955 season and the Philadelphia Ramblers in goals the following season.

Following his playing career, Dorrington settled in Atlantic City, New Jersey, where he worked as an officer for the Atlantic County Sheriff's Department. He retired in 1994 and took a part-time job with the Atlantic City Recreation Department. He created the Arthur Dorrington Ice Hockey Foundation, which supplies underprivileged children with the equipment and ice time necessary to pursue the sport. According to Dorrington, the foundation's "goal is to incorporate life skills with the game of hockey so that the children finish the program with a sense of overall confidence, competence, and well-roundedness." Twenty-five volunteers work year-round to provide the children with two one-and-a-half-hour sessions each week from September through April. Dorrington's wife, Dorothie, a former schoolteacher and administrator, oversees the foundation's education program.

Daniel S. Mason

FURTHER READING

"Art Dorrington Joins Boardwalk Bullies as Community Relations Consultant: The Former Sea Gull Will Provide a Link Between Hockey's Past and Future in Atlantic City" (www.achockey.com/press/dorrington.html).

Kent, B. "Ice Man." *New York Times*, November 30, 1997.

Slate, Ralph. *Internet Hockey Database* (www.hockeydb.com/ihdb/stats/leagues/seasons/teams/0005361951.html).

★ ★ ★

Charles DREW

Born June 3, 1904, Washington, DC
Died April 1, 1950, Burlington, NC
Football player, track and field athlete, doctor

The son of Richard and Nora Drew, Charles Drew was an outstanding all-around athlete at Amherst College whose sports accomplishments were overshadowed by his brief but stellar career in medicine. Upon graduation from Amherst in 1926, Drew served as athletics director and biology instructor at Morgan State College before pursuing graduate studies in medicine.

Drew earned an M.D. and master's of surgery (C.M.) from McGill University in Montreal, Canada, in 1933. He then served stints in Washington, DC, as an instructor of pathology at Howard University, and as an assistant in surgery at the Freedman's

Hospital. Drew continued his graduate studies in New York at Columbia University, earning a doctoral degree in 1940. His research into the storage of blood for transfusion would lead to his greatest accomplishments and fame.

In 1940, Dr. Drew developed a system to produce blood plasma and also served as medical director of a plasma production project in Great Britain. The following year, he became medical director of the first American Red Cross Blood Bank, which produced dried plasma that could be stored for longer periods of time than liquid plasma. His work is credited with saving thousands of American and British soldiers during World War II. Drew was awarded the Spingarn Medal by the NAACP in 1944, and the U.S. Postal Service issued a postage stamp honoring him in 1981. Drew died in an automobile accident in rural North Carolina in 1950.

Robert Epling

FURTHER READING

Adams, Russell, L. *Great Negroes: Past and Present*. Chicago: Afro-Am, 1964, 61.
American Red Cross (www.redcrossaustin.org/historyhtml/drew.html).
Hornsby, Alton, Jr. *Chronology of African American History*. 2d ed. Farmington Hills, MI: Gale Research Group, 1997.
Love, Spencie. *One Blood: The Death and Resurrection of Charles R. Drew*. Chapel Hill: University of North Carolina Press, 1996.
Mabunda, Mpho L., ed. *Reference Library of Black America*. Detroit: Gale Research, 1997.
"Unbound: The Triumph of African Americans" (www.phillyburbs.com/BHM/drew.shtml).

★ ★ ★

Howard DREW

Born June 28, 1890, Lexington, Virginia
Died February 19, 1957, West Haven, Connecticut
Sprinter, lawyer

As a husband and father of two, Drew began high school at twenty-one and later earned his degree (B.A.) from Drake University. He subsequently pursued a law degree and was a member of the bar association in Connecticut and Ohio. At fifty-three, he became an assistant clerk for the city court in Hartford, Connecticut.

Drew gained prominence as a champion sprinter in 1911 while in high school. It was there that he met James Sullivan of the American Athletic Union, who arranged for his participation in the 1912 Olympics. During the trials Drew tied the existing 100-meter record of 10.8 seconds but was unable to compete in the finals due to injury. Later that year he set the 100-meter indoor record of 10.2 seconds. His Olympic hopes ended when the 1916 games were canceled due to World War I, and he failed to qualify in 1920. However, his amateur and intercollegiate career resulted in his being known as the greatest track athlete of the era. Drew was the first to be called "the World's Fastest Human" and holds the world record for the ninety and seventy-yard dashes (9.0 and 7.2 seconds respectively). He held the 1913 world record for the 220 (22.8 seconds) and held AAU titles in the 100 and 220-yard dashes.

In a historical era of legalized discrimination, Drew stood as a testament to the courage of the African-American athlete. He was known for crossing racial barriers in athletics, education, and the legal system.

Debra A. Henderson

See also: Track and Field.

FURTHER READING

Ashe, Arthur R., Jr. *A Hard Road to Glory: A History of the African-American Athlete, 1619–1918*. New York: Warner Books, 1993.

B. Davis Schwartz Memorial Library. *African Americans in the Sports Arena* (www.liu.edu/cwis/cwp/library/aaitsa.html), 1997.

Porter, David L., ed. *The Biographical Dictionary of American Sports*. Westport, CT: Greenwood Press, 1988.

Staff Reporter. "Howard Drew Is Some Sprinter." *Cleveland Advocate*, July 1918.

★ ★ ★

Walter DUKES

Born June 23, 1930, Rochester, New York
Died March 13, 2001, Detroit, Michigan
Basketball player

Dukes was a graduate of Seton Hall Prep, Seton Hall University (B.S.), New York University (M.B.A.), and New York Law School (L.L.B). He spent his professional career as a professional basketball player, an attorney with the U.S. Labor Department, vice president of Vista Travel Services, and president of the Kennedy Development Foundation.

Dukes was a college basketball star as a seven-foot center at Seton Hall University between 1951 and 1953. During his senior year, he led Seton Hall to a 31–2 record and the NIT title. He was selected as the 1953 NIT Most Valuable Player and All-American honors. As a senior he averaged 26.1 points and 22.2 rebounds. Dukes holds the NCAA single season record for most rebounds at 734, and he ranks sixth highest in NCAA career rebounding average (21.1).

In 1953 the New York Knicks drafted Dukes. He opted, however, for a $25,000 contract to play with the Harlem Globetrotters. He played two seasons with the Globetrotters and then joined the Knicks in 1955. After one season with the Knicks, Dukes was traded to the Minneapolis Lakers. In 1957 the Detroit Pistons acquired Dukes; he completed his basketball career with that team in 1963. With the Pistons, Dukes had 4,986 career rebounds and averaged 10.4 points, and he was named twice to the NBA All-Star team (1960 and 1961).

After his basketball career, Dukes was an attorney in Detroit, but in 1975 he was suspended from the Michigan bar. On March 13, 2001, his sister found Dukes dead in his Detroit apartment.

Alar Lipping

FURTHER READING

Addy, Steve. *Detroit Pistons: Four Decades of Motor City Memories*. Champaign, IL: Sagamore, 1997.

"Walter Dukes, 70, a Standout at Seton Hall and the NBA." *New York Times*, March 16, 2001.

"Walter Dukes" (www.ncaa.org/library).

EASTERN COLORED LEAGUE

The Eastern Colored League (ECL) was a circuit of black professional baseball teams. It was established in 1923, largely through the efforts of Edward Bolden, president of the Hilldale Athletic Club. The league began with six teams: the Hilldale A.C., Brooklyn Royal Giants, Lincoln Giants, Bacharach Giants, Baltimore Black Sox, and the Cuban Stars.

The ECL was organized due to a rift between Bolden and Negro National League (NNL) president Andrew "Rube" Foster. Hilldale was an associate member of the NNL, and the league clubs agreed to schedule games with Hilldale and the Bacharach Giants when they traveled east and to refrain from raiding the latter's player rosters. Outside of protection from player raids, the NNL had little to offer either club. Moreover, scheduling weekend games in metropolitan New York was more appealing to Bolden, especially with Sunday ball still prohibited in Philadelphia.

The league elected no president but was governed by six commissioners, one from each club. Bolden was elected chairman, but he was granted far less authority than Foster enjoyed in the NNL. From the outset, the league suffered from two glaring drawbacks that eventually led to its demise—the inability to devise a balanced schedule, and the magnates' overall mistrust of each other. Hilldale emerged as the dominant club in the league, defeating the Kansas City Monarchs in the 1924 and 1925 Colored World Series. In 1928, the Eastern Colored League disbanded.

Michael E. Lomax

See also: Edward Bolden; Negro National League.

FURTHER READING

Lanctot, Neil. "Fair Dealing and Clean Playing: Ed Bolden and the Hilldale Club, 1910–1932," *Pennsylvania Magazine of History and Biography* 67 (January/April 1993): 3–49.

———. *Fair Dealing and Clean Playing: The Hilldale Club and the Development of Black Professional Baseball, 1910–1932*. Jefferson, NC: McFarland, 1994.

Lomax, Michael E. "Black Baseball, Black Community, Black Entrepreneurs: The History of the Negro National and Eastern Colored Leagues, 1880–1930." Ph.D. diss., Ohio State University, 1996.

Ribowsky, Mark. *A Complete History of the Negro Leagues 1884 to 1955*. Secaucus, NJ: Carol, 1995.

★ ★ ★

Harry EDWARDS

Born November 22, 1942, East St. Louis, Missouri
Sports civil rights activist

Edwards, raised by his mother Adelaide and his father Harry, a laborer, is one of the most prominent and outspoken critics of racism in sport and the larger American society. A basketball and track athlete at San Jose State and holder of a Ph.D. in sociology from Cornell University, Edwards first came to national attention in the fall of 1967, when he organized a protest movement of black students that led to the cancelation of the season opening football game between San Jose State and the University of Texas at El Paso. A short time later, Edwards proposed a boycott of the 1968 Olympic games in Mexico City. The mastermind behind an organization named the Olympic Project for Human Rights, Edwards assembled a group of young African-American athletes who threatened not to compete in Mexico City unless certain demands were met, including the restoration of Muhammad Ali's heavyweight boxing title, removal of Avery Brundage as president of the International Olympic Committee, and exclusion of South Africa from competition because of its apartheid policies. The African-American athletes, torn by their desire to compete as athletes while being involved in the civil rights struggle, ultimately decided to express their protest at the games rather than boycott them.

Following the Mexico City games, Edwards assumed a position as professor of sociology at the University of California, Berkeley, and continued to speak out about the racial injustices in American sport while at the same time becoming a part of the sports establishment himself. He was hired in 1987 by baseball commissioner Peter Ueberroth to seek out minority candidates for upper-level administrative positions and has worked for several years as a consultant for the San Francisco 49ers. He has made his views known on sport and wider societal issues through many articles in popular periodicals and academic journals as well as in such books as: *The Revolt of the Black Athlete* (1969), *Black Students* (1970), *The Sociology of Sport* (1973), and *The Struggle That Must Be: An Autobiography* (1980). Edwards is also a widely popular public speaker who is frequently asked to express his views on racial issues and sport at national conferences and on radio and television newscasts.

David K. Wiggins

See also: John Carlos; Civil Rights; Olympic Games; Racial Theories; Tommie Smith.

FURTHER READING

Edwards, Harry. *The Struggle That Must Be: An Autobiography*. New York: Macmillan, 1980.

Matthews, Vince, with Neil Amdur. *My Race Be Won*. New York: Charterhouse, 1974.

Spivey, Donald. "Black Consciousness and Olympic Protest Movement, 1964–1980." In *Sport in America: New Historical Perspectives*, ed. Donald Spivey, 239–259. Westport, CT: Greenwood Press, 1985.

Wiggins, David K. "The Year of Awakening: Black Athletes, Racial Unrest, and the Civil Rights Movement of 1968." *International Journal of the History of Sport* 9 (August 1992): 188–208.

★ ★ ★

Teresa EDWARDS

Born July 19, 1964, Cairo, Georgia
Basketball player

Edwards is the only daughter and oldest of five children of Mildred Edwards, an African American single mother. Edwards has been referred to as the Michael Jordan of women's basketball. Her amateur and professional basketball career spanned a nineteen-year period, beginning with her freshman year at the University of Georgia in 1982 and ending with her retirement after the 2000 Olympics.

At the University of Georgia, Edwards, a five-foot, eleven-inch point guard, led the Lady Bulldogs to three Southeastern Conference (SEC) titles (1983, 1984, 1983), participated in four NCAA tournaments, and led her team to two "Final Four" appearances, 1983 and 1985. In 1983 she was selected as a freshman All-American. In 1984, 1985, and 1986, she was named first team All-SEC and in 1985 and 1986 first team Kodak All-American. She is the University of Georgia's all-time leader in assists, 653, and steals, 342. The University of Georgia honored her accomplishments by retiring her jersey, number five, and naming her to its All-Time Top Ten Female Athletes list.

Edwards played on five U.S Olympic basketball teams (1984, 1988, 1992, 1996, and 2000) winning four gold medals and a bronze. At age twenty, she was the youngest member of the 1984 team, and at age thirty-six the oldest member of the 2000 team.

As a member of twenty-two U.S. international teams, Edwards had an unsurpassed international amateur career. Besides her four Olympic gold medals, she was a member of U.S. women's basketball teams that won gold medals at the 1990 and 1986 Goodwill Games, 1990 and 1986 World Championships, and 1987 Pan American Games. She co-captained the U.S. women's team that won a bronze medal at the 1992 Barcelona Olympic Games and was a member of the U.S. women's teams that won bronze medals at the 1994 World Championships and 1991 Pan American Games.

Her professional career included playing for teams in Italy, 1987–1988; in Japan, 1989–1993; and in Spain and France, 1994. In 1996 she became a founding member, marquee player, and coach for the American Basketball League (ABL), which ended operation in December 1998. She was a three-time winner (1996, 1990, and 1987), of the prestigious USA Basketball's Female Athlete of the Year Award. Her hometown of Cairo, Georgia, honored her in 1988 by naming a street after her.

Gai Ingham Berlage

See also: Olympic Games.

FURTHER READING
Lessa, Christina. *Women Who Win*. New York: Universe, 1998.
Norwood, Robin. "Recognition Is at End of Road." *Los Angeles Times*, September 8, 2000.
"100 Greatest Female Athletes: 22. Teresa Edwards, Basketball." *Sports Illustrated for Women* (www.CNNSI.com), November 30, 1999.
Ponti, James. *WNBA Stars of Women's Basketball*. New York: Pocket Books, 1999.
"Teresa's Bio" (www.teresaedwards.com).
"Teresa Edwards" (www.usabasketball.com/women/edwards_bio.htm).

★ ★ ★

Lee ELDER

Born July 14, 1934, Dallas, Texas
Golfer

Elder's father (Charles) was a coal truck driver and his mother (Sadie) was a housewife. Elder spent his professional life in golf, first as a caddie and after 1959 as a successful tour player.

By the mid-1960s, Elder mastered the United Golf Association's (UGA) black circuit. In 1967 he won eighteen UGA events in twenty-two tries. Later that year, Elder joined the Professional Golf Association Tour. He gained national prominence when he lost to Jack Nicklaus in a play-off at the 1968 American Golf Classic. Elder was slow to win on the PGA Tour, but in 1974 he captured the Monsanto Open. That accomplishment made him eligible for the

Lee Elder, chipping on the 18th green, in the final to help secure his victory in the 1978 Westchester Classic in Harrison, New York. *(AP/Wide World Photos)*

Masters, and in April 1975 Elder became the first African American to compete in the Augusta National Golf Club's prestigious tournament. In 1976 he won the Houston Open, and in 1978 he added victories at the Greater Milwaukee Open and the Westchester Classic. Elder's 1978 performance earned him a spot on the 1979 U.S. Ryder Cup team. He left the PGA Tour in 1984 to join the Senior PGA Tour, where he captured eight tournaments in four years. In 1990 Elder reduced his competitive schedule.

Elder will always be remembered most for his 1975 Masters performance, but his entire career—including regular PGA Tour winnings of more than $1 million and Senior Tour winnings of some $2,500,000—is a testament to the collapse of many racial barriers in professional tour golf in the late 1960s.

Stephen R. Lowe

See also: Golf.

FURTHER READING
Kennedy, John H. *A Course of Their Own: A History of African American Golfers.* Kansas City, MO: Andrews McMeel, 2000.
McDaniel, Pete. *Uneven Lies: The Heroic Story of African Americans in Golf.* Greenwich, CT: American Golfer, 2000.
Sinnette, Calvin. *Forbidden Fairways: African Americans and the Game of Golf.* Chelsea, MI: Sleeping Bear Press, 1998.

★ ★ ★

Carl ELLER

Born February 25, 1942, Winston-Salem, North Carolina
Football player, chemical dependency counselor

Carl Eller, son of Clarence and Ernestine Eller, attended the University of Minnesota from 1960 to 1963; there he was a consensus All-American in 1962 and 1963. Drafted by both the Minnesota Vikings and the Buffalo Bills, he chose to stay in Minneapolis. Eller played defensive end for the Vikings from 1964 through 1978 and for the Seattle Seahawks in 1979. Eller was a dominant player and was named to the All-NFL team as a defensive end every year from 1968 through 1975.

While playing football, Eller developed a substance-abuse problem. In 1981, after receiving treatment and starting the recovery process, he became a health services executive in Minneapolis. He also founded and directed a national institute for sports and human services that focused on developing policies and procedures for alcohol and drug abuse prevention and treatment. In 1982 he became a certified chemical dependency counselor and the following year earned a degree from the Metropolitan State College's Institute of Chemical Dependency. He was a member of the board of directors of the Fellowship of Christian Athletes, the Minnesota Institute of Black Chemical Abuse, the Minneapolis Mayor's Task Force on Chemical Dependency, and the Minnesota State Department of Health and Human Services Chemical Dependency Division. He also served as a consultant to the NFL on matters of drug and alcohol abuse.

As a result of his work in alcohol and drug treatment, Eller was appointed to the White House Special Task Force on Prevention of Chemical Abuse (1982) and was given the Hubert H. Humphrey-Minnesota Labor Award (1982), as well as the WCCO Radio Good Neighbor Award (1984). In 1985 Eller wrote a book about his struggle with chemical dependency, *Beating the Odds*. He was a contributing editor for *Alcoholism & Addiction Magazine*. Eller also produced an educational film about his chemical dependency called "My Fifth Super Bowl."

He was inducted into the Minnesota Sports Hall of Fame in 1989 and into the North Carolina Sports Hall of Fame in 1991.

Keith McClellan

FURTHER READING
Carroll, Bob, Mike Gershman, David Neft, and John Thorn, eds. *Total Football II: The Official Encyclopedia of the National Football League.* New York: HarperCollins, 1999.
Phelps, Shirelle, ed. *Who's Who Among Black Americans 1994/5.* 8th ed. Detroit: Gale Research, 1994.

★ ★ ★

Jimmy ELLIS

Born February 24, 1940, Louisville, Kentucky
Boxer

As an amateur, Jimmy Ellis fought on the same boxing team as Muhammad Ali. He eventually became the sparring partner of Ali and was managed by Ali's manager, Angelo Dundee. When Ali was stripped of his heavyweight title for political reasons, the WBA organized an elimination tournament bout to determine a new champion. In the tournament, Ellis beat Jerry Quarry for the title in fifteen rounds on April 27, 1968. Five months later Ellis successfully defended his title when he beat Floyd Patterson. Though Ellis was inactive during 1969, Ali's absence as champion had created confusion in the boxing world over who the champion "really" was. To name a sole champion, it was determined that Ellis would fight Joe Frazier. The bout was on February 16, 1970, in New York's Madison Square Garden; the favored Frazier knocked out Ellis in round four. After Ali returned to the ring, Ellis met his former sparring partner for the vacant NABF heavyweight title, losing to Ali in the twelfth round.

Ellis retired from the boxing ring in 1975. He thereafter trained young Louisville fighters, hoping to rebuild the city's reputation for producing champion boxers. He also worked for the Louisville Metropolitan Parks and Recreation Department. Currently, he travels across the country making appearances and singing with his gospel group.

Maureen M. Smith

See also: Joe Frazier.

FURTHER READING
Ashe, Arthur R., Jr. *A Hard Road to Glory: A History of the African-American Athlete Since 1945.* New York: Warner Books, 1988.
Jackson, George. *Soul Brother Superfighter.* Placerville, CA: Green Valley Graphics, 1985.
Koerner, Dave. "Ellis Laments Louisville's Decline in Boxing." *Louisville (KY) Courier-Journal,* September 14, 1997.

★ ★ ★

Wayne EMBRY

Born March 26, 1937, Springfield, Ohio
Basketball player, athletic administrator

Embry was a 1958 graduate of Miami (Ohio) University, played eleven years in the National Basketball Association, and held major administrative positions for the Milwaukee Bucks and Cleveland Cavaliers between 1973 and 2000.

Embry attended Tecumseh High School in Clark County, Ohio. Standing six feet, eight inches and weighing 255 pounds, he was a star basketball center for the Miami (Ohio) University Redskins. At one time he held seven individual records at Miami. Upon graduation he was drafted by the Cincinnati Royals, for whom he played

Julius ERVING

Born February 22, 1950, Hempstead, New York
Basketball player

Julius Erving's mother, a domestic and hairdresser, raised him by herself for ten years after his biological father left him at the age of three. By the age of twelve, Julius was playing in a Salvation Army basketball league. His work on the basketball court earned him a scholarship to the University of Massachusetts.

In 1971, he left the University of Massachusetts as a junior to join the American Basketball Association franchise in Richmond, Virginia, where he played for two years bringing respectability to the new league. In 1974 and 1976 he led the ABA's New York Nets to the Championship. From 1976 to 1987, he played for the Philadelphia 76ers, helping them win the NBA championship in 1983.

While in school, Erving was a good student, earning the professorial nickname "Doctor" as a teen. After retiring from professional basketball, his eloquence caused NBC to hire him as a sports commentator and reporter. He was also able to turn his fame into a successful career as a businessman with multiple investments and active roles in management, including as executive vice president of the NBA's Orlando Magic. He also worked with the National Basketball Association on developing plans to increase the popularity of the sport worldwide. As a basketball player, his exciting style of play made him a fan favorite from his freshman year through to his retirement. His popularity has continued through his vocal role as a Christian and through his support of charitable causes, though his reputation was sullied by press reports of personal troubles in 1999 and 2000. His marriage to Turquoise Erving, however, remains strong.

Gregory S. Goodale

eight seasons, thereafter finishing his career with the Boston Celtics and the Milwaukee Bucks. He played in over 800 games in the NBA, scored more than 10,000 points, and snared more than 7,500 rebounds. He earned an NBA championship ring in 1968 with the Celtics as backup center to Bill Russell. Short for an NBA center, he used his bulk and intelligence to good advantage.

He retired as a player in 1969 and assumed a front-office position with the Bucks. In 1973, at age thirty-five, he was appointed general manager of the Bucks, becoming the first African American to hold this position in the NBA. In 1986 he was named general manager of the Cleveland Cavaliers, becoming president in 1994. He was widely acclaimed for his ability to appraise talent and his willingness to make bold trades to improve his teams. In 1992 and 1998 he was named the NBA Executive of the Year by *Sporting News*.

In 2000 he eased into semiretirement, living with his wife Teri in suburban Cleveland, while devoting his attention to his roles as a member of the board of directors of three corporations and as a director of the Federal Reserve Bank in Cleveland.

Richard O. Davies

FURTHER READING
Dayton (Ohio) *Daily News*, September 2, 2000.
Jet, July 12, 1999, 46.
Press releases from files of Miami University Sports Information Office.
Sporting News, May 18, 1998, 13.
"The Wayne and Lenny Show." *Esquire*, June 1989, 61–65.

FURTHER READING

"Dr. J. Operated Above the Rest." *ESPN Greatest Athletes* (espn.go.com/sportscentury/features/00014177.html).

George, Nelson. *Elevating the Game: Black Men and Basketball*. New York: HarperCollins, 1992.

"The NBA at 50: Julius Erving." *The Basketball Hall of Fame* (global.nba.com/nbaat50/greats/erving.html).

Wilker, Josh. *Julius Erving*. New York: Chelsea House, 1995.

★ ★ ★

Lee EVANS

Born February 25, 1947, Madera, California
Runner

An outstanding middle-distance runner, Lee Evans attended Overfelt High School and San Jose State University, where he was the Pan American Games champion in the 400-meter run in 1967 and the NCAA titlist in the same event in 1968. At the Mexico City games in 1968, he won the gold medal in the 400 meters in the world-record time of 43.86 seconds, a record that some track analysts place along side Bob Beamon's long jump of 29 feet 2½ inches. He also won a gold medal as part of the 1,600-meter relay team, which also set a world record of 2:56.1. These were the Olympic Games at which African-American runners Tommie Smith and John Carlos were banned from further Olympic competition for making a civil rights demonstration during their medal ceremony for the 200-meter run; Evans became embroiled in the controversy by publicly stating his support for their actions.

By 1972, Evans had won five AAU titles but did not qualify in the 400 meters for the 1972 U.S. Olympic team. He did earn a place on the 1,600-meter relay team for the Munich Olympics, however, but the team did not compete after two of its members were disqualified for not standing at attention during an earlier medal ceremony. Later in 1972, Evans signed up with a professional track venture that folded after two seasons. He went on to coach track at San Jose State, had his amateur status reinstated in 1980, and ran some excellent times, even though he was in his late thirties. Between 1979 and 1982, he worked for the U.S. Information Service, coaching track in sixteen countries. More recently, he was elected to the National Track and Field Hall of Fame; has coached national track teams in Nigeria, Cameroon, Qatar, and Saudi Arabia; and has worked to establish Special Olympic programs in many countries.

John E. Findling

FURTHER READING

Kirshenbaum, Jerry. "Generating Eclectic Power." *Sports Illustrated*, February 18, 1974, 32–33, 35–36, 41–42.

Moore, Kenny. "Giants on the Earth." *Sports Illustrated*, June 29, 1987, 48–50.

New York Times, October 19, 1968; June 28, 1972; June 4, 1996.

Page, James A., *Black Olympian Medalists*. Englewood, CO: Libraries Unlimited, 1991.

Porter, David L., ed. *Biographical Dictionary of American Sports: Outdoor Sports*. Westport, CT: Greenwood Press, 1988.

★ ★ ★

Patrick EWING

Born August 5, 1962, Kingston, Jamaica
Basketball player

When the New York Knicks selected center Patrick Ewing in 1985 as the first player picked in the original lottery draft, it was widely assumed that he would lead the Knicks to several NBA championships. Instead of being a dominant force at center, however, Ewing left in 2000 under a barrage of criticism from fans and the media, without ever having helped deliver an NBA championship.

Ewing was one of seven children born to Jamaican parents; they moved to Boston when he was eleven. By age sixteen he stood seven feet, one inch and in 1981 was the most highly recruited high school player. He chose Georgetown University, because he believed coach John Thompson was best equipped to prepare him to play center in the NBA. In his junior year he led the Hoyas to the NCAA championship, but Georgetown lost in the finals to North Carolina his freshman year and to Villanova his senior year. He received All-American honors his final three seasons.

Aloof and often showing disdain for journalists, Ewing established a frosty relationship with the hypercritical media and demanding fans of New York from the beginning. Only twice (in 1994 and 1999) did the Knicks reach the NBA finals, losing both times. Despite his intimidating presence on the court, Ewing never won the NBA Most Valuable Player Award. He was severely criticized by sports commentators for his leadership of the Players' Association during the strike of 1999. During his fifteen years with the Knicks he averaged 22.5 points, 10.6 rebounds, and 2.6 blocked shots a game. In 2000 he was traded to the Seattle Super Sonics and played there only sparingly and ineffectively, his age and arthritic knees having caught up with him.

Richard O. Davies

FURTHER READING
Current Biography. 1991, 202–6.
Los Angeles Times, December 8, 2000.
New York Times Bibliographical Service, May 1985.
Sports Illustrated, January 17, 1994, 52–59; February 15, 1999, 76–77.

Mae FAGGS

Born April 10, 1932, Mays Landing, New Jersey
Died January 27, 2000, Cincinnati, Ohio
Runner

Faggs, the first American woman to compete in three Olympics began running in the New York City Police Athletic League. She first competed on the Olympic stage in the 1948 London Games in the 200-meter race. The experience as an Olympian came in handy in 1952 when she won gold as a member of the 400-meter relay team at the Helsinki Games.

With two Olympic competitions already under her belt, Faggs joined the Tennessee State Tigerbelle track team. She was the AAU 200-meter champion in 1954, 1955, and 1956. Her running career culminated in 1956, when she won a bronze medal at the Melbourne Games as a member of the all-Tigerbelle 4 x 100 relay team.

Faggs stayed active in athletics later in life, coaching high school track and field. She devoted more than forty years to children as a teacher and administrator in Cincinnati, Ohio.

Alison M. Wrynn

See also: Ed Temple; Track and Field.

FURTHER READING
Ashe, Arthur R., Jr. *A Hard Road to Glory: A History of the African-American Athlete Since 1946.* New York: Warner Books, 1988.
Bushnell, Asa S., ed. *United States 1952 Olympic Book.* Quadrennial Report of the USOC. New York: U.S. Olympic Committee, 1952.
Davis, Michael D. *Black American Women in Track and Field: A Complete Illustrated Reference.* Jefferson, NC: McFarland, 1992.
United States 1956 Olympic Book. Quadrennial Report of the USOC. New York: U.S. Olympic Committee, 1957.

FENCING

African Americans have participated in fencing to a limited degree at various levels of competition. The first African-American fencers appeared in the early part of the twentieth century, typically receiving their training in the Young Men's Christian Associations (YMCAs) and Young Women's Christian Associations (YWCAs). Unfortunately, African-American fencers, like so many athletes of their race in other sports during this period, were often barred from competitions at the local and national levels by national sporting bodies. This is exactly what happened to the African-American fencer Violet Barker, who was excluded from an open foil meet at the New York Fencers Club by the Amateur Fencers League of America (AFLA) because of her race.

By the midpoint of the twentieth century the AFLA had desegregated, and an increasing number of African Americans found their way into the sport. Some of the most notable of these fencers have been Sophronia Pierce Stent, Bruce Davis, Michael Lofton, Peter Lewison, Uriah Jones, Burt Freeman, Nikki Tomlinson, Sharon Monplaiser, Peter Westbrook, and Terrence Lasker. Of this group, Westbrook is probably the best known, because of his winning the bronze medal in the sabre at the 1984 Olympic Games in Los Angeles.

David K. Wiggins

FURTHER READING
Ashe, Arthur R., Jr. *A Hard Road to Glory: A History of the African-American Athlete.* New York: Amistad, 1993.
D'Asaro, Gay Kirstine Jacobsen. "A History of the Amateur Fencers League of America," Master's thesis, San Jose State University, 1983.
Kirsch, George B., Othello Harris, and Clair E. Nolte, eds. *Encyclopedia of Ethnicity and Sports in the United States.* Westport, CT: Greenwood Press, 2000.

FILMS

Popular feature films, as well as documentaries, have chronicled the history of African-American participation in sport. While sports such as baseball maintained a rigid color line until 1947, professional boxing offered an opportunity for black athletes to compete against their white counterparts. Accordingly, depictions of prize fighting dominated the cinematic treatment of African-American athletes, although many of these films perpetuate racial stereotypes.

In 1909, Jack Johnson was the first black to win the world heavyweight boxing championship. The documentary *Jack Johnson* (1970) contains rare fight footage of Johnson's 1910 bout with James Jeffries and of his 1915 loss to Jess Willard in Havana. Actor Brock Peters provides the voice of Johnson. A 1970 film adaptation of the Broadway play *The Great White Hope* (although the main character's name is Jack Jefferson), with James Earl Jones in the title role, presents a fictionalized treatment of Johnson's controversial life and boxing career.

During the 1930s and 1940s, professional boxing was dominated by Joe Louis, who was featured in the low-budget *Spirit of Youth* (1938) and made a cameo appearance in *Joe Palooka, Champ* (1947). His patriotic image was exploited in the World War II documentary *Sergeant Joe Louis on Tour* (1943). In 1953, Hollywood produced *The Joe Louis Story*, in which Coley Wallace (a former journeyman heavyweight) provided an unconvincing performance in the title role.

While Louis was unable to translate his fighting success into a Hollywood career, other African-American fighters from the 1930s to the 1950s enjoyed more opportunities on the silver screen. Henry Armstrong, who is recorded as having fought in seventy-five bouts in a fifteen-year career, appeared in such films as Keep Fighting (1939) and the *Pittsburgh Kid* (1942). Canada Lee, a welterweight fighter during the 1930s, earned fine reviews for his work in such films as *Lifeboat* (1944) and the boxing classic *Body and Soul* (1947).

Since 1964, when he defeated Sonny Liston for the heavyweight championship, professional boxing has been dominated by Muhammad Ali. The photogenic Ali made a cameo appearance in the 1981 remake of *Body and Soul* and portrayed himself in *The Great* (1977). However, Ali's role as a world-class athlete is best captured in the 1996 Academy Award-winning documentary *When We Were Kings*, chronicling the 1974 championship fight between Ali and George Foreman held in Zaire. Other African-American fighters appearing in Hollywood films in those years include Archie Moore (1960–1966), Sugar Ray Robinson (1969), and Ken Norton (1970).

Racial stereotypes abound in films such as the *Rocky* series (1970–1990), in which white champion Rocky Balboa (Sylvester Stallone) is beset by black opponents like Apollo Creed (Carl Weathers) and Clubber Lang (Mr. T). Yet biographical aptitudes of African-American fighters continue to offer inspiration and move beyond stereotypes. In *Hurricane* (ZOGG 1999), Denzel Washington portrays Rubin "Hurricane"' Carter, whose boxing career was cut short by a murder charge eventually overturned on appeal. Will Smith portrays Muhammad Ali (2002), while African-American filmmaker Spike Lee is producing a film on Joe Louis.

With Hollywood's firm adherence to a color line in earlier decades, African Americans were rarely featured in depictions of the national pastime. All of this changed with Jackie Robinson; Hollywood sought to exploit baseball's integration with *The Jackie Robinson Story* (1950), in which the athlete portrayed himself. The film concludes with Robinson appearing before Congress, responding to critical comments made by Paul Robeson and asserting that African Americans were supportive of the United States. More realistic stories of individuals struggling against racial prejudice in America are told in a series of television biographical baseball pictures: *It's Good to Be Alive* (the 1974 story of Roy Campanella), *One In a Million: The Ron LeFlore Story* (1978), *Don't Look Back: The Story of Leroy "Satchel" Paige* (1981), and *The Court-Martial of Jackie Robinson* (1990). Baseball's years of segregation are considered by Hollywood in Bingo Long's *Traveling All-Stars & Motor Kings* (1976), featuring Billy Dee Williams, Richard Pryor, and James Earl Jones. The film depicts the racism confronted by barnstorming African-American players in the South during the 1930s, but overall the film takes a comic approach to its subject matter. *A Soldier's Story* (1984), in which baseball is a backdrop to a murder investigation, presents a more realistic examination of segregation and racism during the World War II era.

While African-American participation in baseball has declined in the last quarter-century, the African-American presence in football and basketball has helped redefine these sports. This presence is well documented in American cinema.

Football as a film subject is not a Hollywood staple or genre. However, there is a rich tradition of the film capital recruiting football players into the acting profession. This practice dates back to the days of Paul Robeson, who was an All-American football player at Rutgers University in 1917–1918. After establishing a reputation on the New York stage, Robeson starred in such films as *Emperor Jones* (1933), *Sanders of the River* (1935), *Showboat* (1936), and *King Solomon's Mines* (1937), before his career was cut short by the Second Red Scare. Since the 1960s, numerous African-American football stars have attempted to make the transition from the gridiron to Hollywood, including Jim Brown, Tim Brown, Bernie Casey, Joe Greene, Rosey Grier, O.J. Simpson, Bubba Smith, Woody Strode, Carl Weathers, and Fred Williamson. Many of these athletes appeared in exploitive films seeking to tap growing black film audiences. Of these football players turned actors, perhaps the stories of Jim Brown, and O.J. Simpson are most notable. After a superlative career as a running back for the Cleveland Browns, Brown starred in such films as *The Dirty Dozen* (1967), *Ice Station Zebra* (1968), and *Tick Tick Tick* (1970). Following his acting days, Brown has maintained an active role and voice in community activism and fighting racism. Simpson used his fame as a running back for the University of Southern California and Buffalo Bills to fashion a career in commercials and films such as *The Towering Inferno* (1974), *Capricorn One* (1978), and *Naked Gun* (1988). However, Simpson's film roles were cut short by the controversy surrounding his acquittal in the murder of his wife.

Few football films have directed much attention to African-American athletes, those that have tend to give primary focus to white teammates or coaches. Films fitting into this description include *Brian's Song* (1971), depicting the relationship between Chicago Bears teammates Gale Sayers (Billy Dee Williams) and Brian Piccolo (James Caan); *Remember the Titans* (2000), with Denzel Washington as a black coach integrating the white schools of Virginia; and director Oliver Stone's *Any Given Sunday* (2000), examining the relationship between a white coach (Al Pacino) and his black quarterback (Jamie Foxx).

Basketball players have also sought to

use their exploits on the hardwood to form careers in Hollywood, although in general they have been less successful than their football counterparts. Among them are Kareem Abdul-Jabbar, Ray Allen, Wilt Chamberlain, Michael Jordan, Julius Erving, Meadowlark Lemon, Shaquille O'Neal, and Keith Wilkes. Most of their roles have been rather lightweight fare, such as Jordan's *Space Jam* (1996) and *The Fish That Saved Pittsburgh* (1979). In recent years, Hollywood filmmakers have increasingly used basketball as a vehicle to examine the inner-city experience of African Americans, although many of these films perpetuate racial stereotypes. Included in the African-American basketball genre film are: *Above the Rim* (1994), *The Air Up There* (1994), *Final Exam* (1998), and *White Men Can't Jump* (1992). More meaningful fare regarding African Americans and basketball, focusing upon relationships within the African-American community, include: *Heaven Is a Playground* (1991), featuring an inner-city coach and his players; *He Got Game* (1998), a father-and-son drama starring Denzel Washington; and *Love and Basketball* (2000), a more positive look at the African-American athletic and high school experience. The manipulative nature of many high school basketball programs is well chronicled in the documentary *Hoop Dream* (1994).

While black athletes have excelled in track and field, this sport has never been a popular subject for Hollywood. Television biographical features are *Wilma* (1977), with Cicely Tyson in the title role of Wilma Rudolph, who won three gold medals in the 1960 Olympic Games, and *The Jesse Owens Story* (1984), with Darian Harewood portraying Owens. However, the racist nature of the 1936 Berlin Olympic games, dominated by Owens, is best depicted in the Nazi propaganda classic *Olympia*, directed by Leni Riefenstahl.

Tennis and golf are often considered white country-club sports, but the achievements of Arthur Ashe, the Williams sisters, and Tiger Woods should provide new biographical and feature-film subjects for African-American athletes. Just as sport has provided opportunity for some African Americans in the United States, Hollywood has beckoned for many black sport figures. Nevertheless, just as with sport, film careers for black athletes and cinematic depictions of African-American sport heroes have often been exploitive. Yet, cinematic treatment of figures such as Jackie Robinson, Jesse Owens, and Muhammad Ali continue to provide inspiration.

Ron Briley

See also: Kareem Abdul-Jabbar; Jim Brown; Archie Moore; Paul Robeson; Jackie Robinson; Bubba Smith; Woody Strode.

FURTHER READING
Bogle, Donald. *Blacks in American Films and Television: An Encyclopedia.* New York: Garland, 1988.
Davis, Lenwood G., and Belinda S. Daniels, comps. *Black Athletes in the United States: A Bibliography of Books, Articles, Autobiographies, and Biographies on Black Professional Athletes in the United States, 1800–1981.* Westport, CT: Greenwood Press, 1981.
Tudor, Deborah V. *Hollywood's Vision of Team Sports: Heroes, Race, and Gender.* New York: Garland, 1997.
Zucker, Harvey Marc, and Lawrence J. Babich. *Sports Films: Complete References.* Jefferson, NC: McFarland, 1987.

★ ★ ★

George FLIPPIN

Born February 3, 1868, Point Isabelle, Ohio
Died May 15, 1929, Stromsburg, Nebraska
Football player, doctor

George Flippin was one of the first African Americans to play intercollegiate varsity football when he suited up for the University of Nebraska for four seasons in the

1890s. Flippin's father, Charles, an ex-slave, was a medical doctor, and his mother Mahala died while George was still a child. After his football career ended, the younger Flippin followed in his father's footsteps and became a well-respected physician in rural York County Nebraska.

Flippin faced frequent racial prejudice while at the University of Nebraska, but he was, nevertheless, popular with his teammates, who elected him team captain in 1894 over the protests of their white coach. Two years earlier, the University of Missouri was forced to forfeit a scheduled game with Nebraska when the Cornhusker players refused to acquiesce to Missouri's demand to bench its black star.

Flippin left Nebraska in the mid-1890s and received a medical degree from the University of Illinois in 1900. After brief stops in Chicago and Arkansas, Flippin moved to Stromsburg, Nebraska, where, with the help of his father, he opened that town's first hospital and pharmacy.

The headstrong Flippin filed the state of Nebraska's first civil rights lawsuit in 1907, when a local restaurant refused to serve him, and he purchased one of the first automobiles in York County, frequently bedeviling the police with his speedy driving. He remained a well-known and successful doctor until his death in 1929. As a testament to his popularity, Flippin's funeral was reportedly the best attended in Stromsburg history.

Gregory Bond

FURTHER READING
Chalk, Ocania. *Black College Sport.* New York: Dodd, Mead, 1975.
Ochsner, David A. "George Flippin Did It His Way." *Nebraska Magazine* (Spring 1999).
Stromsburg Headlight, May 23, 1929.

★ ★ ★

Curt FLOOD

Born January 18, 1938, Houston, Texas
Died January 20, 1997, Oakland, California
Baseball player

Flood was one of six children born to hospital workers Herman and Laura Flood. Flood was an outstanding baseball center fielder for the St. Louis Cardinals during the 1960s, but his greatest contribution to baseball was his Supreme Court challenge to the sport's reserve clause, a case that altered the financial structure of the game.

In 1940, the Flood family moved to Oakland, California, in search of work. Flood used sport as a vehicle to escape his impoverished background. Discovered by Oakland talent scout and community leader George Powels, Flood was a baseball star for McClymonds and Oakland Technical High Schools. Following graduation in 1956, he was signed by the Cincinnati Reds. Flood spent two seasons with Reds farm teams in the South (Thomasville, North Carolina, and Savannah, Georgia), where he was frequently the target of racial prejudice.

In December 1957, Flood was traded to the St. Louis Cardinals. From 1961 to 1969, he averaged .302 and emerged as one of the best center fielders in the game, earning Gold Gloves for the 1963–1969 seasons. Flood led the Cardinals to National League pennants in 1964, 1967, and 1968, with world championships in 1964 and 1967.

Flood made baseball history when he refused to accept a trade to the Philadelphia Phillies following the 1969 season. Comparing baseball's reserve clause (the inability of players to move from one team to another without the consent of the owners involved) with slavery, Flood informed Baseball Commissioner Bowie Kuhn, "I do not feel that I am a piece of property to be bought and sold irrespective of my wishes." Supported by the Major League

Players Association and with the legal counsel of former Supreme Court justice Arthur Goldberg, Flood appealed his case to the Supreme Court. Flood lost his case in a narrow 5–3 decision in June 1972; however, Flood's challenge paved the way for a collective bargaining agreement that effectively terminated the reserve clause in December 1972.

Flood attempted a baseball comeback with the Washington Senators in 1971, but his skills had deteriorated, and he retired after the season. The intelligent and introspective Flood retreated to the island of Minorca, where he pursued portrait painting and penned one of baseball's outstanding autobiographies, *The Way It Is*. Returning to Oakland, he worked as a broadcaster and head of the Oakland Little League before dying of throat cancer in 1997.

Ron Briley

FURTHER READING
Curt Flood file. *National Baseball Hall of Fame Museum and Library*. Cooperstown, New York.
Dickey, Glenn. "Curt Flood." *Inside Sports*, August 1985, 76–77.
Flood, Curt, with Richard Carter. *The Way It Is*. New York: Pocket Books, 1972.
"Found, an Abe Lincoln of Baseball: Curt Flood's Court Action for Changing the Reserve Clause." *Ebony*, March 1970, 110–11.

★ ★ ★

Tiger FLOWERS

Born August 5, 1895, Camille, Georgia
Died November 16, 1927, New York, New York
Boxer

Born in Georgia, Flowers began his boxing career in Philadelphia, where he relocated to work in a shipbuilding plant. His first professional bout took place when he was twenty-three. The southpaw middleweight boxer weighed in at 157–169 pounds and stood five feet, ten inches tall. Flowers was managed by Walk Miller. Journalists, always eager and able to conjure up unusual monikers for boxers, labeled Flowers "the Georgia Deacon." The holy-man tag was most appropriate as Flowers was an intensely religious man.

Flowers won his first twenty-five contests before being knocked down, and out, by Joe Gans. During 1922 and 1923 Flowers was an erratic performer. While winning more times than he lost, Flowers suffered knockout losses to Kid Norfolk, Sam Langford, and the Jamaica Kid. Despite this, in 1924 *Ring* magazine ranked Flowers as the leading contender to challenge Harry Greb for the world middleweight crown. On February 26, 1926, in New York's Madison Square Garden, the fight took place. Flowers won a unanimous decision, to become the first African American to capture the world middleweight title.

In December 1926 Flowers lost the middleweight championship to Mickey Walter. In November 1927 he died suddenly at the age of thirty-two, following an operation to remove scar tissue from around his eyes. During his short life Flowers fought in 157 bouts and won 115. He was inducted into the International Boxing Hall of Fame in 1993. At his funeral another great boxer, Gene Tunney, said this of Flowers: "He was an inspiration not only to the youth of his race, but to all young men—to live cleanly, speak softly, trust in God, and fight hard and fair."

Scott A.G.M. Crawford

FURTHER READING
Bunce, Steve, and Bob Mee. *Boxing Greats: An Illustrated History of the Legends of the Ring*. Philadelphia: Courage Books, 1998.
Kaye, Andrew M. "'Battle Blind': Atlanta's Taste for Black Boxing in the Early Twentieth Century." *Journal of Sport History* 28 (Summer 2001): 217–32.
———. "The Canonization of Tiger Flowers: A Black

Hero for the 1920s." *Borderlines: Studies in American Culture* 5 (1998): 142–59.

Roberts, James B., and Alexander G. Skutt. *The Boxing Register: International Boxing Hall of Fame Official Record Book*. Ithaca, NY: McBooks Press, 1999.

Sammons, Jeffrey T. *Beyond the Ring: The Role of Boxing in American Society*. Urbana: University of Illinois Press, 1988.

★ ★ ★

Charles FOLLIS

Born February 3, 1879, Cloverdale, Virginia
Died April 5, 1910, Cleveland, Ohio
Football player

One of seven children, Follis moved with his family to Ohio in the early 1880s. A graduate of Wooster (Ohio) High School, Follis was the first African American to play professional football.

As a junior in high school, Follis helped organize the school's first football team and was selected captain. At six feet, 200 pounds, Follis was a powerful runner and a superb defensive player. After graduation in 1901, he attended Wooster College. He played not for the college team but for an amateur team, the Wooster Athletic Association. Follis played well in two games against the northern Ohio champion Shelby Athletic Association team and was recruited by it in 1902. He moved to Shelby and was provided a job at a local hardware store. Follis became known as the "Black Cyclone" as a result of his extraordinary combination of speed and power.

In 1904 Shelby manager Frank Schiffer signed Follis to a professional contract on what was then a semiprofessional team. Follis was often the victim of excessively rough play by opposing teams and taunting by fans. Follis's teammates, including future Brooklyn Dodgers general manager Branch Rickey, often interceded on his behalf to curb the abuse. Follis refused to retaliate against either opponents or fans. He retired in 1906 while still playing for Shelby, due to an injury. Follis was also an excellent baseball player and played professionally for Johnny Bright's Cuban Giants.

John M. Carroll

FURTHER READING
Rathet, Mike, and Don R. Smith. *Their Deeds and Dogged Faith*. New York: Balsam Press, 1984.
Roberts, Milton. "Charles Follis: First Black Gridder Labored in Obscurity." *Black Sports*, November 1975, 42, 57–58.

★ ★ ★

FOOTBALL

American football is an amalgam of British rugby and American "association football." At first played informally in village and college settings, football was first played by college teams in 1869, when Rutgers outscored Princeton in goals, 6–4. In 1874, a team from McGill University in Montreal on a visit to Harvard introduced rugby football, which replaced the largely kicking forms of early college football. The game played at the turn of the twentieth century evolved from British rugby which was transformed by rules committees and conferences from 1880 to 1912. Not until 1920 did professional football emerge as the National Football League (NFL). It would play a secondary role until the 1950s.

For three-quarters of a century, colleges had a virtual monopoly on gridiron attendance and prominence. Beginning in the 1880s, eastern teams led by Yale, Harvard, and Princeton played their "big games" before large crowds in New York and the Boston area under rules that a few former players had drawn up. The possession rule, which decreed that the team with the ball would keep possession if tackled, began the movement away from rugby. Led by Yale's Walter Camp, the "graduate advisers" agreed to a yards and downs rule (three downs to gain five yards), numerical scoring, interference in front of the ball carrier, and tackling below the waist. Players were allowed to move forward before the snap of the ball (momentum plays), and could push, pull, and even catapult the ball carrier through the defense (mass plays). As a result of the rules changes, football gained a reputation for violent and foul play. In the early 1890s, the game came under attack for its alleged danger and brutality.

In the early 1890s, college football spread rapidly to nearly every male and coeducational college in the country, including African-American institutions. Introduced by former players and students from eastern schools, the customs and play closely resembled the big-time contests played in the East, including the rivalries between nearby institutions. As football soared in popularity, criticism among faculty, several college presidents, and crusading journalists grew in intensity, especially when players were killed or seriously injured. On October 7, 1905, just after the beginning of the football season, President Theodore Roosevelt met with six football experts, including Camp, at the White House. He secured their pledge to draw up a statement in which they would agree to eliminate violent and unsportsmanlike play.

Contrary to a widely held belief, Roosevelt did not issue an edict to the colleges, nor did he have a direct role in reforming the rules. In the two months that followed the meeting, the football carnage numbered eighteen deaths (only three college players) and 150 serious injuries. After the death of a Union College player in a game against New York University, Chancellor Henry MacCracken and his faculty invited eighteen schools to consider reforms in the gridiron game. That meeting of twenty-four administrators and faculty led to a second, larger conference on December 28, 1905. The sixty-two colleges appointed a reform rules committee and organized the Intercollegiate Athletic Association of the United States, which would be rechristened the National College Athletic Association in 1910. In the following months, the older big-college rules committee, meeting with the new committee, enacted several important rules changes, including a ten-yard rule (ten yards to be gained in three downs), a line of scrimmage, stiffer penalties to be handed down by better-trained officials, and the forward pass. The number of injuries declined under the new rules, but another round of deaths and injuries in 1909 led to more comprehensive reforms from 1910 to 1912.

Semiprofessional football originated in the coal mining regions of Pennsylvania and took root in the smaller cities of Ohio before World War I. Former college players such as All-Americans Fritz Pollard and Paul Robeson played Sunday afternoon football for Ohio teams. In 1920, as the demand for football outgrew its collegiate facilities, a group of professional teams in midwestern cities met to form what would soon become the National Football League (NFL). In the 1920s and 1930s, the franchises, largely in medium-sized cities, often went bankrupt or moved and played under different names. Only after World War II, with the introduction of televised football, did the professionals challenge the college game.

By the early 1950s, the decline of live attendance at college football games led both the NFL and college football to adopt blackout policies. The NCAA's Game of the Week enabled the association to make money from TV contracts. In 1959, a new league, the American Football League (AFL), was established, its teams based in cities denied franchises by the NFL. A television contract with NBC enabled the new league to survive despite large initial losses. The two leagues merged in 1966; the championship contest between the two leagues, known as the Super Bowl, attained the highest television ratings of any professional sporting event. In 1970, ABC sports innovator Roone Arledge teamed up with NFL commissioner Pete Rozelle to introduce *Monday Night Football,* an instant hit on prime-time evening television.

Following World War II, African-American players appeared in rapidly growing numbers in college football. In the intercollegiate game, a number of players had participated since the 1890s at predominantly white schools outside the South and border states. Subjected to harassment and brutality, the African Americans almost always had to bow out of games played with southern and other white teams. Beginning in 1946, however, most colleges and universities refused to honor these "gentlemen's agreements." Increasing numbers of African Americans were recruited by largely white colleges in the 1950s; only southern teams held out against integration, and they gave way in the late 1960s and early 1970s. In 1961, Ernie Davis of Syracuse became the first African-American Heisman Trophy winner.

African Americans had played semiprofessional football in the early 1900s. A handful played in the early years of the NFL. As a result of racism and the onset of depression, the two remaining black players, Jack Lilliard and Ray Kemp, were forced out of the league after the 1933 season. African Americans would reappear in the predominantly white NFL and newly minted All America Football Conference (AAFC). Their numbers would grow rapidly in the 1950s.

College football enjoyed in the mid-1960s a spurt of prosperity and relative calm, which abruptly ended in the era of the Vietnam War, student protest, and scarce resources. Faced with rising costs and soaring expenditures, big-time college teams opposed sharing TV gridiron revenues with smaller NCAA members. The College Football Association (CFA) formed to negotiate their own TV contract. In 1984, two CFA members, Georgia and Oklahoma, won a Supreme Court decision against the NCAA, thereby ending the association's TV cartel. Though the NCAA survived the defeat, institutions and conferences now gained control of football telecasts.

In the late 1960s, college football coaches shared some of the problems faced by college administrators. The student revolt against traditional curriculums and government policies carried over to college football. Among African-American players, the opposition was most intense. Players presented coaches with lists of demands and threats to boycott games. Student leaders objected to money earmarked for athletics or drawn from student athletic fees. By the early 1970s, most of the gridiron unrest had disappeared.

Unlike professional football and the smaller colleges, the big-time teams in Division IA football have had no playoff championship. The major bowls, sources of revenue and prestige, proved a stumbling block to a playoff system. Beginning in the late 1990s, the NCAA introduced the Bowl Championship System (BCS) to replace the consensus champion chosen by sportswriters and coaches. Using a variety of methods including computer ratings, the NCAA chose two teams to play in one of several prominent bowls rotated from year to year. Critics pointed out that big-time college football was the only college or professional sport that did not choose a national champion by elimination.

Beginning in the late nineteenth century, American football developed far differently than rugby football and association football or "soccer," as Americans have referred to the kicking game. Unlike baseball and basketball, to name just two examples, football has been largely confined to the United States and Canada. It has remained largely a male game, though a women's professional league has fielded teams and female place kickers have competed at the high school and college levels. Whereas baseball was once clearly the American pastime, football has gained preeminence at all levels of play.

John S. Watterson

FURTHER READING

Oriard, Michael. *King Football: Sport & Spectacle in the Golden Age of Radio & Newsreels, Movies & Magazines, the Weekly & the Daily Press*. Chapel Hill: University of North Carolina Press, 2001.

Peterson, Robert W. *Pigskin: The Early Years of Pro Football*. New York: Oxford University Press, 1997.

Ross, Charles K. *Outside the Lines: African Americans and the Integration of the National Football League*. New York: New York University Press, 1999.

Smith, Ronald A. *Sports and Freedom: The Rise of Big-Time College Athletics*. New York: Oxford University Press, 1988.

Watterson, John Sayle. *College Football: History, Spectacle, Controversy*. Baltimore: Johns Hopkins University Press, 2000.

★ ★ ★

Phil FORD

Born February 9, 1956, Rocky Mount, North Carolina
Basketball player

The son of Phil and Mabel Ford, Phil Ford was reared in Rocky Mount, NC, where his parents were schoolteachers. He was a basketball All-American at Rocky Mount High School, from which he graduated in 1974.

Ford attended the University of North Carolina from 1974 to 1978. A six-foot, two-inch point guard, he excelled as a scorer, distributor, and floor general. He was named ACC Player of the Year in 1978, after finishing as runner-up the previous season. Ford won several national Player of the Year awards in 1978, including the Wooden Award. He was named first-team All-ACC 1976–1978 and first-team AP All-America in 1977 and 1978. Ford scored 2,290 points in college, an average of 18.6 per game, and compiled 753 assists. Ford's Tar Heels played in the NCAA Tournament all four of his years at UNC. He led UNC to a second-place finish in 1977. He was a key member of the 1976 U.S. Olympic team, which won the gold medal.

Kansas City made Ford the second pick of the 1978 draft. He won NBA Rookie of the Year honors in 1979 and also was named second-team All-NBA. Injuries and substance abuse began to diminish Ford's effectiveness in the early 1980s. He was traded by Kansas City and completed his career for New Jersey and Milwaukee in 1983 and Houston in 1984 and 1985.

Ford served as an assistant basketball coach at his alma mater from 1988 until 2000, when he became vice president of UNC's Educational Foundation, the school's athletic support group.

Jim L. Sumner

FURTHER READING

Bjarkman, Peter. *ACC: Atlantic Coast Conference Basketball*. Indianapolis, IN: Masters Press, 1996.

Chansky, Art. *The Dean's List: A Celebration of Tar Heel Basketball and Dean Smith*. New York: Warner Books, 1996.

Hubbard, Jan, ed. *The Official NBA Encyclopedia*. 3d ed. New York: Doubleday, 2000.

Morris, Ron. *ACC Basketball: An Illustrated History*. Chapel Hill, NC: Four Corners Press, 1988.

George FOREMAN

Born January 10, 1949, Marshall, Texas
Boxer

Charming, quick-witted, and hard-hitting, George Foreman is an American original. A former street thug from Houston's Fifth Ward, Foreman was the fifth of Nancy Ree and J.D. Foreman's seven kids (actually, Forman's biological father was Leroy Moorehead). A junior high school dropout, Foreman later joined the Job Corps and soon thereafter began an extremely successful amateur boxing career, winning the San Francisco Golden Gloves in 1967, the 1968 Amateur Athletic Union heavyweight title, and eventually the 1968 Olympic heavyweight gold medal in Mexico City.

Eight months later, Foreman turned pro, running his record to 37–0 with thirty-four knockouts before beating Joe Frazier in the second round on January 22, 1973, in Kingston, Jamaica to become the world champion. After defending his title six times, Foreman was knocked out in the eighth round of a bout with former champ Muhammad Ali on October 30, 1974, in Kinshasa, Zaire, in what is known as the "Rumble in the Jungle." It was a huge upset. Demoralized by his loss to Ali, Foreman nonetheless fought thirteen more times before retiring in 1977. The following year, he was ordained at the Church of the Lord Jesus Christ in Houston; he later built his own church and youth center.

Partly to raise money for his religious work, the thirty-eight-year-old Foreman began an improbable comeback by knocking out unheralded Steve Zouski on March 9, 1987. At approximately 250 pounds Foreman was slow, but he still possessed impressive punching ability. Over the next four years, Foreman won twenty-three consecutive fights. Even so, he was the subject of much derision; critics pointed to his opponents' lack of experience and skill, and Foreman's advanced age and apparent lack of conditioning. Foreman combated such criticism with self-deprecating humor and more knockouts. In 1990, he KO'd former contender Gerry Cooney in the second round to position himself for a title shot. Though he lost to then-champion Evander Holyfield in 1991, Foreman's performance was impressive, and he continued to fight. Remarkably, on November 6, 1994, twenty years after he lost the title to Muhammad Ali, Foreman, at the age of forty-five, won the heavyweight championship of the world by KO'ing Michael Moorer in the tenth round, thus becoming the oldest fighter to win the title and an inspiration for millions of aging "baby boomers." Foreman successfully defended his title three times before retiring in 1997 (after a loss to Shannon Briggs) with a record of 76–5, with sixty-eight KOs, and having earned more than $100 million in purses and endorsements.

Daniel A. Nathan

See also: Boxing; Olympic Games.

FURTHER READING
Brooke-Ball, Peter. *The Boxing Album: An Illustrated History*. New York: Smithmark, 1992.
Foreman, George, and Joel Engel. *By George: The Autobiography of George Foreman*. New York: Villard Books, 1995.
Porter, David L., ed. *African-American Sports Greats: A Biographical Dictionary*. Westport, CT: Greenwood Press, 1995.
Sammons, Jeffrey T. *Beyond the Ring: The Role of Boxing in American Society*. Urbana: University of Illinois Press, 1988.

Bob FOSTER

Born December 15, 1938, Albuquerque, New Mexico
Boxer

Foster spent his professional career as a boxer, a member of the U.S. Air Force, and in law enforcement. He was introduced to boxing while in junior high school in his native New Mexico. Foster played football in high school and was offered a football scholarship to the University of New Mexico. Instead, he enlisted in the Air Force, where he boxed as an amateur in the light heavyweight class. At six feet, three inches and weighing between 170 and 188 pounds, he was undefeated in over 100 amateur bouts, and in 1959 he won a place on the Pan American team.

In 1961, Foster turned pro and won his first nine fights before losing to Doug Jones in 1962. After a loss to Zora Folley in 1965, he left boxing to work in a munitions factory in York, PA. Foster was lured back to boxing in 1966 when fight manager Morris Salow purchased his contract. On December 6, 1966, Foster knocked out Leroy Green and then continued on a string of seven victories. On May 24, 1968, Foster was given a title bout against light heavyweight champion Dick Tiger. Foster knocked out Tiger in the fourth round. After gaining the light heavyweight title, Foster defended his crown a record fourteen times. On two occasions Foster had unsuccessful attempts at the heavyweight title. On November 18, 1970, he was knocked out in the second round by Joe Frazier, and on November 21, 1972, Muhammad Ali knocked him out in the eighth round.

In 1974 Foster retired from boxing to become a deputy sheriff in Bernalillo County, NM. In 1975 he returned to boxing but after five bouts decided to retire permanently. Foster ended his boxing career with a record of fifty-six wins, eight losses, and one draw; forty-six of the wins were by knockout. In 1983 he was inducted to the ring's Boxing Hall of Fame.

Alar Lipping

See also: Boxing.

FURTHER READING
Arnold, Peter. *All-Time Greats of Boxing.* Secaucus, NJ: Chartwell Books, 1993.
Porter, David L., ed. *Biographical Dictionary of American Sports: Basketball and Other Indoor Sports.* New York: Greenwood Press, 1989.
Roberts, James B., and Alexander G. Skutt. *The Boxing Register: International Boxing Hall of Fame Official Record Book.* Ithaca, NY: McBooks Press, 1997

★ ★ ★

Rube FOSTER

Born September 17, 1879, Calvert, Texas
Died December 9, 1930, Kankakee, Illinois
Baseball player, manager, and administrator

Foster, son of Andrew Foster, a minister, and Sarah Foster, is considered the father of Negro League baseball. He began his baseball career as a pitcher for the Waco Texas Yellow Jackets. In 1902 the imposing six-foot, four inch Foster won fifty-one games, including one pitching triumph over the great white hurler "Rube" Waddell. This accomplishment earned him the nickname "Rube," which would be his the rest of his life.

In 1903 Foster joined the Cuban X-Giants, with whom he notched fifty-four wins against only one loss. The following season he signed with the Philadelphia Giants and over three years led the team to numerous victories and championships. In 1907 Foster embarked on a new phase of his career by becoming player-manager of the Leland Giants. Four years later he formed a partnership with John Schorling, a white businessman and son-in-law of

Rube Foster (standing in middle of second row), considered the father of Negro League Baseball, posing for a photograph with his 1920 Chicago American Giants. *(National Baseball Hall of Fame Library, Cooperstown, NY)*

Chicago White Sox owner Charles Comiskey, to assemble a team called the Chicago American Giants. The American Giants, with Foster orchestrating play from his managerial position and occasionally pitching, dominated Negro League baseball for over a decade. The team consistently defeated its opponents with an aggressive style of play that emphasized speed, solid base running, sound pitching, and superb fielding.

In 1920 Foster organized the Negro National League (NNL), the first African-American baseball league. Foster served as president and treasurer, developing the NNL into an outstanding organization that originally consisted of the Chicago American Giants, St. Louis Giants, Chicago Giants, Detroit Stars, Taylor ABCs, Kansas City Monarchs and the Cuban Stars. In 1925 Foster resigned as league president, the result of the mental strain and stress of his administrative duties along with other factors. The following year Foster suffered a nervous breakdown and was committed to a mental hospital in Kankakee, Illinois, where he stayed until his death in 1930. In spite of these problems in the latter stages of his life, Foster's many accomplishments and contributions to Negro League baseball resulted in his selection to the Baseball Hall of Fame in 1981.

David K. Wiggins

See also: Baseball; Negro National League.

FURTHER READING

Dixon, Phil, and Patrick J. Hannigan. *The Negro Baseball Leagues: A Photographic History*. Mattituck, NY: Amereon House, 1992.

Holway, John B. *Blackball Stars: Negro League Pioneers*. Westport, CT: Meckler Books, 1988.

Rogosin, Donn. *Invisible Men: Life in Baseball's Negro Leagues*. New York: Atheneum, 1987.

Peterson, Robert W. *Only the Ball Was White*. Englewood Cliffs, NJ: Prentice Hall, 1970.

Porter, David L., ed. *African American Sports Greats: A Biographical Dictionary*. Westport, CT: Greenwood Press, 1995.

★ ★ ★

Joe FRAZIER

Born January 12, 1944, Beaufort, South Carolina
Boxer

The son of Rubin (an overseer) and Dolly Frazier, Joe ended his schooling before the end of his ninth grade year and moved to Philadelphia. Frazier won the Heavyweight Gold Medal at the 1964 Olympic Games in Tokyo, Japan, but he is most famous for his intense rivalry in and out of the ring with Muhammad Ali, whom he faced three times in heavyweight title bouts.

Under the supervision of Yank Durham, Frazier's boxing career blossomed. Refusing to fight in the World Boxing Association elimination tournament to replace Ali, who had been stripped of his championship, Frazier beat Buster Mathis for the vacant New York State Athletic Commission (NYSAC) title on March 4, 1968. He then won the WBA title, beating Jimmy Ellis on February 16, 1970. Ali returned to boxing, and the two met in a sport spectacle organized by theater agent Jerry Perenchio on March 8, 1971. The prefight verbal exchanges took on strong racial and patriotic overtones. Frazier defended his title in fifteen rounds, handing Ali his first loss. Due in part to the prefight antics of Ali, Frazier did not give him a return match, opting to defend his title against George Foreman (to whom he would ultimately lose). Ali and Frazier would meet two more times; Ali beat Frazier in a twelve-round fight for the North American Boxing Federation (NABF) title on January 28, 1974; Ali won again a year later in "Superfight III," also known as the "Thrilla in Manila."

Frazier attempted a comeback in 1980 but finally retired in 1981. He trained young fighters, including two sons, Marvis and Hector. He owns and operates Smokin' Joe Frazier's, a boxing gymnasium in north Philadelphia.

The fights versus Ali continue to be analyzed as dramatic spectacles of sport history. Most recently, the third fight was the topic of Mark Kram's *The Ghosts of Manila*. Frazier was elected to the Boxing Hall of Fame in 1980 and the International Hall of Fame in 1990.

Maureen M. Smith

See also: Boxing; George Foreman.

FURTHER READING

Frazier, Joe with Phil Berger. *Smokin' Joe*. New York: Macmillan, 1996.

Kram, Mark. "'Lawdy, Lawdy, He's Great.'" *Sports Illustrated*, October 3, 1994, 30–33.

Nack, William. "'The Fights Over, Joe.'" *Sports Illustrated*, September 30, 1996, 52–63.

Sammons, Jeffrey T. *Beyond the Ring: The Role of Boxing in American Society*. Urbana: University of Illinois Press, 1988.

★ ★ ★

Walter FRAZIER, JR.

Born March 29, 1945, Atlanta, Georgia
Basketball player

Frazier's parents are Evla Wynn and Walter Frazier, Sr. At David Howard High School in Atlanta, Georgia, Frazier participated in football, baseball, and basketball. Upon graduation from high school in 1963, he went to Southern Illinois University, where he played basketball. He was a Little All-American in his sophomore year. SIU, led by Frazier, became the first small college to participate in the National Invitational Tournament (NIT) in 1967; it defeated Marquette University for the championship. Frazier was the tournament's Most Valuable Player and made the *Sporting News* second-team All-American that year.

Beginning play in the National Basketball Association (NBA) in 1967–1968, he was the league's Rookie of the Year. He went on to play thirteen seasons in the NBA with the New York Knicks, 1967–1977, and the Cleveland Cavaliers, 1977–1979. He played on two NBA championship teams with New York in 1970 and 1973. Frazier was an All-NBA team selection six times and All-Defensive first-team selection seven times. He averaged 18.9 points per game over his career. Frazier was nicknamed "Clyde" by a New York teammate, as he was always nattily dressed, like the character Clyde Barrow of the film *Bonnie and Clyde*.

Frazier's ability to play the game under pressure with calmness and firm leadership earned him lasting praise. He was selected to the Naismith Memorial Basketball Hall of Fame in 1986 and to the NBA's Fiftieth Anniversary team in 1996.

Following his professional basketball career, Frazier lived in St. Croix, Virgin Islands, and maintained interests in New York City, where his Walt Frazier Enterprises represented several professional athletes. He also formed the Walt Frazier Youth Foundation in New York to help inner-city youngsters realize their potential. In the later 1980s, after working with the broadcast media in Atlanta, he joined the Madison Square Garden Network as a color analyst for the New York Knicks cable and radio broadcasts. His son, Walt Frazier, played guard for the University of Pennsylvania in the mid-1980s.

John R. Schleppi

FURTHER READING
Boston Sunday Globe, October 28, 1979.
Hubbard, Jan, ed. *The Official NBA Encyclopedia*. 3d ed. New York: Doubleday, 2000.
News release, Madison Square Garden Network (www.MSGnetwork.com), October 7, 1990.
Walton, David, and John Hareas, eds. *The Sporting News Official NBA Register*, 2000–2001. St. Louis: Sporting News, 2000.

Clarence GAINES

Born May 21, 1923, Paducah, Kentucky
Basketball coach

Clarence "Bighouse" Gaines is a basketball legend. The son of Lester and Olivia Bolen Gaines, he excelled academically and athletically at Lincoln High School in Paducah, KY. Gaines enrolled in 1941 at Morgan State University, where he became an All-American football player and also participated in basketball and track. According to legend, it was at Morgan State that the then six-foot three-inch, 265-pound Gaines gained the famous moniker "Bighouse" when a business manager declared, "I've never seen anything bigger than you but a house."

Upon graduating with a B.S. degree in chemistry in 1945, Gaines decided to delay his plans to become a dentist by taking a temporary coaching position as an assistant at Winston-Salem State University. He never left. When the head coach took another job in 1946, Gaines became athletic director, head football coach, head basketball coach, trainer, and ticket manager. He coached football for three years, but earned his fame as a basketball coach, over a forty-seven-year span.

From 1946 until his retirement in 1993, "Bighouse" Gaines compiled a win/loss record of 828–446. At his retirement, he was the winningest active coach, and second-winningest all-time coach, in NCAA history. In 1967, his greatest team featured dazzling Earl "The Pearl" Monroe; the team won the NCAA Small College Division (Division II) National Championship, becoming the first historically black college to win a national championship. Gaines has received numerous awards and honors, including the Naismith Basketball Hall of Fame (1982), CIAA Hall of Fame (1975), NAIA Hall of Fame (1968), North Carolina Sports Hall of Fame (1978), and U.S. Olympic Committee member (1973–1976).

Robert Epling

FURTHER READING

"Bighouse" Gaines Collection, Winston-Salem State (www.wssu.edu/athletics/menbball/bighouse.htm).

Clarence "Big House" Gaines, *Basketball Hall of Fame* (www.hoophall.com/halloffamers/Gaines.htm).

Isley, Reginald. "A Study of the Professional Life of Clarence E. 'Bighouse' Gaines While at Winston-Salem State University." Unpublished master's thesis, Western Illinois University, 1983.

Reed, W.F. "The House that Roared." *Sports Illustrated*, February 5, 1990, 66.

Whitted, Fred. *The "Big House" on Tobacco Road*. Fayetteville, NC: Resource 2000, 2001.

"Winston-Salem State Coach Clarence 'Bighouse' Gaines Retiring after 47 years." *Jet*, March 15, 1993, 48.

★ ★ ★

Jake GAITHER

Born April 11, 1903, Dayton, Tennessee
Died February 18, 1994, Tallahassee, Florida
Football coach

Gaither received his A.B. degree from Knoxville College (1927) and an M.S. from Ohio State University (1937), and served as head football coach at Florida A & M, 1945–1969.

Gaither was one of six children born to a Methodist minister. Gaither's first coaching experience was as high school football coach at Henderson Institute, in Henderson, NC (1927–1935), followed by a stint at St. Paul Polytechnical Institute in Lawrenceville, Virginia (1935–1937). He joined Florida A & M, in Tallahassee, in 1937 as an assistant football coach, and in 1945 took over as head coach. He also served as the track and field and basketball coach.

Gaither made an immediate impact on Florida A & M's program, taking the black conference championship his initial year. It was the first of his twenty-two titles; he won every year of his tenure except 1951, 1952, and 1966. He also led the school to six national black college championships. An innovative coach, Gaither developed a highly effective T formation by splitting his offensive line, cowriting with his coaching associates an influential book, *The Split-Line T Offense* (1963). A superb motivator, Gaither is famed for his quote, "I like my players mobile, agile, and hostile."

Gaither retired as football coach in 1969, having compiled a 203–36–4 record, the highest winning percentage (.844) of any active coach at the time. He served as athletic director until 1973. In 1975 Gaither was elected to the National Football Foundation Hall of Fame, and he also received the Alonzo Stagg and the Walter Camp awards.

Gaither was a legend even before he retired, and his remarkable success lifted football at black schools into national prominence. As forty-two of his players went into the NFL, he significantly helped advance the African-American athlete in professional football.

Robert Pruter

See also: Historically Black Colleges and Universities.

FURTHER READING
Curry, George E. *Jake Gaither: America's Most-Famous Black Coach*. New York: Dodd, Mead, 1977.
Endsley, Gerald. "Florida A & M's Gaither Was True Football Success Story." *Chicago Tribune*, February 27, 1994.
O'Brien, Richard, and Jack McCallum. "A Man of Influence." *Sports Illustrated*, February 2, 1994, 13.

★   ★   ★

Willie GALIMORE

Born March 30, 1935, St. Augustine, Florida
Died July 26, 1964, Rensselaer, Indiana
Football player

Galimore attended Florida A & M on a basketball scholarship but quickly became a standout halfback for the football team. As a freshman in 1953 he rushed for a total of 1,204 yards and in 1954 ran for 295 yards against Maryland State, capping off the season with a first-team spot on the National Association of Intercollegiate Athletics (NAIA) All-American squad. After two more brilliant seasons (1955–1956), Galimore finished with 3,596 career rushing yards. He was first team All-Conference halfback in the Southern Intercollegiate conference for all four seasons, and his play was recognized with first-team berths on the *Pittsburgh Courier* Black College All-America squads for the seasons of 1954 and 1956.

Selected by the Chicago Bears in the fifth round of the 1956 NFL draft, Galimore scored four touchdowns in a game against Los Angeles in his rookie season, 1957. He led the Bears in scoring for 1958 with twelve touchdowns, was named to the All-Pro team in 1959, and was the Bears' leading rusher in 1961 with 707 yards. After a knee injury early in 1962, Galimore returned to play a key role in the Bears' 1963 NFL championship season, but during training for the 1964 season he and teammate John Farrington were killed in an auto accident.

Galimore—an elusive open-field runner with blazing speed—was considered one of the top backs in the NFL during his seven-year career. He rushed for 2,985 yards and scored thirty-seven touchdowns. He was elected posthumously to the Florida Sports Hall of Fame in 1961 and the College Football Hall of Fame in 1999.

Raymond Schmidt

See also: Gymnastics.

FURTHER READING
Florida A & M Sports Media Guide, 1999, 136.
Haugh, David. "A Big Day for Memories." *South Bend Tribune*, August 13, 1999.
Rollow, Cooper. "Galimore's Car Slips Off Road." *Chicago Tribune*, July 27, 1964.
"Willie Helped Drive to Top." *Chicago Daily News*, July 27, 1964.

★ ★ ★

Joe GANS

Born November 25, 1874, Baltimore, Maryland
Died August 10, 1910, Baltimore, Maryland
Boxer

Born Joseph Gaines of uncertain parentage, Joe Gans may have been the son of Joseph Butts, a successful black baseball player. As a four-year-old, Gans was adopted by Mr. and Mrs. Gant. Mr. Gant worked as a fish-market clerk.

Gans began his career as a professional boxer in 1891. Fighting in the lightweight division, the five-foot six-inch, 131-pound Gans was recognized as a thinking man's boxer who combined punching power with a rare degree of ring craft. He is best remembered for a titanic trio of fights with the white boxer "Battling" Nelson (1906, 1908, 1908) for the world lightweight championship. With Tex Rickard promoting the first fight, the contest became a sad symbol of flagrant racism and discrimination. Despite being the reigning champion, Gans only received one third of the purse. Second, he had to "make" the weight of 133 pounds on three occasions on the day of the fight. Nevertheless, in round forty-two, Nelson was disqualified for hitting Gans with a low punch. In their two following fights Nelson knocked out Gans in rounds seventeen and twenty-one, respectively.

Gans died from tuberculosis in Baltimore. He had married actress Madge Gans. They had two children—James and Julia. His second wife was Margaret. Despite significant career earnings—he had 131 wins in 156 career fights—he was plagued by gambling losses. He was inducted into the International Boxing Hall of Fame in 1990.

Scott A.G.M. Crawford

See also: Boxing.

FURTHER READING
Daniel, Daniel M. "Gans at His Peak." *Ring* (April 1947): 30–35.
Porter, David L., ed. *African-American Sports Greats: A Biographical Dictionary.* Westport, CT: Greenwood Press, 1995.
Roberts, James B., and Alexander G. Skutt. *The Boxing Register: International Boxing Hall of Fame Official Record Book.* Ithaca, NY: McBooks Press, 1997.

★ ★ ★

Mike GARRETT

Born April 12, 1944, Los Angeles, California
Football player

Garrett attended Theodore Roosevelt High School in Los Angeles; he was a star athlete. His athletic talent landed him a scholarship to the University of Southern California, where he excelled in both football and baseball from 1962 to 1965. In 1967 he earned a bachelor of science degree in sociology from that institution.

In 1965 Garrett became the second black athlete, and the second West Coast athlete in history, to win the coveted Heisman Trophy. He was the premier running back in college athletics at the time and set fourteen NCAA records. The Kansas City

Chiefs, of the then American Football League (AFL), signed Garrett to a five-year contract in 1966, reportedly worth $450,000. He remained with the Chiefs until 1970, when he temporarily retired, before being traded to the San Diego Charges. Garrett remained with the Chargers until 1973, when he permanently retired from professional football.

In his first year with the Chiefs, Garrett led the team to the AFL Championship and to the very first Super Bowl, versus the Green Bay Packers of the National Football League (NFL). The Packers won the game 35–10. In 1969 Garrett again led the Chiefs to the AFL Championship, and into Super Bowl IV. This time Garrett and the Chiefs defeated the Minnesota Vikings 23–7 to win the Super Bowl.

Garrett attended Western State Law School in San Diego and twice ran for political office. He was unsuccessful both times. Along with his wife Sherry, he ran a facility for juvenile delinquents and operated a real estate business. He is presently the athletic director at his alma mater, USC.

James R. Coates, Jr.

FURTHER READING
Ashe, Arthur R., Jr. *A Hard Road to Glory: A History of The African-American Athlete.* New York: Warner Books, 1988.
Henderson, Edwin B., with the editors of *Sport* Magazine. *The Black Athlete: Emergence and Arrival.* Cornwall Heights, PA: Pennsylvania Publishers, 1968.
Hickok Sports (www.hickoksports.com/biograph/garrettmike.shtml).
Newsweek, June 22, 1970.
Newsweek, December 12, 1966.

Zina GARRISON

Born November 16, 1963, Houston, Texas
Tennis player

Garrison's father, who was a postman, died when she was a child; she was raised by her mother, a nurse's aide, and her maternal grandmother. Her tennis career began on the inner-city courts of Houston, Texas. Her first coach, John Wilkerson, was a former champion on the predominantly black American Tennis Association (ATA) circuit. Garrison was the first African-American woman to be ranked number-one in tennis in the state of Texas, and in 1981 she won the junior titles at both Wimbledon and the U.S. Open. Garrison was a part of tennis history when in 1986 she and Lori McNeil met in the finals of the Eckerd Open—the first time two black women encountered each other in such a setting.

In 1988 she earned the bronze medal in women's singles at the Olympics, and in 1990 she became the first African-American woman since Althea Gibson in 1958 to reach the singles finals of a Grand Slam event. Garrison's greatest successes, however, came as a doubles player. She won nearly two dozen titles in women's doubles and three Grand Slam titles in mixed doubles. In 1988, at the Seoul Olympics, Garrison teamed with Pam Shriver to win the gold in women's doubles.

Since her playing career ended, Garrison has worked diligently to give back to the community in which she was raised. In 1992 she established the Zina Garrison All-Court Tennis program for inner-city children in her hometown of Houston. It not only helps children learn how to play tennis but helps them develop life skills as well.

Alison M. Wrynn

See also: Tennis.

FURTHER READING

Ashe, Arthur R., Jr. *A Hard Road to Glory: A History of the African-American Athlete Since 1946*. New York: Warner Books, 1988.

Bentley, Ken. *The Story of Black Women in Sports*. Los Angeles: Carnation, 1983.

Garrison, Zina, with Doug Smith. *Zina: My Life in Women's Tennis*. Berkeley, CA: Frog Limited, 2001.

"Zina Garrison: The Success of All-Court Tennis." *Texas Monthly* (www.texasmonthly.com/mag/issues/2001–09–01/sports3.ph), September 2001.

★ ★ ★

Willie GAULT

Born September 5, 1960, Griffin, Georgia
Football player, sprinter

An outstanding college and professional football player, Gault was also a world-class track athlete who earned places on U.S. Olympic teams in two different sports.

Gault was a three-sport star prep athlete, and in 1980 he won a place as a sprinter on the U.S. Olympic team (but never competed because of the boycott of the Moscow Games). Playing football at the University of Tennessee (1979–1982), Gault had his best season in 1982, with fifty pass receptions for 668 yards; he was named first-team All-SEC. He completed his collegiate football career holding twelve school and six conference kick-return records; as a member of the track team he had captured a pair of second-place finishes at the 1982 NCAA Outdoor meet and two titles at the 1983 NCAA Indoors.

Selected by the Chicago Bears in the first round of the 1983 NFL draft, Gault first competed at the 1983 World Track and Field Championships in Helsinki, Finland, where he was a member of the 4 x 100 relay team that set a new world record. Named to the NFL All-Rookie team in 1983, Gault also played a key role in the Bears' winning of the 1986 Super Bowl title.

Gault won a spot as an alternate on the U.S. bobsled team for the 1988 Winter Olympics, but the Bears then traded him to the Los Angeles Raiders. There he had his best NFL season in 1990, completing his eleven-year NFL career in 1993 with career totals of 333 pass receptions and forty-four touchdowns. In the following years he began an acting career that has included movie and television roles.

Raymond Schmidt

FURTHER READING

Cook, Ron. "Gault Is No Dangerfield: He Finally Gets Respect." *Knoxville News-Sentinel*, January 19, 1986.

Pierson, Don. "Gault Added Twist to World Games." *Chicago Bear Report*, August 25, 1983.

Whittingham, Richard. *The Chicago Bears: From George Halas to Super Bowl XX*. New York: Simon and Schuster, 1986.

"Willie Gault: Final Career Summary." *University of Tennessee Sports Information*, 1983.

★ ★ ★

George GERVIN

Born April 27, 1952, Detroit, Michigan
Basketball player

One of six children, Gervin was raised in Detroit. When he was two years old his father left the family in the hands of his mother, who took on various jobs to raise her family. A graduate of Martin Luther King High School (1969), Gervin attended Long Beach (CA) State University (1969–1970) and Eastern Michigan University (1970–1972). Gervin spent his career in professional basketball as a player, assistant coach, and public relations representative. He also founded the George Gervin Youth Center.

Gervin began playing basketball in his Detroit neighborhood. As a high school sophomore, Gervin at five feet, eight inches did not make the school's varsity basketball team. Willie Meriweather, coach of the junior varsity team, saw potential in him, however. Meriweather became an influential coach in Gervin's life and by Gervin's junior year he had made the varsity team. By his senior year, Gervin had grown to a six-foot four-inch school basketball star, averaging thirty-one points and twenty rebounds to lead his school to the state quarterfinals.

In 1969 Gervin accepted a scholarship to play basketball at Long Beach State under Jerry Tarkanian. In 1970 he transferred to Eastern Michigan University, where he averaged 29.5 points as a sophomore forward in 1971–1972. In 1972 Gervin began his professional basketball career with the Pontiac, Michigan, Chaparrals of the Eastern Basketball Association. During the 1972 season he was scouted by Johnny Kerr of the Virginia Squires of the American Basketball Association, and he was signed to a $40,000 a year contract with the Squires.

During the 1973–1974 season Gervin signed a contract with the San Antonio Spurs. It was with the Spurs that Gervin emerged as a basketball star. In 1976 the Spurs joined the National Basketball Association. He played for the Spurs until 1985 and then joined the Chicago Bulls for the 1985–1986 season. Gervin left the Bulls and played one season with Banco Roma of the Italian League. His professional basketball-playing career ended with one year with the Quad City Thunder, of the Continental Basketball Association, in 1990.

Gervin accumulated 26,595 points as an ABA/NBA player and averaged 26.2 points per game. He, Michael Jordan, and Wilt Chamberlain are the only players to win four or more NBA scoring titles. Gervin was selected to the 1979 and 1980 NBA All-Star team and was MVP in the 1980 All-Star Game. On December 5, 1987, the San Antonio Spurs retired his jersey, number forty-four. In 1996 he was inducted into the Naismith Memorial Basketball Hall of Fame.

Alar Lipping

FURTHER READING
"Hall of Famers: George 'Ice Man' Gervin" (www.hoophall.com/halloffamers/Gervin.htm).
Kirkpatrick, Curry. "The Iceman Cometh and Scoreth." *Sports Illustrated*, March 6, 1978, 12–15.
"NBA Legends: George Gervin" (global.nba.com/history/gervinbio.html).
O'Connor, Richard. "The Lonest Star in Texas." *Sports Illustrated*, March 3, 1981, 56–60.
Porter, David L., ed. *Biographical Dictionary of American Sports: Basketball and Other Indoor Sports*. Westport, CT: Greenwood Press, 1989.

★ ★ ★

Althea GIBSON

Born August 25, 1927, Silver, South Carolina
Died September 28, 2003, East Orange, New Jersey
Tennis player

The oldest of five children born to sharecroppers Daniel and Annie Gibson, Althea moved with her family in 1930 to Harlem, where her father worked in a garage. After a troubled childhood marked by school truancy, Gibson graduated from junior high school in 1941 but shortly thereafter dropped out of school and left home. Althea led an erratic life on the streets, in and out of jobs, until she was introduced to tennis through the Police Athletic League and achieved success in the segregated American Tennis Association (ATA). In 1946 she was befriended by two black surgeons, Hubert Eaton of Wilmington, North Carolina, and Robert W. Johnson of Lynchburg, Virginia. Recognizing her potential, they offered her a home and schooling through high school. In 1949 she enrolled at Florida A & M College, graduating in 1952.

Her amateur tennis career blossomed, beginning with a ten-year reign as the ATA women's singles champion, 1947–1956. In 1950, Gibson played in the desegregated National Indoor Championships, losing in the quarterfinals. The following year she lost in the finals. Through the efforts of tennis great Alice Marble, the U.S. Lawn Tennis Association (USLTA) issued Gibson an invitation to the 1950 national championships at Forest Hills, where she lost in the second round. The following year she became the first African American to play at Wimbledon. In 1956, she won the doubles championship at Wimbledon with Angela Buxton. The following year, she won the Wimbledon singles title as well as the national clay court and Forest Hills singles championships. In 1958, she repeated her Wimbledon singles victory and added the doubles title.

Following her tennis career, Gibson had a film role in The Horse Soldiers (1959) and became the first African American to play on the Ladies Professional Golf Association tour (1964–1977). Later, she served as program director for a racquet club, held a seat on the New Jersey State Athletic Commission, and taught in Montclair, New Jersey. Her honors include Associated Press Woman Athlete of the Year, 1957–58; Lawn Tennis Hall of Fame; and the Black Athletes Hall of Fame.

Richard A. Swanson

See also: American Tennis Association; Autobiographies; Historically Black Colleges and Universities; Tennis; Women.

FURTHER READING
Gibson, Althea. *I Always Wanted to Be Somebody*. New York: Harper and Brothers, 1958.
Henderson, Edwin B., and the editors of *Sport* Magazine. *The Black Athlete: Emergence and Arrival*. Cornwell Heights, PA: Publishers Agency, 1978.
Hine, Darlene Clark. *Black Women in America: An Historical Encyclopedia*. Brooklyn, NY: Carlson, 1993.
Lansbury, Jennifer H. "'The Tuskegee Flash' and the 'Slender Harlem Stroker': Black Women Athletes on the Margin." *Journal of Sport History* 28 (Summer 2001): 233–52.
Smith, Jessie Carney, ed. *Epic Lives: One Hundred Black Women Who Made a Difference*. Detroit: Visible Ink Press, 1999.

★ ★ ★

Bob GIBSON

Born November 9, 1935, Omaha, Nebraska
Baseball player

Born the last of seven sons of Pack and Victoria Gibson, he was raised by his mother, who had been widowed a few months prior to his birth. Known also as "Hoot" and "Gibby," Gibson survived poor health as a child to become a star athlete in his teenage years. His baseball and basketball skills were learned on YMCA teams coached by his older brother, Josh. Although he won All-City honors on a Y baseball team that won the American Legion sponsored Nebraska State Championship, he was denied the opportunity to play on the high school team, which had an unwritten whites-only policy. Instead, he participated on the track team during the spring baseball season and in basketball. In his senior year, a new baseball coach was appointed, and Gibson, along with several other African-American players, was welcomed to the team. As a senior, he earned all-city and all-state honors.

Following graduation from Omaha Technical High School in 1953, he turned down an offer to play for the Kansas City Monarchs of the Negro National League and accepted a scholarship to play basketball and baseball at Creighton University. In 1957 he signed a contract with the St. Louis Cardinal organization and also played one season of basketball with the Harlem Globetrotters. Gibson pitched for the Cardinals from 1959 through 1975, compiling a 251–174 record, 3,117 strikeouts, and a career 2.91 ERA. He was elected to the Baseball Hall of Fame in 1981.

Richard A. Swanson

See also: Baseball.

FURTHER READING
Ashe, Arthur R., Jr. *A Hard Road to Glory: A History of the African-American Athlete Since 1946.* New York: Amistad, 1993.
Gibson, Bob, with Lonnie Wheeler. *Stranger to the Game: The Autobiography of Bob Gibson.* New York: Viking Penguin Books, 1994.
Henderson, Edwin B., and the editors of *Sport* Magazine. *The Black Athlete: Emergence and Arrival.* Cornwell Heights, PA: Publishers Agency, 1978.

★ ★ ★

Josh GIBSON

Born December 21, 1911, Buena Vista, Georgia
Died January 20, 1947, Pittsburgh, Pennsylvania
Baseball player

One of the brightest stars of the Negro leagues in the 1930s and '40s, he was the eldest of three children born to Mark and Nancy (Woodcock) Gibson in rural Georgia. In 1926, Gibson, his mother, and sister and brother joined Mark in Pittsburgh, where he had gone to find work in the iron mines. Gibson joined his father in the mines after school and also began to gain recognition as a talented baseball player. The backbreaking work in the mines hardened his body, and by the age of seventeen the six-foot two inch, 200-pound youth commanded respect in the neighborhood as well as on the ball field.

His first organized team was a black amateur club sponsored by Gimble's Department Store. He then played for two other companies in the all-Negro Greater Pittsburgh Industrial League. At the age of sixteen he signed with the professional Pittsburgh Crawfords as a hard-hitting catcher. It was as a long-ball slugger that he proved most valuable and achieved his greatest fame. He played most of his career for the Crawfords but also had brief stints with the Homestead Grays (1930–1932) and Veracruz of the Mexican League (1940–1941). In the 1940s, he continued to excel on the diamond but suffered increasingly from headaches, dizziness, mental instability, and drug and alcohol addiction. He died at the age of thirty-five of a brain hemorrhage. Gibson was elected to the Baseball Hall of Fame in 1972.

Richard A. Swanson

See also: Baseball; Gus Greenlee.

FURTHER READING
Ashe, Arthur R., Jr. *A Hard Road to Glory: A History of the African-American Athlete, 1919–1945.* New York: Amistad, 1993.
Brashler, William. *Josh Gibson: A Life in the Negro Leagues.* Chicago: I.R. Dee, 2000.
Holway, John. *Josh and Satch: The Life and Times of Josh Gibson and Satchel Paige.* Westport, CT: Meckler, 1991.
Ribowsky, Mark. *A Complete History of the Negro Leagues: 1884–1955.* Secaucus, NJ: Carol, 1997.
———. *The Power and the Darkness: The Life of Josh Gibson in the Shadows of the Game.* New York: Simon & Schuster, 1996.

★ ★ ★

Artis GILMORE

Born September 21, 1949, Chipley, Florida
Basketball player

Born to working-class parents—an itinerant fisherman and a housewife—in tiny Chipley, Florida, Artis Gilmore, a dominant seven-foot two-inch, 240-pound center, excelled at every level of competitive basketball en route to a storied career that left his name scattered throughout the record books of professional basketball.

Gilmore burst onto the national scene in 1970–1971, when, after two years at Gardner-Webb Junior College in North Carolina, he led unheralded Jacksonville University to a 27–2 record and a berth in the NCAA championships against UCLA. Although John Wooden's Bruins defeated Jacksonville in its only trip to the "Final Four," Gilmore ended his collegiate career as one of only a handful of players to average more than twenty points and twenty rebounds per game.

After leaving college, Gilmore helped to provide much-needed credibility to the upstart American Basketball Association (ABA) when he joined the Kentucky Colonels in 1971 for a salary of $2.5 million over ten years. The soft-spoken center paid immediate dividends as he was named the ABA'S Rookie of the Year and MVP in leading the Colonels to an ABA-record .810 winning percentage in 1971–1972.

The durable Gilmore played in 670 consecutive games at the start of his professional career, was named to the All-Star team, and helped the Colonels to the playoffs in each of his seasons in the ABA. When the ABA folded after the 1975–1976 season, Gilmore played twelve more seasons for the Chicago Bulls and San Antonio Spurs of the National Basketball Association (NBA). Although Gilmore was never quite able to match his early success in the ABA, he nevertheless retired as the all-time NBA leader in field-goal percentage (.599) and among the all-time professional basketball leaders in points and rebounds.

Gregory Bond

FURTHER READING
Bjarkman, Peter C., ed. *The Biographical History of Basketball*. Dallas: Master's Press, 1998.
"NBA Legends: Artis Gilmore." *NBA.com History* (global.nba.com/history/gilmorebio.html).
Pluto, Terry. *Loose Balls: The Short, Wild Life of the American Basketball Association*. New York: Simon & Schuster, 1991.
Taragano, Martin, ed. *Basketball Biographies: 434 U.S. Players, Coaches, and Contributors to the Game, 1891–1990*. Jefferson, NC: McFarland, 1991.

★ ★ ★

GOLF

It is assumed by many that the contributions of African Americans to the game of golf are neither significant nor long lasting. Both assumptions are incorrect. To begin with, there is convincing, if circumstantial, evidence suggesting that when the game was introduced into the United States in the late eighteenth century, enslaved Africans in the southern states of South Carolina and Georgia were among the nation's earliest caddies. However, after some forty years the "game played with the crooked stick," which Scot and English merchants had brought to the United States, lost its appeal. It did not begin to regain popularity until the end of the Civil War, a half-century later. During the interval, for reasons that are unclear, few of the nation's inhabitants, black or white, showed interest in golf.

A number of developments rekindled enthusiasm for the game. Among the more important were improvements in golf equipment, wider availability of the new equipment, and growth in the construction of both public and private golf courses. Unfortunately, it was also a period of rising hostility toward African Americans, especially those freed from slavery by the Emancipation Proclamation. Increasingly, the majority population excluded black citizens from virtually every sphere of national life—recreation in general, and golf in particular, included. Initially African Americans, with rare exceptions, were excluded from all aspects of the game, but as time passed they gradually were permitted to assume the menial role of caddie. Dr. Francis Grant, Walter Speedy, John Shippen, Joseph Bartholomew, and Dewey Brown were the best known of that select group. Grant, a New England dentist, was issued a patent by the U.S. Patent Office in 1899 for his invention of the wooden golf tee.

John Shippen played in the second U.S. Open in 1899 and played in four more of these events before spending the remainder of his life as a club professional. In 1915, Walter Speedy was instrumental in promoting the first African American golf tournament. A foe of racial discrimination in golf, Speedy was also a leading figure in organizing and supporting the first (and only) national black golfing body. Golf-course architect Joseph Bartholomew built nearly a dozen golf courses in the New Orleans area but because of his race was denied permission to play them. Like many other excellent black golfers, Dewey Brown started his golfing career as a caddie. Later he became a highly sought-after club maker and instructor. He was the first African-American member of the Professional Golfers Association (PGA); when in 1934 his racial identity was discovered by officials of the organization, his membership was withdrawn.

While only a small number of African American golfers achieved a measure of success in the years prior to the First World War, afterward black golfers began to band together and undertake organized activities. The efforts by African Americans during this period to acquire their own golf courses constituted one manifestation of greater collective self-reliance. A small group of black investors opened the Shady Rest Golf and Country Club in Scotch Plains, New Jersey on September 21, 1921; it marked the beginning of African-American attempts to provide additional outlets for black golfers. Although only four are in existence today, at one time or another nearly thirty golf courses have been owned by African Americans. The formation of the United Golfers Association (UGA) in 1925 was the most notable example of this new spirit of collective energy. In keeping with the trend, two historically black institutions of higher learning, Tuskegee Institute in Alabama and Wilberforce University in Ohio, built nine-hole golf courses on their property.

In the ten years before the entry of the United States into the Second World War, three important events took place that had a great impact on black golf. The first occurred in 1934, when the PGA inserted the infamous "Caucasian race" clause into its constitution. This act, which barred African Americans from membership in the organization, would be a source of contention and bitter acrimony until its repeal more than a quarter-century later. The founding of the Wake-Robin Golf Club on April 22, 1937, in Washington, DC, was followed seven months later by the establishment of the Chicago Women's Golf Club. These were the first formal organizations of black women golfers, and both played important roles in increasing the participation of black women in the sport. On August 12, 1941, the last of the three major events took place: the first annual Joe Louis Open, sponsored by the former world's heavyweight boxing champion, was held at Detroit's Rackham Golf Course. An avid golfer himself, Louis used his personal financial resources to provide the purse for the event. Over the next two decades, Louis would continue to be a pillar of support for African-American golf.

It was not until after World War II, however, that the most momentous developments in African-American golf history occurred. These developments were part and parcel of the civil rights movement. Ushered in by the desegregation of the armed forces in 1948, which permitted black servicemen and women to play on the golf courses owned by the military, the struggles of this era focused on racial discrimination in the sport. The second breakthrough occurred in the 1950s, with the passage of landmark civil rights legislation governing public accommodation. As a result, for the first time black golfers gained nationwide access to public golf courses. The next major development followed the removal of the odious "Caucasian race" clause from the PGA constitution in 1961. Although it came too late to benefit talented black professional golfers like the legendary Ted Rhodes, Howard Wheeler, Clyde Martin, or a number of others, since 1961 capable African-American golf professionals have demonstrated that they can compete successfully in PGA events. Among those who achieved success were Charlie Sifford, Lee Elder, Calvin Peete, Jim Dent, and Jim Thorpe.

In 1990, an incident at the Shoal Creek Golf Club in Birmingham, Alabama, drew attention to racial discrimination at privately owned golfing establishments. The uproar over the incident resulted in an announcement by the PGA, the PGA Tour, and the U.S. Golf Association (USGA) that they would no longer use private clubs as tournament sites if their policies barred racial minorities from membership. Only time will tell the extent to which officials in the nation's white country clubs are prepared to accede to the requests for open membership policies.

At the beginning of the new millennium few can seriously question that the superlative performance of Eldrick "Tiger" Woods fully deserves the plaudits he has received from the golfing public as one of the world's best golfers. But as we enter the new century, it is important to be aware that Tiger is the only person of African descent currently playing on the PGA Tour.

With considerable fanfare, new programs have recently been announced that are intended to provide less financially favored youth with wider opportunities to become involved with golf. Their success in correcting the present imbalance will deserve close attention in the years ahead.

Calvin H. Sinnette

See also: Shady Rest Golf and Country Club; United Golfers Association.

FURTHER READING
Dawkins, Marvin P., and Graham C. Kinloch. *African American Golfers During the Jim Crow Era*. Westport, CT: Praeger, 2000.
Howell, Donna W. *I Was a Slave*. Washington, DC: American Legacy, 1995.
Morgan, Philip D. *Slave Counterpoint*. Chapel Hill: University of North Carolina Press, 1998.
Price, Charles, and George C. Rogers, Jr. *The Carolina Low Country Birthplace of American Golf 1786*. Hilton Head Island, SC: Impression, 1980.
Sinnette, Calvin H. *Forbidden Fairways*. Chelsea, MI: Sleeping Bear Press, 1998.

★ ★ ★

Ed GORDON, JR.

Born July 1, 1908, Gary, Indiana
Died September 1971, Detroit, Michigan
Long jumper

The son of two schoolteachers, Ed Gordon, originally took up athletics to fill out his six-foot, three-inch frame, and he eventually became an amateur, collegiate, and Olympic champion in the broad jump (now known as the long jump).

Gordon got his start in track and field at Froebel High School in Gary, Indiana, where he competed in the high jump and hurdles events. After matriculating at the University of Iowa, Gordon concentrated on the long jump, and while still a freshman he won a spot on the 1928 U.S. Olympic team. Hampered by an injury in

Amsterdam, he finished seventh in the broad jump, an event he had only begun to learn.

Returning to Iowa City, Gordon went undefeated in three years of Big Ten competition and captured three consecutive (1929–1931) NCAA titles in the broad jump. He added an Amateur Athletic Union championship in 1929 and made his second U.S. Olympic team in 1932. Competing in Los Angeles, Gordon won the gold medal in the broad jump with a leap of 25 feet ¾ inches. At the 1932 games, Gordon and teammate Eddie Tolan became the third and fourth African Americans to capture Olympic gold medals.

After his Olympic triumph, Gordon moved to New York City, competing for the Grand Street Boys Club and driving a city bus. In 1956, the former Olympic champion moved to Detroit, where he finally completed his college degree at Wayne State University and taught science until he suffered a fatal heart attack in 1971.

Gregory Bond

FURTHER READING

Ashe, Arthur R., Jr. *A Hard Road to Glory: A History of the African-American Athlete, 1919–1945.* New York: Amistad, 1988.

White, Maury. "Gordon Leaped into Shrine Spot." *Des Moines Register*, April 7, 1974.

Williams, Charles H. "Negro Athletes in the Tenth Olympiad." *Southern Workman* 61 (November 1932): 330–34.

Ned GOURDIN

Born 1898, Jacksonville, Florida
Died July 21, 1966, Boston, Massachusetts
Long jumper, lawyer, National Guard officer

Ned Gourdin was the son of a meat cutter (Walter), who was part black and part Seminole, and a mother (Felicia) who was black. One of nine children, Ned showed early promise, graduating as his high school's valedictorian. He then moved to Boston, where he soon became an undergraduate and a law student at Harvard, lettering in baseball, basketball, and track. During his senior year, he became the first man to jump over twenty-five feet, a feat that made him a hero on the sports pages of black and white newspapers. He then won the AAU National Pentathlon Championship two years in a row (1921 and 1922) and won the silver medal in the long jump at the 1924 Olympic Games.

His accomplishments away from track and field were even more significant. Because no white law firm would hire him, he set up his own practice. During the early 1930s he switched his political affiliation from the Republican to the Democratic Party and in 1936 won appointment by President Franklin D. Roosevelt to an assistant U.S. attorney post. He served as a colonel in a segregated unit assigned to the Pacific theater during the Second World War and eventually rose to become brigadier general in the National Guard. Gourdin opposed segregation and complained that white officers had little regard for black troops.

In 1958, he was the first African American appointed to the Massachusetts Superior Court, thus winning the attention of the press thirty-seven years after his athletic feats.

Gregory S. Goodale

FURTHER READING

Abeel, Daphne. "VITA: Edward Orval Gourdin." *Harvard Magazine* (November–December 1997).

Ashe, Arthur R., Jr. *A Hard Road to Glory*. Vol. 2. New York: Amistad, 1993.

Chalk, Ocania. *Black College Sport*. New York: Dodd, Mead, 1976.

Frenette, Gene. "Athletes of the Century: Discover Jacksonville's Hidden Treasure." *Florida Times-Union* (www.jacksonville.com/special/athletes_of_century/stories/gourdin.shtml).

★ ★ ★

Frank GRANT

Born August 1, 1865, Pittsfield, Massachusetts
Died May 27, 1937, New York, New York
Baseball player

The youngest of seven children, Grant was given the name "Ulysses F.," but his parents began calling him "Frank," probably because his father, Franklin, died when Grant was four months old. Sometimes referred to as a "Spaniard" to make his presence more acceptable, he still periodically encountered racial prejudice.

He began his baseball career as a catcher with a semipro team and advanced to the professional ranks in 1886 with Meriden, CT. He later joined a Buffalo club and was the best all-around player in the city's baseball history. However, when the International League eliminated the use of black players in 1889, he signed with the Cuban Giants. To avoid injuries, he began wearing wooden shin guards for protection from runners sliding into second base with spikes high, and on occasion he was moved to the outfield for his own protection.

He later played with Harrisburg, PA, then the big Gorhams team of New York, and later returned to the Cuban Giants. In 1898, he played with the Page Fence Giants, completing his career with the Philadelphia Giants ball club in 1902–1903.

Grant was the first black player to be made into not-quite-legal "analogue" of the game's greatest white players. He was the "black Dunlap" after Fred Dunlap, the St. Louis Browns' second baseman, whose talents had earned him baseball's first $10,000 salary.

Sporting Life called him "a great all-around player." After leaving baseball, he worked for a catering service. He died in New York City of arteriosclerosis.

Clyde Partin

FURTHER READING

Holway, John B. *Blackball Stars: Negro League Pioneers*. Westport, CT: Meckler Books, 1988.

Ribowsky, Mark. *A Complete History of the Negro Leagues, 1884 to 1955*. New York: Birch Lane Press, 1995.

Riley, James A. *The Biographical Encyclopedia of the Negro Baseball Leagues*. New York: Carroll and Graf, 1994.

Shatzkin, Mike, and Jim Chariton. *The Ball Players*. New York: Arbor House, 1990.

★ ★ ★

Edward GRAY

Born October 3, 1888, Aquasco, Maryland
Died May 20, 1943, Cincinnati, Ohio
Football, baseball, basketball player, sprinter

The son of Samuel and Martha Gray, his schooling took place in Washington, DC, public schools. As an undergraduate he attended Amherst College in Massachusetts. Records on his years at college are somewhat confused. The Amherst College Library Archives and Special Collections has a short obituary notice that places Gray at

Amherst only in the period 1908–1909. There is also a yearbook entry (1912), however, that clearly points to Gray's having been a student in residence at Amherst in 1906. The latter has to be correct, for in that year Gray was named by Walter Camp as an outstanding halfback and nominated to Camp's All-American third team.

The *Encyclopedia of African American Culture and History* makes the point that at the start of the twentieth century several athletes of color played football for northern and midwestern schools. Gray is described as one of "the most talented stars." Gray was a stellar running back at Amherst from 1906–1908 and was a very successful sprinter on the college track and field team.

Gray entered Howard University Medical College in September 1908. Although remembered most for his football exploits, he also played top level baseball and basketball. He originally played basketball for the YMCA Twelfth Street team. At this time (1911) the black press began to select All-American teams. The selectors were Edwin B. Henderson and Matthew W. Bullock. One of the standout athletes nominated was Edward B. Gray (All-American team, 1911). Two years later Gray graduated MED and M.D. in 1913 from Howard University.

Gray interned at the General Hospital, Kansas City, Missouri. In 1914 he doubled as football coach and physician at Wiberforce University. In 1915 he began to practice medicine in Cincinnati, Ohio, and eventually was chief of staff at Mercy Hospital. He was president of the Model Drug Company, a Mason, and a member of the Methodist Episcopal Church.

Scott A.G.M. Crawford

FURTHER READING
Ashe, Arthur, Jr. *A Hard Road to Glory*. Vol. 1. New York: Amistad, 1988.
Chalk, Ocania. *Black College Sport*. New York: Dodd, Mead, 1976.
Nelson, Peter. Amherst College Library Archives and Special Collections.
Salzman, Jack, David L. Smith, and Cornel West, eds. *Encyclopedia of African-American Culture and History*. New York: Macmillan, 1996.

★ ★ ★

Joe GREENE

Born September 24, 1946, Temple, Texas
Football player

Raised by his mother (Cleo), Greene compiled a lengthy career as a prominent professional football player and coach.

Attending North Texas State University, Greene was first-team defensive tackle on the Missouri Valley All-Conference squad for three seasons (1966–1968). After the 1968 season he was also named consensus first-team All-America defensive tackle and the Missouri Valley Athlete of the Year.

Selected by the Pittsburgh Steelers in the first round of the 1969 NFL draft, Greene was the 1969 NFL defensive Rookie of the Year. He later received the NFL's Most Valuable Defensive Player award in 1972 and 1974, as he spearheaded Pittsburgh's legendary "steel curtain" defense. He was named All-Pro on eight occasions as the Steelers captured four Super Bowl championships during his thirteen-year career. Retiring after the 1981 season, Greene was inducted into the College Football Hall of Fame in 1984 and the Pro Football Hall of Fame in 1987.

Greene received a CLIO Award for his appearance in the popular 1980 Coca-Cola "jersey" commercial, and after retiring he worked one season as a football analyst for CBS. In 1982, in private business, Greene was appointed to a term on the North Texas State Board of Regents—the first African American to hold that position. After

1986 he served as a defensive line coach, working with the Pittsburgh Steelers, Miami Dolphins, and the Arizona Cardinals.

During his playing career Greene brought strength, quickness, agility, and emotion to the defensive tackle position. He is considered one of the greatest defensive lineman in professional football history, as evidenced by his selection for the NFL's seventy-fifth anniversary All-Time team.

Raymond Schmidt

FURTHER READING
Arizona Cardinals Online Media Guide, 2001.
Blount, Roy, Jr. "He Does What He Wants Out There." *Sports Illustrated*, September 22, 1975, 96–104.
Fox, Larry. *Mean Joe Greene and the Steelers Front Four.* New York: Dodd, Mead, 1975.
Husar, John. "Joe's Not Mean, He's Just Ornery." *Football Digest*, March 1975, 39–44.
Porter, David L., ed. *Biographical Dictionary of American Sports: Football*. Westport, CT: Greenwood Press, 1987.

★ ★ ★

Gus GREENLEE

Born December 26, 1895, Marion, North Carolina
Died July 7, 1952, Pittsburgh, Pennsylvania
Negro leagues team owner and administrator

His African-American father (Samuel) was a brick mason, and his racially mixed mother (Julia) was a housewife. Greenlee, the numbers king of black Pittsburgh, owned the Pittsburgh Crawfords, one of black baseball's greatest teams. He founded the second Negro National League (NNL) and was its first president (1933–1938). He created black baseball's showpiece event, the East-West All-Star game, in 1933. Greenlee Field, one of the few black-owned ballparks, was built for the Crawfords in 1932. He also controlled a stable of boxers, including John Henry Lewis, the first African-American light heavyweight champion.

As a young man, Greenlee migrated to Pittsburgh and after service in World War I solidified control of the rackets in the Hill District. In 1925, "Big Red" purchased the Crawford Grill, which became Pittsburgh's leading restaurant and entertainment venue. Beginning in 1930, he bankrolled the semipro Crawfords, which from 1932 to 1936 dominated black professional play. The 1933 team was awarded a disputed championship by league president Greenlee. The 1935 Crawfords, featuring future Hall of Famers Oscar Charleston, Josh Gibson, Judy Johnson, and "Cool Papa" Bell, defeated the New York Cubans in a championship playoff and are generally considered to have been the greatest black team. The 1936 Crawfords led the NNL, but no playoffs were held. The city then shut down Greenlee's numbers operation, and he broke up the team. He formed the short-lived United States League in 1945.

Greenlee was admired as a sportsman and leader of Pittsburgh's black community despite his criminal activities. He revitalized the Negro leagues and helped them survive the depression.

David C. Skinner

See also: Baseball.

FURTHER READING
Bankes, James. *The Pittsburgh Crawfords: The Lives & Times of Baseball's Most Exciting Team*. Dubuque, IA: Wm. C. Brown, 1991.
Brashler, William. *Josh Gibson: A Life in the Negro Leagues*. New York: Harper & Row, 1978.
Holway, John B. *Blackball Stars: Negro League Pioneers*. Westport, CT: Meckler Books, 1988.
Paige, Leroy ("Satchel"), and David Lipman. *Maybe I'll Pitch Forever*. Garden City, NY: Doubleday, 1962.
Ruck, Rob. *Sandlot Seasons: Sport in Black Pittsburgh*. Urbana: University of Illinois Press, 1987.

★ ★ ★

Hal GREER

Born June 26, 1936, Huntington, West Virginia
Basketball player

Raised by his father William Chester, a railroad machinist, and his stepmother, Tula, Greer graduated from Huntington (WV) Douglass High School and Marshall College. He is best known for his successful fourteen-year career as a professional basketball player.

Greer led Huntington Douglass High School to the 1951 and 1953 state championships in the segregated West Virginia Athletic Union tournament. Shortly after the 1954 *Brown v. Board of Education* Supreme Court decision, he was recruited to integrate Marshall College in his hometown. Integration was peaceful, but difficult. Marshall was a member of the Mid-American Conference, with colleges in Ohio and Michigan that had been integrated at least superficially. Huntington remained mostly segregated during Greer's college career. He was very successful on the basketball court, leading Marshall to a conference championship and an NCAA bid in 1956. In 1958 he led the team in scoring with a 23.8 average.

The Syracuse Nationals drafted the six-foot two-inch, 176-pound Greer in the second round of the National Basketball Association (NBA) draft. In 1967 Greer averaged 22.1 to help the Philadelphia 76ers (the franchise had moved to Philadelphia in 1963) to the NBA championship. Greer played in eight NBA All-Star Games and was named the MVP in the 1968 game. He retired after the 1972 season and was elected to the Naismith Memorial Basketball Hall of Fame in 1981. Huntington's Hal Greer Boulevard now runs through his old neighborhood and Marshall University.

C. Robert Barnett

FURTHER READING

Bjarkman, Peter J. *The Encyclopedia of Pro Basketball Team Histories.* New York: Carroll & Graf, 1994.
Hal Greer file, Marshall University Sports Information Office, Huntington, WV.
Kirsch, George, Othello Harris, and Claire E. Nolte, eds. *Encyclopedia of Ethnicity and Sports in the United States.* Westport, CT: Greenwood Press, 2000.
National Basketball Association (www.nba.org).
Neft, David, et al. *The Sports Encyclopedia: Pro Basketball.* 5th ed. New York: St. Martin's Press, 1992.

★ ★ ★

Ann GREGORY

Born July 25, 1912, Aberdeen, Mississippi
Died February 5, 1990, Gary, Indiana
Golfer

Gregory, the daughter of Henry and Myra Moore, moved to Gary, Indiana from Aberdeen, Mississippi at age eighteen and was married eight years later. Although years earlier she had demonstrated her athletic ability in tennis, it was not until after her husband, an avid golfer, went into the navy in 1942 that Ann became interested in golf. Then in her early thirties, she soon developed a remarkable aptitude for golf. Less than one year after she began playing, she won second place in a local women's tournament.

Over the next two decades Gregory so dominated the segregated black women's golf circuit that on at least one occasion her competitors sought a handicap from tournament officials (their requests were denied). In the African-American press the long-hitting amateur was referred to as "the Queen of Negro Golf Women." But she was also the first black woman to compete on the national scene. In 1947 she was invited by the Chicago golf promoter George S. May to play in his Tam O'Shanter Open Tournament. Nine years later she became the first black golfer to enter the U.S. Golf Association (USGA) Women's Amateur Championship. Despite her acknowledged prowess on the golf course, she had to endure the indignities of racial prejudice at the 1959 Women's Amateur Championship held at the Congressional Country Club in Bethesda, Maryland, and again the next year at the same event in Tulsa, Oklahoma. Undaunted, she continued playing (and occasionally winning) USGA senior women's events until the year before her death on February 5, 1990.

Inducted into the Hall of Fame of the (African American) United Golfers Association (UGA) in 1966, Ann Gregory also enjoyed a reputation as a devoted wife and mother, active churchgoer, respected civic volunteer, and role model for aspiring black and white women golfers.

Calvin H. Sinnette

See also: Golf.

FURTHER READING
Cowans, Russ. "Sifford, Jones, Gregory Win CWGC [Chicago Women's Golf Club] Titles." *Chicago Defender*, August 25, 1951.
Glenn, Rhonda. *The Illustrated History of Women's Golf*. Dallas: Taylor, 1991.
McDaniel, Pete. *Uneven Lies*. Greenwich, CT: American Golfer, 2000.
Overstreet, Joann Gregory. Correspondence with author, June 6, 1997.
Strong, Audra. "Golfing Champ Keeps Swinging at 76." *Post-Tribune* (Gary, Indiana), July 6, 1989.

★ ★ ★

George GREGORY, JR.

Born November 22, 1906, New York, New York
Died May 11, 1994, New York, New York
Basketball player, social activist

The first African-American college basketball All-American selection, Gregory was the star center for the Columbia University varsity team from 1928 to 1931. He led the Lions to back-to-back league titles before embarking on a long career as a Harlem community activist.

The six-foot, four-inch Gregory learned the game in local YMCA gymnasiums and as a member of the starting five of DeWitt Clinton High School in the Bronx. Gregory enrolled at Columbia in 1927, and after a season on the freshman squad became a three-year starter for the Lions' varsity. Among the team's and the league's leading scorers each season, he led Columbia to the school's first Eastern Intercollegiate League (a forerunner of the modern Ivy League) basketball championship in 1929–1930.

Prior to his senior season, his teammates and coaches elected Gregory as the team captain. He responded by leading Columbia to a 21–2 record and a second league title. Gregory's collegiate career ended with his selection to the 1930–1931 Helms Foundation All-American team.

After graduation, Gregory financed a law degree from St. John's University by playing for several local semiprofessional basketball teams. Throughout his career he remained active in the local African-American community, fighting juvenile delinquency, and championing civil rights. For more than twenty years he served as a director for numerous settlement houses and youth organizations, such as the Harlem Youth Center. From 1950 to 1965 Gregory served as chairman of a Harlem Community Planning Board, which oversaw extensive redevelopment and public works programs in the area. He retired from active political life in 1970 but remained a fixture in the community until his death in 1994.

Gregory Bond

FURTHER READING
Ashe, Arthur R., Jr. *A Hard Road to Glory*. Vol. 2. New York: Warner Books, 1988.

Chalk, Ocania. *Black College Sport*. New York: Dodd, Mead, 1975.

Lyons, Richard D. "George Gregory, Jr." *New York Times*, May 21, 1994.

★ ★ ★

Rosey GRIER

Born July 14, 1932, Cuthbert, Georgia
Football player

Grier was a college athlete, professional football player, activist, artist, and entertainer. He was the seventh of eleven children born to Joseph and Ruth Grier. The family moved north to Roselle, New Jersey, and Rosey attended Roselle High School. After graduating in 1950 Rosey attended Penn State University, where he participated in football and track and field. In 1955 Grier was drafted by the New York Giants of the National Football League. At six feet, five inches, and 300 pounds, Grier was an imposing and dominant NFL defensive tackle. In 1964 he was traded to the Los Angeles Rams of the NFL.

Grier, along with fellow defensive tackle Lamar Lundy and defensive ends Deacon Jones and Merlin Olsen, formed a unit that became known as the "Fearsome Foursome." Rosey's career lasted from 1955 to 1968, including time in the U.S. Army. Grier also has talents as a musician, actor, and needlepoint artist. As a political activist, serving on Senator Robert F. Kennedy's presidential campaign staff in 1968, Grier captured Sirhan Sirhan immediately after he assassinated Kennedy during a speech in California. Rosey has been married three times, twice to the same person, Marge Grier, and once to Beatrice Lewis. He has a daughter, Denise, from his first wife (Beatrice) and a son, Roosevelt Kennedy, from Marge. Grier was very active in politics during the 2000 presidential election.

James R. Coates, Jr.

FURTHER READING

Grier, Rosey. *Rosey, An Autobiography: The Gentle Giant*. Tulsa, OK: Honor Books, 1986.

Porter, David L., ed. *Biographical Dictionary of American Sports: Football*. Westport, CT: Greenwood Press, 1987.

Rosey Grier's All American Heroes: Multicultural Success Stories. MasterMedia Publishing, 1993.

★ ★ ★

Ken GRIFFEY, JR.

Born November 21, 1969, Donora, Pennsylvania
Baseball player

Son of former major league star Ken Griffey, Ken Jr. was drafted out of Cincinnati Moeller High School by the Seattle Mariners as the number-one pick in June 1987. He was traded to Cincinnati in 2000. As of 2000, Griffey had played in ten All-Star games, won ten Gold Gloves, won seven Silver Slugger awards, had been voted Most Valuable Player (MVP) in the American League (in 1997, when he became only the ninth unanimous American League MVP winner, while leading the AL in home runs, runs batted in, runs, total bases, and slugging percentage), and had been the All-Star MVP (in 1992). He is the third-youngest player ever to reach 150 home runs, the fourth-youngest ever to hit 250 home runs, the second-youngest ever to reach 300 home runs, and the youngest in baseball history to reach 400 home runs. In 1999 he was voted the Players' Choice Player of the Decade. He and his dad were the first father-son duo to play simultaneously in the major leagues. Griffey shares the major league record for consecutive games with one or more home runs (eight), set in 1993. He also holds the Seattle Mariners franchise all-time records for most runs (1,063), hits (1,742), home runs (398), and runs batted in (1,152). Griffey is deeply involved with the Make-A-Wish Foundation, which presented him with its 1994 Celebrity Recognition Award.

Larry S. Bonura

FURTHER READING
"Biography on Ken Griffey Jr." *Ken's Klubhouse* (griffeyjr.com/biography/).
Holway, John B., and Bob Carroll. "The 400 Greatest," *Baseball Almanac* (www.baseball-almanac.com/legendary/li400gr.shtml).
Ken Griffey Jr. (www.kgjonline.com/info.html).
"Ken Griffey Jr." *Sporting News: Baseball* (www.sportingnews.com/baseball/players/4305).
Shatzkin, Mike, ed. *The Ballplayers: Baseball's Ultimate Biographical Reference.* New York: Arbor House, 1990.

★ ★ ★

Florence GRIFFITH-JOYNER

Born December 21, 1959, Los Angeles, California
Died September 21, 1998, Mission Viejo, California
Sprinter

Few athletic careers have burned as brightly but briefly as Florence Griffith-Joyner's. "Flo Jo," as she was called, turned in a brilliant performance at the 1988 Olympics, only to retire shortly afterward and die suddenly at age thirty-eight. Few athletes have combined skill and style like Griffith-Joyner did.

Griffith-Joyner grew up poor in the Watts section of Los Angeles, the seventh of eleven children. At age seven she began running track and regularly beating her male counterparts. As an adolescent she exhibited the flair and eccentricities that marked her style as a track star. Griffith-Joyner graduated from LA's Jordan High in 1978 and entered Cal State-Northridge that fall. She was forced to quit after her freshman year due to lack of funding, and she took a job as a bank teller. In 1980, she followed Bob Kersee, a Northridge sprint coach, to UCLA.

After winning an NCAA championship in the 200 meters, Griffith-Joyner won the silver medal in that event at the 1984 Los Angeles Olympics. She dropped out of track for a time after the games, and in 1987 she married Al Joyner, the 1984 Triple Jump champion. Joyner's sister, Jackie, was the wife of Bob Kersee and the reigning heptathlon champion.

Griffith-Joyner's star reached its zenith at the 1988 Seoul Olympics. After shaving more than a quarter of a second off the world 100-meter record at the U.S. Olympic trials, she went to Seoul and won gold medals in the 100, 200, and 400-meter races and a silver medal in the 4 x 400-meter relay. She also captured the world record for the 200 in Seoul. Griffith-Joyner's accomplishments on the track were magnified by her long, iridescent fingernails, flowing hair, and exotic beauty.

Her meteoric rise and dominating performance at the Olympics raised whispers of drug usage, especially in light of Canadian sprinter Ben Johnson's disqualification for a positive drug test. These rumors continued when Griffith-Joyner suddenly retired from the sport just five months after the games, even though she passed eleven drug tests in 1988. After her retirement, Griffith-Joyner developed her own beauty and clothing lines, wrote children's books, and became a mother. She died in her sleep of asphyxiation from an epileptic seizure on September 21, 1998. Ironically, she was serving as spokeswoman for the President's Council on Physical Fitness at the time of her death.

Richard D. Loosbrock

See also: Olympic Games; Track and Field.

FURTHER READING

"My Flo Jo" *Florence Griffith Joyner: The World's Fastest Woman* (www.cmgww.com/sports/aljoyner/myflojo.html); (www.florencegriffithjoyner.com/).

Noden, Merrell. "FloJo Lived Her Life in Fast Forward." *Sports Illustrated*, September 22, 1998.

Stewart, Mark. *Florence Griffith-Joyner.* New York: Scholastic Library, 1996.

★ ★ ★

Tony GWYNN

Born May 9, 1960, Los Angeles, California
Baseball player

The second of three sons of Charles, a warehouseman, and Vendella, a postal clerk. After graduating from Long Beach (CA) Polytechnic High School and San Diego State University, he became a professional baseball player and just the twenty-second player to record more than 3,000 base hits.

Gwynn attended college on a basketball scholarship but excelled in baseball too and was drafted by the San Diego Padres of the National League (NL) and the San Diego Clippers of the National Basketball Association on the same day. Choosing baseball, he spent parts of three seasons in the minor leagues before joining the Padres, with whom he played his entire twenty-year career.

Batting better than .300 nineteen years in a row, including .394 in 1994, he led the league in hits seven times and won eight batting championships, four of them consecutively (1994–1997), to tie Honus Wagner's NL record. He appeared in postseason play three times, batting .368 in the 1984 National League Championship Series and .500 in the 1996 World Series.

Gwynn used video technology to study his swing and practiced hard to improve his fielding. He won five Gold Glove awards for fielding excellence and was an NL All-Star fifteen times. He got his 3,000th hit on August 6, 1999.

Known for his outgoing and generous personality, Gwynn returned to San Diego State as a baseball coach following his retirement.

Steven P. Gietschier

See also: Baseball.

FURTHER READING

Attner, Paul. "Boggs and Gwynn, Masters of Trade, Tell How They Put Bat on Ball." *Sporting News*, September 18, 1989.

Collier, Phil. "He's a Big Hit with the Padres." *Sporting News*, July 23, 1984.

Gwynn, Tony, with Jim Geschke. *Tony!* Chicago: Contemporary Books, 1986.

★ ★ ★

GYMNASTICS

The first black gymnast of national acclaim was Mike Carter, from Louisiana State University (1973–1975). A three-time All-American, Carter's specialties included floor exercises (third in 1974), the all-around (sixth in 1974 and third in 1975), and the parallel bars (eleventh in 1973).

Ron Galimore, son of Chicago Bears football player Willie Galimore, became the only gymnast to win NCAA individual titles in four different years, between 1978 and 1981. Matriculating at Louisiana State in 1977, he transferred to Iowa State, where he was holder of seven records, including scoring a perfect "ten" in the 1980 Big Eight Championships. His specialties included vaulting (NCAA champion in 1978, 1980, and 1981) and floor exercises (AAU champion). Internationally, he was a member of the 1980 U.S. Olympic Team, Coca Cola International Invitation in Canada,

1977 World University Games, and the 1977 United States tour to Bulgaria.

The first internationally ranked female gymnast was Diane Durham from Houston, Texas. Beginning at an early age, she won the United States Junior Championships in 1981 and 1982 in floor exercises, vault, parallel bars, and the balance beam. She was National Senior winner the following year in the same events. She might have been the winner of the Los Angeles Olympic games instead of Mary Lou Retton, but injury before the 1984 Olympic trials prevented her participation. Durham trained alongside Retton with legendary coach Bela Karolyi in Houston. The leg injury kept her off the 1984 team. Durham influenced many young African-American girls to join gymnastics, most notably Olympians Betty Okino and Dominique Dawes.

Other greats have included Charles Lakes from St. Louis, Missouri, the first black gymnast to compete in the Olympics (1988), and Okino and Naomi Hewitt-Courtourier, Olympic contenders. Dominique Dawes came on the scene in 1992 as an Olympic bronze medalist, 1992 national uneven bars champion, and 1992 World Championships team member.

Dawes won the 1996 Olympic Trials and all four events at the 1996 Coca Cola National Championships. A four-time world championships medalist, she has won more national championships since 1983 (fifteen) than any other athlete, male or female. She swept the 1994 Coca Cola National Championships, winning the all-around and all four-event titles, the first gymnast to accomplish this feat since Joyce Tanac Schroeder won the all-around and all four events at the 1969 AAU National Championships. Dawes won the 1995 Arch McDonald Award, presented by the Touchdown Club of Washington, DC. She also won the 1995 Henry P. Iba Citizen Athlete Award, presented annually to two outstanding athletes who have demonstrated good citizenship. She was named 1994 Sportsperson of the Year by USA Gymnastics and was a finalist for the 1994 AAU Sullivan Award, which recognizes the USA's top amateur athlete. Her coach and teammates call her "Awesome Dawesome."

Dawes returned to gymnastics in April 2000 in an attempt to make her third Olympic team with longtime coach Kelli Hill. After the 1996 Olympics, Dawes decided to attend the University of Maryland. She is also pursuing a career in television production.

Tasha Schwikert is currently ranked number one in the country and fifth in the world. In the beginning of 2000, she competed at the 2000 RCA Challenge, 2000 American Cup, and won the 2000 American Classic. Becoming a member of the 2000 Olympic team after Morgan White had broken her foot, Tasha helped Team USA place fourth. In 2001 she won the 2001 U.S. Classic, 2001 U.S. Nationals, and 2001 World Championships.

Success for most gymnasts has come from training early with private coaches in gyms rather than introduction to the sport in public school programs. The expense may have been a constraint for children of color, but as the sport grows, especially at the college level, so does the number of black varsity athletes.

Brenda P. Wiggins

See also: Dominique Dawes.

FURTHER READING
Ashe, Arthur R., Jr. *A Hard Road to Glory: A History of the African-American Athlete Since 1946.* Vol. 3. New York: Amistad, 1993.
"Breaking the Barriers." *Houston Chronicle Special Section* (www.chron.com/content/chronicle/sports/special/barriers/others80s.html).
"Dominique Dawes." 2000. *U.S.A. Gymnastics Online* (www.usa-gymnastics.org/athletes/bios/d/ddawes.html).
Official Website of Tasha Schwikert (www.tashaschwikert.com).

Marvin HAGLER

Born May 23, 1954, Newark, New Jersey
Boxer

For most of the 1980s, prizefighter Marvelous Marvin Hagler (his legal name since 1982) dominated the middleweight division. Noted for his shaved head, menacing demeanor, and rugged fighting style, Hagler ranks among the best middleweights in history.

The oldest of Robert and Ida Mae Hagler's seven children, Hagler moved with his family from Newark, New Jersey, to Brockton, Massachusetts, after race riots engulfed his hometown in the late 1960s. Soon thereafter, he quit high school, got a job to help support his family, and began boxing. Hagler won fifty-seven fights as an amateur and the 1973 Amateur Athletic Union middleweight championship before turning professional.

By 1976, Hagler had won his first thirty-four fights, before losing close decisions to Philadelphians Bobby Watts and Willie Monroe in Philadelphia. Hagler later avenged both losses with knockouts. On November 30, 1979, Hagler fought Vito Antuofermo for the middleweight title, but the fight ended in a draw. In London's Wembley Stadium, on September 27, 1980, after three more successful fights, Hagler dominated middleweight champion Alan Minter, winning on a technical knockout in the third round.

Hagler defended his title twelve times over the next six years, including victories over Roberto Durán and Thomas Hearns. The fight with Hearns, the World Boxing Council (WBC) junior-middleweight champion, on April 15, 1987, was particularly exciting, though it lasted just over eight minutes. From the fight alone, Hagler reportedly earned at least $7.5 million. Following a successful defense against John Mugabi, Hagler fought former welterweight and junior middleweight champ Sugar Ray Leonard, who had been retired for three years. Leonard won the controversial split decision for the WBC middleweight title. It was Hagler's first loss in eleven years. Leonard refused to give Hagler a rematch.

Shortly thereafter, a frustrated Hagler retired from boxing, with a 62–3–2 record (including fifty-two KOs), and moved to Milan, Italy, where he occasionally acts in Italian action movies. He was inducted into the International Boxing Hall of Fame in 1993.

Daniel A. Nathan

See also: Boxing; Thomas Hearns; Sugar Ray Leonard.

FURTHER READING
Arnold, Peter. *The Illustrated Encyclopedia of World Boxing.* New York: Gallery Books, 1989.
Berger, Phil. *Punch Lines: Berger on Boxing.* New York: Four Walls Eight Windows, 1993.
Brooke-Ball, Peter. *The Boxing Album: An Illustrated History.* New York: Smithmark, 1992.
Kimball, George. "The 20th Century's Top 10 Middleweights." *Boston Herald,* July 24, 1999, 70.
Marvelous Marvin Hagler (www.ibhof.com/hagler.htm).
Porter, David L., ed. *African-American Sports Greats: A Biographical Dictionary.* Westport, CT: Greenwood Press, 1995.

★ ★ ★

HARLEM GLOBETROTTERS

The Harlem Globetrotters are a barnstorming, African-American basketball team founded in Chicago in 1926. In the post–World War II era, the team became world famous for its fancy dribbling, passing, and comedy antics on the court. The Globetrotters are known as the "Clown Princes of Basketball."

The Globetrotters were formed from the nucleus of the Wendell Phillips High School team, the first African-American squad to win the Chicago city championship. Dick Hudson, an ex-National Football League player, arranged for the team to play games at the famed Savoy Ballroom in Chicago; it became known as the Savoy Big Five. Unable to book games in the Midwest because of the racial climate of the era, Hudson and Walter Ball, a former Negro League pitcher, arranged for Abe Saperstein, a white promoter, to take the team on the road. Saperstein dressed the players in bright red, white, and blue uniforms and renamed the team the Harlem Globetrotters.

The Globetrotters were highly successful barnstorming the Midwest during the late 1920s and the early 1930s, winning nearly 90 percent of their games. After several seasons, Saperstein realized that small-town fans did not enjoy watching their local teams lose by often large margins. He began to include various gimmicks, stunt plays, fancy passing and dribbling, and comedy routines to keep the fans entertained and interested. The popularity of the team soared, and comedy became a Globetrotters' trademark. The team later developed a warmup drill to the musical accompaniment of "Sweet Georgia Brown"; it became a signature routine. The Globetrotters, however, could play excellent "straight" basketball. From 1939 to 1945, they competed in the World Professional Basketball Tournament held in Chicago Stadium and won the championship in 1940. After World War II, the Globetrotters also defeated the world champion Minneapolis Lakers in exhibition games before sellout crowds in Chicago.

By the 1950s the Globetrotters were the most popular basketball team in the world. In 1951, they played before a record crowd of 75,000 at the Olympic Stadium in Berlin. The Globetrotters were also a huge draw in large arenas in the United States. When the National Basketball Association (NBA) was formed in 1949, the owners banned African-American players, in part, because they feared offending Saperstein, who played in their arenas and controlled the best black professional players. The ban was overturned in 1950 at the insistence of New York Knickerbocker owner Ned Irish, who immediately signed the Globetrotters' star, Nat "Sweetwater" Clifton. With the NBA integrated, Saperstein could no longer depend on signing the best African-American players for the Globetrotters.

Over the years, the Globetrotters have had numerous talented and entertaining players. The first showman was Inman Jackson, who could palm the ball and roll it up his arms and across his shoulders, and was an excellent faker. He was followed by Reece "Goose" Tatum, Meadowlark Lemon, and many others. Marques Haynes earned a reputation as "the world's greatest dribbler" as a member of the Globetrotters. In addition to Clifton, future NBA stars Wilt Chamberlain and Connie Hawkins played with the Globetrotters. The Harlem Globetrotters continue to tour the U.S. and have played in nearly 100 countries.

John M. Carroll

See also: Basketball; Wilt Chamberlain; Connie Hawkins; Meadowlark Lemon; Reece "Goose" Tatum.

FURTHER READING
Gould, Todd. *Pioneers of the Hardwood: Indiana and the Birth of Professional Basketball.* Bloomington: Indiana University Press, 1998.
Nack, William. "On the Road Again." *Sports Illustrated*, April 22, 1985, 78–92.

Peterson, Robert W. *Cages to Jump Shots: Pro Basketball's Early Years.* New York: Oxford University Press, 1990.

★ ★ ★

Franco HARRIS

Born March 7, 1950, Fort Dix, New Jersey
Football player

The third of nine children born to an African-American serviceman (Cad Harris) and an Italian immigrant "war bride" (Gina Parenti), Franco Harris graduated from Rancocas Valley Regional High School and Penn State University and went on to become one of the greatest NFL running backs of all time.

In 1972, after a distinguished football career in high school and college, Franco Harris was drafted by the Pittsburgh Steelers in the first round, thirteenth overall. In his first season, Harris's cutting, deceptive style earned him over 1,000 yards rushing and the AFC Rookie of the Year award. Over his next eleven seasons with the Steelers, Harris was selected to nine Pro Bowl appearances, led the team to four Super Bowl victories, and was named Most Valuable Player of Super Bowl IX (1975). Coupled with his gridiron prowess, Harris's mixed ethnic ancestry made him a celebrity in both the African-American and Italian-American communities of Pittsburgh, the latter creating a highly publicized fan group called Franco's Italian Army.

Off of the field, Harris developed a reputation for a kind, caring nature and frequent acts of charity. He spent much of his free time raising money for a variety of charities and often consoled ill and disabled children at Pittsburgh area hospitals. In recognition of his humanitarian efforts and service to the community, Harris received the NFL Man of the Year Award in 1976 and the Byron "Whizzer" White Humanitarian Award in 1982. After a long career with the Steelers, Harris played the 1984 season, his last, with the Seattle Seahawks. Upon retirement from football, Harris returned to Pittsburgh and became a successful businessman. In 1990, Harris was inducted into the Pro Football Hall of Fame.

Nicholas P. Ciotola

FURTHER READING
Anderson, Dave. "Breakthrough in Pittsburgh: Franco Harris and His Italian Army." *Sport*, November 1973, 60–71.
Ciotola, Nicholas P. "Spignesi, Sinatra, and the Pittsburgh Steelers: Franco's Italian Army as an Expression of Ethnic Identity, 1972–1977." *Journal of Sport History* 27 (Summer 2000): 271–89.
Franco Harris: Good Luck on Sunday, prod. Richard Rubenstein, dir. George Romero, 46 min., Hinzman Production Company, 1999, videocassette.
Kowet, Don. *Franco Harris*. New York: Coward, McCann and Geoghegan, 1977.
Reid, Ron. "Black and Gold Soul with Italian Legs." *Sports Illustrated*, December 11, 1972, 36–37.

★ ★ ★

Frank HART

Born 1857, Haiti
Died Unknown
Pedestrian racer

Hart resided in Boston and worked as a grocery store clerk for six years before becoming a professional pedestrian racer. He entered his first pedestrian race in April 1879 at the Boston Music Hall and completed 119½ miles in thirty hours. He hired Fred Englehardt as his trainer and Daniel O'Leary, the legendary pedestrian, as his financial backer. Given his relationship with O'Leary and his promise, Hart was nicknamed "Black Dan." Hart placed fourth in the 1879 Astley Belt Race held at

Madison Square Garden, completing 482 miles and earning $2,730. During this race, it was rumored that a fan had poisoned Hart, but that was strongly denied by Englehardt and O'Leary.

Hart competed in many pedestrian races, often earning prize and gate money. He set an American record for 131 miles in twenty-four hours at the 1880 O'Leary race and won the six-day race, completing 565 miles. This distance beat the previous record by twelve miles and earned Hart approximately $17,000.

Hart and other blacks participated in numerous pedestrian races. Hart was popular with many fans and frequently received flowers during races. However, he faced racism, including the unwillingness of other racers to shake his hand at the starting line. Additionally, he confronted racial taunts and violent threats from spectators.

Sara A. Elliott

FURTHER READING
Collins, Kelly. "Old Time Walk and Run." *Ultramarathon Running* (www.lehigh.edu/dmd1/public/www-data/kelly.html), December 11, 1996.
"The Contest for the Belt." *New York Times*, September 18, 1879.
"Frank Hart the Winner." *New York Times*, April 11, 1880.
"Hart First in the Race." *New York Times*, December 28, 1879.
Osler, Tom, and Ed Dodd. *Ultra-Marathoning: The Next Challenge*. Mountain View, CA: World, 1979.

★ ★ ★

Connie HAWKINS

Born July 17, 1942, Brooklyn, New York
Basketball player

The son of Iziah and Dorothy Hawkins, Hawkins was one of the greatest high school basketball players ever to play in New York City. Rejected by the National

Connie Hawkins, recently traded from the Phoenix Suns, shows off his new Los Angeles Lakers' uniform prior to a 1973 game against the New York Knicks. *(AP/Wide World Photos)*

Basketball Association (NBA) because of his alleged involvement in a 1961 college basketball scandal, Hawkins entered the American Basketball League (ABL), where after averaging 27.5 for the champion Pittsburgh Rens he was voted the league MVP. After playing five years with the Globetrotters, Hawkins joined the newly formed American Basketball League (ABL), from 1967 to 1969 parlaying two outstanding seasons into one MVP award and two first All-ABL selections. The book *Foul: The Connie Hawkins Story* is a classic treatise on Hawkins' life growing up in a squalid environment, the unsavory aspects of college basketball in the 1950s, and his professional career.

After prevailing in a multimillion dollar lawsuit in 1969 forcing the NBA to open its doors to him, he joined Phoenix as a twenty-seven-year-old rookie. Playing in the NBA for seven years, clearly in the twilight of his career, Hawkins was still named to the All-NBA first team in 1970, averaging 24.6 points, and played in four NBA All-Star Games. In 1992 he was elected to the Naismith Memorial Basketball Hall of Fame. Hawkins is often credited by those who saw him play in his prime with introducing "showmanship," including the slam dunk, to professional basketball.

Albert J. Figone

See also: Harlem Globetrotters.

FURTHER READING
Figone, Albert J. "Jack Molinas and the 1951–61 College Basketball Scandals." Paper read at the annual meeting of the North American Society for Sport History, Auburn, AL, May 1996.
George, Nelson. *Elevating the Game: Black Men and Basketball.* New York: HarperCollins, 1992.
Goodrich, Jim. "Sun Finally Rises for Connie Hawkins." *Ebony*, February 1970, 36–38.
Hollander, Zander, ed. *Modern Encyclopedia of Basketball.* Rev. ed. Garden City, NY: Dolphin Books, 1979.
Wolf, David. *Foul: The Connie Hawkins Story.* New York: Holt, Rinehart and Winston, 1972.

★ ★ ★

Bob HAYES

Born December 20, 1942, Jacksonville, Florida
Died September 18, 2002, Jacksonville, Florida
Sprinter, football player

Once regarded as the "world's fastest human," Bob Hayes, the son of John and Mary Hayes, was an all-around athlete in high school, playing football and basketball in addition to running track. At Florida A & M University, he was a running back and kick returner for the football team but quickly became better known for his accomplishments in track. He won three AAU championships in the 100-yard dash

Bob Hayes breaking the world record in the 100-meters (with a time of 9.1) at the National A.A.U. Track and Field Championships in St. Louis in 1963. *(AP/Wide World Photos)*

and one NCAA outdoor title in the 200-yard dash. During the 1963 and 1964 seasons, he was undefeated at 100 yards, and he won a gold medal at the Tokyo Olympics of 1964 by the largest margin (seven feet) in the history of the games. He won a second gold medal for running the anchor leg on the 400-meter relay team.

In 1966, he joined the Dallas Cowboys of the National Football League as a pass receiver and kick return specialist. He played nine seasons with the Cowboys (1966–1974) and finished his football career with the San Francisco 49ers in 1975. His speed caused NFL defensive coaches to install zone-defense systems, since defensive backs could not keep up with Hayes in man-to-man coverage.

After his retirement from football, Hayes held various jobs. In 1979, he was convicted of selling cocaine to an undercover agent and served nearly eleven months of a five-year jail sentence. In more recent years, he battled health problems, notably prostate cancer, but was able to attend his induction into the Dallas

Cowboy's Ring of Honor in September 2001.

John E. Findling

See also: Track and Field.

FURTHER READING
Dallas Morning Herald, September 23, 2001.
New York Times, October 14, 1979; February 28, 1980.
Page, James A. *Black Olympian Medalists.* Englewood, CO: Libraries Unlimited, 1991.
Porter, David L., ed. *Biographical Dictionary of American Sports: Outdoor Sports.* Westport, CT: Greenwood Press, 1988.

★ ★ ★

Elvin HAYES

Born November 17, 1945, Rayville, Louisiana
Basketball player

During his formative years, Elvin Hayes's father fought racism in segregated Rayville, Louisiana, by teaching his son to earn and demand respect. When Hayes was laughed at for his poor basketball skills as an eighth-grader, he responded by practicing long hours and by becoming a starting center for his high school basketball team. In his senior year, he led his team to the state championship.

The newly desegregated University of Houston provided him a scholarship to play; he was the first black athlete to play on the Cougars basketball team. His college career was capped by one of the most thrilling of all college basketball games. In 1968, he helped the Cougars defeat the favored UCLA Bruins, who were led at the time by Lew Alcindor (Kareem Abdul-Jabbar). Ten years later, Hayes earned one of the rarest of trifectas, when he led his professional team, the Washington Bullets, to the NBA championship.

After retiring from the NBA in 1984, Hayes spent two years at the University of Houston, completing degrees in speech and recreation. He next purchased a Texas ranch and a Houston car dealership, which he renamed Elvin Hayes Ford. He has also remained active with the National Basketball Association as a spokesperson and participated in the 2000 All-Star Game activities as the coach of the second-year players NBA class.

Gregory S. Goodale

FURTHER READING
"Elvin Hayes," *NBA.com* (www.nba.com/history/hayes_bio.html).
Herskowitz, Mickey. "Jordan Will Need a Wizard's Touch." *Houston Chronicle*, January 21, 2000.
"NBA's Young Players Need Guidance from Old Guard." *Slam Sports* (www.canoe.ca/Slam010212/nba_fut-st.html), February 12, 2001.

★ ★ ★

Marques HAYNES

Born October 3, 1926, Sand Springs, Oklahoma
Basketball player

Often called the greatest dribbler of all time, Marques Haynes learned his trade as a child on the sidelines of playgrounds near Tulsa, Oklahoma. The older children did not pick him for their teams; he practiced his craft while they played. He learned so well that he earned second-team All-American honors while leading Booker T. Washington High School to a black high school national championship.

Haynes played basketball at Langston University in Oklahoma, where he was the Most Valuable Player of his conference, leading his team to a 112–3 record. His patented routine was first displayed in the last two minutes of a conference championship game. While a player there, Langston defeated two professional teams, including the Harlem Globetrotters. Beating the Globetrotters caught the attention of Abe Saperstein. After graduating from college in 1946, he began touring with the Kansas City Stars before being called up to the Globetrotters later that year. During his six years playing with the team, the Globetrotter beat George Mikan's Lakers twice (1948 and 1949) and also the College All-Stars of 1950. They were billed as the world champions.

In 1953, Haynes had a contract dispute with Saperstein. Saperstein reportedly said, "A black man didn't need as much money as a white man." Incensed by their treatment, both Haynes and teammate Goose Tatum left the Globetrotters. As partners they started their own team, the Magicians. They remained partners for two years, until Tatum started his own team.

In 1972 Haynes came back to the Globetrotters as player and coach after nineteen years as owner, manager, coach, player, and bus driver of his own team. In 1979 he left them again but remained in basketball until 1992, playing for the Bucketeers, the Harlem Wizards, and again with the Magicians before retiring.

His early years were dominated by oppressive racial segregation. Haynes has been accused of being an "Uncle Tom" because he seemingly pandered to largely white audiences, but his reputation as a person of integrity in business and positive demeanor may have had an important role in the process of racial desegregation. In 1998 Haynes was enshrined in the Basketball Hall of Fame. He holds membership in five other halls of fame, including the NAIA's.

Rick Knott

FURTHER READING
Basketball Hall of Fame (www.hoophall.com/halloffamers/Haynes.htm).

Deford, Frank. "The Bouncing Ball." *Sports Illustrated*, December 3, 1973, 108–28.
Nack, William. "On the Road Again and Again and . . ." *Sports Illustrated*, April 22, 1985, 78–92.
Vecsey, George. *Harlem Globetrotters*. New York: Scholastic Books, 1970.
Young, A.S. "Doc." "Basketball's Black Entrepreneur." *Ebony*, March 1971, 96–103.

★ ★ ★

Spencer HAYWOOD

Born April 22, 1949, Silver City, Mississippi
Basketball player

Haywood, whose father was a carpenter, graduated from Detroit Pershing High School. He then attended junior college at Trinidad State in Colorado from 1967 to 1968 and college at the University of Detroit (1968–1969).

Haywood led his high school to the Class A Michigan State Championship in 1967. After averaging twenty-eight points per game at Trinidad State, he transferred to the University of Detroit. He averaged thirty-two points per game for his one season at the university and was selected for the 1968 U.S. Olympic basketball team, which won a gold medal.

At the end of his sophomore year, he was drafted by the Denver Rockets of the American Basketball Association (ABA). He was ABA Rookie of the Year and the League's Most Valuable Player. He was a first-team All-Star and MVP of the All-Star Game in 1970, averaging thirty points per game for the season. He left the ABA after one season for the National Basketball Association (NBA), where he played for the Seattle SuperSonics (1970–1975), the New York Knicks (1975–1979), the New Orleans Jazz (1979), and the Los Angeles Lakers (1979–1980). He was a member of the Lakers NBA Championship team. He finished his NBA career in 1981–1983 with the Washington Capitols and played professional basketball in Italy during 1980–1982.

A period of substance abuse and subsequent rehabilitation led to an unsuccessful reentry into the NBA in the mid-1980s. However, following his positive association with Detroit mayor Whitney Young and several Detroit businessmen, Haywood redirected his life to business and philanthropy. He founded the Spencer Haywood Foundation for media projects and substance abuse-prevention programs and was associated with a computer training program company that aided prison education programs. He was financially involved with a multi-unit apartment complex near downtown Detroit and continued these endeavors through the 1990s.

John R. Schleppi

FURTHER READING
Detroit News, April 8, 1991.
Haywood, Spencer. *The Spencer Haywood Story*. New York: Tempo, 1972.
Hubbard, Jan, ed. *The Official NBA Encyclopedia*. 3d ed. New York: Doubleday, 2000.
Walton, David, and John Hareas, eds. *The Sporting News Official NBA Register*. 2000–2001 ed. St. Louis: Sporting News, 2000.

★ ★ ★

Thomas HEARNS

Born October 18, 1958, Memphis, Tennessee
Boxer

Thomas Hearns was the third child born to John and Lois Hearns. When his parents separated, he moved with his grandfather, mother, and two older siblings to Detroit, Michigan. His mother's second marriage produced six more children.

Hearns began boxing at age ten, and by age fourteen he was traveling across town in order to train at the well-known Kronk's Gym under the tutelage of Emanuel Stewart. Hearns lost three of his first four amateur fights, and Stewart saw very little natural ability. By the time he turned professional, however, his amateur record was 155-8. Hearns had fought two AAU championship fights, losing the first but winning the second with a broken nose.

At six feet, two inches and with a 78½-inch reach, he had an advantage over nearly every fighter he ever faced in the ring. His reach advantage gave him knockout power he never seemed to have had as an amateur. Hearns came to be known as Thomas "Hit Man" Hearns and the "Motor City Cobra," nicknames he always attempted to live down. At one time he held six different titles in five different weight classes, from the welterweight (147-pound) through the light heavyweight (175-pound) division.

His professional career lasted twenty-three years and included famous fights with Marvin Hagler and Ray Leonard. Although his second fight against Leonard ended in a draw, it will be remembered as one of the greatest fights of the century. After he lost a second fight in 1992 to Iran Barkley, considered by many experts to be a club fighter (second-rate fighter), he dropped out of the national scene. Hearns continued fighting occasionally through April 2000, because, he claimed, he enjoyed it. At the age of forty-one, Hearns retired to become a fight promoter. Throughout his career, he was involved in helping underprivileged youth in the Detroit area.

Rick Knott

See also: Boxing; Marvin Hagler; Sugar Ray Leonard.

FURTHER READING
Gordon, Randy. "Pulling No Punches: An Interview with Thomas Hearns." *Ring*, October 1980, 37–39.

King, Peter, ed. "Closeup on Thomas Hearns. *KO Magazine*, December 1983, 35.
Putnam, Pat. "The Last of the Legends." *Sports Illustrated*, June 17, 1991, 61–65.
Seconds Out (www.secondsout.com/legends).
"Thomas 'Hit Man' Hearns." *Ebony*, February 1981, 137–42.

★ ★ ★

Edwin Bancroft HENDERSON

Born November 24, 1883, Washington, DC
Died February 3, 1977, Tuskegee, Alabama
Educator, coach, administrator, activist

The son of William, a government worker, and Louisa, a housewife, Henderson graduated from the famous M Street School in Washington, DC, attended Dudley Allen Sargent's celebrated Harvard Summer School of Physical Education, and took degrees from Howard University (BA) and Columbia University (MA). A man of diverse talents and many interests, Henderson spent his professional life as a physical educator, coach, athletic administrator, civil rights activist, and historian of African-American athletes.

Henderson headed the Department of Physical Education in the segregated Washington, DC, school systems from 1925 until his appointment some twenty-six years later as director of physical education, safety and athletics. He held many offices as well and either founded or cofounded several professional organizations within and outside sports. He was, among other things, a member and officeholder in such organizations as the Committee for Coordinating Recreational Plans in the District of Columbia, the Joint Army and Navy Committee on Recreation, and the District of Columbia's 12th Street Branch of the Young Men's Christian Association. He introduced basketball to the Washington school system and organized the Public School Athletic League. He cofounded the Washington, DC, Pigskin Club and established such organizations as the Inter-Scholastic Athletic Association of Middle Atlantic States, the Washington, DC, chapter of the American Alliance for Health, Physical Education, Recreation, and Dance (AAHPERD), and the Falls Church, Virginia, branch of the National Association for the Advancement of Colored People.

Henderson was also a prolific writer. He published many articles and book chapters on African Americans in sport and co-edited the *Official Handbook: Inter-Scholastic Athletic Association of Middle Atlantic States*. He has the distinction of writing the first books on the history of African-American athletes. *The Negro in Sports* (1939, 1949) and *The Black Athlete: Emergence and Arrival* (1968) have served as models for subsequent books on the subject. Henderson fought, moreover, various forms of racial discrimination throughout his life. He battled against segregated transportation facilities in Virginia, led fights to eliminate segregated recreational and sports programs in Washington, DC, and attempted to stop southern states from excluding African Americans from membership in local AAHPERD chapters.

Henderson was honored for his many accomplishments. He was a recipient of the YMCA Distinguished Service Award, was given a Presidential Citation and honor award by AAHPERD, was selected honorary president of the North American Society for Sport History, and in 1974 was chosen as a charter member of the Black Athletes Hall of Fame.

David K. Wiggins

See also: Basketball; Historiography.

FURTHER READING

Coursey, Leon N. "The Life of Edwin Bancroft Henderson and His Professional Contributions to Physical Education." Ph.D. diss., Ohio State University, 1971.

Henderson, James H.M., and Betty F. Henderson. *Molder of Men: Portrait of a 'Grand Old Man': Edwin Bancroft Henderson.* Washington, DC: Vantage Press, 1985.

Stuart, Greg. "The Beginning of Tomorrow." *Black Sports*, February 1972, 62–67.

Wiggins, David K. "Edwin Bancroft Henderson: Physical Educator, Civil Rights Activist and Chronicler of African American Athletes." *Research Quarterly for Exercise and Sport* 70 (June 1999): 91–112.

———. *Glory Bound: Black Athletes in a White America.* Syracuse, NY: Syracuse University Press, 1997.

★ ★ ★

Rickey HENDERSON

Born December 25, 1957, Chicago, Illinois
Baseball player

Henderson graduated in 1976 from Oakland's Technical High School, where he played baseball, basketball, and football. He received two dozen scholarship offers to play college football. The A's were his favorite team as a youngster, and he now wears number twenty-four because "of the great Willie Mays."

He broke Lou Brock's record of 939 stolen bases on May 7, 1991, and he continues to play more than ten years after that date. He also continues to play twelve years after breaking Barry Bonds' record for leadoff home runs (Henderson is the all-time leader, with seventy-five leadoff home runs). He was selected as the American League's MVP in 1990.

The 2001 season was a memorable one. Three days before the end of the season, he broke Ty Cobb's career record for runs, scoring his 2,246th run. On the last day of the 2001 season, he lofted the first pitch off Colorado's John Thomson toward the right-field line; the ball dropped in about ten feet inside the line, and he became the twenty-fifth member of the 3,000-hit club. Henderson is the leader in bases on balls, with 2,141, and has 1,395 stolen bases. Henderson holds the distinction, moreover, of being one of just two players to play for a team four different times.

Henderson coauthored his autobiography, *Off Base: Confessions of a Thief*, following the 1991 season. Henderson and his wife Pam live with their daughters, Angela, Alexis, and Adrianne, in Hillsborough, California.

Clyde Partin

FURTHER READING

Ashe, Arthur R., Jr. *A Hard Road to Glory.* Vol. 3. New York: Warner Books, 1988.

Holway, John B. *Blackball Stars: Negro League Pioneers.* Westport, CT: Meckler Books, 1988.

Ribowsky, Mark. *A Complete History of the Negro Leagues, 1884 to 1955.* New York: Citadel Press, 2002.

★ ★ ★

Stephanie HIGHTOWER

Born July 19, 1958, Louisville, Kentucky
Hurdler

Stephanie Hightower is the daughter of James and Barbara Hightower and a graduate of Ohio State University. In 1975, while at Stuart High School, she set the Kentucky High School Athletic Association record in the 110-yard hurdles with a time of 14.3 seconds, and the sixty-yard hurdles in a record 8.0 seconds.

As a member of the Ohio State University (OSU) track team from 1977 to 1980, Hightower achieved outstanding accomplishments. She won Big Ten athletic conference championships fifteen times while at OSU, went undefeated in four years of

Stephanie Hightower capturing another title in the high hurdles at a Mobil indoor track and field meet in the early 1980s. *(AP/Wide World Photos)*

collegiate competition, and was named to the All-American team each year. Hightower earned a spot on the 1980 Olympic team in the 100-meter hurdles. In 1980 she set a world record of 7.47 seconds in the sixty-yard hurdles. Two years later she set an American record in the 100-meter hurdles with a time of 12.79 seconds. She was a five time Millrose Games hurdles champion (1980, 1982–1985).

Hightower's nickname was "little sticks," because of her relatively short stature, just over five feet, four inches. While this may seem a physical disadvantage for a hurdler, Hightower's quickness at the start and determination propelled her to the ranks of world-class athletes.

Following her athletic career Hightower served on the Columbus (OH) Board of Education. From 1996 to 1999 she served as an assistant to the mayor in charge of sports development. In 2001 she began a term as the special assistant to the president of Columbus College of Art and Design, in charge of external relations. Hightower is a member of the Ohio State University Athletic Hall of Fame and in 1993 was inducted into the Millrose Games Hall of Fame.

Rita Liberti

FURTHER READING
"Best Bets from the U.S." *Women's Sports and Fitness*, May 1984, 33–40.
Hendershott, Jon. "America's Leading Women Hurdlers: Stephanie Hightower and Benita Fitzgerald." *Track and Field News*, June 1982, 41.
Millrose Games (www.millrosegames.com).
Neff, Craig. "A Matched Pair and a Matchless Miler." *Sports Illustrated*, February 22, 1982, 18.

★ ★ ★

Calvin HILL

Born January 2, 1947, Baltimore, Maryland
Football player

Calvin Hill, the son of Henry and Elizabeth Hill, attended high school at Riverdale Country Day School in New York and was a member of the Yale University class of 1969, earning a B.A. in history. He attended Southern Methodist University from 1969 to 1971.

A big, tall athlete of great talent, Calvin Hill was tried at tight end, linebacker, and running back at the Dallas Cowboy's training camp in 1969, when he was a rookie. However, when Calvin returned to training camp after the College All-Star Game in Chicago, Coach Tom Landry decided to leave him at the running back position. In his first year with the Cowboys, Hill outperformed the NFL's number-one draft pick, O.J. Simpson, until he injured a foot late in the season; he consequently fell short of 1,000 rushing yards. In 1972 and 1973 Hill had 1,000-yard rushing seasons, and after six seasons he ranked second only to Don Perkins on the all-time Dallas rushing chart. He also led the Cowboys in receiving two years. Hill played for the Cowboys from 1969 until 1975, when he signed a contract with the Hawaiians of the World Football League. When the World Football League faltered, Hill joined the Washington Redskins for the 1976 and 1977 seasons. He was brought to the Cleveland Browns by coach Sam Rutigliano four weeks into the 1978 season to shore up an injury-depleted backfield and to provide veteran leadership for his young team. Hill played for the Browns until the close of the 1981 season, an integral part of the "Kardiac Kids'" success. He caught 107 passes in his four seasons with the Browns.

During the player's strike in 1982, Hill helped younger players weather the storm by providing financial support himself and getting players who were financially secure to help those who were less fortunate. Hill had married Janet McDonald in 1969, and their son Grant became an All-American basketball player at Duke University before becoming a superstar in the National Basketball Association with the Detroit Pistons and the Orlando Magic. Calvin Hill was on the board of directors of the Baltimore Orioles and the RAND Corporation Drug Policy Research Center. He was a member of the Yale Club of Washington, DC, and the Yale University Council. He currently is on the payroll of the Dallas Cowboys as a consultant with the team.

Keith McClellan

See also: Grant Hill.

FURTHER READING
Phelps, Shirelle, ed. *Who's Who Among Black Americans 1994/5*. 8th ed. Detroit: Gale Research, 1994.
Ridenour, Marla. "Calvin Hill: A Man of All Seasons." *Akron Beacon Journal*, August 8, 1999.

Zang, David W. "Calvin Hill Interview." *Journal of Sport History* 15 (Winter 1988): 334–55.

★ ★ ★

Grant HILL

Born October 5, 1972, Dallas, Texas
Basketball player

The only child of Calvin Hill, Yale graduate and NFL All-Pro running back, and Janet Hill, a graduate of Wellesley College, Grant Hill was brought up in the wealthy Washington, DC, suburb of Reston, Virginia, where he was challenged to be the best athlete he could by his talented and disciplined father. Hill rejected football for basketball and made the varsity team his freshman year at South Lakes High School.

Hill chose to attend Duke University, where he graduated with a B.A. in history in 1994. He helped Duke win NCAA championships in 1991 and again in 1992. At six feet, eight inches and 225 pounds, Hill was drafted number-three overall by the Detroit Pistons in 1994. At forward, he helped resurrect a declining Pistons team. He shared Rookie of the Year honors in 1995 and was the first rookie ever to lead in fan voting for the All-Star Game. In 1996 he led in All-Star votes again and was also named to the "dream team" that won a gold medal at the 1996 Olympics.

At a time when NBA players were becoming more flamboyant, Hill stood out as the ultimate "nice guy," exhibiting the good manners and sportsmanship he had learned from his father. Hill is a consistent All-Star, leading his team in triple doubles in 1999 for the third time, one of only three players (behind Elgin Baylor and Wilt Chamberlain) to have led their teams in all three categories at least three times.

Hill has been honored for his involvement in community service and his dedication to the prevention of child abuse. He married Tamia Washington, a well-known Canadian recording artist, in 1999.

Donna Abruzzese

See also: Calvin Hill.

FURTHER READING
Christopher, Matt. *On the Court with Grant Hill.* New York: Chelsea House, 1996.
Markiewicz, David A. "Grant Hill, Inc." *Detroit News*, February 12, 1995.
McCallum, Jack. "The Man." *Sports Illustrated*, 1996, 40.
National Basketball Association (www.nba.com/playerfile/grant_hil).
Plummer, William. "Shooting Star: Detroit Piston Rookie Is a Breath of Fresh Air." *People Weekly*, 1995, 74.
Who's Who in America, 2001. 55th ed. Chicago: Marquis Who's Who.

★ ★ ★

Jim HINES

Born September 10, 1946, Dumas, Arkansas
Sprinter, football player

The ninth of twelve children of Charlie, a construction worker, and Minnie West Hines, a canner, Jim Hines graduated from McClymonds High School in Oakland, California, in 1964 and from Texas Southern University in 1970. He became a world-record and Olympic champion sprinter, professional football player, and community activist.

Hines equaled the national high school record of 9.4 seconds for 100 yards and established a California state high school record of 20.7 seconds in the 220-yard dash. He won AAU national championships in the 220-yard dash in 1966 and in the 100-yard dash in 1967. Hines tied the world record of 9.1 seconds for 100 yards in 1967 and established a world record of 9.9 seconds in the 100 meters in 1968, to become the first man officially to break ten seconds for the distance. His 1968 Olympic gold medal performance in the 100 meters resulted in an electronically timed world record of 9.95 seconds. Hines garnered a second Olympic gold medal by anchoring the U.S. 4 x 100 meter relay team in the world-record time of 38.24 seconds. His world record in the 100 meters stood for nearly fifteen years, until Calvin Smith clocked 9.93 seconds in 1983.

After the Olympic Games, Hines played two seasons in the National Football League, with the Miami Dolphins and the Kansas City Chiefs, before establishing the Jim Hines Foundation to assist battered women, abused children, and the homeless in Oakland, California.

Adam R. Hornbuckle

See also: Track and Field.

FURTHER READING
Ashe, Arthur R., Jr. *A Hard Road to Glory.* Vol. 3. New York: Warner Books, 1988.
Hettenhausen, Amy. "Hines Takes Strides to Create a Better World." *Austin* (Texas) *American Statesman*, August 26, 1994.
Menke, Frank G. *The Encyclopedia of Sports.* 4th rev. ed. New York: Barnes, 1969.
Quercetani, Roberto L. *Athletics: A History of Modern Track and Field Athletics (1860–1990) Men and Women.* Milan: Vallardi & Associati, 1990.
Wallechinsky, David. *The Complete Book of the Summer Olympics.* Sydney 2000 ed. Woodstock, NY: Overlook Press, 2000.

★ ★ ★

HISTORICALLY BLACK COLLEGES AND UNIVERSITIES

The sport legacy at historically black colleges and universities (HBCU) in the

Morris Brown College baseball team, circa 1900. Morris Brown, like many other historically black colleges and universities, had highly competitive athletic programs in a variety of sports. *(Library of Congress)*

United States is a distinguished one dating back to the late nineteenth century. In 2001 the number of HBCU stands at eighty-eight, down from a high of 122 at the peak of the civil rights movement in the 1960s. The history of the HBCU themselves begins in the early nineteenth century with Cheyney State College in Pennsylvania, founded in 1837; Lincoln University in Pennsylvania, in 1854; Wilberforce University in Ohio, in 1856; and others that followed. The HBCU fully embraced the tenets of "muscular Christianity," that a sound mind could not be achieved without a sound body. Before the end of the century, virtually every HBCU in existence at the time boasted a burgeoning athletic program.

Baseball was the first intercollegiate sport played at HBCU, with Morehouse College in Atlanta hosting the inaugural game in 1890. Clark University and Morris Brown College joined with Morehouse in forming the Atlanta League in 1896; Morehouse dominated league play for the remainder of the decade. By 1910 intercollegiate baseball was immensely popular throughout HBCU; high-quality teams included those of Fisk University, Virginia Union, Howard University, Hampton Institute, Wiley College, Tuskegee Institute, Shaw University, Livingstone College, Johnson C. Smith, and Prairie View A & M. Tuskegee took the Negro Southern Intercollegiate Baseball Championship in 1911, and Morris Brown captured it in 1915. Baseball's popularity on black campuses peaked in the 1920s, by then four school rivalries had grown to such importance that they drew record crowds of more than a thousand spectators to the big games: Howard versus Lincoln, Fisk versus Tuskegee, Wiley versus Prairie View, and Livingstone versus Johnson C. Smith.

Despite baseball's early prominence and appeal, football rapidly usurped its mantle as the most popular team sport and the largest spectator draw at HBCU. The gridiron game was nearly as old as baseball on black campuses and had never been far behind in popularity even during the early years. The first HBCU intercollegiate football game pitted Livingstone College against Johnson C. Smith on December 27, 1892; Johnson C. Smith won 4–0. Later that year Howard University fielded its first team. Howard and Lincoln University played their first game on Thanksgiving Day in 1894. Theirs was to become a classic rivalry. Tuskegee Institute and Atlanta University squared off against each other that same year. Morehouse played its first game in 1900, and when it took the field against Tuskegee there began what would become one of the oldest rivalries in collegiate gridiron history, lasting a century. Fisk University, in Nashville, Tennessee, won the Negro Southern Intercollegiate Football Championship seven times between 1910 and 1929.

Basketball, the premier indoor sport, caught on quickly at HBCU. Howard University put the first varsity team on the court in 1910, followed by Hampton Institute. Howard and Hampton dominated the sport on black campuses over the next decade and a half, and Morgan State, Virginia State, and Xavier University led the pack from the late 1920s through the 1930s.

Basketball was also the first team sport on college campuses played by women. The HBCU led the way in women's basketball with industrial schools—Hampton, Tuskegee, and Tennessee A & I—in the forefront. Liberal arts colleges (Fisk, Spelman, and Howard) soon followed suit with women's teams of their own. Tuskegee, Shaw University, and Johnson C. Smith were perennial powerhouses in women's basketball from the late 1920s through 1940s.

The overall popularity and importance of sport on black campuses necessitated that the schools form their own leagues; the first one was a loose confederation of regional conferences in the Southeast and Southwest. The Negro Southern Intercollegiate Athletic Conference (SIAC), with nine member associations, can claim 1910 as the approximate year of its founding. The largest and recognized first formal association, with eleven member institutions, was the Colored Intercollegiate Athletic Association (CIAA), founded in 1912. The CIAA changed its name from "Colored" to "Central" when it gained associate status in the National Collegiate Athletic Association. Other HBCU conferences include the Mid-Eastern Athletic Conference (MEAC), with seven member schools, and the Southwestern Athletic Conference (SWAC), with eight.

Athletics at HBCU grew and prospered during the 1920s, a golden era in sports. Virtually all athletic programs nationwide expanded during these years. The participation of African Americans in track and field was first established at predominantly white colleges and universities (PWCU) in the North with their superior facilities and higher national athletic visibility compared to HBCU. Most of the early black stars of track and field were students at PWCU, including the first black Olympian, George Poage of the University of Wisconsin, who participated in the 1904 games and won a bronze medal in the 400-meter hurdles; John Baxter Taylor of the University of Pennsylvania, who in the 1908 Olympics in London ran the third leg on the championship U.S. 400-meter relay team; and DeHart Hubbard of the University of Michigan, who became the first African American to win an individual Olympic championship when he captured the gold medal in the broad jump at the 1924 games in Paris. In this era HBCU began developing track programs in earnest. The institutions competed against themselves and, on occasion, against some white schools in the North. In the South, interracial sports of any kind were taboo. In 1920 the famous Penn Relays, hosted at the University of Pennsylvania, afforded Lincoln University, Howard University, and Morgan State, the opportunity to compete against teams from Temple University and New York University, among others.

The golden era in sport came to an abrupt end with the stock-market crash of 1929. Athletic programs at most HBCU were casualties of the national and worldwide economic collapse of the Great Depression of the 1930s; the schools were forced to take austerity measures to survive. This downturn in sport was short-lived, however. Sporting activities nationwide rose in the aftermath of World War II and the economic recovery of the 1940s. At HBCU only baseball proved to be a permanent casualty of the Depression era and unable to regain any semblance of its past glories on campus.

Women's track and field actually advanced during the Depression, with Tuskegee Institute's program at the pinnacle. The women's track program at Tuskegee began in earnest in 1929 and over the next two decades became the strongest program in the country, winning eleven of twelve AAU championships in track and field between 1937 and 1948. Tuskegee's remarkable Alice Coachman, a premier athlete of the 1940s, brought home the Olympic gold medal in 1948 while establishing a new world record in the high jump. Tennessee State University dominated women's track in the 1950s and 1960s; Wilma Rudolph soared as the fastest woman in the world, garnering three gold medals in the 1960 Olympic Games in Rome. There would be a long list of HBCU women stars of track and other sports, such as the great Althea Gibson in tennis, a product of Florida A & M University. The long list of outstanding male athletes produced in track and field and, most notably, in football from HBCU is also impressive. That production hit its peak in the 1960s and 1970s.

The immense economic rewards and increased access to higher education for African Americans today have ushered in a profound change in the role and future of sport programs at HBCU. Predominantly white colleges and universities increasingly siphon off African-American athletes who, in the era before desegregation, would have had no choice but to attend an all-black school. The better-funded programs at PWCU and the greater media exposure they receive make it relatively easy for them to recruit the best of the African-American student athletes. Long gone are the days when the National Football League looked almost exclusively to coach Eddie Robinson's Grambling Tigers and Jake Gaithers's Florida A & M teams for black players. The marching bands at these institutions are still the greatest in all of college sports, but their athletic programs are now rarely the first choice of blue-chip players who dream of careers in professional ball. Neither can HBCU teams generate the spectator support they once did in their Orange Blossom and Bayou Classics. These bowl games still draw respectable audiences, by HBCU standards, but only the Heritage Bowl, initiated in 1991, has proven able to attract a large enough audience to win national television coverage. The revenue and program visibility generated by one annual bowl game that draws national attention will not stop the breaking away of top African-American players from HBCU and their embrace of PWCU. The challenges of higher academic requirements for athletic participation imposed by the NCAA's Proposition 48 has further slanted the playing field for HBCU, which in the past prided themselves on their unique ability to admit student-athletes with less than sterling academic backgrounds and nurture them to maturity and college degrees. The erasing of the color line has given African-American men and women athletes and nonathletes a wider choice of higher educational opportunities and has posed severe challenges to HBCU.

Donald Spivey and Cecile Houry

See also: Central Intercollegiate Athletic Association; Alice Coachman; Jake Gaither; Althea Gibson; George Poage; Eddie Robinson; Wilma Rudolph; John Taylor.

FURTHER READING
Ashe, Arthur R., Jr. *A Hard Road to Glory: A History of the African-American Athlete.* Vols. 1 and 2. New York: Warner Books, 1988.
Duval, Earl H. "An Historical Analysis of the Central Intercollegiate Athletic Association and Its Influence on the Development of Black Intercollegiate Athletics, 1912–1984." Ph.D. diss., Kent State University, 1985.

Hurd, Michael. *Black College Football: One Hundred Years of History, Education, and Pride.* Virginia Beach, VA: Donning, 1998.

Liberti, Rita Marie. "'We Were Ladies, We Just Played Basketball Like Boys': A Study of Women's Basketball at Historically Black Colleges and Universities in North Carolina, 1925–1945." Ph.D. diss., University of Iowa, 1998.

Miller, Patrick B. "To Bring the Race Along Rapidly: Sport, Student Culture, and Educational Mission at Historically Black Colleges During the Interwar Years." *History of Education Quarterly* 35 (Summer 1995): 111–33.

Watts, Langston. "The CIAA Has Grown." *Sports Review*, February 1995.

★ ★ ★

HISTORIOGRAPHY

The first person to write extensively about the involvement of African Americans in sport was Edwin B. Henderson, an influential physical educator and civil rights activist from Falls Church, Virginia. Sometimes referred to as the "father of black sports history," Henderson traced the evolution of African-American athletes through a number of articles, book chapters, and the frequently cited monographs *The Negro in Sports* (1939, 1949) and *The Black Athlete: Emergence and Arrival* (1968). Henderson's writings were all patterned after the scholarship of the famous historian Carter G. Woodson, in that they were intended to inspire, and prove the worth of, African Americans by chronicling athletic successes in a society marked by racial discrimination and inequality.

Many of the subsequent historical surveys on African-American athletes were also meant to instill a sense of pride and furnish examples of success in the black community. These writings, while varying in format and organization, are all marked by their emphasis on the accomplishments of African-American athletes, without much regard for historical context and larger societal issues. Included among this group are such monographs as Wally Jones and Jim Washington's *Black Champions Challenge American Sports* (1972), Andrew S. "Doc" Young's *Negro Firsts in Sports* (1963), Ocania Chalk's *Pioneers of Black Sport* (1975), Arna Bontemp's *Famous Negro Athletes* (1964), Jack Orr's *Black Athlete: His Story in American History* (1969), and Arthur Ashe's *A Hard Road to Glory: A History of the African American Athlete* (1978).

Biographical studies have dominated much of the writings on African-American athletes. These studies have been devoted almost exclusively to male rather than female athletes, an unfortunate but unsurprising fact that reflects a general trend in the sport history literature. Tellingly, the story of even well-known black female athletes have been relegated to children's literature. Perhaps the most notable biographical studies of black male athletes are David W. Zang's *Fleet Walker's Divided Heart: The Life of Baseball's First Black Major Leaguer* (1995), Andrew Ritchie's *Major Taylor: The Extraordinary Career of a Champion Bicycle Racer* (1988), Randy Roberts' *Papa Jack: Jack Johnson and the Era of White Hopes* (1983), Chris Mead's *Champion: Joe Louis, Black Hero in White America* (1985), William J. Baker's *Jesse Owens: An American Life* (1986), Jules Tygiel's *Baseball's Great Experiment: Jackie Robinson and His Legacy* (1983), and David Remnick's *King of The World: Muhammad Ali and the Rise of a Hero* (1998).

Rivaling biographical studies for the attention of historians have been works dealing with separate black sporting institutions. The most famous and most-written-about of these separate sports organizations were the black baseball teams and leagues that sprang up in various parts of the country during the latter stages of the nineteenth century and first half of the twentieth. Important studies of baseball in the African-American community are Donn Rogosin's *Invisible Men: Life in Baseball's Negro Leagues* (1987), Neil Lanctot's *Fair Dealing and Clean Playing: The Hilldale Club and the Development of Black Professional Baseball 1910–1932* (1994), Janet Bruce's *Kansas City Monarchs: Champions of Black Baseball* (1985), Rob Ruck's *Sandlot Seasons: Sport in Black Pittsburgh* (1987), Robert Peterson's *Only the Ball Was White* (1970), John Holway's *Voices from the Great Negro Baseball Leagues* (1975), and Michael E. Lomax's "Black Baseball's First Rivalry: The Cuban Giants versus the Gorham's of New York and the Birth of the Colored Championship" in *Sport History Review* (1997) and "Black Entrepreneurship in the National Pastime: The Rise of Semiprofessional Baseball in Black Chicago, 1890–1915" in *Journal of Sport History* (1998).

Historians have paid far less attention to other all-black sporting organizations. There has, however, been some impressive work done on both professional and amateur sport behind the walls of segregation. Examples of these studies are Rob Ruck's "Soaring Above the Sandlots: The Garfield Eagles," *Pennsylvania Heritage* (1982); Gerald R. Gems "Blocked Shot: The Development of Basketball in the African American Community of Chicago," *Journal of Sport History* (1995); Randy Roberts' *But They Can't Beat Us! Oscar Robertson's Crispus Attacks Tigers* (1999); Richard Pierce's "More than a Game: The Political Meaning of High School Basketball in Indianapolis," *Journal of Urban History* (2000); Rita Liberti's "'We Were Ladies, We Just Played Basketball Like Boys': African American Womanhood and Competitive Basketball at Bennett College 1928–1942" *Journal of Sport History* (1999); and Patrick B. Miller's "To Bring the Race Along Rapidly: Sport, Student Culture, and Educational Mission at Historically Black Colleges During the Interwar Years," *History of Education Quarterly* (1995).

An increasing amount of attention has been devoted to the experiences of African-American athletes who competed in predominantly white college sport between the two world wars. Utilizing black and white newspapers, presidential papers, NAACP documents, and a variety of other primary materials, historians have charted both the triumphs and incidents of racial discrimination experienced by the select number of outstanding African-American athletes who competed at such well-known institutions as UCLA, Michigan, Harvard, and Syracuse. Some of the more intriguing of these types of studies are John Carroll's *Fritz Pollard: Pioneer in Racial Advancement* (1992); Donald Spivey's "End Jim Crow in Sports: The Protest at New York University, 1940–1941," *Journal of Sport History* (1988); David Wiggins' "Prized Performers but Frequently Overlooked Students: The Involvement of Black Athletes in Intercollegiate Sports on Predominantly White University Campuses, 1890–1972," *Research Quarterly for Exercise and Sport* (1991); John Behee's *Hail to the Victors! Black Athletes at the University of Michigan* (1974); and Patrick Miller's "Harvard and the Color Line: The Case of Lucien Alexis," in *Sports in Massachusetts: Historical Essays* (1991).

Historians have written extensively about the shattering of the color line in major league baseball. Recognizing the symbolic importance of baseball integration and its effect on both the black and white communities in this country, historians have written with great passion and insight about Jackie Robinson's signing with the Brooklyn Dodgers and his Hall of Fame career as well as his life after baseball. The best known works on Robinson and baseball integration include Stephen Norwood and Harold Brackman's "Going to Bat for Jackie Robinson: The Jewish Role in Breaking Baseball's Color Line," *Journal of Sport History* (1999); David Wiggins' "Wendell Smith, the *Pittsburgh Courier-Journal* and the Campaign to Include Blacks in Organized Baseball, 1933–1945," *Journal of Sport History* (1983); William Simons's "Jackie Robinson and the American Mind: Journalistic Perceptions of the Reintegration of Baseball," *Journal of Sport History* (1985); Ronald Smith's "The Paul Robeson–Jackie Robinson Saga and a Political Collision," *Journal of Sport History* (1979); Joseph Dorinson and Joram Warmund's *Jackie Robinson: Race, Sports, and the American Dream* (1998); Arnold Rampersad's *Jackie Robinson: A Biography*; and Jules Tygiel's *Baseball's Great Experiment: Jackie Robinson and His Legacy* (1983).

The elimination of the color line in other professional sports has garnered far less coverage from academicians. There are, however, important studies that examine the integration processes in football, basketball, and golf. These consist of such works as Calvin Sinnette's *Forbidden Fairways: African Americans and the Game of Golf* (1998); Pete McDaniel's *Uneven Lies: The Heroic Story of African Americans in Golf* (2000); Nelson George's *Elevating the Game: Black Men and Basketball* (1992); Charles Salzberg's *From Set Shot to Slam Dunk: The Glory Days of Basketball in the Words of Those Who Played It* (1987); Gerald Gems "Shooting Stars: The Rise and Fall of Blacks in Professional Football," *Professional Football Research Association Annual Bulletin* (1988); and Thomas Smith's "Civil Rights on the Gridiron: The Kennedy Administration and the Desegregation of the Washington Redskins," *Journal of Sport History* (1987) and "Outside the Pale: The Exclusion of Blacks from the National Football League, 1934–1946," *Journal of Sport History* (1988).

A number of historians have focused on the elimination of the color line in intercollegiate sport. The best and largest number of studies have dealt with the integration of southern schools and conferences. The most frequently cited of these studies are Joan Paul et al., "The Arrival and Ascendance of Black Athletes in the Southeastern Conference, 1966–1980," *Phylon* (1984); Ronald Marcello's "The Integration of Intercollegiate Athletics in Texas: North Texas State College as a Test Case, 1956," *Journal of Sport History* (1987); Richard Pennington's *Breaking the Ice: The Racial Integration of Southwest Conference Football* (1987); and Charles Martin's "Jim Crow in the Gymnasium: The Integration of College Basketball in the American South," *International Journal of the History of Sport* (1993); "Racial Change and Big-Time College Football In Georgia: The Age of Segregation, 1892–1957," *Georgia Historical Quarterly* (1996); and "Integrating New Year's Day: The Racial Politics of College Bowl Games in the American South," *Journal of Sport History* (1997).

Historians have been fascinated with the involvement of African-American athletes in the black power movement and larger civil rights struggle of the late 1960s and early 1970s. The specific focus of most of these investigations has been the political activism of African-American athletes on predominantly white college campuses and in Olympic competition. Significant works of this type are Adolph Grundman's "Image of Intercollegiate Sports and the Civil Rights Movement: A Historian's View," *Arena Review* (1979); Donald Spivey's "Black Consciousness and Olympic Protest Movements, 1964–1980," in *Sport In America: New Historical Perspectives*, edited by Donald Spivey (1985); Richard Lapchick's *Broken Promises: Racism in American Sports* (1984); and David Wiggins's "The Year of Awakening: Black Athletes, Racial Unrest, and the Civil Rights Movement of 1968," *International Journal of the History of Sport* (1992), and "The Future of

College Athletics Is at Stake: Black Athletes and Racial Turmoil on Three Predominantly White University Campuses, 1968–1972," *Journal of Sport History* (1988).

African-American women athletes, once relegated to children's literature in regard to full-scale biographies, have drawn more attention from scholars in the recent past. Historians have charted with insight and sensitivity the triumphs and the various forms of racial discrimination experienced by African-American women athletes. For examples of these works see Patricia Vertinsky and Gwendolyn Captain's "More Myth than History: American Culture and Representations of the Black Female's Athletic Ability," *Journal of Sport History* (1998); Alfred Dennis Mathewson's "Black Women, Gender Equity and the Function at the Junction," *Marquette Sports Law Journal* (1996); Yvonne Smith's "Women of Color in Society and Sport," *Quest* (1992); Susan Birrell's "Women of Color, Critical Autobiography, and Sport," in *Sport, Men, and the Gender Order: Critical Feminist Perspectives*, edited by Michael Messner and Donald Sabo (1990); Linda Williams's "Sportswomen in Black and White: Sports History from an Afro American Perspective," in *Women, Media and Sport: Challenging Gender Values*, edited by Pamela Creeden (1994); Susan Cahn's *Coming On Strong: Gender and Sexuality in Twentieth-Century Women's Sport* (1994); Jennifer Lansbury's, "'The Tuskegee Flash' and 'the Slender Harlem Stroker': Black Women Athletes on the Margin," *Journal of Sport History* (2001); and Cindy Gissendanner's "African American Women and Competitive Sport, 1920–1960," in *Women, Sport, and Culture*, edited by Susan Birrell and Cheryl Cole (1993), and "African American Women Olympians: The Impact of Race, Gender, and Class Ideologies, 1932–1968" *Research Quarterly for Exercise and Sport* (1996).

The most recent years have seen a proliferation of research concerned with the relationship between race, social structure, and sport orientation as well as the questions of racial differences and sport performance. A topic of special interest to many academicians is the question of supposed black athletic superiority. The best and most balanced studies dealing with this topic are Laurel R. Davis's, "The Articulation of Difference: White Preoccupation with the Question of Racially Linked Genetic Differences Among Athletes," *Sociology of Sport Journal* (1990); David Wiggins's "Great Speed but Little Stamina: The Historical Debate over Black Athletic Superiority," *Journal of Sport History* (1989); Patrick Miller's "Anatomy of Scientific Racism: Racialist Responses to Black Athletic Achievement," *Journal of Sport History* (1998); and Mark Dyreson's "American Ideas About Race and Olympic Races from the 1890s to the 1950s: Shattering Myths or Reinforcing Scientific Racism?" *Journal of Sport History* (2001).

David K. Wiggins

See also: Arthur Ashe, Jr.; Edwin Bancroft Henderson; Wali Jones; Andrew S. "Doc" Young.

FURTHER READING
Marable, Manning. "Black Athletes in White Men's Games, 1880–1920." *Maryland Historian* 4 (Fall 1973): 143–49.
McPherson, Barry D. "Minority Group Involvement in Sport: The Black Athlete." *Exercise and Sport Science Reviews* 2 (1974): 71–101.
Sammons, Jeffrey T. "'Race' and Sport: A Critical Historical Examination." *Journal of Sport History* 21 (Fall 1994): 203–98.
Wiggins, David K. "The African American Athletic Experience." In *The African American Experience: An Historiographical and Bibliographical Guide*, ed. Arvarh E. Strickland and Robert E. Weems, Jr. Westport, CT: Greenwood Press, 2001.

Jerome Brud HOLLAND

Born January 9, 1916, Auburn, New York
Died January 13, 1985, Bronxville, New York
Football player, educator, diplomat

Son of a handyman and one of thirteen children, Holland attended public schools in New York and then attended Cornell University. Holland maintained honors status in his work toward his B.S. and M.S. degrees and was twice named All-American at Cornell—its first African-American football player. After obtaining his Ph.D. from the University of Pennsylvania, Holland launched an impressive career that included college teaching, research, administration, diplomatic service, and business.

Holland was head of Delaware State College for seven years and then became president of Hampton Institute in Hampton, Virginia, from 1960 to 1970. Holland was named ambassador to Sweden in 1970 and upon his return to the United States in 1972 became the first African American to serve on the board of the New York Stock Exchange. He served as director of several corporations, including American Telephone and Telegraph, the Chrysler Corporation, General Foods, and Union Carbide.

Holland was also active in numerous humanitarian efforts and was the vice chairman of both the National Conference of Christians and Jews and the New York Advisory Board of the Salvation Army. He was also a trustee of the Foreign Policy Association.

Holland, a strong advocate for education and job training as the keys for advancement for African Americans, wrote numerous articles on the socio-economic issues of his race and wrote the book *Black Opportunity*. He was inducted into the National Football Foundation Hall of Fame and received the Distinguished American Award in 1972.

Trisha M. Hothorn

FURTHER READING
Chalk, Ocania. *Black College Sport*. New York: Dodd, Mead, 1976.
Cook, Joan. "Jerome Holland, Former U.S. Envoy." *New York Times*, January 14, 1985.
"Dr. Jerome (Brud) H. Holland." *American Red Cross* (www.redcross.org).
Rywell, Martin, ed. *Afro-American Encyclopedia*. North Miami, FL: Educational Book Publishers, 1974.
Smith, Thomas G. "Outside the Pale: The Exclusion of Blacks from the National Football League, 1934–1946." *Journal of Sport History* 15 (Winter 1988): 255–81.

Steve HOLMAN

Born March 2, 1970, Indianapolis, Indiana
Runner

The son of a Baptist minister and a guidance counselor, Holman grew up in one of the few African-American families in middle-class Richfield, MN. He graduated from Richfield High School (1988) and Georgetown University (1992) with a degree in English.

Holman became one of the most successful middle-distance runners in the United States during the 1990s. He realized his most significant accomplishments in his senior year at Georgetown. He won the NCAA 1,500-meter, finished second at the Olympic Trials, and finished ninth in the semifinals at the 1992 Olympics. With personal bests of 3:34.95 (1,500 meters) and 3:52.73 (1,600 meters), Holman finished 1992 as the number-two-ranked American miler. As a professional, Holman competed consistently among the top middle-distance runners in the world (posting personal bests of 3:31.52 and 3:50.40). In 1999, Holman won his first outdoor title in the U.S. Outdoor 1,500-meter.

Holman's emergence as one of the top American milers gave African Americans a presence in middle-distance track. Graduating with a 3.4 GPA, he was honored with the Georgetown Big East Scholar Athlete of the Year award and the prestigious NCAA Top Six Award. Continuing to live in Washington, DC, Holman has become actively involved in the Big Brother program and raises funds for inner-city educational ventures.

Holman has fought to improve international track and field's image. He has consistently lobbied for tougher drug-testing procedures for athletes in order to "clean" the sport and enhance public acceptance.

Gregory H. Duquette

FURTHER READING
Layden, Tim. "First at Last." *Sports Illustrated*, July 5, 1999, 88.
"On the Road to Sacramento with Steve Holman." *LetsRun.com* (www.runwiththebluffs.com/pages/holman.html), June 28, 2000.
Patrick, Dick. "Head of the Class." *Runner's World*, May 1993, 78–87.
USA Track and Field Biographies (www.usatf.org/athletes/bios/Steve_Holman.shtml).

★ ★ ★

Larry HOLMES

Born November 3, 1949, Cuthbert, Georgia
Boxer

The Holmes family left Cuthbert, Georgia in the 1950s. It moved to Easton, Pennsylvania, where Larry grew up. Not having much interest in education, Larry quit school and turned to the streets of Easton. He was taught how to box at the St. Anthony Youth Center in Easton. He began his amateur boxing career in 1970, winning the New Jersey AAU (Amateur Athletic Union) light-heavyweight championship and the Eastern Olympic Championship.

Holmes began his professional boxing career in March 1973. He served as a sparring partner for Muhammad Ali, who was the champion and most popular figure in the sport. On June 10, 1973, Holmes received the opportunity to box Ken Norton for the WBC version of the heavyweight championship. In what turned out to be a very controversial bout, Holmes became the champion. After winning this championship, Holmes went on to forty-eight consecutive victories, defeating the likes of Ali, Ernie Shavers, Leon Spinks, and Gerry Cooney. He lost the championship to Michael Spinks in September of 1985. In 1986 Michael Spinks again defeated Holmes. After this defeat Holmes retired, for the first of several times.

Holmes, at six feet, three inches and 215 pounds, was not considered a knockout puncher, but he had an excellent jab and quick hands. While he was not formally educated, Holmes avoided the financial pitfalls of many other athletes by investing his money wisely. The major benefactor from Holmes's investments was his adopted hometown of Easton. He also gave large financial contributions to the local Boys Club and the NAACP. At the time of his first retirement Holmes professional career record was forty-eight wins and three defeats.

James R. Coates, Jr.

See also: Boxing; Ken Norton; Leon Spinks.

FURTHER READING
Holmes, Larry, and Phil Berger. *Against the Odds*. New York: St. Martin's Press, 1998.
Izenberg, Jerry. "Angry Man in Search of Ali." *Sport*, July 1980, 40–43.
Newsweek, March 25, 1985.

Reverson, Derek A. "Other Heavyweight Champion." *Ebony*, February 1979, 112–15.

★ ★ ★

HORSE RACING

Horse racing was initially hugely popular, America's initial national pastime, attracting hundreds of thousands of fans in pre–Civil War days and in the first half of the twentieth century. Within a year of taking possession of New York from the Dutch in 1664, the British established a racetrack in what is now Nassau County, Long Island. More than a dozen racetracks existed in Virginia before 1700, and South Carolinians founded the Jockey Club of Charleston in 1734. British artist Benjamin Robert Haydon once noted, "Wherever the British settle, wherever they colonize, they carry, and will always carry, trial by jury, horse racing and portrait painting."

Traveling from New York to New Orleans between 1832 and 1872, Edward Troye immortalized in paintings many of America's greatest race horses, with their black jockeys and trainers. After the American Revolution anti-nobility sentiment led to attempts to abolish horse racing—the "sport of kings." Fundamentalist religious leaders opposed to frivolous sports and sinful gambling pressured governments to enact repressive legislation. Ironically, black lawmakers during Reconstruction unsuccessfully proposed prohibiting horse racing on Sundays, continuing the assault on racing. Boston, Philadelphia, and New York banned racing in 1802. However, the sport continued to flourish in the South. Although New York lifted the ban in 1821, racing's stronghold remained in the South until the Civil War. Racing boomed in the 1830s in Virginia, Maryland, the Carolinas, Georgia, Tennessee, Kentucky, Alabama, Louisiana, and Mississippi.

African-American jockeys competed side by side with white jockeys predominantly in the South, which boasted sixty-three official racecourses compared to six tracks in the Northeast at the end of the 1830s. Blacks dominated American horse racing as jockeys, grooms, and trainers from the early 1700s until the 1910s. In the South, professional jockeys were mostly slaves who grew up on plantations caring for horses. By 1800, the South had produced the majority of black jockeys seen at the major racetracks. Recognized for their skills with horses, the jockeys traveled alone and across state lines—despite slave laws—to ride in races. Even during the Civil War, racing continued at the Metairie racecourse in New Orleans until December 1861 and in Kentucky in 1862, as well as in Paterson (New Jersey) and Saratoga (New York) in 1863, with southern black jockeys riding at all the tracks.

After the Civil War, some of the wealthiest jockeys were African American. In the first Kentucky Derby, in 1875, the majority of the fifteen riders were black. Black jockeys, most of them from the newly crowned racing center of Kentucky, won the Derby fifteen times in its first twenty-eight years. Black trainers conditioned five of those winners. Not until 1989 did another black trainer, Hank Allen, start a horse in the Derby. Within the sporting newspaper, *Spirit of the Times*, and the mainstream paper, *New York Herald*, coverage of the feats of African-American jockeys, while often couched in racist terms, conveyed admiration for their professionalism and expertise. Reporters routinely interviewed the prominent black jockey Isaac Murphy.

The rise of Jim Crow laws at the turn of the twentieth century began driving blacks from Kentucky and Tennessee horse farms to seek other forms of employment in urban areas and excluded African-American trainers and jockeys from the leading racetracks in the South. Starting around 1894 in other areas of the country, most black jockeys were denied state licenses to ride at the major racetracks. The Ku Klux Klan targeted some prominent black jockeys, and increasing Klan violence may have frightened some away. Higher purses attracted more white riders. Racism as well as outright rough riding discouraged trainers from using black jockeys, whose white counterparts would gang up during a race to prevent them from winning. Premier black jockey Jimmy Winkfield would recall, "In the old days, where if you ran twelve horses, from six to eight of the jockeys were always black. And it remained that way until more money got in the game. Now, then, when a lot of money got in the game, the white men then, like they do now and like they've always been, wanted his people to have, not only the money, but also the reputation." The last time a black jockey won a major-stakes race was 1908, when Jimmy Lee took the Travers at Saratoga. The Kentucky Derby had not had an African-American rider between Henry King, tenth in 1921, and Marlon St. Julien, who finished seventh in 2000. Some former jockeys became trainers or rode in steeplechase races when they could no longer keep their weight down, but these career paths also dead-ended for African Americans. Ex-jockeys Jimmy Winkfield and his son Robert became successful and prominent trainers—in France.

Farm-trained Kentucky jockeys faced increasing competition from new urban jockeys. Coney Island, New York, trainer Bill Daly ran a jockey school for immigrants' children and boys from orphanages. He turned out some of the meanest riders in the business; they gradually replaced the more skillful black riders. Without ethics or loyalties, these newcomers were easily bribed and did whatever it took to win—or lose—even if it meant abusing their horses. Racing's higher profile among the moneyed elite and the general public and the rise in financial stakes associated with racing contributed to the easing out of black jockeys out as purse money and jockeys' shares increased.

With the decline in participation by African Americans as jockeys and trainers, the racing world came to see black faces only on the backside of racetracks as grooms, hot walkers (hired to keep the horses in condition), and exercise riders. By the end of the twentieth century, black involvement in horse racing as owners was the exception, with the most notable example being Oaktown Stable's Lewis Burrell and his sons Louis Jr., Chris, and Stanley (rap singer M.C. Hammer) during a brief period in the early 1990s. Hispanic jockeys began to overtake whites in the 1960s, while women broke the gender barrier in 1973. The few African-American jockeys riding at the turn of the twenty-first century work the small tracks in Louisiana and Texas, dreaming of one day getting their shot at the Kentucky Derby.

Susan Hamburger

FURTHER READING

Hotaling, Edward. *The Great Black Jockeys: The Lives and Times of the Men Who Dominated America's First National Sport.* Rocklin, CA: Forum, 1999.

Robertson, William H.P. *The History of Thoroughbred Racing in America.* Englewood Cliffs, NJ: Prentice Hall, 1964.

Woodham, Martha. "The Forgotten Riders: They're Rare Today, but Black Jockeys Once Dominated U.S. Horse Racing." *Atlanta Journal-Constitution,* April 30, 1995.

William Dehart HUBBARD

Born November 25, 1903, Cincinnati, Ohio
Died June 23, 1976, Cleveland, Ohio
Long jumper, sprinter

William Dehart Hubbard was the son of William A. Hubbard and a 1922 graduate of Walnut Hills High School in Cincinnati, Ohio, in 1922, and a 1926 graduate of the University of Michigan. A national and Olympic champion and world record holder in the long jump, Hubbard pursued a career in public administration.

Hubbard won six AAU national championships in the long jump (1922–1927) and two national championships in the triple jump (1923–1924). He captured two NCAA long-jump titles in 1923 and 1925, with the latter resulting in a world record of 25 feet, 10-7/8 inches. Prior to becoming the world record holder, Hubbard had won the long jump in the 1924 Olympic Games, becoming the first African American to win an individual Olympic gold medal. In 1925 he won the NCAA championship in the 100-yard dash and, in 1926, equaled the world record of 9.6 seconds for 100 yards. An improper long-jump landing pit cost Hubbard a world record of 26 feet, 2½ inches in 1927. Competing injured in the 1928 Olympic Games, he finished eleventh in the long jump.

Hubbard supervised Negro athletic leagues for the Cincinnati Public Recreation Commission from 1926 to 1941. He became the manager of Cincinnati's Valley Homes Public Housing Project in 1941. After serving as a race relations adviser to the Federal Public Housing Authority in Cleveland from 1942 to 1947, he became the regional adviser on minority affairs to the Federal Housing Authority.

Adam R. Hornbuckle

See also: Olympic Games; Track and Field.

FURTHER READING
Ashe, Arthur R., Jr. *A Hard Road to Glory.* Vol. 2. New York: Warner Books, 1988.
Hanley, Reid M. *Who's Who in Track and Field.* New Rochelle, NY: Arlington House, 1973.
Mallon, Bill, and Ian Buchanan. *Quest for Gold: The Encyclopedia of American Olympians.* New York: Leisure Press, 1984.
Menke, Frank G. *The Encyclopedia of Sports.* 4th rev. ed. New York: A.S. Barnes, 1969.
Nelson, Cordner. *Track and Field: The Great Ones.* London: Pelham Books, 1970.
Quercetani, Roberto L. *A World History of Track and Field Athletics, 1864–1964.* London and New York: Oxford University Press, 1964.
Wallechinsky, David. *The Complete Book of the Summer Olympics.* Sydney 2000 ed. Woodstock, NY: Penguin Books, 2000.

★ ★ ★

Martha HUDSON

Born March 21, 1939, Eastman, Georgia
Sprinter

Hudson was an AAU, Pan American, and Olympic record holder in track and field. She ran a leg of the 400-meter relay team that won a gold medal in the 1960 Olympics in Rome, Italy, along with teammates Lucinda Williams, Wilma Rudolph, and Barbara Jones.

She experienced success early, winning as an eighth-grader in McRae, Georgia, district races for the fifty, seventy-five, and 100-meter dash. She finished third in the Tuskegee Relays at the age of fifteen and set a Pan American Games record in 1955 in Mexico City. Hudson attended Tennessee State University and ran track under the legendary coach Edward Temple; she graduated in 1962 with a B.S. degree in education. She served as an elementary school teacher for many years in Thomaston, Georgia, and was inducted into the Georgia Hall of Fame in 1986.

Alison M. Gavin

FURTHER READING

Ashe, Arthur R., Jr. *A Hard Road to Glory: A History of the African American Athlete Since 1946.* New York: Amistad, 1988.

Atlanta Olympics 1996 Calendar. "Martha Hudson Pennyman." Tennessee State University, Hall of Fame Archives, Clippings from Martha Hudson File.

★ ★ ★

Eddie HURT

Born February 12, 1883, Brookneal, Virginia
Died March 24, 1989, Baltimore, Maryland
Coach

A one-time All-American end at Howard University, Eddie Hurt was best known for his academic and coaching prowess at Morgan State. He was among a few black college coaches to enjoy a successful career, despite inadequate facilities and budgets. Hurt coached football, basketball, and track and field at Morgan State for forty years, beginning in 1929.

Coach Hurt's Morgan State Thinclads won fifteen CIAA open and closed track and field championships and sixteen individual national championships. In Penn relays competition, a well-recognized event during the era, the track team earned several college-class mile-relay victories, one freshman mile-relay championship, one 400-meter championship, and one Class A mile-relay championship.

Under Hurt's coaching, Morgan State's football teams won thirteen CIAA championships and several national titles. Eleven of Hurt's teams had undefeated seasons, including a fifty-four-game non-losing streak from 1932 to 1938. The 1943 team completed its season without ever being scored against, while scoring 166 points itself in five games.

Hurt also coached Morgan State's basketball team from 1929 to 1947. His team consistently placed among the top clubs in the CIAA. Hurt won four CIAA basketball titles, including top honors in three consecutive years (1931, 1932, and 1933).

For Hurt's accomplishments at Morgan State, he was awarded coaching positions in both the 1959 Pan American Games and the 1964 Olympic Games. Additionally, the Morgan State gymnasium, built in 1952, was appropriately named after him.

Eddie Comeaux and C. Keith Harrison

FURTHER READING

Ashe, Arthur R., Jr. *A Hard Road to Glory: A History of the African-American Athlete, 1919–1945.* New York: Warner Books, 1983.

Associated Press. "Ed Hurt Among Weekend Hall of Fame Inductees." *Afro American Newspaper*, October 14, 1989.

Lindsey, Fred. *Afro American Newspaper*, October 14, 1987, C5. Located in Maryland football hall of fame.

★ ★ ★

Lula Mae HYMES

Born Unknown
Died Unknown
Sprinter

Hymes graduated from Booker T. Washington High School in Atlanta, Georgia, and attended Tuskegee Institute, where she was captain of the track team from 1937 to 1939. She ran anchor on the team's championship 400-meter relay team for three years. In 1937 and 1938 she was the AAU champion in the long jump and in 1939 was the top AAU woman in the 100-meter race.

Hymes solitary chance at Olympic fame came in 1936 during the U.S. trials. Hymes, only a freshman at Tuskegee, froze in the starting blocks and failed to make the team. Hymes was at the top of her competitive world, and very likely would have won Olympic medals, in 1940 and 1944, when the Games were canceled as a result of World War II.

Alison M. Wrynn

FURTHER READING
Ashe, Arthur R., Jr. *A Hard Road to Glory*. Vol. 2. New York: Warner Books, 1988.
Davis, Michael D. *Black American Women in Track and Field: A Complete Illustrated Reference*. Jefferson, NC: McFarland, 1992.

ICE HOCKEY

Ice hockey developed in eastern Canada during the last decades of the nineteenth century. Since that time, few black players have played at an elite level, although very recently there has been an influx of talented black athletes playing in the National Hockey League (NHL). A number of reasons have been suggested for the absence of black players in hockey, including the financial barriers and lack of facilities that preclude low-income, inner-city families from encouraging their children to play at an early age; a lack of black players at the NHL level who act as role models for younger players; and racial barriers that, while not as pronounced as in other sports, have existed in the sport since its inception. However, the most likely reason for the few black players in the sport has been that the country that has historically produced the most players, Canada, has not had a large population of blacks. For example in 1971, only 34,445 (or 0.02 percent of the population) were black; at that time, only one player in the NHL was not Canadian.

Despite this, several prominent players have had an impact on the sport, starting in 1899, when Hipple "Hippo" Galloway played for Woodstock, and later Charlie Lightfoot for Stratford, in the Central Ontario Hockey Association. At the same time, the Colored Hockey League of the Maritimes was founded in 1900 in Atlantic Canada, featuring teams from Dartmouth, Halifax, Amherst, Truro, and Africville. Meanwhile, other black players pursued the sport, including a Nova Scotia team composed of five black players from one family and two from another. Several black players and teams continued to play in eastern Canada throughout the first two decades of the twentieth century, including Fred "Bud" Kelly. In 1916, Kelly played for Frank Selke's 118th Battalion team in London, Ontario, in the Ontario Hockey Association's intermediate division; however, Kelly did not perform well when the general manager of the Toronto St. Pats (later Maple Leafs) scouted him for the NHL.

By the 1940s three talented black players, Herb and Ossie Carnegie, and Manny McIntyre, were playing together on a single forward line on a team in the Quebec Senior Hockey League, considered one of the highest-caliber leagues in the country. Because there were only six teams in the NHL at that time, many gifted players played at the senior level and were not given the chance to play in the NHL. Herb and brother Ossie were from Toronto, while McIntyre hailed from Fredericton, New Brunswick. During the 1944–1945 season playing for the Shawinigan team, the line held three of the four top-scoring positions on the team. Herb Carnegie was considered the most talented of the three and later played with future NHL star Jean Beliveau for the Quebec Aces. In 1947, Carnegie was offered a tryout with the NHL's New York Rangers, but the team wanted him to work his way through the minor leagues to make the club. Carnegie opted to return to the Quebec League, which paid salaries that rivaled the NHL. Despite suggestions that the NHL was without the same prejudices of the other major sports leagues, many felt that the only factor keeping Carnegie out of the NHL was his race. This fact was not lost on Toronto Maple Leafs' magnate Conn Smythe, who is alleged to have said, "I'll give any man $10,000 who can make Herb Carnegie white."

However, it was not long before a black player made an NHL lineup. On January

ICE HOCKEY

18, 1958, Willie O'Ree of Fredericton played for the Boston Bruins, playing in two games during the 1957–1958 season and forty-three games in 1960–1961 before returning to the minor leagues for the remainder of his career. It was thirteen years before another black player played in the NHL, when Mike Marson was drafted by the Washington Capitals. Marson found it isolating as the only black player, and subsequent players had similar experiences. Through 1990, less than twenty black players had played in the NHL, and only two, Grant Fuhr and Tony McKegney, had significant impacts as players.

Since the early 1990s, blacks have had an increasing presence in the sport, as players, coaches, and owners. The Edmonton Oilers' Mike Grier became the first U.S. born and trained black player to play in the NHL, following a successful collegiate career in which he was nominated as a finalist for the Hobey Baker award as U.S. college hockey's outstanding player. Indeed, the Edmonton Oilers featured no less than five black players on their roster during the 2000–2001 season, and the NHL reports that there are between thirty and forty black players in the NHL or its minor-league system. One reason for this increase could be the increase in blacks in the Canadian population: by 1996, 2 percent of the Canadian population was black (573,860).

In the meantime, John Paris of Windsor, Ontario, coached the Atlanta Knights of the International Hockey League to that league's championship in 1994, and in 1997, 51 percent of the East Coast Hockey League's New Orleans Brass franchise was bought by four African-American entrepreneurs. The NHL and USA hockey have worked in concert to try to create opportunities for minority and disadvantaged youths to play hockey, creating the NHL/USA Hockey Diversity Task Force, which operates twenty-eight developmental programs across the United States. This program has been in place since the mid-1990s, and Willie O'Ree has since become director of youth development. In addition, programs like Hockey in Harlem have provided young black players with new opportunities to pursue the sport.

Despite the increasing presence of blacks in hockey, some prejudices have remained. During the 1997–1998 and 1998–1999 seasons, three NHL players were suspended for using racially inappropriate language toward black players. Since then, the NHL has implemented its own diversity training program. Despite the relatively small presence of black players in the sport since its inception, hockey should continue to see an increase in the number and prominence of black players in the years to come, as urban centers in Canada historically producing top players see increases in the population of black families, more black NHL players act as role models for young black athletes, and initiatives provide access to the sport that were unavailable to children in previous years.

Daniel S. Mason

See also: Willie O'Ree.

FURTHER READING
Carnegie, Herb, and Robert Payne. *A Fly in a Pail of Milk: The Herb Carnegie Story.* Toronto, ON: Mosaic Press, 2000.
Farber, Michael. "Soul on Ice: A Growing Number of Black Players Are Making Their Mark in a League that Until Recently Has Been Known for Its Insensitivity." *Sports Illustrated,* October 4, 1999, 62–69.
Graves, Gary. "Shift Change: More and More Black Players Making Presence Known in NHL." *USA Today,* January 10, 2001, 1C–2C.
Hocker, Cliff, and Eric L. Smith. "Turning Brass into Gold." *Black Enterprise* 28 (March 1998): 20.
Humbers, William. "Black Hockey History." In *Total Hockey,* ed. D. Diamond, J. Duplacey, and I. Kuperman. Kansas City, MO: Andrews and McMeel, 1998.

INTERNATIONAL AFRO-AMERICAN SPORTS HALL OF FAME AND GALLERY

The International Afro-American Sports Hall of Fame and Gallery was established to preserve the contributions made by athletes from among all race and ethnic groups. The International Afro-American Sports Hall of Fame and Gallery, originally located in Detroit, Michigan, was founded on January 9, 1982, by Elmer Anderson (ex-semipro baseball player) and Arthur Finney (editor, UAW Local 63 newspaper). The founders established the Hall of Fame and Gallery to educate youth about the contributions made by athletes of African heritage. Records indicate this was the first International Afro-American Sports Hall of Fame and Gallery.

The International Afro-American Sport Hall of Fame and Gallery has positioned itself to become a nationally and internationally recognized attraction. The gallery's primary function is to preserve the history of Negro league baseball and document the sport contributions made by African-American coaches, administrators, educators, student athletes, and professional sport celebrities.

The gallery features over 500 inductees, including Muhammad Ali, Jackie Robinson, Wilma Rudolph, Paul Robeson, Lem Barney, Thomas Hearns, Spencer Haywood, and Joe Louis. Visitors to the gallery will see uniforms and other sports memorabilia. In addition to honoring outstanding African-American athletes, it maintains a scholarship program for African American youth.

Dedicated to the public commemoration of an African-American athletic heritage, it is a visible challenge to the community to narrow the gap between the ideals of equality and the reality of today's society.

Dana D. Brooks and Ronald Althouse

FURTHER READING
Brooks, Dana D., and Ronald Althouse. "African American Sport: Halls of Fame, Museums, and Associations." In *The African American Athletic Resource Directory*, ed. Dana Brooks and Ronald Althouse. Morgantown, WV: Fitness Information Technology, 1996.
"International Afro-American Sports Hall of Fame" (www.sportshalls.com/Template.cfm).
Singer, Christopher M. "Halls of Glory." *Detroit News*, February 16, 2000.

INTERNATIONAL LEAGUE OF BASEBALL CLUBS IN AMERICA AND CUBA

The International League of Baseball Clubs in America and Cuba (ILBCAC) was a semiprofessional circuit composed of black clubs primarily from New York and Cuba. The ILBCAC was formed in 1907 and consisted of six clubs: Cuban X Giants, Quaker Giants of New York, Cuban Stars, Havana Stars of Cuba, Philadelphia Professional, and Riverton Palmyra. The Quaker Giants and the Havana Stars disbanded in the league's first season and were replaced by the Philadelphia Giants and the Wilmington Giants. In 1908, the Brooklyn Royal Giants and the Genuine Cuban Giants joined the league.

The ILBCAC functioned primarily as a booking agent rather than a traditional league, with teams competing for pennants and championships. Nat Strong—president of the Ridgewood Club, a white semiprofessional team—served as the league's business manager. The formation of the ILBCAC was also instrumental in creating a business alliance with the Chicago City League. The formation of the National Association of Colored Professional Base Ball Clubs (NACPBBC) established scheduling commitments between eastern and western black clubs and simultaneously curbed the destructive practice of player raiding. The formation of the ILBCAC and NACPBBC made Nat Strong the booking power in New York.

In 1910 the ILBCAC disbanded. Several black baseball magnates had complained that their clubs were not given proper consideration in regard to playing dates throughout New York's park system. Philadelphia Giants manager Sol White attempted to persuade both black and white baseball magnates to form a new league and book their own games. However, since none of these moguls owned or leased ballparks in the greater New York area, White's efforts ended in failure.

Michael E. Lomax

FURTHER READING

Lanctot, Neil. "Fair Dealing and Clean Playing: Ed Bolden and the Hilldale Club, 1910–1932," *Pennsylvania Magazine of History and Biography* 67 (January/April 1993): 3–49.

———. *Fair Dealing and Clean Playing: The Hilldale Club and the Development of Black Professional Baseball, 1910–1932*. Jefferson, NC: McFarland, 1994.

Lomax, Michael E. "Black Baseball, Black Community, Black Entrepreneurs: The History of the Negro National and Eastern Colored Leagues, 1880–1930." Ph.D. diss., Ohio State University, 1996.

Ribowsky, Mark. *A Complete History of the Negro Leagues 1884 to 1955*. Secaucus, NJ: Carol, 1995.

★ ★ ★

INTERSCHOLASTIC ATHLETIC ASSOCIATION OF MIDDLE ATLANTIC STATES

The Interscholastic Athletic Association of Middle Atlantic States was founded in 1906 in Washington, DC, by Messrs. William A. Joiner, Ralph Cook, R.N. Mattingly, G.C. Wilkinson, William J. Decatur, Benjamin Washington, Edwin B. Henderson, Haley G. Douglass, and C.C. Cook. Charter representatives included Howard University, the M Street High School (now Dunbar), the Armstrong Manual Training School of Washington, DC, the Douglass High School of Baltimore, and the Howard High School of Wilmington, Delaware. An outgrowth of track and field events, the ISAA was the first organization of schools to foster athletics. The first track and field meet was held May 30, 1906, at Howard University.

The ISAA sponsored a fourteen-week basketball league; participating teams included the M Street High School, LeDroit Park, Howard College, Howard Prep, Crescent A.C., Oberlin A.C., Howard Medical, and Armstrong School. Games were played at True Reformers Hall in Washington, DC. Officers of the basketball league were William A. Joiner, president; R.N. Mattingly, vice president; Ralph Cook, 2nd vice president; G.C. Wilkinson, treasurer; E.B. Henderson, general manager; and Haley G. Douglass, corresponding secretary.

The ISAA published an official handbook, edited by Edwin B. Henderson, William A. Joiner, and G.C. Wilkinson. It was the only book dealing with general athletics for blacks at the time. Fifteen thousand copies of the ISAA handbook were published and sold, with 10,000 copies sold in the South. The ISAA is considered to have been the model for historically black college and university athletic conferences.

Danielle A. Mincey White

See also: Edwin Bancroft Henderson.

FURTHER READING

Coursey, Leon N. Box 44–2, Manuscript Division, Moorland-Springarn Research Center, Howard University. Ph.D. diss., Ohio State University, 1971.

Henderson, Edwin B. *The Negro in Sports*. Washington, DC: Associated, 1949.

William A. Joiner Papers, Box 148–4, folder 8, Manuscript Division, Moorland-Spingarn Research Center, Howard University.

★ ★ ★

Monte IRVIN

Born February 25, 1919, Halesburg, Alabama
Baseball player

Monte Irvin had the great fortune of being able to play with some of the best athletes in both the Negro leagues and the major leagues during his career. In the Negro National League (NNL) Irvin won two batting titles and helped his Newark Eagles win the World Series over Kansas City in 1946. He joined the New York Giants at the end of the 1949 season and finished his first full season with them in 1950, hitting .299. He finished his eight-year major-league career in 1956 with the Chicago Cubs, leaving with a career .293 batting average. His accomplishments led to his election to the National Baseball Hall of Fame in 1973. Since retiring as an active player, Irvin has remained connected with the game, serving as a scout, in the commissioner's office, and on the Veteran's Committee for the Hall of Fame.

Irvin's career is even more amazing when one realizes that he lost four years during World War II, when he enlisted. He hit .395 in 1941 before he left the

Monte Irvin holding up four fingers to indicate the number of hits he made in the opening World Series game against the New York Yankees in 1951. *(AP/Wide World Photos)*

Newark Eagles and .404 in 1946 when he returned.

Leslie A. Heaphy

FURTHER READING

Clark, Dick, and Larry Lester. *The Negro Leagues Book*. Cleveland: Society for American Baseball Research, 1994.

Green, Paul. "An Interview with Monte Irvin." *Sports Collectors Digest*, September 16, 1983, 42–50.

Porter, David L., ed. *Biographical Dictionary of American Sports: Baseball*. Westport, CT: Greenwood Press, 1987.

Riley, James A. *The Biographical Encyclopedia of the Negro Baseball Leagues*. New York: Carroll and Graf, 1994.

"Rajo" JACK

Born July 28, 1905, Tyler, Texas
Died February 27, 1956, Ridgecrest, California
Race driver

The life of "Rajo" Jack, one of the few black racing drivers in the years before World War II, is shrouded in mystery. Jack got his nickname when he was the top salesman on the Pacific Coast for the Rajo cylinder head used on Model T Fords. His real name was, according to himself, Roger Jack DeSoto; his wife Ruth said it was Dewey Gatson. His death certificate lists him only as Rajo Jack.

The family moved from Texas to California, and Jack settled in Los Angeles, where he lived the rest of his life. Inspired by driver Barney Oldfield, he began racing around 1923. Little is known of his career until the early 1930s, when he competed very successfully in Southern California. Throughout the decade he was a top driver on the West Coast. Around 1941 Jack traveled east and raced on the Midwest circuit, where he was billed as "Rajah Ramacus, the Portuguese Dirt Track Champion" because of the racist atmosphere at the tracks. In 1954, as one of fifteen drivers representing the western area of the North American continent, he won two races sponsored by the Honolulu Chamber of Commerce. Jack was a gifted mechanic and a hard-charging driver, and he suffered many wrecks and injuries. He lost his right eye in a wreck in a 1938 race in Oakland, California, and had an arm permanently bent, so that he could hardly reach the steering wheel. Most major prewar races were sanctioned by the American Automobile Association, which barred drivers of color from membership. By the time blacks were accepted he could not meet the physical requirements, so he never fulfilled his lifelong dream of competing in the Indianapolis 500. Late in his life Jack took long auto trips for no apparent reason. On one of these rambles he began to feel unwell and pulled off the road. He died near Ridgecrest in the Mojave Desert at the wheel of his truck, possibly of a heart attack or a cerebral hemorrhage.

Suzanne Wise

FURTHER READING
Ashe, Arthur R., Jr. *A Hard Road to Glory: A History of the African-American Athlete, 1919–1945*. New York: Warner Books, 1988.
Radbruch, Don. "Mystery Man Rajo Jack." *Secrets Magazine*, April 1999, 32.
"Rajo Jack." *Four Banger*, January 1975, 7–9, 20.
"Rajo Jack: Biography." *National Speed Sport News*, June 1944, 5.
Young, A.S. "Doc." *Negro Firsts in Sports*. Chicago: Johnson, 1963.

★ ★ ★

Bo JACKSON

Born November 30, 1962, Bessemer, Alabama
Football player, baseball player, decathlete

"Bo," nicknamed by his family, was an outstanding all-around athlete from an early age. At McAdory High in McCalla, Alabama, Jackson lettered in football, baseball, and track and field. He was a two-time state champion in the decathlon. He set a national high school home run record (twenty) in baseball as a senior and stole ninety bases in ninety-one attempts in his career. In football he was an All-State running back in his senior year, gaining 1,173 yards.

Jackson continued his prolific performance as a multisport athlete for Auburn University, lettering in track, baseball, and football. In baseball he was considered one of the top professional prospects in the nation; 1985 was his highlight year, with a .401 batting average. But it was football that brought him to national recognition. During his four-year career he rushed for 4,303 yards and forty-three regular-season touchdowns. He culminated his collegiate career in 1985 with four 200-yard games, 1,786 yards rushing and seventeen touchdowns. The Downtown Athletic Club of New York selected Jackson as the Heisman Trophy winner for 1985. In 1998 he was inducted into the National Football Foundation and College Hall of Fame.

In 1986 Jackson was selected with the first pick in the National Football League draft. But he turned down the multimillion dollar offer to pursue a career in professional baseball. Jackson made his major league baseball debut with the Kansas City Royals in 1986. In 1987 while playing for the Royals, Jackson made his professional football debut with the Los Angeles Raiders. As a multisport professional athlete Jackson became a media icon. In 1989 Jackson's performance in the major league All-Star Game gained him the Most Valuable Player award. During the next year he was selected to the football Pro Bowl, becoming the first ever All-Star player in two different professional sports. Jackson's success was cut short by a career-shattering hip injury during a 1991 playoff game for the Raiders. He would never be the same. His football career was over, and his baseball career was brought to a premature end.

David W. Hunter

FURTHER READING
Auburn University, *Bo Jackson 1985 Heisman Trophy Winner* (www.auburn.edu/athletics/fball/bo.html).
Devaney, John. *Bo Jackson: A Star for All Seasons*. New York: Walker, 1992.
Jackson, Bo, and Dick Schapp. *Bo Knows Bo*. New York: Doubleday, 1990.
Knapp, Ron. *Sports Great Bo Jackson*. Hillside, NJ: Enslow, 1990.

★ ★ ★

Levi JACKSON

Born August 22, 1926, Branford, Connecticut
Died December 7, 2000, Detroit, Michigan
Football player, business executive

Jackson was the son of George Jackson, a Yale University chef, and his wife, Adeline, a university custodial worker. A graduate of Yale (B.A.), Jackson was that university's first African-American football player and the first black player to be elected team captain. He was also the first black executive at Ford Motor Company and a key figure in Detroit's recovery after the riot of 1967.

Jackson would have been among the first professional black football players in postwar America had he accepted a $10,000 offer from the New York Giants, whom he helped defeat while playing on an army post team during World War II. He also turned down a football scholarship from Indiana University to play running back for Yale. His election in 1948 as Yale's captain came the same day that the Associated Press named him to its All-Eastern Team. By the time he graduated in 1950 he held or shared thirteen Yale records. Jackson also played varsity basketball for Yale.

At Ford, Jackson worked in personnel and labor relations and was instrumental in building the automaker's minority dealership program. Following the riot of 1967, he spent a year counseling Ford and city and private agencies on ways to reform hiring and training for minorities. In 1967 Ford named him Citizen of the Year, and in 1987 he received the Walter Camp Man of the Year Award from the Walter Camp Foundation.

Mary Jo Binker

FURTHER READING
May, Jeanne. "Levi Jackson: The First Black Executive at Ford." *Detroit Free Press*, December 9, 2000.
Schiff, Judith Ann. "Levi Jackson: Hometown Hero." *Yale Alumni Magazine*, October 1999, 104.
"Yale Elects First Negro Captain as Jackson Heads Football Team" *New York Times*, November 23, 1948.

★ ★ ★

Mannie JACKSON

Born May 4, 1939, Illmo, Missouri
Basketball player and owner

Mannie Jackson was the son of Emmett and Margaret Jackson and a graduate of Edwardsville High School in Edwardsville, Illinois, the University of Illinois (B.A.), and the University of Detroit (MBA). His remarkable career took him from a small town of 8,000 in southern Illinois to the board rooms of America's most successful corporations.

Jackson's family moved to Edwardsville when he was four years old. His father, a factory worker, was an articulate leader of the black community, which successfully integrated the Edwardsville public schools in 1952. A football, basketball, and track star, Jackson and his lifelong friend Govoner Vaughn led Edwardsville to the Illinois state championship finals in 1956 before it fell to Rockford High School 61–59. As Illinois's "Mr. Basketball" in 1956, Jackson was nationally recruited but decided, along with Vaughn, to accept a basketball scholarship to the University of Illinois. They were the first African-American basketball players to earn varsity letters at the university. Elected team captain as a senior, Jackson finished his three-year career with 922 points and earned All-Big Ten and All-American recognition.

Upon graduation he played one year with the New York Technical Tape Corporation in the National Industrial Basketball League and two years, 1961–1963, for the Harlem Globetrotters. After working for General Motors for three years, Jackson joined Honeywell, where he became senior vice president for marketing and administration. In 1993 Jackson put together an investment group that purchased the Harlem Globetrotters, which made him the first African American to own a major sports organization.

Besides reviving the Globetrotters, Jackson is director of four *Fortune 500* companies and the recipient of numerous awards and distinctions. In 1993 *Black Enterprise* magazine named him one of the nation's forty most powerful and influential black executives. In 1995 he was one was one of twelve nominees for the Archbishop Desmond Tutu Award for Human Rights. He is a charter member of the Illinois Basketball Hall of Fame, and the University of Illinois honored him in 1996 with its lifetime Achievement Award. Jackson and his wife, Catherine, have two daughters and live in Scottsdale, Arizona.

Adolph H. Grundman

FURTHER READING
Biographical Sketch, Department of Sports Information, University of Illinois. Biographical Sketch, Harlem Globetrotters.
Phone Interview, September 11, 2001.

★ ★ ★

Peter JACKSON

Born July 3, 1861, St. Croix, Virgin Islands
Died July 13, 1901, Roma, Australia
Boxer

The son of a fisherman and his wife, Jackson was a famous heavyweight boxer in

Boxing champion Peter Jackson toward the latter stages of his career. Frustrated in his attempts to secure a bout with John L. Sullivan and living a bit too extravagantly, Jackson died at the rather young age of 40 in Australia. *(Courtesy of Bill Schutte)*

the late nineteenth century who fought several important bouts against many of the world's best fighters. Known as "Black Prince Peter" for his gentlemanly deportment, the six-foot, 200-pound Jackson represented a new breed of fighter who used ring generalship rather than the mauling tactics of earlier boxers. He was a scientific fighter who relied on strategy as well as the quickness of his feet and power of his punching to beat his opponents.

Jackson was born in the West Indies but at the age of twelve moved with his parents to Australia, where he learned the art of boxing from American ship owner Clay Callahan and then later from Larry Foley at his White Horse Saloon, in Sydney. His first great triumph was a thirty-round victory over Tom Lees at Foley's Saloon in 1886 for the Australian heavyweight championship. Unable to find any worthwhile opponents in Australia following the Lees match, Jackson journeyed to America in 1888 for the express purpose of securing a fight with the world champion, "the Boston Strong Boy," John L. Sullivan. Unfortunately, Sullivan steadfastly refused to cross the color line, which forced Jackson to fight nonchampionship, yet important bouts against other great pugilists. In 1891 Jackson fought a much-publicized bout against "Gentleman" James J. Corbett at the California Athletic Club in San Francisco. The bout, which ended in a draw after sixty grueling rounds, raised Corbett's stock considerably in the eyes of boxing aficionados and catapulted him, ironically enough, into a championship fight with Sullivan one year later. In 1892 Jackson defeated Frank Slavin in a viciously contested fight in London's National Sporting Club. In front of some 1,300 spectators, which included promoters, journalists, and various members of London's ruling class, Jackson pummeled Slavin before finally knocking him out with a minute left in the tenth round. Jackson's last fight was a humiliating defeat by the future heavyweight champion Jim Jeffries in 1898 in San Francisco's Woodward Pavilion.

As with so many boxers, Jackson's postfight career was a relatively short and unhappy one. Physically drained from years in the ring and too much alcohol, Jackson returned home to Australia in 1900. He occasionally gave boxing exhibitions and traveled with the Fitzgerald Brothers Circus for a time. The following year, however, he was stricken with tuberculosis and died in the arms of his close friend, the black comedian Ernest Hogan. He was only forty years old.

David K. Wiggins

See also: Boxing.

FURTHER READING
Fleischer, Nathaniel S. *Black Dynamite: The Story of the Negro in the Prize Ring from 1782 to 1938.* 3 vols. New York: Ring Book Shop, 1938.
Hales, A.G. *Black Prince Peter: The Romantic Career of Peter Jackson.* London: Wright and Brown, 1931.
Langley, Tom. *The Life of Peter Jackson: Champion of Australia.* Leicester, England: Vance Harvey, 1974.
Wiggins, David K. "Peter Jackson and the Elusive Heavyweight Championship: A Black Athletes Struggle Against the Late Nineteenth Century Color-Line." *Journal of Sport History* 12 (Summer 1985): 143–68.

Reggie Jackson, slugging outfielder of New York Yankees, taking a gigantic swing for a strike in a 1977 game against the Toronto Blue Jays. *(AP/Wide World Photos)*

★ ★ ★

Reggie JACKSON

Born May 18, 1946, Wyncote, Pennsylvania
Baseball player

Over his twenty-one-year career, Reggie Jackson, "Mr. October," epitomized the power hitter for a generation of baseball fans. He broke into professional baseball in 1967 with the Kansas City Athletics and moved with the team to Oakland the next year. Over the next eight years, the Athletics won the American League West pennant from 1971 to 1975 and the World Series in 1972, 1973, and 1974. Individually, Jackson won both the American League and World Series MVP awards in 1973.

In 1975, Oakland traded Jackson to the Baltimore Orioles. He spent one year in Baltimore before signing as a free agent with the New York Yankees. During his five-year stint with New York, Jackson helped the team win four divisional titles and two World Series titles.

Game six of the 1977 World Series proved to be Jackson's defining moment—he hit three consecutive home runs. The feat made him the first person since Babe Ruth to hit three home runs in one World Series game and the first person to hit five home runs in a single postseason series.

In 1982, he signed with the California Angels. That same year he led the league in home runs and helped the Angels win their division. He returned to Oakland in 1987 for his final season. Jackson compiled a .262 lifetime batting average and collected 563 home runs. He also struck out a record 2,597 times. In 1993, he was inducted into the National Baseball Hall of Fame.

Rob Fink

FURTHER READING
Baseball Encyclopedia: The Complete and Definitive Record of Major League Baseball. 10th ed. New York: Macmillan, 1996.
Hahn, James, and Lynn Hahn. *Reggie Jackson, Slugger Supreme.* St. Paul: EMC Corporation, 1979.
Jackson, Reggie, with Mike Lupica. *Reggie: The Autobiography.* New York: Villard Books, 1984.

Joe JEANNETTE

Born August 26, 1879, North Bergen, New Jersey
Died July 2, 1958, Weehawken, New Jersey
Boxer

As a young man, Jeannette's first pugilistic experiences were bloody and brutal neighborhood brawls in which it was the survival of the fittest. The winner was, more often than not, the fighter able to absorb the most punishment.

Although he did not become a professional boxer until he was twenty-five, Jeannette had a career that was both rapid and successful. In his career, Jeannette fought all of the great black boxers—Jack Johnson, Sam Langford, Morris Harris, Black Bill, Battling Jim Johnson and Harry Wills. He outpointed the white French European champion Georges Carpentier in 1914. Jeanette's real disappointment was that Jack Johnson never allowed him a title fight. Steven Bunce and Bob Mee describe a cultural climate in which racial discrimination manifested itself by the subtle strategy of stonewalling black contenders: "In those days waiting for a fight was itself hazardous business. It was all to easy to succumb to injury or ill health before you had your shot at the title."

Jeannette retired at the age of forty in 1919. While official records list 157 career fights, Jeannette claimed that he had taken part in some 400 bouts. Jeannette appeared in the 1921 boxing movie *Square Joe* and starred with another black boxer, John Lester Johnson. His most intriguing film record is in a *Jack Johnson* (1970) documentary that showed Jeannette fighting Johnson in a November 27, 1945, exhibition (three one-minute rounds) in New York. In his later years, Jeannette worked as a referee, ran a limousine rental firm, and operated a gymnasium. He was inducted into the Hall of Fame in 1997.

Scott A.G.M. Crawford

See also: Boxing; Harry Wills.

FURTHER READING

Bunce, Steve, and Bob Mee. *Boxing Greats: An Illustrated History of the Legends of the Ring.* Philadelphia: Courage Books, 1998.

Roberts, James B., and Alexander G. Skutt. *The Boxing Register: International Boxing Hall of Fame Book.* Ithaca, NY: McBooks Press, 1999.

Sammons, Jeffrey T. *Beyond the Ring: The Role of Boxing in American Society.* Urbana: University of Illinois Press, 1988.

Zucker, Harvey M., and Lawrence J. Babich. *Sports Films: A Complete Reference.* Jefferson, NC: McFarland, 1987.

Bernie JEFFERSON

Born January 12, 1918, Grand Rapids, Michigan
Died August 1991, Scottsdale, Arizona
Football player and coach

A graduate of Ottawa Hills High School in 1935, Bernie Jefferson attended Northwestern University in Evanston, Illinois, from 1935 to 1939. He received his undergraduate degree in education. While attending Northwestern University, Jefferson was a star halfback/defensive back on the football team for the 1936–1938 seasons. He led Northwestern to its last Big Ten championship in 1936. His play in the scoreless tie with the University of Michigan made him one of the all-time defensive backs developed at Northwestern University under head coach Lyn Waldorf. Over 70,000 fans packed Michigan Stadium in the contest with Northwestern in 1936. They saw Jefferson play a career game as an aggressive, quick-thinking defender. He batted down all but one of the passes thrown into his zone; the one he did not ground, he intercepted.

After graduation in 1939 from Northwestern, Jefferson was sought out by many historically black colleges and universities (HBCUs) to serve as head coach. He eventually organized and served as player coach of an all-Negro semiprofessional football team in Chicago, the Brown Bombers. In 1942, Jefferson joined the Army Air Corps and was a member of the 33rd Fighting Group, also known as the Tuskegee Airmen. He flew more than 100 missions over Europe and was awarded the Distinguished Flying Cross. He was honored for destroying two key enemy radar stations in Toulon, France. He also received the Air Medal and six oak leaf clusters.

After World War II, Jefferson received his master's degree from the Chicago Teachers' College, now Chicago State University. He served as a public school teacher for more than thirty-five years and completed his education career as the principal at Cook Country Jail School from 1971 to 1980. He was the school's first black principal, and he enlarged the school's General Education Development Program, brought in new teachers, and expanded its teaching staff from nineteen to forty. He combined the County Jail School with the House of Corrections School and changed the name to The School to Meet Special Needs. Jefferson retired in 1980 and moved to Georgia. In 1987, he settled in Scottsdale, Arizona, where he passed away in 1991.

Gary A. Sailes

FURTHER READING

Ashe, Arthur R., Jr. *A Hard Road to Glory: A History of The African-American Athlete.* New York: Warner Books, 1983.

Athletic Department at Northwestern University, Evanston, IL.

Lawson, Edward "Who Will Be All-American?" *Opportunity* 16 (October 1938): 300–301.

Nace, Ed. "Negro Grid Stars, Past and Present." *Opportunity* 17 (September 1939): 272–73.

Wilkins, Roy. "Negro Stars on Big Grid Teams." *Crisis* 43 (December 1936): 362.

★ ★ ★

Cornelius JOHNSON

Born August 21, 1913, Los Angeles, California
Died February 15, 1946, San Francisco, California
Sprinter, high jumper

The son of Shadreak Johnson, a plasterer, Cornelius Johnson graduated from Los Angeles Senior High School in 1933 and attended Compton Junior College. A national and Olympic champion in the high jump, he later worked as a letter carrier and served in the U.S. merchant marine.

Johnson dominated high school track and field competition in the sprints and the high jump. He won the AAU national outdoor championship in the high jump in 1933, 1935, and 1936, and he tied for the title in 1932 and 1934. In 1935 Johnson won the AAU indoor title outright. As a high school junior, he finished fourth in the 1932 Olympic high jump. Before the 1936 Olympic Games, Johnson established a high jump world record of 6 feet, 9¾ inches. Triumphant in the high jump in the 1936 Olympic Games, he established an Olympic record of six feet, eight inches. While Johnson's Olympic triumph, the first of several by African Americans at the 1936 Olympic Games, may have temporarily undermined the Nazi notion of Aryan superiority, it accomplished little in weakening American racism.

Johnson retired from athletics in 1938

and became a letter carrier for the U.S. Post Office in Los Angeles. In 1945 he joined the merchant marine, serving as a baker on the *Santa Cruz.* Johnson became gravely ill at sea and died en route to the San Francisco Harbor Emergency Medical Center in 1946.

Adam R. Hornbuckle

See also: Track and Field.

FURTHER READING
Ashe, Arthur R., Jr. *A Hard Road to Glory—Track and Field: The African-American Athlete in Track and Field.* New York: Warner Books, 1988.
Baker, William J. *Jesse Owens: An American Life.* New York: Free Press, 1986.
Mandell, Richard D. *The Nazi Olympics.* New York: Macmillan, 1971.
Menke, Frank G. *The Encyclopedia of Sports.* 4th rev. ed. New York: Barnes, 1969.
Quercetani, Roberto L. *A World History of Track and Field Athletics.* London and New York: Oxford University Press, 1964.
Wallechinsky, David. *The Complete Book of the Summer Olympics.* Woodstock, NY: Overlook Press, 2000.
Wiggins, David K. "The 1936 Olympic Games in Berlin: The Response of America's Black Press." *Research Quarterly for Exercise and Sport* 54 (1983): 279–82.

★ ★ ★

Jack JOHNSON

Born March 31, 1878, Galveston, Texas
Died June 10, 1946, Raleigh, North Carolina
Boxer

Jack Johnson was born in Galveston, Texas, to Henry and Tina Johnson. Henry had been a slave and after the Civil War worked as a woodcutter and janitor. At the age of ten Jack stopped attending school and began to earn money for his family.

In 1897 Johnson became a professional boxer, a career that lasted until 1945. For years Johnson was regarded as the best boxer in the world, but he was not given an opportunity until 1908 to challenge the

Controversial heavyweight champion Jack Johnson reading his scrapbook just three years prior to his 1946 death in an auto accident just north of Raleigh, North Carolina. *(AP/Wide World Photos)*

world champion. In that year he defeated Tommy Burns in Australia. This bout produced a seven-year search for the "Great White Hope," a white man who could defeat Johnson. Racial riots occurred in various cities across the United States after former champion James Jeffries failed to defeat Johnson during a bout staged in Reno, Nevada, in 1910. In 1915 Johnson may have allowed a white boxer to defeat him during the sixteenth round of a match held in Cuba, in order to reduce threats against him that were caused by his title and his marriage to a white woman.

Johnson resented white racism, often flaunting his wealth and fame in order to offend his many white detractors. Over the course of his life he married three white women. His second marriage (after the suicide of his first wife) caused Johnson to run afoul of the Mann Act, prohibiting the transportation of women across state borders for immoral purposes. This caused Johnson to flee the country in 1913. He continued his boxing career in Europe and Mexico, where he occasionally fought bulls as well. Upon his return in 1920, he was arrested and sent to Leavenworth Federal Penitentiary.

Johnson's winnings were spent on a fast-paced life. During the 1920s and 1930s he operated nightclubs in Chicago and Harlem. He also appeared in movies and drove racecars, a hobby that cost him his life in 1946.

Gregory S. Goodale

See also: Autobiographies; Boxing; Films; Joe Jeannette; Sam Langford; Sam McVey; Harry Wills.

FURTHER READING
Gilmore, Al-Tony. *Bad Nigger! The National Impact of Jack Johnson.* Port Washington, NY: Kennikat, 1975.
Johnson, Jack. *Jack Johnson in the Ring and Out.* 1927. Reprint, Chicago: Bicentennial, 1977
Roberts, Randy. *Papa Jack: Jack Johnson and the Era of White Hopes.* New York: Free Press, 1983.
Sammons, Jeffrey T. *Beyond the Ring: The Role of Boxing in American Society.* Urbana: University of Illinois Press, 1988.
Van Den Bergh, Tony. *The Jack Johnson Story.* London: Panther Books, 1956.

★ ★ ★

John Henry JOHNSON

Born November 24, 1929, Waterproof, Louisiana
Football player

Johnson attended high school in Pittsburg, California, where his athletic accomplishments were remarkable. Besides gaining numerous honors in football, he competed in basketball, baseball, track, and wrestling. Johnson was a three-year All-Contra Costa County Athletic League selection in football, basketball, and track. Taking advantage of his athletic talents, Johnson went on to become a football and track star at Arizona State University.

After receiving his degree from Arizona State, Johnson played in the Canadian Football League with Calgary for a year. In his first season, Johnson was awarded the Most Valuable Player trophy for his contributions to the team. Continuing his athletic pursuits, Johnson later joined the San Francisco 49ers in 1954, where he played alongside another Hall of Famer, Hugh McElhenny, to make one of the most feared backfield tandems in the National Football League (NFL).

In 1957, he was traded to the Detroit Lions and helped them win the 1957 championship. Johnson continued his successful NFL career with the Pittsburgh Steelers from 1960 to 1965. While a member of the Steelers, he surpassed 1,000 yards in 1962 and 1964 and became the first Steeler to rush for 200 yards in a single game. In 1966, he joined the Houston Oilers for a year before retiring.

Johnson's career accomplishments included three Pro Bowls, 6,803 rushing yards, and forty-eight touchdowns, earning him induction into the Professional Football Hall of Fame in 1987.

Eddie Comeaux and C. Keith Harrison

FURTHER READING
Ashe, Arthur R., Jr. *A Hard Road to Glory: A History of the African-American Athlete, 1919–1945.* New York: Warner Books, 1983.
Eger, Bob. *Maroon and Gold: A History of Sun Devil Athletics.* Phoenix: Sports Publishing, 2001.
Hickok, Ralph. *Sport Champions.* New York: Houghton Mifflin, 1995.

★ ★ ★

Magic JOHNSON

Born August 14, 1959, Lansing, Michigan
Basketball player

After leading Michigan State to a national collegiate basketball championship, Johnson became the premier point guard in the National Basketball Association (NBA), playing for the Los Angeles Lakers (1979–1996).

Johnson was the middle of seven children born to Earvin Sr. (an auto plant worker) and Christine (school cafeteria worker). At Lansing Everett High School, Johnson led his team to a state Class A basketball championship in 1977 and was named the UPI Prep Player of the Year.

Johnson enrolled in Michigan State University, where as a freshman he helped the Spartans achieve a 25–5 record and win a Big Ten title. In 1979, Johnson led Michigan State to the National Collegiate Athletic Association national championship, defeating the Larry Byrd–led Indiana State team.

Johnson left for the NBA at the end of his sophomore year and made an immediate impact on the league, leading Los Angeles to the league championship, averaging eighteen points, over seven rebounds, and seven assists per game. Johnson showed in that season and in subsequent seasons how a point guard through brilliant passing and assists could raise the level of play of his teammates. Johnson led the Lakers to four more NBA titles—1982, 1985, 1987, and 1988. He was the league's Most Valuable Player three times—1987, 1989, and 1990, and an All-Star twelve times.

In 1991 Johnson retired from the NBA because he had contracted human immunodeficiency virus (HIV), but he played in the 1992 Olympic Games. He made three short returns to the Lakers, twice as a player during the 1992–1993 and 1995–1996 seasons, and once as a coach, in the 1993–1994 season. Johnson was elected to the Naismith Memorial Basketball Hall of Fame in 2002.

Johnson, with his dazzling play, ebullient personality, and infectious smile, was one of the marquee players in the 1980s and helped significantly to make the professional game, which had become dominated by African-American players, accepted and popular with mainstream America.

Robert Pruter

Los Angeles Lakers' star Magic Johnson making one of his many assists during his Hall of Fame NBA career. *(AP/Wide World Photos)*

See also: Autobiographies; Basketball; Olympic Games.

FURTHER READING
Bigelow, Barbara Carlisle, ed. *Contemporary Black Biography.* Vol. 3. Detroit: Gale Research, 1993.
Donnelly, Sally B., and Dick Thompson. "It Can Happen to Anybody, Even Magic Johnson." *Time*, November 18, 1991, 26–27.
Johnson, Earvin "Magic," with William Novak. *My Life.* New York: Random House, 1992.
Smith, Eric L. "The Magic Touch!" *Black Enterprise*, May 1999, 74–82.

★ ★ ★

Michael JOHNSON

Born September 13, 1967, Dallas, Texas
Sprinter

Youngest of five children born to Paul Johnson, Sr., a truck driver, and Ruby Johnson, an elementary school teacher, he holds the world record in both the 200 (19.32 seconds) and 400-meter (43.18 seconds) sprint events and is world record coholder in the 4 x 400-meter relay (2:54.20 seconds). Although he ran with an atypical stiff and upright technique, he is considered one of the greatest multidistance sprinters of all time.

Johnson grew up in a fairly strict home, and his parents stressed the importance of getting a good education. He ran track and played football in junior high school but gave up the latter sport after two years. He continued running track at Skyline High School in Dallas and in 1986 placed second at 200 meters in a Texas State High School meet. He majored in accounting and marketing at Baylor University in Waco, Texas, and was a member of the track team coached by Clyde Hart. He began his international career in 1990 by competing at the Goodwill Games in Seattle, Washington. He won twenty of twenty-one races that year and became the first male sprinter to be ranked number-one in the world in both the 200 and 400-meter dashes. He continued his number-one ranking in both distances the following year, went undefeated, and made a stunning impression at the World Track and Field Championships. Johnson was expected to win two gold medals in these same events in 1992 at the Barcelona Olympic Games. Unfortunately, he was weakened severely from food poisoning two weeks before the games, and his individual medal hopes did not materialize. He did, however, win a gold medal as a member of the 4 x 400-meter relay team with a world-record time of 2:55.74.

After the 1992 Olympics Johnson fell in the rankings, but he regained his number-one spot at 400 meters the following year; a title he held for most of the decade. Beginning in 1994, he received the Jesse Owens Memorial Award as the most outstanding U.S. track and field athlete three consecutive times. His most spectacular victories occurred at the 1996 Atlanta Olympic Games. Johnson became the first man to win a gold medal in both the 200 and 400-meter sprint events. His 200-meter time of 19.32 still stands as a world record. That same year he received the Amateur Athletic Union's (AAU) James E. Sullivan Memorial Award, as well as the International Amateur Athlete Federation's (IAAF) Jesse Owens International Trophy for best amateur athlete in the world. He won the Owens International Trophy the following year after winning his third consecutive world championship title at 400 meters. In 1998, at the Goodwill Games in Uniondale, New York, he ran the last leg for the 4 x 400-meter relay team that set a new and existing world record of 2:54:20. At the 2000 Sydney Olympic Games he became the first man to repeat a gold medal victory at the 400-meter distance and won a second gold medal on the 1,600-meter relay team.

Johnson retired from competitive track at the age of thirty-four in September 2001 after participating in his fourth Goodwill Games in Brisbane, Australia. That November in Monaco he was honored by the International Athletic Foundation with its Distinguished Career Award for exemplary performance and sportsmanship. He presently lives with his wife and daughter in Mill Valley, California.

Danny Rosenberg

FURTHER READING
Agence France-Presse. "Johnson to Receive Career Award"(www.sportserver.com/track_field/story/T73595p-1683027c.html).
Baum, Greg. "Farewell Superman, You'll be Missed" (www.theage.com.au/sport).
Burfoot, Amby, Dave Kuehls, Marty Post, and Bob Wischnia. "Bound for Glory." *Runner's World* (September 1996): 54, 55, 58.
"Johnson, Michael." *Encarta* (www.encarta.msn.com/index/conciseindex/AB/0ABDB000.html).
"Michael Johnson." *USA Track and Field* (www.usatf.org/athletes/bios/Johnson_Michael.shtml).
Rosenthal, Bert. "Michael Johnson Ends Career with Relay Win." (www.usatoday.com/olympics/summer/2001-09-07–goodwill.htm).
Runner's World, November 1992, 86.
Sports Illustrated, July 22, 1996, 74–84.
"The Top Runners of the 20th Century: Men, #2 Michael Johnson, USA, 200 and 400 Meters" (www.coolrunning.com/20century/20th02m.shtml).

★ ★ ★

Rafer JOHNSON

Born August 18, 1935, Hillsboro, Texas
Decathlete

One of six children of handyman Lewis and domestic Elma (Gibson) Johnson, he rose from an impoverished background to attend college and become a decathlon silver medalist at the 1956 Melbourne, Australia, Olympic Games and a gold medalist at the 1960 Olympics in Rome, Italy.

Johnson began his schooling in Texas until his family moved to Kingsburg, California, when he was eleven. He attended Kingsburg High School and demonstrated his prowess as an all-around athlete. He ran track for four years, played forward in basketball for three years, and led his team to three championships as halfback in football. He batted over .400 in the one year he played baseball, in center field. At the 1954 California State Track Meet, Johnson finished first in the high hurdles and placed second in the low hurdles. Although he excelled in several sports, at the age of sixteen he decided to focus on the decathlon. As a high school senior he placed third in the 1954 Amateur Athletic Union (AAU) decathlon championships. Johnson received a football scholarship to the University of California at Los Angeles (UCLA) but declined to play football to pursue his track career and in order to avoid serious injury. In 1955 he captained the freshman track team, broke or equaled five freshman track records, and lettered in freshman basketball.

In March of the same year, Johnson gained international recognition by winning a gold medal in the decathlon at the Pan American Games with a score of 6,994 points. Kingsburg hosted the AAU decathlon championships in June 1955, and before a hometown crowd Johnson won the title with a world-record score of 7,983 points. In 1956 he led UCLA to its first National Collegiate Athletic Association (NCAA) track and field title, even though he was hampered by an old football injury. He earned All-American status and became a member of the U.S. Olympic track and field team in the decathlon and broad jump. He was favored to win a gold at the Melbourne Olympics in the decathlon but came in second.

After recovering from knee surgery in 1957, Johnson returned to compete in decathlon events. In August of 1958, he participated in Moscow's "Little Olympics" and defeated rival Vasily Kuznetsov with a world decathlon record of 8,302 points. In the same period, Johnson kept up an A average at UCLA, played basketball for two years under legendary coach John Wooden, was president of the student body, became the first African American to pledge at a white fraternity, and headed three campus honorary societies. He also befriended fellow UCLA decathlete C.K. Yang, a Chinese student from Formosa; the two developed a fierce but amicable rivalry. In 1959, Kuznetsov regained the decathlon world title because Johnson suffered a back injury in an automobile accident and could not compete. After a complete recovery, Johnson edged out Yang to win the decathlon at the 1960 Olympic Games in Rome.

After the Rome Olympics, Johnson retired from track. He received the James E. Sullivan Memorial Trophy, an annual national award given to the amateur athlete who best exemplifies sportsmanship. In 1960, he was honored as the Associated Press's Athlete of the Year. He was an executive with Continental Telephone, served as director of the Kennedy Foundation, and engaged in community service. At one time he served as chair of the Olympian Citizens Advisory Commission, president of the board of directors of the California Special Olympics, and national head coach of the Washington, DC, Special Olympics, Inc. He was a member of the Los Angeles Olympic Organizing Committee and on the board of the Amateur Athletic Foundation. At the opening ceremonies of the 1984 Los Angeles Olympics, Johnson was given the honor of lighting the Olympic cauldron in Memorial Coliseum. He is a member of the U.S. Track Hall of Fame.

Danny Rosenberg

See also: Track and Field.

FURTHER READING

Hanley, Reid M. *Who's Who in Track and Field.* New Rochelle, NY: Arlington House, 1973.

Henderson, Edwin B., with the editors of *Sport* Magazine. *The Black Athlete: Emergence and Arrival.* New York: Publishers, 1968.

Johnson, Rafer, with Philip Goldberg. *The Best That I Can Be: An Autobiography.* New York: Doubleday, 1998.

Orr, Jack. *The Black Athlete: His Story in American History.* New York: Lion Books, 1969.

Page, James A. *Black Olympian Medalists.* Englewood, CO: Libraries Unlimited, 1991.

★ ★ ★

Robert L. JOHNSON

Born April 8, 1946, Hickory, Mississippi
NBA franchise owner

Johnson, the recipient of a B.A. in history from the University of Illinois and M.A. in public affairs from Princeton University, is a media mogul who has the distinction of being the first African-American billionaire. In 1980, with a forty-thousand-dollar second mortgage on his home in Washington, DC, Johnson started Black Entertainment Television (BET), which offers sitcoms, comedies, public affairs, news, music videos, and youth programming. In addition to BET, which reaches approximately 90 percent of African-American cable households, according to Nielson Media Research, Johnson has investments with U.S. Airways, Vanguard Media, and lottery business on six Caribbean Islands. He is also a board member for U.S. Airways, Hilton Hotels Corporation, United Negro College Fund, General Mills, American Film Institute, and National Cable Television Association.

In 2002 Johnson made history when he became the first African American to own a professional sports franchise, by purchasing the National Basketball Associations (NBA) expansion team in Charlotte, NC. Outbidding a group led by basketball legend Larry Bird, Johnson paid three hundred million dollars for a franchise set to begin play during the 2004–2005 season. Johnson also has made plans, along with several other investors, to purchase a major league baseball team and bring it to the Northern Virginia/Washington, DC area.

Johnson has received numerous honors and awards for his many accomplishments. He has, for instance, been given the NAACP Image Award, the National Women's Political Caucus's Good Guy Award, the Broadcasting and Cable Magazine's Hall of Fame Award, and the President's Award from the National Cable Television Association.

David K. Wiggins

FURTHER READING
Taylor, Phil. "93 Franchise Player." *Sports Illustrated*, May 5, 2003, 35–37.
USA Today, December 19, 2002.
Washington Post, December 19, 2002.
Who's Who in America. Vol. 1. New Providence, NJ: Reed, 1993.

★ ★ ★

William "Judy" JOHNSON

Born October 26, 1899, Snow Hill, Maryland
Died June 5, 1989, Wilmington, Delaware
Baseball player

The son of Annie Lee and William Henry, a sailor, licensed boxing coach, and athletic director of the Negro Settlement House in Wilmington, Johnson was groomed to be a boxer, but he opted for baseball instead; he would bat .309 for his career. This intelligent and sure-handed third baseman was considered the top third baseman in the Negro leagues in his time, with excellent range and a strong arm. He was a key member of some of the greatest teams in Negro league history. While he had little power, he was a skilled contact hitter who consistently batted .300 or better. In the inaugural Negro league World Series in 1924, he led the Hilldale club with a .341 average.

A smart, soft-spoken, and well-respected player, Johnson later served as team captain of the 1930s Pittsburgh Crawfords, which boasted four other future Hall of Famers. In 1935, he captained the Crawfords to the Negro National League championships. Many consider that team to be the most talented and dominant team ever in the Negro leagues. After leaving Hilldale, Johnson became the player-manager of the Homestead Grays. After retiring from active playing, Johnson remained active as a scout and coach for the Philadelphia Athletics and Phillies for nearly fifty years. *Total Baseball* lists Johnson as one of the 400 greatest baseball players of all time. In 1999, members of the Society for Baseball Research chose Johnson as the fifteenth-greatest Negro league player. Often compared with Brooks Robinson, Johnson was elected to the National Baseball Hall of Fame in 1975 by the Committee on Negro leagues.

Larry S. Bonura

FURTHER READING
Clark, Dick, and Larry Lester, eds. *The Negro Leagues Book*. Cleveland: Society for American Baseball Research, 1984.
"40 Greatest Negro League Figures by SABR." *Baseball Almanac* (www.baseball-almanac.com/legendary/lisabr40.shtml).
Harvin, Al. "Historically Speaking: Judy Johnson." *Black Sports* (April 1975): 52–54, 60.
Holway, John B., and Bob Carroll. "The 400 Greatest." *Baseball Almanac* (www.baseball-almanac.com/legendary/li400gr.shtml).
National Baseball Hall of Fame (www.baseballhalloffame.org/hofers_and_honorees/hofer_bios/johnson_judy.htm).

Shatzkin, Mike, ed. *The Ballplayers: Baseball's Ultimate Biographical Reference.* New York: Arbor House, 1990.

★ ★ ★

Barbara JONES

Born 1937, Chicago, Illinois
Sprinter

Jones was a member of the 1952 gold medal–winning 400-meter relay team. What was unique about this accomplishment was that at the time she was only fifteen years old. For three years in the 1950s (1953, 1954, 1955), she was a member of the Catholic Youth Organization (CYO) of Chicago's AAU championship relay teams. In 1953 and 1954 she was also the AAU outdoor champion at 100 meters. At the 1955 Pan American Games, held in Mexico City, Jones won gold in the 400 meters and as a member of the 400-meter relay team.

Her running career hit a snag in 1956 when she did not qualify for the U.S. Olympic team. Jones shifted her focus and enrolled at Tennessee State to train with the legendary Tigerbelles track team. The hard work paid off; she returned to form in 1957 with a victory in the 100-yard dash at the

Tennessee State's Barbara Jones capturing the 100-meter dash in the United States-Russia track meet in 1958. (AP/Wide World Photos)

AAU National Championships. She completed her return to top form in the 1960 Rome Olympics, where she won a gold in the 400-meter relay once again.

Today Jones teaches in DeKalb, Georgia, and is on the board of the Heart Association and the Martin Luther King Center. She was also a member of the Paralympic Games Committee, as well as the Atlanta Committee for the Olympic Games Youth Advisory Committee's Educational Council in 1996.

Alison M. Wrynn

FURTHER READING
Ashe, Arthur R., Jr. *A Hard Road to Glory: A History of the African-American Athlete.* New York: Warner Books, 1988.
Bushnell, Asa S., ed. *United States 1952 Olympic Book.* Quadrennial Report of the USOC. New York: U.S. Olympic Committee, 1952.
Davis, Michael D. *Black American Women in Track and Field. A Complete Illustrated Reference.* Jefferson, NC: McFarland, 1992.
United States 1956 Olympic Book. Quadrennial Report of the USOC. New York: U.S. Olympic Committee, 1957.

★ ★ ★

David "Deacon" JONES

Born December 9, 1938, Eatonville, Florida
Football player

A four-sport athlete at Orlando (FL) Hungerford High, Jones attended Mississippi Vocational College for one year and also played football at South Carolina State for three seasons (1958–1960). It was at State that he earned his nickname, for leading pregame team prayers. Selected by the Los Angeles Rams in the fourteenth round of the 1961 NFL draft, Jones struggled through his first few pro seasons until he shifted to defensive end. He became one of the top players in the league as part of the Rams' "Fearsome Foursome"—considered to be one of the greatest defensive lines in football history.

Jones was named defensive end on the all-NFL team on six occasions (1965–1970) and made eight appearances in the Pro Bowl. In 1967 he was named NFL Defensive Player of the Year, receiving the award again in 1968. Jones appeared in 143 consecutive NFL games before suffering a leg injury in 1971; he was then traded to the San Diego Chargers. Jones finished his fourteen-season pro career in 1974 with the Washington Redskins. After retiring, Jones was involved in several business ventures, eventually becoming a football analyst for Fox Sports. A long time advocate of improving educational opportunities for inner-city youth, in 1997 he organized the Deacon Jones Foundation, which provides scholarships and other assistance to needy students. He was inducted into the Pro Football Hall of Fame in 1980.

Raymond Schmidt

FURTHER READING
Hano, Arnold. "The Awesome Power of Deacon Jones." *Sport*, January 1969, 59–64.
Klawitter, John, and "Deacon" Jones. *Headslap: The Life and Times of Deacon Jones.* Amherst, NY: Prometheus Books, 1996.
Oates, Bob. "Deacon Jones: A Lineman's Case for Most Valuable." *Quarterback*, January 1970, 38–42.
Porter, David L., ed. *Biographical Dictionary of American Sports: Football.* Westport, CT: Greenwood Press, 1987.

★ ★ ★

Hayes JONES

Born August 4, 1938, Starkesville, Mississippi
Hurdler

Jones graduated from Pontiac (Michigan) High School in 1957 and Eastern Michigan University in 1961. He began hurdling as a high school sophomore in 1955 and within two years established a junior world record of 13.7 seconds in the 120-yard high hurdles. He won five AAU national championships in the high hurdles from 1958 to 1964, finishing second in 1959 and 1962. Jones won both the 120-yard high hurdles and 220-yard low hurdles in the 1959 NCAA championships. A six-time AAU indoor champion in the sixty-yard high hurdles (1958, 1960–1964), he established indoor world records in the fifty, sixty, and seventy-yard high hurdles and shared the world record for forty-five yards.

Jones won a gold medal in the 1959 Pan American Games and a bronze medal in the 1960 Olympic Games in the 110-meter high hurdles. As a member of the U.S. national 4 x 100-meter relay team, he ran the opening leg of its world record performance of 39.1 seconds to defeat the Soviet Union in 1961. After establishing a personal best of 13.4 seconds in the 110-meter high hurdles in the 1964 U.S. Olympic Trials, Jones won the gold medal at the Olympic Games. After retirement, he became a municipal recreation director and businessman.

Adam R. Hornbuckle

FURTHER READING
Henderson, Edwin B., with the editors of *Sport* Magazine. *The Black Athlete: Emergence and Arrival*. Cornwall Heights, PA: Pennsylvania Publishers, 1968.
Wallechinsky, David, *The Complete Book of the Summer Olympics*. Sydney 2000 ed. Woodstock, NY: Overlook Press, 2000.

K.C. JONES

Born May 25, 1932, Taylor, Texas
Basketball player and coach

A product of San Francisco's Commerce High and the University of San Francisco, Jones teamed with Bill Russell to lead USF to a fifty-five-game consecutive win streak and two consecutive national titles, in 1955 and 1956. Selected by the Boston Celtics in the second round of the 1956 NBA draft, Jones played with the Celtics for nine seasons, which included eight consecutive NBA championships. He was the last individual from the great Celtic dynasty to be inducted into the Hall of Fame in 1989. His offensive statistics were only 7.4 points per game and a shooting percentage of .387, but his defensive play, play-making, and leadership skills had been key ingredients in the Celtics' success.

Following his playing career, Jones applied his extraordinary leadership skills in coaching and wherever he coached was no less successful than as a player in compiling championships and winning percentages. One of his outstanding seasons was in 1971–1972, when he assisted former Celtic great Bill Sharman with the Los Angeles Lakers, a team that produced an incredible .841 winning percentage and a NBA championship. After a stint in the ABA, Jones coached the Washington Bullets for two years, leading them to the finals in 1975. After assisting with the Celtics from 1978 through 1983, he was named Boston's head coach in 1983, serving in that position until the 1987–1988 season and leading the team to four consecutive NBA final appearances and to championships in 1984 and 1986.

Albert J. Figone

FURTHER READING
Auerbach, Red, and Paul Sann. *Winning the Hard Way*. Boston: Little, Brown, 1966.

Cousy, Bob, and Bob Ryan. *Cousy on the Celtic Mystique.* New York: McGraw-Hill, 1988.
George, Nelson. *Elevating the Game: Black Men and Basketball.* New York: Dolphin Books, 1992.
Hollander, Zander, ed. *Modern Encyclopedia of Basketball.* Rev. ed. Garden City, NY: Dolphin Books, 1979.
Ryan, Bob. "Jones Joins Hall of Fame." *Boston Globe,* February 11, 1989.

★ ★ ★

Marion JONES

Born October 12, 1975, Los Angeles, California
Track and field athlete

Jones's mother, Marion Toler, originally from Belize, is a legal secretary. George Jones, her biological father, left the family in 1975. Toler in 1983 married Ira Toler, who raised Jones until 1987. Jones attended Rio Mesa High School until 1991 and graduated from Thousand Oaks High School in 1993. She attended the University of North Carolina at Chapel Hill (UNC-CH) and graduated in 1997. Jones married C.J. Hunter in 1998.

Jones's track career began in high school; she won both the hundred and two-hundred-meter dashes in the California State High School Championships 1990–93. She continued winning the hundred and two-hundred-meter at the USA Juniors in 1991 and was California's High School Athlete of the Year for 1991 and 1992.

Jones, a dual sport athlete at UNC-CH in basketball and track and field, helped lead North Carolina to the 1994 NCAA women's basketball championship. She participated in both sports until 1996, when she endured a fracture in her fifth metatarsal. Jones decided to give up basketball and focus on track and field. She won the hundred-meter and long jump at the Atlantic Coast Conference Championships in 1994 and long jump in 1995.

In 1998, Jones success continued, as she won thirty-five out of thirty-six competitions she entered. She set the women's record for winning the most medals at a single Olympics by capturing three gold and two bronzes in 2000 in Sydney, Australia. Jones team broke the 4 x 200-meter world record at the USA versus the World at the Penn Relays in 2000.

Sue Scaffidi

FURTHER READING
International Amateur Athletic Federation. *Athlete Biographies: Marion Jones* (www.iaaf.org/Results/Bio/62739.html).
SportsLine.com Wire Reports. 2000. "Marion Jones' Final Count: Three Gold's, Two Bronzes" (www.sportsline.com/u/ce/multi/0,1329,2859234_182185,00.html).
USA Track and Field. "Marion Jones" (www.usatf.org/athletes/bios/Jones_Marion.shtml).

★ ★ ★

Sam JONES

Born June 24, 1933, Wilmington, North Carolina
Basketball player

Sam Jones was the only child of Mrs. Louise Davis. Growing up in poverty, he worked a number of jobs in order to help support his family and aid his financial status as a student. Jones was a four-year letter winner and both All-Conference and All-State his senior year at Laurinburg Institute. Although he had other scholarship offers, he chose to play for all-black North Carolina Central College, which was closest to his home. At North Carolina Central, Jones was again a four-year letter winner, averaging 18.6 points per game over his career, and he earned All-Conference honors three times.

In 1957 the Celtics took Jones in the first round of the NBA draft. Because of a stint in the army, he was older and more mature than most of the other rookies. At six feet, four inches tall and 200 pounds, he was one of the NBA's first big guards. He was known for his outstanding speed, being able to run the floor with the guards and battle for rebounds with the forwards. He was one of the best shooters the game has known, by virtue of his patented bank shot. Over his twelve-year career, he amassed 15,380 points, which translates to 17.7 points per game. Five times he was an NBA All-Star, and he was an instrumental link on ten Boston Celtic NBA championship teams.

In 1971 the NBA honored Jones as a member of its silver-anniversary team, meaning one of the twenty-five best players of all-time. In 1996 he was honored again as part of the NBA's fiftieth anniversary team. In 1969, during his last season, the Boston Celtics retired his number, twenty-four. Jones was enshrined in the Basketball Hall of Fame in 1984. He also holds membership in the NAIA Hall of Fame, and he was the first black entry into the North Carolina Hall of Fame. After his retirement, Jones coached college basketball at Federal City College and North Carolina A & T University, scouted for the Celtics, and has been a spokesman for black education.

Rick Knott

FURTHER READING
Basketball Hall of Fame (hoophall.com/halloffamers/Jones/S.htm).
Deford, Frank. "And That Old Celtic Wheel Rolls Again: Boston Goes Into Finals Against Los Angeles." *Sports Illustrated*, April 28, 1969, 24–25.
Mandell, Ronald L. *Who's Who in Basketball*. New Rochelle, NY: Arlington House, 1973.
Walsh, George. "Jones and Jones at Court." *Sports Illustrated*, March 20, 1961, 49–52.

★ ★ ★

Wali JONES

Born February 14, 1942, Philadelphia, Pennsylvania
Basketball player

Wali Jones graduated from the famous Overbrook High School in Philadelphia, Pennsylvania, in 1960. He was a high school teammate of Walt Hazzard and had been the Most Valuable Player of the city championship game. Recruited to play for Villanova, he was an All-American in 1964. His Villanova team was one of the nation's best. Villanova was 22–3 during Jones's senior season.

At six feet, two inches and 180 pounds, Jones was known throughout his career as both a play maker and a defensive specialist. Later in his career Jones was given the nickname "Attila the Hun," due not only to his relentless and aggressive defensive attitude but also to his intimidating presence, with his long hair, as well as facial hair. In 607 NBA games, he averaged 3.2 assists and 10.1 points per game. Originally drafted by the Detroit Pistons, Jones was traded to the Baltimore Bullets. He spent the majority of his career, however, playing for the Philadelphia 76ers. He also played for the Milwaukee Bucks, the ABA Utah Stars, and the Pistons. In his eleven-year professional career, Jones seemed to always be a part of very successful teams. He played in seventy NBA playoff games, in addition to five ABA playoff games. Jones was a critical part of the 1966–1967 Philadelphia 76ers, one of the best teams in history. The 76ers that year concluded their regular season with a 68–13 record and later won the NBA championship.

After playing for the Bucks for a year, Jones was suspended and then waived in December 1972 due to allegations of drug usage. Jones had been helping the league with their drug education. Jones had a physical exam and based on the results appealed to the league commissioner. He won his appeal, received most of his salary from the Bucks, and was declared a free agent.

Rick Knott

See also: Historiography.

FURTHER READING

Deford, Frank. "New Spirit of the 76ers: Defeat of Celtics in the Eastern Division Pro Playoffs." *Sports Illustrated*, April 17, 1967, 28–31.

Hubbard, Jon, ed. *The Official NBA Encyclopedia*. New York: Doubleday, 2000.

Mendell, Ronald L. *Who's Who in Basketball*. New Rochelle, NY: Arlington House, 1973.

New York Times, May 25, 1973.

Underwood, John. "Wally's Cue: Sidney! Sidney!" *Sports Illustrated*, February 10, 1964, 26–28.

★ ★ ★

Michael JORDAN

Born February 17, 1963, Brooklyn, New York
Basketball player

The son of Deloris and James, a professional couple, Jordan grew up in Wilmington, North Carolina, where he starred on the high school basketball team. After graduation from high school, Jordan went to the University of North Carolina to play for the legendary Dean Smith. His collegiate career was filled with enormous success. As a freshman in 1982 he was a member of the North Carolina NCAA Championship basketball team. He was named the NCAA College Player of the Year in both 1983 and 1984 and was also a unanimous selection to the first-team All-American basketball squad the same two years. He was, moreover, the winner of the Naismith Award and Wooden Award in 1984.

Jordan's professional career has perhaps been even more impressive. His scoring average for his career is 31.5 points per game.

Michael Jordan drives to the basket to score in a 1991 game against the Houston Rockets. *(AP/Wide World Photos)*

He has ten scoring titles in thirteen years. He was named the NBA's Most Valuable Player in 1988, 1991, 1992, 1996, and 1998 and Most Valuable Player of the All-Star Games in 1988, 1996, and 1998. He scored the first triple-double in All-Star Game history, with fourteen points, eleven rebounds, and eleven assists, in the 1997 Classic. In 1996 he was selected as one of the fifty greatest players in NBA history, and ESPN named him Sportsman of the Century. In all, Jordan led the Chicago Bulls to six NBA titles. Jordan became the Washington Wizards' president of basketball operations in 2000. He returned to the NBA as a player in 2001, signing a two-year contract with the Wizards.

Jordan has also been a big success off the

court. He may well be the busiest pitchman ever, selling everything from hamburgers (McDonald's) to cool drinks (Gatorade) and men's underwear (Hanes). He has his own fragrance line, made by Bijan Fragrances. He holds the title of honorary CEO of Brand Jordan, a division of Nike that sells shoes and sportswear and earns him an estimated $16 million a year. Jordan signed his first Nike shoe contract in 1984 and currently is paid an estimated $40 million a year for marketing products, with some contracts not ending until 2007. He is involved in several restaurant ventures; his most famous restaurant is in Chicago, but he also has them in North Carolina and New York. Jordan also serves on the corporate boards of Oakley and Divine Interventures.

Earl Smith

See also: Basketball; Olympic Games.

FURTHER READING
Dupree, David. "Matching Up with Jordan." *USA Today*, September 27, 2001.
Halberstam, David. *Playing for Keeps: Michael Jordan and the World He Made*. New York: Random House, 1999.
"Jordan's Midlife Ad Crisis." *Wall Street Journal*, September 27, 2001.
LaFeber, Walter. *Michael Jordan and the New Global Capitalism*. New York: W.W. Norton, 1999.
McCarthy, Michael. "Marketers Jump with Jordan's Return." *USA Today*, September 26, 2001.
Wise, Mike. "Jordan Makes Official What Most Expected." *New York Times*, September 26, 2001.

★ ★ ★

Jackie JOYNER-KERSEE

Born March 3, 1962, East St. Louis, Illinois
Jumper, hurdler, heptathlete

Second of four children and named by her grandmother after First Lady Jacqueline Kennedy, Joyner-Kersee is the daughter of

Jackie Joyner-Kersee long jumping in a qualifying round at the 1995 World Track and Field Championships in Goteborg, Sweden. *(AP/Wide World Photos)*

Alfred Joyner, a Springfield, Illinois, railroad switch operator, and Mary Joyner, a nurse's assistant. Joyner-Kersee overcame difficult surroundings as a youth by excelling in sport and doing well in school. The all-around athlete captured six Olympic track and field medals; some consider her to be "the greatest female athlete" in the modern era.

Joyner-Kersee attended John Robinson Elementary School, and her running prowess was noticed at the age of nine at the Mary Brown Center. While attending Lincoln High School between 1977 and 1980, Joyner-Kersee received All-City honors in track, volleyball, and basketball. She won the Amateur Athletic Union (AAU) Junior Pentathlon Championship at age fourteen and as a junior set a state long jump record with a distance of 20 feet, 7½ inches. She was named to the All-State Basketball Team in her senior year. Joyner-Kersee won the long jump at the 1979 Pan American Junior Games and at the 1980 The Athletic Congress (TAC) Junior Championships. She finished in the top 10 percent of her high school graduating class and accepted a basketball scholarship from the University of California at Los Angeles (UCLA), where she majored in history and minored in communications.

Joyner-Kersee became a star forward on the UCLA basketball team and excelled in track and field. She ranks in the top ten among the Lady Bruins in assists, rebounding, and scoring. In track and field, Joyner-Kersee competed in the long jump, broad jump, 400-meter hurdles, and triple jump. Although she did not win a National Collegiate Athletic Association (NCAA) or TAC title in these events, in 1985 she set a U.S. long-jump record with a distance of twenty-three feet, nine inches at a meet in Switzerland. An accomplished student-athlete, in 1983 and 1985 Joyner-Kersee received the All-University Student Athlete Award, the Broderick Award for track and field in 1983, and the Broderick Trophy as Collegiate Sportswoman of the Year in 1985.

Before she graduated from UCLA in 1986, and because few opportunities existed for females in basketball after college, her future husband Bob Kersee encouraged Jackie to train in the seven-event heptathlon, where the full range of her track and field skills could be developed. As a result, she won the 1982 TAC heptathlon crown and the NCAA titles in 1982 and 1983. In each year between 1982 and 1985 she set new collegiate heptathlon records, beginning with a score of 6,099 points and finishing with 6,718 points. At the 1984 Olympic trials, she set the U.S. heptathlon record with a score of 6,520 points and also qualified to compete in the long jump. Her brother Al Joyner, Jr., earned a spot on the same U.S. Olympic team in the triple jump. At the Los Angeles Olympic Games, where brother Al won a gold medal in the triple jump, Joyner-Kersee settled for fifth in the long jump and won a silver medal in the heptathlon, just five points short of becoming a gold medal winner. Following the Olympics, Joyner-Kersee lost the heptathlon title to former record holder Jane Frederick, who set a new U.S. record of 6,803 points.

In 1986, Joyner-Kersee reclaimed the U.S. record at a meet in Austria with a score of 6,841 points. Even more impressive was her breaking the 7,000-point mark (7,148 points) at the Moscow Goodwill Games and becoming the first American woman to set a world record in a multi-event contest since Babe Didrickson's triathlon world record in 1936. In the same year she won the Sullivan Memorial Trophy as the nation's top amateur athlete and the 1986 Jesse Owens Award, and became the *Track and Field News* Female Athlete of the Year, and the U.S. Olympic Committee sportswoman of the year.

At the 1988 Seoul Olympic Games, Joyner-Kersee became the first female athlete to win gold medals in the long jump and the heptathlon, setting a new world mark of 7,291 points in the latter event. Over the next few years she continued to win long-jump and heptathlon competitions despite recurring injuries. She also received numerous awards, including an honorary doctorate, endorsement contracts from many leading corporations, and began to get involved in community service projects. At the Barcelona, Spain, Olympic Games the thirty-year-old Joyner-Kersee captured an unprecedented second gold medal in the heptathlon and a bronze medal in the long jump. Four years later at the Olympic Games in Atlanta, Georgia, Joyner-Kersee competed again in the heptathlon but had to withdraw due to a hamstring injury. She still managed to win a second consecutive bronze medal in the long jump.

After the Olympics, Joyner-Kersee played briefly with the Richmond Rage of the newly formed American Basketball League. She officially retired from track in the summer of 1998 but tried to make a comeback to participate in her fifth Olympic Games in 2000. At the U.S. Olympic trials, the thirty-eight-year-old came sixth in the long jump finals and did not earn a place on the team. Joyner-Kersee has many successful business ventures, including Elite Sports Marketing, Gold Medal Rehab, a NASCAR team sponsorship, and the JJK Youth Community Foundation. She serves on the St. Louis Sports Commission and is one of the most sought-after motivational speakers in the United States.

Danny Rosenberg

See also: Olympic Games; Track and Field.

FURTHER READING
Davis, Michael D. *Black American Women in Track and Field: A Complete Illustrated Reference.* Jefferson, NC: McFarland, 1992.
Hine, Darlene Clark, ed. *Black Women in America: An Historical Encyclopedia.* Brooklyn, NY: Carlson, 1993.
Page, James A. *Black Olympian Medalists.* Englewood, CO: Libraries Unlimited, 1991.
Porter, David L., ed. *Biographical Dictionary of American Sports: Outdoor Sports.* Westport, CT: Greenwood Press, 1988.
Salem, Dorothy C., ed. *African American Women: A Biographical Dictionary.* New York: Garland, 1993.
USAToday. "Jackie-Joyner-Kersee: Extended Biography" (www.usatoday.com/olympics/otf/otfmsc21.htm), July 17, 1996.

Leroy KELLY

Born May 20, 1942, Philadelphia, Pennsylvania
Football player

A talented and versatile halfback, Kelly was regarded as one of the premier offensive players in the NFL.

A two-sport star at Simon Gratz High School in Philadelphia, Kelly attended Morgan State University, where he played four seasons of football (1960–1963). A standout on both offense and defense, Kelly was named to the All-Conference squad of the Central Intercollegiate Athletic Association for 1963.

Selected by the Cleveland Browns in the eighth round of the 1964 NFL draft, Kelly found himself behind legendary running back Jimmy Brown. Playing primarily on special teams during his first two seasons, Kelly led the NFL in punt returns in 1965 with an average of 15.6 yards. Brown retired before the 1966 season, and Kelly immediately established himself as one of the league's top running backs, rushing for 1,141 yards. In 1967 and 1968 he was the NFL's leading rusher, with respective totals of 1,205 yards and 1,239 yards.

Kelly also led the league in rushing touchdowns and was named to the All-NFL team for all three seasons—also leading in total scoring in 1968. Hampered by a leg injury, he retired after the 1973 season, having scored ninety touchdowns and rushed for 7,274 yards during his ten-year NFL career.

After playing briefly in 1974 for the Chicago Fire of the World Football League, Kelly went into the restaurant business in the Philadelphia area. An avid golfer, he makes frequent appearances on behalf of charitable organizations. He was inducted into the Pro Football Hall of Fame in 1994.

Raymond Schmidt

FURTHER READING
Cartwright, Gary. "Leroy Kelly: His Own Man Now." *Sport*, November 1968, 67–72.
Heaton, Chuck. *The Cleveland Browns: Power and Glory.* Englewood Cliffs, NJ: Prentice Hall, 1974.
Lebovitz, Hal. "A Little Cat Named Leroy." *Sport*, February 1967, 33, 77–78.
Logan, Joe. "In the Shadow of a Legend." *Cleveland Plain Dealer Magazine*, January 22, 1989.

★ ★ ★

Ray KEMP

Born April 7, 1907, Rassing, Pennsylvania
Football player, coach

Ray Kemp was the son of Ona, a farmer and coal miner, and Hattie Perkins, a housewife. A graduate of Cecil (PA) High School and Duquesne University in Pittsburgh, Kemp was a college and professional football player during the 1930s. He was later a successful football coach at three historically black colleges.

From 1927 through 1931 Kemp, as a college football lineman at Duquesne, was one of the few African-Americans who played for a predominantly white college during that period of uneven segregation in the North. For example, when Duquesne played against West Virginia University in Morgantown, West Virginia, Kemp was permitted to play in the game but had to stay in segregated housing the night before. In 1933, when Kemp joined the Pittsburgh Pirates (renamed the Steelers in 1941), he and Joe Lilliard (of the Chicago Cardinals) were the only two African Americans in the National Football League (NFL). The following season the NFL was segregated and remained so until 1946.

Kemp was not invited to rejoin the Pirates in 1934 but was hired as the football coach at segregated Bluefield (WV) State College. He led Bluefield to an undefeated season and an 8–0–1 record. Kemp subsequently had a thirty-nine-year career at Bluefield, Lincoln (MO) University, and Tennessee State University, where he worked as a coach, athletic administrator, and teacher.

C. Robert Barnett

See also: Football.

FURTHER READING
Barnett, C. Robert. "The First Black Steeler," *Pittsburgh Courier*, August 27, 1983.
———. Personal interview with Ray Kemp, June 26, 1981.
Neft, David, et al. *Pro Football: The Early Years*. New York: Sports Products, 1978.

★ ★ ★

Leroy KEYES

Born February 18, 1947, Newport News, Virginia
Football player

A native of Newport News, Virginia, Keyes attended Carver High School and subsequently Purdue University. Keyes established himself as a workhorse running back and a dependable receiver for the Boilermakers and helped lead his team in its most successful era. Keyes was twice nominated for the Heisman trophy (1967 and 1968) and was voted the Most Valuable Player in the 1967 Big Ten Conference. He was selected as Purdue's MVP in 1967 and 1968.

Keyes was the third overall pick by Philadelphia in the 1969 National Football League draft and played for the Eagles until 1972, leaving to join the Kansas City Chiefs for a year. In 1987, Keyes was named Purdue University's All-Time Greatest Player and in 1994 was named to the university's Athletic Hall of Fame.

Keyes left football to become a desegregation specialist with the Philadelphia School District for sixteen years. He returned to Purdue as running back coach for the Boilermakers (1995–1996) and administrative assistant for the team (1997–1999). In July 2001, Keyes was named assistant director of the John Purdue Club, a fundraising arm of the school's athletic department. Keyes maintains his connection to the Purdue team by assisting in the Boilermaker's recruiting efforts. He has four children and resides with his wife in West Lafayette, Indiana.

Trisha M. Hothorn

FURTHER READING
"Keyes to Join Purdue Club." *Purdue Boilermakers Official Athletic Site* (www.purduesports.fansonly.com).
"NCAA's 'Silver' Stars." *Christian Science Monitor*, January 20, 1994, 14.
Rywell, Martin, ed. *Afro-American Encyclopedia*. North Miami, FL: Educational Book Publishers, 1974.

★ ★ ★

Don KING

Born December 6, 1932, Cleveland, Ohio
Boxing promoter

A product of the mean streets of Cleveland, Ohio, Don King beat the odds and is now the most successful and powerful boxing promoter. King's career, devoted to staging the best in world-championship boxing, spans three decades and comprises over 500 fights. His flamboyant public image, flashy jewelry, wild hairdo, booming laugh, inimitable vocabulary, and evangelical monologues, in which he embellishes quotes from Shakespeare and other literary immortals, make him easily recognizable.

A former numbers czar, King was arrested, convicted, and jailed for manslaughter, having beat a man to death over a debt. He became a millionaire two years after his release from prison in 1974 when he promoted a fight between George Foreman and Ken Norton in Caracas, Venezuela. King went on to promote several pugilistic extravaganzas that created unprecedented wealth for himself and his fighters.

In his first ten years as a fight promoter, Don King shifted control of the power structure of boxing from traditional white brokers and promoters to black entrepreneurs. He expanded boxing to Third World countries, which created unprecedented purses. Some of King's most famous bouts were the Ali-Foreman "Rumble in the Jungle," the Ali-Frazier "Thrilla in Manila," the Holmes-Cooney "The Pride and the Glory," and the double header fight known as "The Crown Affair." His promotions have entertained billions around the world.

King was inducted into the Boxing Hall of Fame in 1997. He was the only boxing promoter named to *Sports Illustrated*'s list of the "40 Most Influential Figures of the Past 40 Years." The *New York Times* credited King as one of the 100 African Americans who helped shape this country's history during the past century. When asked what he would like on his epitaph, King responded, "'He worked for the day when all people would be clothed in dignity.'" This statement illustrates the fact that at heart King is a social and civil rights activist. He was awarded the National Association for the Advancement of Colored People's highest honor, the President's Award. Grambling State University granted him its Lifetime Achievement Award. He has earned several honorary doctoral degrees from colleges and universities, and all three major boxing organizations—the IBF, WBA, and WBC—have proclaimed Don King the "Greatest Boxing Promoter in History."

Gary A. Sailes

FURTHER READING
Dempsey, David. "Man in the Middle." *New York Times Magazine*, July 10, 1949.
"From Killer to King: Promoter Don King." *Time*, June 30, 1975, 55–56.
Sammons, Jeffrey T. *Beyond the Ring: The Role of Boxing in American Society*. Urbana: University of Illinois Press, 1988.
South-Western (www.swcollege.com/booktour/don_king).
Wilson Web (www.hwwilson.com).

★ ★ ★

William "Dolly" KING

Born 1917, New York, New York
Died January 29, 1969, Binghamton, New York
Basketball player

A celebrated all-around athlete, William "Dolly" King starred on the basketball court at Long Island University (LIU), played for some of the best independent professional teams in the country, and in 1946 helped to reintegrate the National Basketball League when he signed with the Rochester Royals.

The 6-foot-tall King was a three-sport letter winner (basketball, baseball, and football) at Brooklyn's Alexander Hamilton High School, twice garnering All-City honors in both basketball and football. After high school, King moved on to LIU, where he helped legendary basketball coach Clair Bee lead the Blackbirds to a perfect 25–0 record and the second National Invitational Tournament title in 1939.

Upon completing his college eligibility in 1941, King turned professional, playing for the Washington Bears and the Harlem Renaissance, two of the country's best all-black barnstorming teams. In 1943, King and the Bears won the *Chicago Herald-American*'s World Professional Basketball Tournament; King was named to the All-Tournament team.

In 1946–1947, the National Basketball League, formerly a regional league of small midwestern cities, went nationwide and claimed major-league status. King, signed by the Rochester Royals, was one of four African Americans to play in the league that year, helping to break the color line in professional basketball.

After retiring in the 1950s, King worked for fifteen years at Harlem's Riverton Housing Project. In 1964 he was named head basketball coach at Manhattan Community College. In five years at MCC King compiled a 50–7 record before dying of a heart attack with his team on the road in Binghamton, NY.

Gregory Bond

See also: Basketball.

FURTHER READING
Bjarkman, Peter C., ed. *The Biographical History of Basketball*. Dallas: Master's Press, 1998.
Chalk, Ocania. *Black College Sport*. New York: Dodd, Mead, 1975.
———. *Pioneers of Black Sport*. New York: Dodd, Mead, 1975.
"Dolly King" (Obituary). *New York Times*, January 30, 1969.

LACROSSE

African Americans have been underrepresented in the sport of lacrosse. Its limited geographical appeal, the presence of few nationally known role models, and a host of other socioeconomic factors, have limited the involvement of African Americans in a sport that originated with Native Americans. In spite of this fact, individual African-American athletes have found success in the sport and realized much acclaim and notoriety.

Perhaps the first two well-known African-American lacrosse players were Simeon Moss, who competed in 1939 for Rutgers University, and Lucien Alexis, Jr., who competed for Harvard University in 1941 and 1942. A number of other African Americans followed Moss and Alexis into lacrosse after World War II, a period that witnessed a dramatic increase in the number of players and growth of popularity in the sport. The most famous of these players was Syracuse University's Jim Brown, the great all-around athlete who would become perhaps professional football's greatest running back. Brown, who had not played the sport prior to his arrival at Syracuse, revolutionized the style of play, combining a level of speed and power that had never been seen before in lacrosse. Playing the midfield position, Brown overwhelmed his opponents and seemingly handed out assists and scored goals at will. In 1957 Brown became the first African American to play in the North-South Game, scoring five goals and having two assists in the North's 14–10 victory.

The last several decades have seen a number of outstanding African Americans participating in lacrosse at both predominantly white and historically black colleges and universities. Included among these athletes are Wendell Thomas of Towson University, John Sheffield of the University of Pennsylvania, Ed Howard of Hobart College, Rick Sowell of Washington College, Tina Sloan Green of West Chester University, James Ford and Albert Ray of Rutgers University, and Miles Harrison, Wayne Jackson, and Joe Fulks of Morgan State University. Of this group, Green is perhaps the most noteworthy, in that she competed for four years on the U.S. Women's Lacrosse Team and then coached the Temple University Women's Lacrosse Team to three national championships and eleven consecutive national collegiate athletic association final four appearances. Green's accomplishments gained her entry into the Lacrosse Hall of Fame.

David K. Wiggins

See also: Jim Brown.

FURTHER READING
Ashe, Arthur R., Jr. *A Hard Road to Glory*. New York: Amistad, 1993.
Brooks, Dana, and Ronald Althouse. *Racism in College Athletics: The African American Athlete's Experience*. Morgantown, WV: Fitness Information Technology, 2000.
Roberts, Milton. "Lacrosse." *Black Sports*, May 1976, 18–19.

★ ★ ★

Sam LACY

Born October 23, 1903, Mystic, Connecticut
Died May 8, 2003, Washington, DC
Journalist

Lacy was born in Connecticut but grew up in Washington, DC, with his parents, Rose and Sam. He attended Henry Armstrong High School and excelled as an athlete in baseball, basketball, and football. After graduating from Howard University, Lacy briefly played semiprofessional baseball.

His journalism career began in the 1930s at the *Washington Tribune* under the direction of editor Lewis Lautier. From 1934 to 1939, Lacy served as the newspaper's sports and managing editor. In 1940, he became a writer and assistant national editor for the black-owned newspaper the *Chicago Defender*. In 1944, Lacy became a weekly columnist and sports editor for the *Baltimore Afro-American*. His popular column "A to Z" was published from 1944 to 1991.

Throughout his career, Lacy was an influential pioneer in the fight to integrate major league baseball. He served on the Major League Committee of Baseball Integration and relentlessly campaigned against segregation in sport. In 1948, Lacy was the first African American admitted as a member of the U.S. Baseball Writers Association. Lacy was inducted into the Maryland Media Hall of Fame in 1984 and awarded the Lifetime Achievement Award by the National Association of Black Journalists in 1991. In 1997, Lacy was named the forty-ninth recipient of the J.G. Taylor Spink Award, named in honor of the esteemed publisher and editor of the *Sporting News*. Lacy was inducted as a writer in the National Baseball Hall of Fame in 1998.

Tracey M. Salisbury

See also: Baseball; Sportswriters.

FURTHER READING

Kirsch, George B., Othello Harris, and Claire E. Nolte, eds. *Encyclopedia of Ethnicity and Sports in the United States*. Westport, CT: Greenwood Press, 2000.

Lacy, Sam, with Moses J. Newson. *Fighting for Fairness: The Life Story of Hall of Fame Sportswriter Sam Lacy*. Centreville, MD: Tidewater, 1999.

Steadman, John, "As Usual. Lacy Gets to Point, with Strong Message." *Baltimore Sun*, July 27, 1998.

★ ★ ★

Betty Jean LANE

Born 1923
Sprinter

After graduating from high school in the late 1930s, Lane took the opportunity to compete on the Wilberforce University (OH) track and field team. Future Olympic coach Tom Harris and "Country" Lewis trained Lane to compete in national and international track and field events. In 1942 she was declared the greatest athlete ever to have attended Wilberforce University.

Majoring in health and physical education, Lane took great pleasure in defeating her opponents, especially those who ran for rival Tuskegee Institute of Alabama. Although she excelled in the fifty and 100-meter events, the 200-meter dash proved to be her area of expertise. At the twelfth annual Senior Women's Track and Field Championships, she set a record in the 200-meter race. The Chenault Trophy was presented to her for this exceptional performance. She also thrived at a national meet at the young age of seventeen. In 1940, in Ocean City, New Jersey, Lane won the fifty-meter dash and 100-meter against the Polish Olympic star Stella Walsh. One year later, Lane defeated Walsh again in the 200-meter race, harsh weather conditions making this victory especially sweet. She also took first place in the 100-meter dash. She was presented a gold key to the city from Atlantic City's mayor, Tomas D. Taggert, Jr. Unfortunately, in 1942, she was unable to defend previously held titles, for unknown reasons. However, she competed at the Knights of Columbus Invitational Indoor Meet, where she captured the championship in the sixty-five-yard dash.

Sara B. Washington

FURTHER READING

Ashe, Arthur R., Jr. *A Hard Road to Glory: The African-American Athlete in Track & Field*. New York: Amistad, 1993.

Brower, William A. "Betty Jean Lane, Wilberforce's Mercurial Maiden." *Opportunity* 19 (June 1941): 172–73.

Tricard, Louise M. *American Women's Track and Field: A History, 1895 through 1980.* Jefferson, NC: McFarland, 1985.

Wilberforce University Yearbook, 1942.

★ ★ ★

Dick LANE

Born April 16, 1928, Austin, Texas
Football player

Dick Lane was raised in poverty by a foster mother, "Mama Ella" Lane, who also had four children of her own. Lane would play cornerback for three professional football teams in a fourteen-year career.

After competing in high school football and basketball in Austin, Lane enrolled at Scottsbluff Junior College in 1946 and 1947, his natural mother having moved to Scottsbluff, Nebraska. After dropping out of Scottsbluff (now Western Nebraska Community College) in 1948, he joined the U.S. Army and played football for four years at Fort Ord, California.

After his discharge in 1952, he appeared at the offices of the Los Angeles Rams and as a walk-on rookie defensive back set a NFL record of fourteen interceptions that has stood for half a century. He received his colorful nickname "Night Train" because he frequently visited a teammate's room to listen to the popular recording by the same name.

Regarded as "difficult" by his coaches, he was first traded to the Chicago Cardinals in 1954 and then to the Detroit Lions in 1960. In his first four years at Detroit, he was All-NFL. Lane was known for his fierce "necktie" tackles. Vince Lombardi called him the best cornerback he had ever seen and cautioned his quarterback, Bart Starr, never to throw near him. Lane's sixty-eight interceptions and 1,207 interception yards led to six Pro Bowls and induction into the Pro Football Hall of Fame in 1974.

Possessed of a flamboyant personality and remarkable natural talent, Lane was the most effective—and feared—defensive back of his era. He helped to define the position of cornerback and remains arguably the best ever to play at that position.

John S. Watterson

FURTHER READING
Anderson, Dave. *Great Defensive Players of the NFL.* New York: Random House, 1967.
The Official Site of Dick Lane (www.cmgww.com/football/lane/bio).
Porter, David L., ed. *African-American Sports Greats: A Biographical Dictionary.* Westport, CT: Greenwood Press, 1995.
———. *Biographical Dictionary of American Sports: Football.* Westport, CT: Greenwood Press, 1987.

★ ★ ★

Sam LANGFORD

Born March 4, 1883, Weymouth, Nova Scotia
Died January 12, 1956, Boston, Massachusetts
Boxer

Langford ran away from home at the age of twelve and made his way to Boston, where he found a janitorial job at the Lenox Athletic Club. The owner, Joe Woodman, found that Langford had a knack for taking punches during training sessions with established boxers. At the age of fifteen, Langford turned professional, with Woodman as his manager.

Langford probably boxed in over 600 matches during his career, most of them unrecorded. Though only five feet, six inches, he boxed in almost every weight category, relying on his long reach and his ability to take punches. Sadly, he never fought for a world title, in large part because he fought during the Jim Crow period. The few black boxers, like Jack Johnson, who did win titles refused to fight Langford. He was suspended from boxing at least once—in New Jersey, for failing to show up for a fight.

After retiring in 1926, Langford experienced a series of ups and downs. He had begun to lose his eyesight before 1920 and underwent a series of unsuccessful eye operations. In 1931 he was struck by a car near his home in Boston. He was again struck by a car in 1935, this time in New York City. Mayor Fiorello La Guardia, learning of the accident and of Langford's poverty, provided the former boxer with a job; however, by 1938 Langford was destitute again. A charitable fund for him was started in 1944. Wendell Wilkie, Joe Louis, and Jack Dempsey, among others, contributed to the fund. Langford died in Boston in 1956, a year after being inducted into *Ring* Magazine's Hall of Fame.

Gregory S. Goodale

See also: Boxing; Joe Jeannette.

FURTHER READING
"Amazing Career of Sam Langford, Boxer." *Ebony*, April 1956, 97–105.
Canada: Our Century in Sport: Feature Moments (www.ourcenturyinsport.com/website/english/moments/silver_langford.html).
Cromwell, Blair. *Sam E. Langford: "The Boston Terror."* Ottawa: Environment Canada, Park Service, Historic Sites and Monuments Board of Canada, n.d.
Davis, Luckett, and Tim Leone. *Sam Langford (the "Boston Tar Baby")*. International Boxing Research Organization (www.infotechnology.org/blair/langford.html).
Sammons, Jeffrey T. *Beyond the Ring: The Role of Boxing in American Society*. Urbana: University of Illinois Press, 1988.

★ ★ ★

Bob LANIER

Born September 10, 1948, Buffalo, New York
Basketball player

After starring at St. Bonaventure University, Lanier played in the National Basketball Association (NBA), for the Detroit Pistons (1970–1979) and the Milwaukee Bucks (1980–1984).

Lanier grew up in Buffalo, New York, and led Bennett High to consecutive city titles. His choice of college was St. Bonaventure, in Olean, New York, and in his sophomore year (1968) he led the school to a 22–0 regular-season record and number-three national ranking. In his three-year college career, he set school records for scoring (2,067 points) and rebounding (1,180), while averaging 27.5 points and 15.7 rebounds. He graduated in 1970 with a business administration degree.

The Detroit Pistons made Lanier their number-one pick in the 1970 draft, and he immediately helped turn the team around in his first season, making the All-Rookie team for 1970–1971. The following season he was selected for the NBA All-Star Game, the first of eight All-Star Games during his career.

Physically healthy the first four years at Detroit, Lanier was hampered in later years by injuries. The team was struggling as well, and Lanier asked to be traded. He joined the Milwaukee Bucks midway in the 1979–1980 season. He helped lead his new team to five consecutive division titles, from 1980 to 1984. In his fourteen-year career he averaged 20.1 points and 10.1 rebounds per game, while scoring 19,248 points and 9,698 rebounds. He also served as president of the NBA Players Association.

In 1985 he founded Bob Lanier Enterprises, an advertising promotions business. Lanier briefly served as an assistant and then interim coach for the Golden State Warriors during the 1994–1995 season.

Lanier lacked speed and jumping ability, but he used his large muscular frame and an aggressive physical style of play to become the prototype big center who dominated the low post. His bronzed size-twenty-two sneakers preceded him into the Naismith Memorial Basketball Hall of Fame, to which he was elected in 1992.

Robert Pruter

FURTHER READING
"Bob Lanier." *NBA Legends* (www.nba.com/history/lanier_bio.html).
"Lanier Looks Back at What Might Have Been: He Put in 14 Seasons in the NBA But Has No Championships to Show for Efforts." *Los Angeles Times*, May 19, 1985.
Porter, David L., ed. *Dictionary of American Sports: Basketball and Other Indoor Sports*. Westport, CT: Greenwood Press, 1989.

★ ★ ★

LEAGUE OF COLORED BASE BALL CLUBS

The League of Colored Base Ball Players was organized in Baltimore, Maryland, on December 5, 1886, by Walter S. Brown. Prospects for the new league looked bright. Mr. Brown was elected president; J.J. Callis of Baltimore, vice president; and C. Howard Johnson, secretary. Owners of six clubs paid the $100 franchise entry fee: the Pittsburgh Keystones, Boston Resolutes, New York Gorhams, Philadelphia Pythians, Baltimore Lord Baltimores, and the Louisville Falls Citys. Representatives of the Cuban Giants and the Cincinnati Browns were undecided.

On March 14–15, 1887, league officials and delegates again met in Baltimore to finalize playing schedules and appoint umpires. Reach Sporting Goods agreed to provide the league's official ball and award gold medals for the highest batting and fielding averages. The Cuban Giants declined membership; the Cincinnati Browns and Washington, DC, Capitols were accepted, but neither paid the entry fee, and they never officially joined the league.

Heavy rains delayed the season a week until May 6, when the host Pittsburgh Keystones lost to the New York Gorhams 11–8 before a crowd of 1,200. An exceptionally cold and rainy spring severely hampered the league's schedule. On May 16, the once-promising league folded after only thirteen games. Aside from the weather, the league's expansive geography was a significant factor, necessitating long and expensive travel. The failure of investors to honor their commitments, along with the small monetary guarantees assured visiting teams, was compounded by small gate receipts. Despite its brief existence, the league helped foster a greater awareness of talented black ball players and black baseball as worthwhile entertainment.

Jerry J. Wright

FURTHER READING
Chadwick, Bruce. *When the Game Was Black and White: The Illustrated History of Baseball's Negro Leagues*. New York: Abbeville Press, 1992.
Dixon, Phil, and Patrick J. Hannigan. *The Negro Baseball Leagues: A Photographic History*. Mattituck, NY: Ameron, 1992.
New York Freeman, March 26, 1887.
White, Sol. *Sol White's Official Baseball Guide*. Philadelphia: H. Walter Schlichter, 1907.

★ ★ ★

Meadowlark LEMON

Born Lexington County, South Carolina
Basketball player

Meadowlark Lemon never revealed his age, always claiming simply to be between eighteen and 100 years old. He was an All-State athlete in both basketball and football at Wilmington High School in Wilmington, NC, and attended Florida A & M University. Lemon is affectionately known as the "Clown Prince of Basketball." He has been the creative juice and center of attention of international comedic basketball since he began his career with the Harlem Globetrotters more than four decades ago. *Los Angeles Times* sportswriter Jim Murray described Meadowlark Lemon as "an American Institution whose uniform should hang along side the *Spirit of St. Louis* and the Gemini Space Capsule in the halls of the Smithsonian Institute." Lemon was famous for his "no-look, wrap-around pass" for an easy slam-dunk. His hook shots from half-court and his ability to turn hapless game referees into confounded buffoons was priceless and unsurpassed.

Lemon had twenty-four memorable seasons with the Globetrotters. He has entertained kings, popes, queens, and presidents in addition to millions of fans around the world. Lemon played in more than 7,500 consecutive basketball games in more than ninety-four countries and in more than 1,500 North American cities. His love affair with the Globetrotters began in 1952, when he wrote the team's front office requesting a tryout. In 1954, after serving two years in the U.S. Army, Lemon signed a contract and was assigned to the Globetrotter's developmental team, the Kansas City Stars. He was at the time the youngest basketball player ever to join the Globetrotters. When Reece "Goose" Tatum, then the "Clown Prince of Basketball," announced his retirement from the Globetrotters, Lemon stepped in. He was assigned to understudy "Rookie" Brown on a southern tour and later changed his name (George) to "Meadowlark." He officially became the Globetrotters "Clown Prince" in 1956.

In 2000, the Naismith Basketball Hall of

Harlem Globetrotters star Meadowlark Lemon in 1978. *(AP/Wide World Photos)*

Fame honored Lemon with the prestigious John W. Bunn Award during Enshrinement Weekend in Springfield, Massachusetts. The John W. Bunn Award, established in 1974 to recognize outstanding lifetime achievements and contributions to basketball, is named in honor of the Hall of Fame's first executive director. It is the highest award presented by the Basketball Hall of Fame short of enshrinement. Lemon joined Marques Haynes and Wilt Chamberlain as the only players in Harlem Globetrotter history to have their jerseys retired. Lemon now resides in Scottsdale, Arizona, where he serves as an ordained minister and motivational speaker.

Gary A. Sailes

See also: Harlem Globetrotters.

FURTHER READING
George, Nelson. *Elevating the Game: Black Men and Basketball.* New York: HarperCollins, 1992.
Lemon, Meadowlark, with Jerry B. Jenkins. *Meadowlark.* Nashville, TN: Nelson, 1987.
Naismith Memorial Basketball Hall of Fame (www.hoophall.com).

★ ★ ★

Buck LEONARD

Born September 8, 1907, Rocky Mount, North Carolina
Died November 27, 1997, Rocky Mount, North Carolina
Baseball player

This smooth-fielding, sweet-swinging first baseman was the backbone of the Homestead Grays' dynasty of the 1930s and 1940s. Leonard was the son of John, a railroad fireman, and Emma. He left school at age fourteen to work as a shoeshine boy and a mill hand. At age twenty-five, Leonard left his home to become one of the finest first basemen in the game. The left-handed half of the Gray's power tandem, Leonard paired with Josh Gibson to lead the Grays to nine consecutive Negro National League championships, from 1937 to 1945. He was a favorite of the fans and became a fixture in the annual East-West All-Star classic, in which he played in a record twelve games, hitting .317 and belting three home runs to establish another record. His seventeen-years with the Grays constituted the longest tenure with one team in Negro league history.

Leonard compiled an unofficial lifetime .341 average in the Negro National League and a .382 mark in exhibitions against major leaguers. Washington Senators owner Clark Griffith approached Leonard and Gibson about playing in the majors. Griffith backed down, deciding not to disturb the status quo. When the color line was finally broken, Bill Veeck contacted Leonard about playing in the majors, but Leonard felt he was too old. After the Grays dissolved in 1950, Leonard spent five seasons in the Mexican leagues.

Total Baseball lists Leonard as one of the 400 greatest baseball players of all time. In 1999, the Society for Baseball Research chose him in a tie with Satchel Paige as the greatest Negro league player. In 1972, he became the second player elected by the Committee on Negro leagues to the National Baseball Hall of Fame, after Satchel Paige's selection in 1971. Leonard is the only Negro league first baseman enshrined in Cooperstown. In 1962 he helped organize the Rocky Mount (Carolina League) club and served as its vice president.

Larry S. Bonura

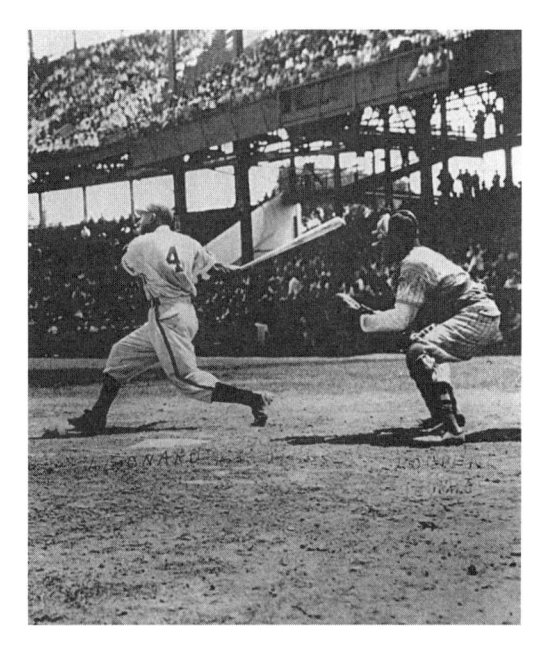

Homestead Gray's Buck Leonard hitting against the New York Cuban stars in a 1944 game in Washington, DC's Griffith Stadium. *(National Baseball Hall of Fame Library, Cooperstown, NY)*

FURTHER READING

"Buck Leonard." *CBS Sportsline* (cbs.sportsline.com/u/baseball/bol/ballplayers/L/Leonard_Buck.html).

"40 Greatest Negro League Figures by SABR." *Baseball Almanac* (www.baseball-almanac.com/legendary/lisabr40.shtml).

Holway, John. *Voices from the Great Black Baseball Leagues*. Rev. ed. New York: De Capo, 1992.

Holway, John B., and Bob Carroll. "The 400 Greatest." *Baseball Almanac* (www.baseball-almanac.com/legendary/li400gr.shtml).

Leonard, Buck, and James A. Riley. *Buck Leonard: The Black Lou Gehrig*. New York: Carroll and Graf, 1995.

National Baseball Hall of Fame (www.baseballhalloffame.org/hofers_and_honorees/hofer_bios/leonard_buck.htm).

Riley, James A. "Buck Leonard." In *The Ballplayers: Baseball's Ultimate Biographical Reference*, ed. Mike Shatzkin. New York: Arbor House, 1990.

"Walter Fenner (Buck) Leonard." *A Look At the Negro Leagues* (www.execpc.com/sshivers/leonard.html).

★ ★ ★

Sugar Ray Leonard, one of the world's most charismatic boxers, shortly before his 1987 victory against Marvin Hagler for the middleweight championship. *(AP/Wide World Photos)*

Sugar Ray LEONARD

Born May 17, 1956, Wilmington, North Carolina
Boxer

Named after the famous blues singer Ray Charles and nicknamed after the legendary prizefighter Sugar Ray Robinson, Ray Charles Leonard was born to Cicero and Getha Leonard. Cicero, a produce market employee, and Getha, a nursing assistant at a convalescent center, moved their family from North Carolina to the Washington, DC, area in 1960.

Possessing tremendous technical skill and speed, the clean-cut and ebullient Leonard enjoyed a meteoric career as an amateur boxer, winning the 1973 National Golden Gloves, the 1974 AAU title, the 1975 Pan American Games gold medal, and the 1976 Olympic gold medal as a light-welterweight.

After briefly retiring from boxing, Leonard turned professional in 1977 and won his first twenty-seven fights, including a November 30, 1979, bout with Wilfred Benitez to win the World Boxing Council (WBC) welterweight belt. On June 20, 1980, Leonard lost his first pro fight and his title in a fifteen-round decision to Roberto Durán. Five months later, on November 25, Leonard avenged the loss. With sixteen seconds left in the eighth round of their rematch, Durán gave up the title when he turned his back on Leonard and famously said, "*No más.*"

The next year, Leonard temporarily moved up a weight class, knocked out Ayub Kalule, and thus earned the World Boxing Association (WBA) junior middleweight title. Three months later, on September 16, 1981, Leonard and Thomas Hearns fought for the undisputed welterweight crown; Leonard held the WBC title and Hearns the WBA version. After fourteen tough rounds, Leonard was awarded a technical knockout over the previously undefeated Hearns. It was among the richest sports events in history up to that point, grossing approximately $35 million. In recognition of these accomplishments, *Sports Illustrated* named Leonard Sportsman of the Year.

Following a successful title defense, Leonard retired from boxing in 1982 due to a detached retina. His retirement was short-lived, however. In 1984, with a surgically repaired retina, Leonard returned to the ring, beat Kevin Howard, and again retired. Three years later, Leonard agreed to fight WBC middleweight champion Marvelous Marvin Hagler. On April 6, 1987, having fought only once in the previous five years, Leonard beat the rugged Hagler, winning a controversial split decision in one of the richest bouts in boxing history—reportedly grossing over $100 million.

On November 7, 1988, Leonard beat Donny Lalonde to claim the WBC light-heavyweight and super-middleweight titles. In 1989, the thirty-three-year-old Leonard again took on Hearns and Durán: he fought Hearns to a draw and outpointed Durán. Leonard retired again, but in 1991 he fought WBC super-welterweight champion Terry Norris; knocked down twice, Leonard lost a unanimous decision and retired. In March 1997, the former champ attempted yet another unsuccessful comeback, which ended with a technical knockout by Hector Camacho.

All told, Leonard held world championship titles in five weight classes and earned in excess of $100 million from fight purses, television contracts, and endorsements. He also won a great deal of praise as a boxer of rare grace, intelligence, strategy, and surprising toughness. Indeed, Leonard's career was even more impressive than his statistics (36–3–1, with twenty-five KOs) suggest. Leonard was voted Fighter of the Year three times by *Ring* magazine and was inducted into the International Boxing Hall of Fame in 1997.

Daniel A. Nathan

See also: Boxing; Marvin Hagler; Thomas Hearns.

FURTHER READING
Berger, Phil. *Punch Lines: Berger on Boxing*. New York: Four Walls Eight Windows, 1993.
Brooke-Ball, Peter. *The Boxing Album: An Illustrated History*. New York: Smithmark, 1992.
Early, Gerald. "Hot Spicks versus Cool Spades: Three Notes Toward a Cultural Definition of Prizefighting." In *Tuxedo Junction: Essays on American Culture*, Gerald Early. New York: Ecco Press, 1989.
Sugar Ray Leonard (www.ibhof.com/srleon.htm).

★ ★ ★

Lisa LESLIE

Born July 7, 1972, Hawthorn, California
Basketball player

Lisa Leslie was raised by her mother (Christine) after her father (Walter) left the family shortly after her birth. Her mother worked as a truck driver for many years to support the family. Leslie is a 1994 graduate of the University of Southern California (USC).

Leslie's basketball career began when she was eleven. During her senior year at Morningside High School she scored 101 points in a single half of play. She earned All-America honors three of the four years of eligibility at USC and was the unanimous choice for National Player of the Year in 1994. Leslie represented the United States on several national teams, including the gold medal-winning team at the 1996 Olympic Games in Atlanta. In Atlanta she averaged 19.5 points per game. During the three games in the medal round Leslie

Lisa Leslie, one of the most popular and talented WNBA players. *(AP/Wide World Photos)*

made nearly three-quarters of all her shooting attempts.

The six-foot, five inch Leslie played one year in Italy and was then drafted by the Los Angeles Sparks of the Women's National Basketball Association (WNBA) for the league's inaugural season in 1997. One of the league's most prominent players, Leslie won the Most Valuable Player trophies for the All-Star Game and the season in 2001. She helped lead the Sparks to their first WNBA championship, averaging over twenty-two points and twelve rebounds during the 2001 playoffs.

Leslie's athletic accomplishments as an amateur and professional women's basketball player make her a positive role model for young African-American girls who aspire to participate in athletics at all levels.

Rita Liberti

FURTHER READING
Anderson, Kelli. "Woman Possessed." *Sports Illustrated*, September 10, 2001, 46–47.
Moran, Malcolm. "In the Center in Two Worlds: Leslie is a Model Performer and a Performing Model." *New York Times*, July 17, 1996.
Women's National Basketball Association (www.wnba.com).

★ ★ ★

Jerry LeVIAS

Born September 5, 1946, Beaumont, Texas
Football player

The youngest of ten children born to Charles and Leura LeVias, and an all-district performer in football for Hebert High in Beaumont, LeVias played at the positions of quarterback, wide receiver, running back, and kick returner. Blessed with exceptional speed, he was clocked at 9.5 seconds in the 100-yard dash as a sophomore. He scored forty-three touchdowns in his junior and senior years and was highly sought after by many of the top universities in the country.

In March 1965, LeVias changed the face of college football, becoming the first African American to receive a football scholarship in the Southwest Conference, by signing with Southern Methodist University. In spite of facing many racial taunts both on and off the field, including hate mail, death threats, bomb threats, requiring at times state highway patrol and Federal Bureau of Investigation protection, he excelled both athletically and academically. In 1966, LeVias led Southern Methodist to its first conference title in eighteen years. Though only five feet, nine inches tall and weighing 177 pounds, LeVias made numerous athletic and academic All-American teams, including consensus All-American in 1968, Most Valuable

Player in the Senior Bowl in 1969, and All-Southwest Conference in 1966, 1967, and 1968. He set school records for most passes caught in a game, a season, and career. His 1,131 yards receiving in the 1968 season, 213 yards receiving, and fifteen receptions in a game still stand as Mustang records. He ended his career with 2,275 yards and twenty-two touchdowns. After obtaining his degree in finance it was time for the professional ranks.

The Houston Oilers selected LeVias in the second round of the 1969 American Football League draft. As a wide receiver and kick returner, he was awarded Rookie of the Year honors by setting a league record for combined punt and kickoff returns in a season. One of the most exciting players of his era, LeVias played a total of six seasons for the Oilers and the San Diego Chargers before he injured a knee. He was inducted into the Texas Sports Hall of Fame in 1995.

David W. Hunter

FURTHER READING
Fry, Hayden, and George Wine. *Hayden Fry: A High Porch Picnic*. Champaign, IL: Sports Publishing, 1999.
Miller, Geralda. *The Story and Struggle of SMU's Pioneer Black Athlete* (sdc.htrigg.smu.edu/HTMLPages/Spring98/DC.03–25–98/DC.03–25–98–s.smu.html).
Pennington, Richard. *Breaking the Ice: The Racial Integration of the Southwest Conference*. Jefferson, NC: McFarland, 1987.

★   ★   ★

Carl LEWIS

Born July 1, 1961, Birmingham, Alabama
Sprinter, jumper

Born to William and Evelyn Lewis, themselves athletes and coaches, Lewis was raised in the middle-class Philadelphia suburbs. He graduated from Willingboro High School and attended the University of Houston, majoring in communication. He retired from competition in 1997 and is pursuing a professional broadcasting and acting career.

Lewis was a dominant sprinter and long jumper throughout his track and field career. In high school he set a national long-jump record and was the New Jersey Long Jumper of the Year. At the University of Houston, Lewis developed his unique double-hitch long-jump technique and was ranked number-one nationally in the long jump and 100-meter, matching the 1936 performance of Jesse Owens by winning indoor/outdoor titles in both events. In 1982 Lewis left college and joined the Santa Monica Track Club, setting records in the 100-meter dash and winning gold medals in the first World Championships. He rose to fame during the 1984 Olympics, equaling Jesse Owens's record of four gold med-

Carl Lewis, one of the most decorated track and field athletes in Olympic history, capturing the gold medal in the long jump at the 1996 Atlanta Olympic games. *(AP/Wide World Photos)*

als (long jump, 100-meter, 200-meter, 400-meter relay) and setting Olympic records in the 200 meters (19.80) and 400-meter relay (37.83). In 1988 he won silver in the 200-meter and gold medals in the long jump and 100-meter (9.92). His success continued in 1992, when he won gold in the long jump and 400-meter relay. At his final Olympic competition (1996), Lewis won a gold medal in the long jump (27 feet 10¾ inches).

Lewis retired with ten Olympic medals (nine gold, one silver), ten world records, and eight world championships. He received the Sullivan Award (1981), Jesse Owens Award (1982), *Track and Field News* World Athlete of the Year (1982, 1984), Associated Press Male Athlete of the Year (1983, 1984), and World Sports Awards of the Century (1999) and is a U.S. Olympic Hall of Fame inductee (1985).

A longtime advocate of amateur-athlete rights and an outspoken adversary of performance-enhancing drugs in athletics, Lewis currently aids abused and neglected children as a National Court Appointed Special Advocate Association spokesperson.

Debra A. Henderson

See also: Track and Field.

FURTHER READING
"A Champion for the Children." *Essence*, November 1998, 16.
Lewis, Carl. "The Athletes Are the Games." *Newsweek*, February 1999, 56.
McGovern, Mike. "Lewis, Carl." In *The Encyclopedia of Twentieth-Century Athletes*, ed. M. McGovern. New York: Facts On File, 2001.
Porter, David L., ed. *African American Sports Greats: A Biographical Dictionary*. Westport, CT: Greenwood Press, 1995.
Sienkewicz, Thomas J. "Carl Lewis." In *Great Athletes*, eds. D.P. Dawson, R.K. Rasmussen, A. Miller, and E. Slocum. Pasadena, CA: Salem Press, 2002.

★ ★ ★

John Henry LEWIS

Born May 1, 1914, Los Angeles, California
Died April 18, 1974, Berkeley, California
Boxer

John Henry Lewis was born to be a boxer. His great granduncle was Tom Molineaux, a former slave who achieved fame as a bare-knuckle fighter in nineteenth-century England. Lewis was a genuine ring pioneer. He became the first African-American light heavyweight champion, and his meeting with Joe Louis in 1939 marked the first time two black men fought for the heavyweight championship.

Described by Joe Louis as "cagey, fast, and brainy," Lewis won the light heavyweight championship on November 31, 1935, in St. Louis with a unanimous decision over Bob Olin. He held the title for four years and never lost, as the 175-pound division champion. In a 1932 bout in San Francisco against heavyweight Jim Braddock, Lewis's speed and boxing ability proved too much for the bigger man. In a rematch two years later in New York City, though, Braddock earned a ten-round decision.

By the time he fought Louis in Madison Square Garden on January 25, 1939, Lewis was at the end of his career. He had lost lateral vision in one eye and was hoping for one more good payday before he retired. Louis had already defeated all the heavyweight contenders, so promoter Mike Jacobs was taking a financial gamble on the first heavyweight title bout between two blacks. Despite Jacobs's fears of a white backlash at the gate, the fight sold out. The two fighters were good friends; not wanting to prolong the fight, Louis knocked down his lighter opponent three times before the referee stopped the bout just 2:09 into the first round. It was the first time in

117 fights that Lewis had been knocked out. He never fought again. Lewis was inducted into the International Boxing Hall of Fame in 1994.

Dennis Gildea

See also: Boxing.

FURTHER READING
Fleischer, Nat. *The Heavyweight Championship: An Informal History of Heavyweight Boxing from 1719 to the Present Day*. New York: Putnam, 1949.
Louis, Joe. *My Life Story*. New York: Duell, Sloan, and Pearce, 1947.
Mead, Chris. *Champion: Joe Louis, Black Hero in White America*. New York: Penguin Books, 1985.

★ ★ ★

Oliver LEWIS

Born Unknown
Died Unknown
Jockey

Little is known about African-American jockey Oliver Lewis's early and later years. At the inaugural meet at Churchill Downs in Louisville, Kentucky, Lewis won three races and was honored as the leading rider. He won the first running of the Kentucky Derby in 1875, aboard Aristides. Sent out to set the pace for stablemate Chesapeake, Aristides proved the better horse despite Lewis's strong hold on him. When owner H. Price McGrath waved Lewis on to win, the jockey guided Aristides on to a record-setting finish. In June, under the owner's orders, Lewis held back Aristides to let McGrath's Calvin win the Belmont Stakes in New York. Lewis never rode in another Derby, but he attended the 1907 running as a spectator. As did many former jockeys, Lewis became a trainer, managing a stable in Lexington, Kentucky. He later worked for a bookmaker, which was legal at the time, and provided detailed information on how the horses ran. He developed a race-result form that was the forerunner of the Daily Racing Form and Equibase charts.

Susan Hamburger

FURTHER READING
"African Americans in the Derby." *Churchill Downs* (www.churchilldowns.com).
Hotaling, Edward. *The Great Black Jockeys: The Lives and Times of the Men Who Dominated America's First National Sport*. Rocklin, CA: Forum, 1999.
Logan, Rayford W., and Michael R. Winston, eds. *Dictionary of American Negro Biography*. New York: W.W. Norton, 1982.

★ ★ ★

William Henry LEWIS

Born November 28, 1868, Berkeley, Virginia
Died January 1, 1949, Boston, Massachusetts
Football player, attorney

Lewis was the son of freed slaves, Ashley H. Lewis (a Baptist minister) and Josephine Baker Lewis. A graduate of Amherst College (B.A.) and Harvard Law School (LL.B), Lewis was a well-known college football player, lawyer, and politician in Massachusetts. He also served as U.S. attorney for Boston (1903–1906) and as an assistant attorney general of the United States (1911–1913).

The first center in football to block, Lewis was also the first African American to be elected captain of the football teams at Amherst and Harvard, although his Harvard captaincy was only for the 1893 game against the University of Pennsylvania. His feats on the field earned him a spot on Walter Camp's "All-American Football Team" in 1892 and 1893; he was the first African American to be so listed.

After graduation Lewis continued to pioneer as a coach and as an arbiter of the game. His nearly ten years as an assistant coach with Harvard made him the country's first black coach at a predominantly white university, while his book *A Primer on College Football* (1896) is one of the sport's earliest books. He also wrote the chapter on line play in Camp's *How to Play Football* (1903).

Lewis, who had been part of Harvard's infamous 1892 "flying wedge" formation, was equally active in efforts to make football safer. His suggestion to create a neutral zone at the line of scrimmage was one of a number of major changes instituted in 1906.

Mary Jo Binker

FURTHER READING
Beale, Morris A. *The History of Football at Harvard.* New York: Webberprint, 1948.
Chalk, Ocania. *Black College Sport.* New York: Dodd, Mead, 1976.
Ewing, Addison A. "William H. Lewis." *Amherst Graduate Quarterly* 38 (February 1949).
Oriard, Michael. *How the Popular Press Created an American Spectacle.* Chapel Hill: University of North Carolina Press, 1993.
Smith, Ronald A., ed. *Big-Time Football at Harvard 1905.* Urbana: University of Illinois Press, 1994.
Sullivan, George. "A Memorable Day for a Great Man." Harvard vs. Pennsylvania Game Program, November 13, 1993.
Wade, Harold Jr. *Black Men of Amherst.* Amherst, MA: Amherst College Press 1976.
"William H. Lewis, Noted Attorney, Stricken Fatally." *Boston Globe,* January 2, 1949.

★ ★ ★

Joe LILLARD

Born June 15, 1905, Tulsa, Oklahoma
Died September 18, 1978, New York, New York
Football player

Professional athlete in three sports, Lillard played football under considerable adversity in the NFL as one of the last two African Americans in the league before the unofficial ban against nonwhite players in 1934.

A three-sport prep star at Mason City, Iowa, Lillard was twice named all-state in football and basketball. After graduation in 1927, he played semi-pro baseball for the Chicago-based Gilkerson Union Giants, and in the winters played basketball with the Savoy Big Five. Lillard was recruited for football by the University of Oregon in 1931, but the Pacific Coast Conference declared him ineligible early in the season.

Lillard played two seasons (1932–1933) with the Chicago Cardinals of the National Football League, and was one of the league's top backfield men. The target of constant rough play by opposing players, teammates frequently refused to help Lillard when he was injured. He also began a two-year stint with the Chicago American Giants baseball team in 1932, and continued to play basketball with the touring Savoy Big Five.

After playing pro football in Los Angeles in 1934, Lillard joined the New York Brown Bombers for three seasons (1935–1937), before moving to the American Association. He also continued his baseball career with the Cincinnati Tigers (1936) and the American Giants (1937). Retiring from athletics in the early 1940s, Lillard served as a social counselor for juveniles in the New York area; later working twenty-two years for a Harlem sporting goods store.

Raymond Schmidt

See also: Football.

FURTHER READING
Gill, Bob, and Tod Maher. "Black Players in Minor League Football, 1933–46." *Coffin Corner* 11 (1989): 1–2.
"Lillard vs. Cards." *Chicago Defender,* December 9, 1933.
Stiles, Maxwell. "Oregon, Minus Lillard." *Los Angeles Examiner,* October 17, 1931.
Ziemba, Joe. *When Football Was Football: The Chicago Cardinals and the Birth of the NFL.* Chicago: Triumph Books, 1999.

★ ★ ★

Gene "Big Daddy" LIPSCOMB

Born August 9, 1931, Uniontown, Alabama
Died May 10, 1963, Baltimore, Maryland
Football player

Gene Lipscomb was born into a family of cotton pickers; his father died when he was three. His mother (Carrie) moved herself and her only child to the "Black Bottom" ghetto in Detroit and was stabbed to death when Lipscomb was eleven years old. Lipscomb, living with his often-abusive maternal grandfather and subject to teasing by his classmates because of his size and lack of academic skills, dropped out of school and joined the U.S. Marine Corps in 1949. Establishing himself as a football phenomenon while in the Marines, Lipscomb was drafted by the Los Angeles Rams in 1953.

Lipscomb, at six feet, seven inches and 290 pounds, was a formidable defensive tackle on the field, combining size and amazing speed to become a dependable roadblock. Lipscomb's off-field behavior was as predictable but not as admirable, involving bouts of womanizing, drinking, and violence, a pattern that led the Rams to place him on waivers after three years. He was picked up by the Baltimore Colts in 1956, responded well to their training regimen, and helped lead the team to two successful championships (1958 and 1959). Despite his growing maturity on the field, Lipscomb's private life continued to be one of self-destruction. He was traded to the Pittsburgh Steelers in 1961 and delivered one of the greatest performances of his career in the Pro Bowl of 1963; he died that same year of a drug overdose. His friends deny that his death was self-induced.

Trisha M. Hothorn

FURTHER READING

Carroll, Bob. *When the Grass Was Real: The Best Ten Years of Pro Football.* New York: Simon & Schuster, 1993.

Linn, Ed. "Sad End of Big Daddy Lipscomb." *Saturday Evening Post,* July 27, 1963, 73–74.
Lipscomb, Eugene. "Big Daddy: I'm Still Scared." *Saturday Evening Post,* November 12, 1960, 36.
Nack, William. "The Ballad of Big Daddy." *Sports Illustrated,* January 11, 1999.
Rywell, Martin, ed. *Afro-American Encyclopedia.* North Miami, FL: Educational Book Publishers, 1974.

★ ★ ★

Sonny LISTON

Born May 8, 1932, Forest City, Arkansas
Died December 30, 1970, Las Vegas, Nevada
Boxer

Sonny Liston was the twenty-fourth of twenty-five children; his father (Tobey) was a tenant farmer and mother (Helen) a housewife. Liston did not enjoy school and did not attend after he joined his mother in St. Louis as a young teen. Liston was to become a physically strong fighter and hold the heavyweight title for two years.

In 1950, Liston was charged with robbery and sentenced to five years in Missouri State Penitentiary, where he learned to box. Throughout his career Liston was to be linked with organized-crime figures, such as John Vitale, Frankie Carbo, and Blinky Palermo. Because of these ties and his own criminal background (over twenty arrests), Liston's application to fight Floyd Patterson for the heavyweight title was the subject of great debate and controversy. New York denied Liston a license, so the championship bout was held in Chicago, on September 25, 1962. Liston knocked Patterson out in the first round for the title. Liston defended his title against Patterson, knocking him out in the first round on July 22, 1963, in Las Vegas. His next challenger was a young fighter named Cassius Clay, whom Liston was expected to beat handily. On February 25, 1964, Clay beat the heavily favored Liston in the seventh round when Liston failed to answer the bell. On May

25, 1965, Liston challenged Muhammad Ali (as Cassius Clay was by then known) for the title, this time losing on a phantom punch (not easily seen) in the first round. Many claimed that he had thrown the fight. Liston fought second-rate fighters for several years before retiring from the ring. In his last fight, on June 29, 1970, Liston knocked out Chuck Wepner.

Liston's retirement was short; he died on December 30, 1970. He was inducted into the International Boxing Hall of Fame in 1990.

Maureen M. Smith

See also: Boxing; Films; Floyd Patterson.

FURTHER READING
Nack, William. "O Unlucky Man." *Sports Illustrated*, February 14, 1994, 152–160.
Roberts, Randy. "Self-Defeated." *National Review*, October 9, 2000, 55–57.
Tosches, Nick. *The Devil and Sonny Liston*. New York: Little, Brown, 2000.
Young, Andrew S. "Doc." *Sonny Liston: The Champ Nobody Wanted*. Chicago: Nelson, 1963.

★ ★ ★

Floyd LITTLE

Born July 4, 1942, New Haven, Connecticut
Football player

Little was a three-time All-American running back for Syracuse University (1964–1966) and had a successful career in the National Football League (NFL) with the Denver Broncos (1967–1975). Little, whose 2,704 yards at Syracuse were the most by Orangemen running backs (ahead of Jim Brown and Ernie Davis) as of when he graduated, was inducted into the College Football Hall of Fame in 1983.

Following the 1948 death of his father (Fred), Little was raised on welfare by his widowed mother (Lula), along with five siblings. Little was the first African American to attend Bordentown (NJ) Military Academy, where he became a prep school football All-American in 1962. At Syracuse, Little was a collegiate football All-American in his three varsity seasons, gaining 5,529 total yards (rushing, receiving, kick returns). In 1999, Little was named to the Syracuse All-Century team.

In the NFL, Little played for the Broncos and was nicknamed "The Franchise." Little retired in 1975 as the team's all-time leader in rushing yards (6,323) and touchdowns (54). The Broncos retired Little's number and named him as an inaugural member of the team's "Ring of Fame" in 1984.

Little has been a successful businessman since his retirement from the NFL. He currently owns and operates a Ford dealership in Seattle, WA. During the late 1980s, Little attempted to become the first African American to become a majority owner of an NFL team when he led a group that bid for the Seattle Seahawks.

Michael T. Friedman

FURTHER READING
Denver Broncos. "Ring of Fame: Floyd Little" (www.denverbroncos.com/history/ringoffame/little.php3).
McGrath, John. "A Football Legacy—and Much More." *News (Tacoma, WA) Tribune*, January 24, 1999.
Porter, David L., ed. *Biographical Dictionary of American Sports: Football*. Westport, CT: Greenwood Press, 1987.
Saunders, Patrick. "1960–2000 Mile High Memories: Floyd Little." *Denver Post*, October 1, 2000.
Withers, Bud. "Whatever Happened to . . . Floyd Little—Bronco Legend in Our Midst." *Seattle Times*, June 9, 2000.

★ ★ ★

Earl LLOYD

Born April 3, 1928, Alexandria, Virginia
Basketball player

On October 31, 1950, Earl Lloyd became the first African American to play in a National Basketball Association game when his Washington Capitols visited the Rochester (NY) Royals. Lloyd, Chuck Cooper, and Nat "Sweetwater" Clifton are generally linked as the three pioneering African Americans in the NBA. Cooper was the first black player drafted (Boston Celtics), Clifton the first to sign a contract (New York Knicks, from the Harlem Globetrotters), and Lloyd the first actually to play in a game.

Lloyd downplayed his pioneering role, noting that the situation in the NBA was not comparable to that faced by Jackie Robinson in major league baseball in 1947. Lloyd described as "ho-hum" the nondescript NBA of that era and problems he faced as an early black player. He heard some taunts and was unable to eat in some hotel restaurants, but he encountered no racial hostility from teammates or opponents.

Lloyd played college basketball at West Virginia State, which he led to back-to-back national Colored Invitational Athletic Association titles in 1948–1949. His rookie season of 1950 lasted only briefly before he was drafted into the army, serving two years during the Korean War. Lloyd returned to the NBA in 1952, spent six seasons with the Syracuse Nationals, then played with the Detroit Pistons from 1958 to 1960. In 1960, he became an assistant coach with the Detroit Pistons and later their head coach. Lloyd was nominated for the Naismith Basketball Hall of Fame in 2001. He is also a member of the Central Intercollegiate Athletic Association Hall of Fame. He averaged 8.4 points and 6.4 rebounds during his NBA career.

Robert Epling

See also: Basketball.

FURTHER READING

Broussard, Chris. "3 Pioneers Hailed for Breaking Color Line." *New York Times*, November 1, 2000.

Dixon, Oscar. "NBA Not Forgetting Barrier-Breakers Trio Integrated All-White League." *USA Today*, October 30, 2000.

"Earl Lloyd Says He's No Robinson." *Verve* (www.canoe.ca/Slam001030/nba_lloyd-ap.html).

Mitchell, John. "Uneventful Game, Memorable Man." *Washington Times*, March 29, 1999.

Nance, Roscoe. "Integrating 'Ho-hum' Basketball Was Much Easier." *USA Today*, April 16, 1997.

"The Reason for the Season: NBA Pioneer Earl Lloyd!" *Black Web Portal* (www.blackwebportal.com/wire/DisplayArticle.cfm?ArticleID 23).

Sullivan, George. "NBA Color Line Fell 50 Years Ago." *USA Today*, April 25, 2000.

"Time Trail." *West Virginia March Programs* (www.wvculture.org/history/timetrl/ttmar.html).

★ ★ ★

John Henry LLOYD

Born April 25, 1884, Palatka, Florida
Died March 19, 1965, Atlantic City, New Jersey
Baseball player

John Henry Lloyd was a premier Negro league shortstop and thought by many to be the greatest player ever. Left without a father as an infant, he left school at an early age to work as a delivery boy to help meet the family's financial needs. He was discovered in 1905 on the sandlots of Jacksonville, Florida, where he was playing on a team called the "Old Receivers."

He played on at least a dozen different teams in his twenty-six year career. Lloyd was a complete ballplayer, who could hit, field, run, throw, and hit with power. While playing in Cuba, his play on the field earned him the nickname of "El Cuchara," Spanish for "shovel," for the way he dug balls out of the dirt. In 1913, Lloyd's team compiled a phenomenal 101–6 record and soundly defeated Foster's Chicago American Giants in the playoffs.

In twenty-nine recorded games against white major leaguers, Lloyd batted .321. In 1911, Lloyd was honored by being named to the first black All-Star team, which was selected by the *Indianapolis Freeman* newspaper. After retiring in 1932, he settled in Atlantic City, where he stayed close to baseball by continuing as a manager and first baseman of sandlot teams until age sixty. He worked as a custodian for the post office and schools system.

In 1949, the John Henry Lloyd Park for baseball was dedicated in his honor in Atlantic City. Lloyd was voted into the National Baseball Hall of Fame in 1977.

Clyde Partin

FURTHER READING
Ashe, Arthur R., Jr. *A Hard Road to Glory, 1619–1918.* New York: Penguin Books, 1988.
Holway, John B. *Blackball Stars: Negro League Pioneers.* Westport, CT: Meckler Books, 1988.
Ribowsky, Mark. *A Complete History of the Negro Leagues, 1884–1955.* New York: Birch Lane Press, 1995.
Riley, James A. *The Biographical Encyclopedia of the Negro Baseball Leagues.* New York: Carroll and Graf, 1994.
Shatzkin, Mike, and Jim Charlton. *The Ball Players.* New York: Arbor House, 1990.

★ ★ ★

Ronnie LOTT

Born May 8, 1959, Albuquerque, New Mexico
Football player

Ronnie Lott is the son of Roy D. Lott (a career U.S. Air Force serviceman) and Mary (Carroll) Lott. Lott's formative years were spent in his town of birth, then Washington, DC, and, from 1969 through high school in Rialto, California.

At Eisenhower High School, Lott lettered in baseball, basketball, and football. In 1977, he was a *Parade* magazine High School All-American in football. Lott entered the University of Southern California in 1977. In his sophomore year he lettered as a guard in basketball. While he was a skilled college basketball player, Lott's most notable athletic feats at USC occurred on the football field. He was a member of the 1978 and 1979 Rose Bowl-winning Trojan teams. Among other honors, Lott was elected to the All-Pac Ten team and was USC's 1980 MVP. He won All-American awards as a defensive back during both his junior and senior years. In 1981, Lott graduated with a B.A. in public administration.

In the 1981 National Football League draft, the six-foot, 200-pound Lott was the first-round choice (eighth player selected overall) of the San Francisco 49ers. His career with the 49ers lasted ten years. During his time in San Francisco, as a cornerback (1981–1984) and a free safety (1985–1990), Lott was a part of four Super Bowl-winning teams (1982, 1985, 1989, and 1990). In March 1991, Lott signed to play with the Los Angeles Raiders. Two years later, he joined the New York Jets, finishing his playing career with them in 1994. Lott was selected to ten Pro Bowls as a player. He was named to the NFL's Seventy-fifth Anniversary team and inducted into the Professional Football Hall of Fame in 2000.

In 1991, Lott married Karen Collmer. They have one daughter. Lott also has a son, born in 1979. Since 1996, Lott has worked as a football analyst for Fox Broadcasting Corporation. He has various business interests in Northern California and is active in local charitable organizations.

Deane A. Lamont

FURTHER READING
Henderson, Ashyia N., ed. *Who's Who Among African Americans.* Detroit: Gale Group, 2000.
Porter, David L., ed. *Biographical Dictionary of American Sports: 1992–1995 Supplement for Baseball, Football, Basketball and Other Sports.* Westport, CT: Greenwood Press, 1995.
Professional Football Hall of Fame (www.profootballhof.com).
Who's Who in America, 2001. New Providence, NJ: Marquis Who's Who, 2001.

★ ★ ★

Joe LOUIS

Born May 13, 1914, Lafayette, Alabama
Died April 12, 1983, Las Vegas, Nevada
Boxer

Son of Munn Barrow (a farmer) and his wife Lillie Barrow, Louis was arguably the greatest boxer in history. He was an enormously powerful and physically gifted boxer who realized heroic status among large segments of both the white and African-American communities for his many ring triumphs. Under the direction of Detroit businessman John Roxborough, Louis turned professional in 1934 and just three years later captured the heavyweight championship by defeating James Braddock. He defended his title a record twenty-five times over his career, seemingly unafraid to fight any boxer and under any circumstances. Perhaps the most memorable and historically significant of Louis's sixty-nine professional victories was his first-round knockout of Max Schmeling in 1938. The victory avenged a twelve-round defeat to Schmeling just two years earlier and was a symbolic nail in the coffin of the doctrine of racial superiority espoused by Adolf Hitler and his Nazi regime.

Louis retired from the ring in 1949. Serious financial problems, however, forced him to make a brief return to the "squared circle." Unfortunately, Louis's boxing skills had so deteriorated that he was no match for his subsequent bouts with new champion Ezzard Charles and Rocky Marciano. Louis's postretirement career was similar to those many other former boxers who possessed little formal education and few marketable skills. Married four times and continuing to be wracked by money troubles caused by bad investments and poor choices of advisers, Louis struggled to the very end of his life to make ends meet and carve out a meaningful existence. He performed for a time as a professional wrestler, failed as a fast-food entrepreneur, and acted as a front man for boxing promoter James Norris. In 1970 he spent several months in a mental hospital and in the last years of his life served as an official greeter at Caesar's Palace in Las Vegas, Nevada. He died in Las Vegas in 1983 and seven years later was elected to the International Boxing Hall of Fame.

David K. Wiggins

Joe Louis having his hand raised following his first round knockout of Germany's Max Schmeling in the much written about rematch between the two fighters at New York's Yankee Stadium in 1938. *(AP/Wide World Photos)*

See also: Autobiographies; Boxing; Charles Ezzard; Films; Historiography.

FURTHER READING
Capeci, Dominic J., Jr., and Martha Wilkerson. "Multifarious Hero: Joe Louis, American Society and Race Relations During World Crisis, 1935–1945." *Journal of Sport History* 10 (Winter 1983): 5–25.

Davis, Lenwood G. *Joe Louis: A Reference of Articles, Books, Pamphlets, Records, and Archival Material*. Westport, CT: Greenwood Press, 1983.

Edmonds, Anthony O. *Joe Louis*. Grand Rapids, MI: William B. Eerdmans, 1973.

Mead, Chris. *Champion: Joe Louis, Black Hero in White America*. New York: Scribner's, 1985.

Sammons, Jeffrey T. *Beyond the Ring: The Role of Boxing in American Society*. Urbana: University of Illinois Press, 1988.

★ ★ ★

James LuVALLE

Born November 10, 1912, San Antonio, Texas
Died January 30, 1993, New Zealand
Sprinter, scientist

James LuValle was the son of James Arthur Garfield (a newspaper reporter) and Isabel Ellis LuValle (a music teacher). He was a graduate of the University of California, Los Angeles, in 1931, the University of California at Los Angeles in 1936 and 1937, and the California Institute of Technology in 1940. An intercollegiate and Olympic championship runner, LuValle also garnered success as an inventor, scientist, and teacher.

LuValle began running in the 220- and 440-yard dashes in junior high school. In 1934 he posted 20.8 seconds for 220 yards, the fastest time for the furlong that year. LuValle, who captained the UCLA track team in 1935, won the 440-yard dash in the National Collegiate Athletic Association (NCAA) championship that year in 47.7 seconds. In 1936, he posted lifetime bests of 47.1 seconds in the quarter-mile and 46.3 seconds for its metric equivalent. At the 1936 Olympic Games in Berlin, Germany, LuValle's bronze medal-winning performance in the 400 meters was one of several by African Americans that cast doubt upon Nazi notions of Aryan superiority.

A Phi Beta Kappa scholar, LuValle earned a bachelor's degree in chemistry in 1936 and two master's degrees (in chemistry and physics) in 1937. One of the first graduate teaching assistants in the UCLA chemistry department, he served as the first president of the school's Graduate Students Association. In 1940, LuValle completed doctorate degrees in chemistry and mathematics and became the first African American appointed to the research staff of the Eastman Kodak Company, joining its technical operations division in 1953. He became the director of basic research at the Fairchild Camera and Instrument Corporation in 1959 and the director of the microstatics laboratory at Smith-Corona Merchant in 1968.

In 1975, LuValle became the director of the undergraduate chemistry laboratories at Stanford University. He retired in 1982 but remained at Stanford, conducting research in the chemical basis of memory. The author of at least thirty-five scientific papers, LuValle held nine patents in the United States and Europe. In 1985 UCLA named the LuValle Commons, a new student center, in his honor. He died of a heart attack while vacationing in New Zealand.

Adam R. Hornbuckle

See also: Track and Field.

FURTHER READING

LuValle, Dr. Phyllis, Calgary, Alberta, Canada, letter to author, April 9, 2001.

Mallon, Bill, and Ian Buchanan. *Quest for Gold: The Encyclopedia of American Olympians*. New York: Leisure Press, 1980.

Quercetani, Roberto L. *A World History of Track and Field Athletics*. London and New York: Oxford University Press, 1964.

UCLA Alumni Association, letter to Adam R. Hornbuckle, February 26, 2001.

Wallechinsky, David. *The Complete Book of the Summer Olympics*. Woodstock, NY: Overlook Press, 2000.

GENERAL INDEX

Aaron, Hank, **1:**1–2; **2:**229, 230
AAU. *See* Amateur Athletic Union
Abbott, Cleveland, **1:**2; **2:**231, 373
Abdul-Jabbar, Kareem (Lew Alcindor), **1:**3–4, 26, 35, 40, 102, 142; **2:**297, 303–4
Above the Rim (film), **1:**102
Adams, Lucinda, **1:**4–5
Adderley, Herb, **1:**5
African American Tennis Association, **2:**335
Agents, **1:**6–7
  Nehemiah, Renaldo, **2:**256
Air Up There, The (film), **1:**102
Albritton, David, **1:**7–8; **2:**372, 386
Alcindor, Lew. *See* Abdul-Jabbar, Kareem
Alexander, Alpha, **1:**35
Alexander, Grover Cleveland, **2:**405
Alexis, Lucien, Jr., **1:**199
Ali, Muhammad (Cassius Clay), **1:**8–9, 16, 17, 45–46, 69, 91, 95, 100, 109, 110, 112, 158, 167, 197, 213–14; **2:**241, 260, 266, 277, 312, 343
All-Americans (college basketball)
  Bellamy, Walter, **1:**32–33
  Bing, Dave, **1:**33
  Boozer, Bob, **1:**39–40
  Cooper, Chuck, **1:**75
  Dantley, Adrian, **1:**77–78
  Dukes, Walter, **1:**89
  Ewing, Patrick, **1:**97–98
  Ford, Phil, **1:**108
  Jackson, Mannie, **1:**173
  Jordan, Michael, **1:**190–91
  Leslie, Lisa, **1:**207–8
  Manning, Danny, **2:**224
  Monroe, Earl, **2:**239–40
  Murphy, Calvin, **2:**246
  O'Neal, Shaquille, **2:**268–69
  Russell, Cazzie, **2:**319–20
  Sampson, Ralph, **2:**321
  Scott, Charlie, **2:**324
  Stallworth, Dave, **2:**346
  Thompson, David, **2:**367–68
  Thompson, John, **2:**368–69
  White, Jo Jo, **2:**398–99
  Woodward, Lynette, **2:**415–16
  Worthy, James, **2:**418
All-Americans (college football)
  Adderley, Herb, **1:**5
  Bass, Dick, **1:**26–27
  Campbell, Earl, **1:**58–59
  Carter, Cris, **1:**62–63
  Davis, Ernie, **1:**78–79

All-Americans (college football) *(continued)*
  Dickerson, Eric, **1:**83–84
  Drew, Charles, **1:**87–88
  Eller, Carl, **1:**94–95
  Greene, Joe, **1:**128–29
  Holland, Jerome Brud, **1:**157
  Hurt, Eddie, **1:**162
  LeVias, Jerry, **1:**208–9
  Lewis, William Henry, **1:**211–12
  Little, Floyd, **1:**214
  Lott, Ronnie, **1:**216
  Marshall, Bob, **2:**225–26
  Marshall, Jim, **2:**226
  Matson, Ollie, **2:**227
  Newsome, Ozzie, **2:**259
  Parker, Jim, **2:**276
  Perkins, Don, **2:**281
  Pollard, Fritz, **2:**283–84
  Reed, Dwight, **2:**296
  Renfro, Mel, **2:**297–98
  Rice, Jerry, **2:**301
  Robeson, Paul, **2:**304–5
  Rodgers, Johnny, **2:**313–14
  Rogers, George, **2:**315–16
  Rozier, Mike, **2:**316
  Sanders, Deion, **2:**322
  Sayers, Gale, **2:**323
  Simmons, Ozzie, **2:**330
  Simpson, O. J., **2:**331
  Smith, Bruce, **2:**335–36
  Smith, "Bubba," **2:**336–37
  Smith, Emmitt, **2:**337–38
  Swann, Lynn, **2:**352–53
  Tatum, Jack, **2:**357–58
  Taylor, Lawrence, **2:**360–61
  Walker, Herschel, **2:**384–85
  Warfield, Paul, **2:**388–89
  Washington, Gene, **2:**389–90
  West, Charlie, **2:**396
  White, Reggie, **2:**399–400
  Willis, Bill, **2:**407–8
  Young, Buddy, **2:**422
Allen, Hank, **1:**159–60
Allen, Marcus, **1:**9–10
Allen, Ray, **1:**102
Amateur Athletic Union (AAU), **2:**371, 392–94
Amateur Fencers League of America, **1:**99
Ambers, Lou, **1:**11–12
American Bowling Congress, **1:**42, 69; **2:**252
American Football League, **1:**107
American Negro League, **2:**253

GENERAL INDEX

American Tennis Association (ATA), **1**:10, 118, 120–21; **2**:363–64, 391, 394
Amsterdam News (newspaper), **2**:345
Anderson, Dave, **2**:400
Anderson, Elmer, **1**:167
Anderson, Raymond, **1**:7
Angott, Sammy, **2**:405
Antuofermo, Vito, **1**:137
Any Given Sunday (film), **1**:101
Apartheid, **1**:69, 92
Archibald, Nate, **1**:11
Arguello, Alexis, **1**:46
Arledge, Roone, **1**:107
Armstrong, Henry, **1**:11–12, 45, 100
Armstrong Manual Training School, **1**:168
Armstrong, Sherman, **2**:300
Ashe, Arthur, Jr., **1**:12–13, 16, 17, 102, 153; **2**:291, 363, 364
Ashford, Emmett, **1**:13–14
Ashford, Evelyn, **1**:15; **2**:265, 372
Associated Negro Press, **1**:54
Association football, **1**:105
Association Tennis Club of Washington, **1**:10
Atkins, W. E., **1**:63
Atlanta Daily World (newspaper), **2**:303
Atlanta University, **1**:150
Auerbach, Red, **2**:247, 318
Autobiographies, **1**:15–17, 104

Babilonia, Tai, **2**:267
Bach, Joe, **2**:296
Baillet-Latour, Henri de, **2**:265
Baird, Tom, **2**:252
Baker, Buck, **2**:325
Baker, Dusty, **1**:72
Baker, William J., **1**:153
Baldwin, Jerry, **1**:72
Ball, Robert "Pat," **2**:377
Ball, Walter, **1**:138
Balls, Iolanda, **2**:231
Baltimore Afro-American (newspaper), **1**:41, 200; **2**:303, 345
Bankhead, Sam, **1**:32
Banks, Ernie, **1**:19; **2**:270
Barco, J. W., **1**:63
Barker, Violet, **1**:99
Barkley, Charles, **1**:19–20; **2**:266
Barkley, Iran, **1**:144
Barksdale, Don, **1**:20–21, 25; **2**:266
Barnett, Dick, **2**:297
Barney, Lem, **1**:167
Barron, Allan P., **1**:35
Bartholomew, Joseph, **1**:124
Basilio, Carmen, **1**:45
Bass, Dick, **1**:26–27
Baton twirling, **2**:246
Baylor, Don, **1**:27, 72
Baylor, Elgin, **1**:28, 148; **2**:297
Beamon, Bob, **1**:28–29, 42; **2**:372
Beer, Klaus, **1**:42

Behee, John, **1**:154
Beliveau, Jean, **1**:165
Bell, Bill, **1**:29–30
Bell, Bobby, **1**:30–31
Bell, James "Cool Papa," **1**:22, 31–32, 129; **2**:254
Bell, "Puggy," **1**:24
Bellamy, Walter, **1**:32–33, 39
Bench, Johnny, **2**:243
Benitez, Wilfred, **1**:206
Berbick, Trevor, **2**:375
Berra, Yogi, **1**:58
Bikila, Abebe, **2**:265
Bing, Dave, **1**:33
Bird, Larry, **1**:184
Birrell, Susan, **1**:156
Black Athlete, The: Emergence and Arrival (Henderson), **1**:145, 153
Black Bill, **1**:176
Black Coaches Association (BCA), **1**:33–34; **2**:293, 302
Black Entertainment Television, **1**:183
Black Newspaper Publishers Association, **1**:69
Black Sports (magazine), **1**:35
Black Women in Sports Foundation, **1**:35
Black World Championship Rodeo, **1**:36; **2**:313
Blair, George E., **1**:36
Blount, Mel, **1**:36–37; **2**:261
Body and Soul (film), **1**:100
Body and Soul (film, remake), **1**:100
Bolanos, Enrique, **2**:405
Bolden, Edward, **1**:37–38, 91
Bonds, Barry, **1**:38–39, 146
Bonds, Bobby, **1**:38
Bontemp, Arna, **1**:153
Boozer, Bob, **1**:39–40
Borican, John, **1**:40
Bostic, Joseph, **1**:22, 41; **2**:345
Boston, Ralph, **1**:41–42; **2**:372
Boswell, Sonny, **1**:24
Bowie State University, **1**:63
Boxing Hall of Fame
 Armstrong, Henry, **1**:11–12
 Foster, Bob, **1**:110
 Frazier, Joe, **1**:112
 Jeannette, Joe, **1**:176
 King, Don, **1**:196–97
 Moore, Archie, **2**:241–42
 Patterson, Floyd, **2**:276–77
 See also International Boxing Hall of Fame
Boycotts and protests
 against Brigham Young University, **1**:29
 college football in 1960s, **1**:107
 Harry Edwards and, **1**:91–92
 historians on, **1**:155
 Moscow Olympics (1980), **1**:81–82
 against National Negro League, **1**:76
 1965 AFL All-Star Game, **1**:31
 1929 NYU-Georgia basketball game, **1**:68
 Olympic black-power protest (Mexico City, 1968), **1**:17, 29, 60, 69–70, 97; **2**:265, 266, 340, 372
Brackman, Harold, **1**:154

Braddock, James, **1:**44, 210, 217
Bradford, Jim, **2:**392
Bradley, Bill, **2:**297
Bragan, Bobby, **2:**409
Branham, George, **1:**42
Bratton, Johnny, **2:**405
Braun, Carl, **2:**400
Brian's Song (film), **1:**101
Bright, John, **1:**105; **2:**251
Brisco-Hooks, Valerie, **1:**46–48; **2:**372
Brock, Louis, **1:**48; **2:**270
Brodie, John, **2:**273
Brokaw, Tom, **2:**291
Broughton, Jack, **1:**43
Brown, Delmar, **1:**60
Brown, Dewey, **1:**124
Brown, Godfrey, **2:**403
Brown, Jim, **1:**16, 49–50, 101, 195, 199, 214; **2:**237
Brown, Joe, **1:**45
Brown, Larry, **1:**50–51
Brown, Mary K., **1:**6
Brown, Panama Al, **1:**44
Brown, Paul, **2:**237, 246
Brown, Roger, **1:**51
Brown, "Rookie," **1:**204
Brown, Roosevelt, **1:**52
Brown, Tim, **1:**101
Brown, Walter, **1:**75
Brown, Walter S., **1:**203
Bruce, Janet, **1:**154
Brumel, Valery, **2:**367
Brundage, Avery, **1:**69, 91
Bryant, Bear, **2:**307
Bryant, Kobe, **1:**52–53
Bullock, Matthew, **1:**53–54, 128
Bunce, Steven, **1:**176
Bunche, Ralph, **1:**24
Burley, Daniel, **1:**54; **2:**345
Burley, Darryl, **2:**418
Burns, Isaac. *See* Murphy, Isaac
Burns, Tommy, **1:**44, 178
Burrell, Chris, **1:**160
Burrell, Lewis, **1:**160
Burrell, Louis, Jr., **1:**160
Burrell, Stanley (M. C. Hammer), **1:**160
Burwell, Bryan, **2:**345
Butler, Sol, **1:**55
Buxton, Angela, **1:**121
Byrd, Larry, **1:**180

Caan, James, **1:**101
Caddies (golf), **1:**123–24
Cahn, Susan, **1:**156; **2:**413–14
Calhoun, Lee, **1:**57
Callahan, Clay, **1:**174
Callis, J. J., **1:**203
Camacho, Hector, **1:**207
Camp, Walter, **1:**106
Campanella, Roy, **1:**16, 57–58, 101; **2:**219
Campbell, Earl, **1:**58–59

Campbell, Milt, **1:**59; **2:**372
Campos, Manuel, **2:**251
Capricorn One (film), **1:**101
Captain, Gwendolyn, **1:**156
Carbo, Frankie, **1:**213; **2:**404
Carey, Harry, **2:**398
Carey, Max, **2:**409
Carlos, John, **1:**29, 60, 70, 97; **2:**265, 266, 340, 372
Carmichael, Harold, **1:**61
Carnegie, Herb, **1:**165
Carnegie, Ossie, **1:**165
Caroline, J. C., **1:**61–62
Carpentier, Georges, **1:**176
Carr, Austin, **2:**403
Carr, Nate, **2:**419
Carroll, John, **1:**154
Carter, Butch, **1:**62–63, 72
Carter, Cris, **1:**62–63
Carter, Jack, **2:**238
Carter, Jimmy, **1:**74; **2:**267
Carter, Mike, **1:**134
Carter, Rubin "Hurricane," **1:**100
Casey, Bernie, **1:**101
Castro, Fidel, **2:**389
Catto, Octavius, **2:**287–88
CBS (Columbia Broadcasting System), **2:**291
Center for the Study of Sport and Society, **2:**291, 293
Central Intercollegiate Athletic Association (CIAA), **1:**24, 63–64, 151; **2:**233, 234
Cepeda, Orlando, **2:**230
Chalk, Ocania, **1:**153
Chamberlain, Wilt, **1:**16, 25, 64–65, 102, 120, 138, 148, 205; **2:**297
Chandler, Happy, **2:**303
Chaney, John, **1:**65–66, 71
Channels, Isadore, **2:**363
Chaplin, Oscar, III, **2:**394
Charity, Ron, **1:**12
Charles, Ezzard, **1:**45, 66, 217; **2:**384
Charleston, Oscar, **1:**22, 67, 129; **2:**219, 254
Chase, Jack, **2:**241
Cheyney State College, **1:**150
Chicago Bee (newspaper), **1:**54
Chicago Defender (newspaper), **1:**54, 76, 200; **2:**345, 421, 422
Chicago Herald-American (newspaper), **2:**341
Chicago Women's Golf Club, **1:**124
City Dump (documentary), **2:**400
Civil rights, **1:**67–70
  and golf, **1:**124–25
  historians on athletes and, **1:**155
  and integration in athletics, **2:**253
  See also Boycotts and protests; Segregation and integration
Clark, Dwight, **2:**256
Clark, Nathan, **2:**354
Clark University, **1:**150
Clay, Cassius, Jr. *See* Ali, Muhammad
Cleveland Advocate (newspaper), **2:**401
Cleveland Call and Post (newspaper), **2:**421

GENERAL INDEX

Clifton, Nat "Sweetwater," **1:**25, 69, 71, 138, 214–15; **2:**400
Coaches and managers, **1:**23, 71–72
   Baylor, Don, **1:**27
   Bell, Bill, **1:**29–30
   Chaney, John, **1:**65–66, 71
   Daniels, Isabelle, **1:**77
   Embry, Wayne, **1:**95–96
   Gaines, Clarence "Bighouse," **1:**115
   Gaither, Jake, **1:**115–16
   Green Bay Packers (1999), **2:**299
   Green, Tina Sloan, **1:**199
   Hurt, Eddie, **1:**162
   Jones, K. C., **1:**187
   Kemp, Ray, **1:**195–96
   Lewis, William Henry, **1:**211–12
   McLendon, John, **2:**233–34
   Miller, Cheryl, **2:**236
   Newsome, Ozzie, **2:**259
   Nunn, William, Jr., **2:**261
   Pollard, Fritz, **2:**284
   Raveling, George, **2:**295–96
   Reed, Dwight, **2:**296
   Rhodes, Ray, **2:**298–99
   Richardson, Nolan, **2:**301–2
   Robinson, Eddie, **2:**307
   Robinson, Frank, **2:**308–9
   Russell, Bill, **2:**318–19
   segregation and integration, **2:**301–2
   Shell, Art, **2:**326–27
   Silas, Paul, **2:**329–30
   Smith, John, **2:**338–39
   Snowden, Fred, **2:**341–42
   Stringer, Vivian, **2:**350–51
   Temple, Ed, **2:**362
   Thomas, Isiah, **2:**366–67
   Thompson, John, **2:**368–69
   in track and field, **2:**373
   Tunnell, Emlen, **2:**374
   Unseld, Wes, **2:**378
   Walker, Leroy, **2:**385–86
   Williams, Doug, **2:**404
   women as, **2:**414
Coachman, Alice, **1:**72–74, 152; **2:**265, 372, 373, 414
Cobb, Ty, **1:**146; **2:**409
Cobb, William Montague, **1:**74; **2:**290
Coburn, Ruth, **1:**42
Coetzee, Gerrie, **2:**343
Coleman, Ronnie, **2:**393
College athletics, segregation and integration, **1:**68, 103, 107, 130, 142, 151, 195, 208–9; **2:**229, 328, 396
College Football Association, **1:**107
Collett, Wayne, **2:**266, 338
Color barrier. *See* Boycotts and protests; Civil rights; Segregation and integration
Colored Hockey League, **1:**165
Colored Intercollegiate Athletic Association. *See* Central Intercollegiate Athletic Association
Colored World Series. *See* Negro World Series

Comiskey, Charles, **1:**111
Conlan, Jocko, **2:**315
Connors, John, **2:**251
Cook, C. C., **1:**168
Cook, Ralph V., **1:**10, 168
Coolidge, Calvin, **2:**228
Coon, Carleton S., **2:**290
Cooney, Gerry, **1:**109, 158, 197
Cooper, Chuck, **1:**25, 69, 75, 214–15; **2:**261
Cooper, Cynthia, **2:**267
Cooper, Michael, **1:**16
Cooper, "Tarzan," **1:**24
Corbett, Jim, **1:**43, 85, 174
Corbitt, Ted, **1:**75–76
Cosby, Bill, **2:**300
Cosell, Howard, **1:**8
Court-Martial of Jackie Robinson, The (television film), **1:**101
Cousy, Bob, **2:**318
Cowans, Russ, **1:**76
Cream, Arnold Raymond. *See* Walcott, Joe
Crescent Athletic Club, **1:**168
Cribb, Tom, **1:**43; **2:**238, 302, 334
Crockett, Rita, **2:**381
Cromwell, Dean, **2:**289–90
Crutchfield, Jimmie, **1:**32
Culbreath, William, **2:**256
Cumberland, Duke, **1:**24

Daly, Bill, **1:**160
D'Amato, Cus, **1:**45, 46; **2:**276, 375
Dandridge, Ray, **1:**22
Daniels, Cheryl, **1:**42
Daniels, Isabelle, **1:**77; **2:**228
Dantley, Adrian, **1:**77–78
Davenport, Willie, **2:**267
Davies, Lynn, **1:**41
Davis, Al, **2:**326, 327
Davis, Bronco Jim, **2:**312
Davis, Bruce, **1:**99
Davis, Dwight, **1:**10
Davis, Ernie, **1:**78–79, 107, 214; **2:**237
Davis, Jack, **1:**57
Davis, John Henry, **1:**79; **2:**266, 392
Davis, Laurel R., **1:**156
Dawes, Dominique, **1:**80, 135; **2:**267
De Frantz, Anita, **1:**81–82; **2:**267, 414
De Zonie, Hank, **1:**25
DeBusschere, Dave, **2:**297
Decatur, William J., **1:**168
Dehnert, Dutch, **2:**258
Dempsey, Jack, **1:**202; **2:**408–9
Dent, Jim, **1:**125
Detroit Tribune (newspaper), **1:**76
Devers, Gail, **1:**82–83
DiBiase, Mike, **2:**241
Dickerson, Chris, **2:**393
Dickerson, Eric, **1:**83–84
Didrickson, Babe, **1:**192
Dightman, Myrtis, **2:**313

GENERAL INDEX

Dihigo, Martin, **2:**395
Dillard, Harrison, **1:**84–85; **2:**372
DiMaggio, Joe, **1:**54; **2:**286
Dirty Dozen, The (film), **1:**101
Ditka, Mike, **2:**220
Dixon, George, **1:**43, 85–86
Doby, Larry, **1:**86; **2:**219, 395, 409
Don't Look Back: The Story of Leroy "Satchel" Paige (television film), **1:**101
Dorinson, Joseph, **1:**155
Dorrington, Arthur, **1:**69, 87
Dougherty, Romeo, **2:**345
Douglas, Bob, **1:**24; **2:**257
Douglas, Buster, **1:**46; **2:**375
Douglas, Robert, **2:**256, 418
Douglass, Haley G., **1:**168
Douglass High School, **1:**168
Downing, Al, **1:**1
Drew, Charles, **1:**24, 87–88
Drew, Howard, **1:**88; **2:**371
DuBois, W. E. B., **1:**17; **2:**326
Dukes, Walter, **1:**89
Dundee, Angelo, **1:**95
Dunlap, Carla, **2:**393
Dunn, Willie, **2:**327
Duran, Roberto, **1:**46, 137, 206, 207
Durham, Diane, **1:**135
Durham, Yank, **1:**112
Dwyer, Michael F., **2:**330
Dwyer, Philip J., **2:**330
Dyreson, Mark, **1:**156; **2:**292

East-West All-Star Game, **1:**22, 129; **2:**252
East-West League, **2:**253, 254
Eastern Colored League, **1:**91; **2:**253, 254
Easton, James, **1:**81–82
Eaton, Hubert, **1:**120; **2:**363
Ebony (magazine), **1:**54; **2:**421
Edwards, Harry, **1:**60, 69, 91–92; **2:**266, 291, 340
Edwards, Teresa, **1:**92–93; **2:**267
Elder, Lee, **1:**93–94, 125; **2:**417
Elizabeth City State University, **1:**63
Eller, Carl, **1:**94–95
Ellis, Jimmy, **1:**95, 112
Embry, Wayne, **1:**95–96
Emperor Jones (film), **1:**101
Englehardt, Fred, **1:**139–40
Entine, John, **2:**292
Ervin, Anthony, **2:**267
Erving, Julius, **1:**35, 96, 102
Evans, Fred, **2:**354
Evans, Lee, **1:**97; **2:**372
Everett, Danny, **2:**339
Ewing, Patrick, **1:**97–98; **2:**369

Faggs, Mae, **1:**99; **2:**362, 373
Farrell, Charles, **2:**293
Farrington, John, **1:**116
Fayetteville State University, **1:**63
Ferenczy, Alex, **1:**49; **2:**240

Fiall, George, **1:**24
Films and television, **1:**100–102
　Abdul-Jabbar, Kareem as actor, **1:**3–4, 102
　Ali, Muhammad as actor, **1:**100
　Armstrong, Henry as actor, **1:**100
　baseball, **1:**100–101
　basketball, **1:**101–2
　boxing, **1:**100
　Brown, Jim as actor, **1:**50, 101
　Brown, Tim as actor, **1:**101
　Butler, Sol as actor, **1:**55
　Casey, Bernie as actor, **1:**101
　Chamberlain, Wilt as actor, **1:**65, 102
　Erving, Julius as actor, **1:**102
　football, **1:**101
　Frazier, Walter, Jr. as sports announcer, **1:**113
　Gault, Willie as actor, **1:**119
　Gibson, Althea as actress, **1:**121
　about golf, **1:**102
　Greene, Joe as actor, **1:**101, 129
　Grier, Rosey as actor, **1:**101, 132
　Hagler, "Marvelous" Marvin as actor, **1:**137
　Jeannette, Joe as actor, **1:**176
　Johnson, Jack as actor, **1:**179
　Jordan, Michael as actor, **1:**102
　Lee, Canada as actor, **1:**100
　Lemon, Meadowlark as actor, **1:**102
　Louis, Joe as actor, **1:**100
　Moore, Archie as actor, **1:**66; **2:**241
　Moore, Lenny as announcer, **2:**243
　Morgan, Joe as commentator, **2:**244
　Norton, Ken as actor, **1:**100
　O'Neal, Shaquille as actor, **1:**102
　Perkins, Don as sportscaster, **2:**281
　racial theories and television, **2:**291–92
　Rashad, Ahmad as sportscaster, **2:**294–95
　Robeson, Paul as actor, **2:**304
　Robinson, Jackie as actor, **1:**100–101; **2:**310
　Robinson, Sugar Ray as actor, **1:**100
　Simpson, O. J. as actor, **1:**101; **2:**331
　Smith, "Bubba" as actor, **1:**101; **2:**337
　Strode, Woody as actor, **1:**101; **2:**351
　Swann, Lynn as sports announcer, **2:**352–53
　tennis, **1:**102
　Thompson, John as commentator, **2:**369
　track and field, **1:**102
　White, Bill as announcer, **2:**398
　Williamson, Fred as actor, **1:**101
Final Exam (film), **1:**102
Finney, Arthur, **1:**167
Firpo, Luis Angel, **2:**408
Fish That Saved Pittsburgh, The (film), **1:**102
Fisk University, **1:**150, 151
Fitzgerald, Ella, **2:**326
Flippin, George, **1:**102–3
Flood, Curt, **1:**103–4
Flores, Jesse, **2:**405
Flores, Tom, **2:**326
Florida A & M University, **1:**152
Flowers, Tiger, **1:**44, 104

GENERAL INDEX

Foggs, Mae, **1:**77
Foley, Larry, **1:**174
Folley, Zora, **1:**110
Follis, Charles, **1:**105
Ford, Gerald, **2:**421
Ford, James, **1:**199
Ford, Phil, **1:**108
Foreman, George, **1:**46, 100, 109, 112, 197; **2:**241, 260, 266
Foster, Andrew "Rube." *See* Foster, Rube
Foster, Bob, **1:**46, 110
Foster, Rube, **1:**22, 91, 110–11; **2:**253, 254
Fowler, Bud, **1:**22
Foxx, Jamie, **1:**101
Franke, Nikki, **1:**35
Franklin Evening News (newspaper), **2:**410
Frazier, Charles R., **1:**63
Frazier, Hector, **1:**112
Frazier, Joe, **1:**46, 95, 109, 110, 112, 197; **2:**266
Frazier, Marvis, **1:**112
Frazier, Walter, Jr., **1:**112–13; **2:**297
Frederick, Jane, **1:**192
Freeman, Burt, **1:**99
Freeman, Henry, **1:**10
Frick, Ford, **1:**69
Fryar, Irving, **2:**316
Fuhr, Grant, **1:**166
Fulks, Joe, **1:**199
Fuller, William, **2:**238
Fullmer, Gene, **1:**45
Futch, Eddie, **2:**260

Gaines, Clarence "Bighouse," **1:**115
Gaines, Joseph. *See* Gans, Joe
Gaither, Jake, **1:**115–16, 152
Galiber, Joe, **1:**25
Galimore, Ron, **1:**134
Galimore, Willie, **1:**116, 134
Gallatin, Harry, **2:**400
Galloway, Hipple "Hippo," **1:**165
Gans, Joe, **1:**44, 104, 117
Gant, Lamar, **2:**394
Garcia, Ceferino, **1:**12
Garrett, Mike, **1:**117–18
Garrison, Zina, **1:**118; **2:**364
Garvey, Marcus, **2:**228
Gates, "Pop," **1:**24
Gatewood, Bill, **1:**31
Gault, Willie, **1:**119
Gavilan, Kid, **2:**405
Gehrig, Lou, **2:**229
Gems, Gerald R., **1:**154, 155
Gentry, Alvin, **1:**72
George, Nelson, **1:**155
George V, King of England, **2:**312
Gervin, George, **1:**119–20
Ghosts of Manila, The (Kram), **1:**112
Gibbs, Joe, **2:**239
Gibson, Althea, **1:**10, 12, 16, 69, 118, 120–21, 152; **2:**326, 363–64, 394, 406, 407, 414

Gibson, Bob, **1:**121–22
Gibson, Josh, **1:**22, 67, 122, 129, 205; **2:**219
Gill, Turner, **2:**316
Gilliam, Joe, **2:**261
Gilmore, Artis, **1:**122–23
Gissendanner, Cindy, **1:**156
Glickman, Marty, **2:**328
Goldberg, Arthur, **1:**104
Golden Gloves, **1:**44, 45
Gordon, Ed, Jr., **1:**125–26
Gordy, Fuller, **1:**42
Gore, Al, **2:**342
Gottlieb, Eddie, **1:**37
Gourdin, Ned, **1:**126–27
Graham, Otto, **1:**5; **2:**237, 246
Grambling State College, **1:**152; **2:**307
Grange, Harold "Red," **1:**6; **2:**422
Grant, Francis, **1:**124
Grant, Frank, **1:**127
Grant, George, **2:**377
Graves, William, **1:**40
Gray, Edward, **1:**127–28
Greased Lightning (film), **2:**325
Great, The (film), **1:**100
Great White Hope, The (film), **1:**100
Greb, Harry, **1:**104
Green, Leroy, **1:**110
Green, Pumpsie, **1:**22
Green, Tina Sloan, **1:**35, 199
Greene, Joe, **1:**101, 128–29
Greenlee, Gus, **1:**22, 67, 129
Greenwood, L. C., **2:**261
Greer, Hal, **1:**130
Gregory, Ann, **1:**130–31
Gregory, George, **1:**24
Gregory, George, Jr., **1:**131
Grier, Mike, **1:**166
Grier, Rosey, **1:**101, 132
Griffey, Ken, **1:**132
Griffey, Ken, Jr., **1:**132–33
Griffith, Clark, **1:**69, 205
Griffith-Joyner, Florence, **1:**133; **2:**265, 372
Grundman, Adolph, **1:**155
Gwynn, Tony, **1:**134

Hagen, Walter, **2:**417
Hagler, "Marvelous" Marvin, **1:**46, 137, 144, 207
Halas, George, **2:**307
Halliard, Wendy, **1:**35
Halls of fame. *See* Boxing Hall of Fame; International Boxing Hall of Fame; Naismith Memorial Basketball Hall of Fame; National Baseball Hall of Fame; Professional Football Hall of Fame; U.S. National Track and Field Hall of Fame
Hamilton, Bobby, **2:**300
Hammer, M. C. (Stanley Burrell), **1:**160
Hampton Institute, **1:**63, 150, 151
Haney, Lee, **2:**393
Hard Road to Glory, A (Ashe), **1:**13, 153
Harding, Ben, **1:**42

GENERAL INDEX

Harewood, Darian, **1:**102
Hargrave, H. P., **1:**63
Harlem Globetrotters, **1:**24, 25, 64, 71, 89, 121, 137–38, 143, 173, 204–5; **2:**358, 415
Harlem Magicians, **1:**75, 143
Harris, Alphonso, **1:**42
Harris, Arthur, **2:**393
Harris, Ed, **2:**345
Harris, Franco, **1:**139
Harris, James, **2:**307
Harris, Morris, **1:**176
Harris, Tom, **1:**200; **2:**277
Harrison, Miles, **1:**199
Hart, Clyde, **1:**181
Hart, Frank, **1:**139–40
Haskins, Don, **2:**301
Havemeyer, Theodore F., **2:**327
Hawkins, Connie, **1:**138, 140–41
Hawkins, Robert, **2:**377
Hawkins, Tommy, **2:**290
Haydon, Benjamin Robert, **1:**159
Hayes, Bob, **1:**141–42; **2:**372
Hayes, Elvin, **1:**142
Hayes, Wilbur, **2:**252
Haynes, Marques, **1:**138, 142–43, 205; **2:**358
Haywood, Spencer, **1:**143–44, 167
Hazzard, Walt, **1:**189
He Got Game (film), **1:**102
Hearns, Thomas, **1:**46, 137, 144, 167, 207
Heaven Is a Playground (film), **1:**102
Heisman Trophy
   Allen, Marcus, **1:**9–10
   Campbell, Earl, **1:**58–59
   Davis, Ernie, **1:**78–79
   Garrett, Mike, **1:**117–18
   Jackson, Bo, **1:**171–72
   Rodgers, Johnny, **2:**313–14
   Rogers, George, **2:**315–16
   Rozier, Mike, **2:**316
   Sanders, Barry, **2:**321
   Simpson, O. J., **2:**331
   Walker, Herschel, **2:**384–85
   Ward, Charlie, **2:**387–88
Henderson, Edwin Bancroft, **1:**23, 53–54, 128, 145, 153, 168; **2:**363
Henderson, Rickey, **1:**146
Henriquez de Zubiera, Constantin, **2:**264
Heritage Bowl, **1:**152
Hewitt-Courtourier, Naomi, **1:**135
High school athletics, segregation and integration, **1:**121
Hightower, Stephanie, **1:**146–47
Hill, Calvin, **1:**147–48
Hill, Fitz, **1:**72
Hill, Grant, **1:**148–49
Hill, Jimmy, **1:**55
Hill, Kelli, **1:**135
Hines, Jim, **1:**149; **2:**372
Historically black colleges and universities (HCBU), **1:**149–52; **2:**354

Historiography, **1:**153–56
Hitler, Adolf, **2:**265
Hoberman, John, **2:**292
Hoffman, Bob, **2:**392
Hogan, Ernest, **1:**175
Holdsclaw, Chamique, **2:**267
Holland, Jerome Brud, **1:**157
Holman, Nat, **1:**25; **2:**258
Holman, Steve, **1:**157–58
Holmes, Larry, **1:**46, 158, 197; **2:**260, 343, 344
Holmes, Talley, **1:**10; **2:**363
Holston, Isabelle. *See* Daniels, Isabelle
Holt, Johnny, **1:**24
Holtz, Lou, **2:**357
Holway, John, **1:**154
Holyfield, Evander, **1:**109; **2:**375
Homer, **2:**371
Hoop Dreams (film), **1:**102
Horse Soldiers, The (film), **1:**121
Hotaling, Ed, **2:**291
Howard, Ed, **1:**199
Howard High School, **1:**168
Howard, Kevin, **1:**207
Howard Medical School, **1:**168
Howard University, **1:**63, 150, 151, 168; **2:**354, 363
Hubbard, William Dehart, **1:**42, 151, 161; **2:**265, 371
Huckleberry Finn (film), **2:**241
Hudson, Dick, **1:**138
Hudson, Martha, **1:**161
Hue (magazine), **2:**421
Hunt, Edward E., Jr., **2:**290
Hunter, C. J., **1:**188
Hurricane (film), **1:**100
Hurt, Eddie, **1:**162
Hyman, Flo, **2:**381
Hymes, Lula Mae, **1:**162–63; **2:**414

Ice Station Zebra (film), **1:**101
Iliad (Homer), **2:**371
Indianapolis Freeman (newspaper), **1:**215
Integration. *See* Segregation and integration
Intercollegiate Athletic Association of the United States, **1:**106
International Afro-American Sports Hall of Fame Gallery, **1:**167
International Boxing Club, **1:**45
International Boxing Hall of Fame
   Flowers, Tiger, **1:**104
   Frazier, Joe, **1:**112
   Gans, Joe, **1:**117
   Hagler, "Marvelous" Marvin, **1:**137
   Leonard, Sugar Ray, **1:**207
   Lewis, John Henry, **1:**211
   Liston, Sonny, **1:**213–14
   Louis, Joe, **1:**217
   McVey, Sam, **2:**234
   Moore, Archie, **2:**241–42
   Norton, Ken, **2:**260
   Patterson, Floyd, **2:**276–77
   Robinson, Sugar Ray, **2:**311–12

GENERAL INDEX

International Boxing Hall of Fame *(continued)*
   Walcott, Joe, **2:**383–84
   Williams, Ike, **2:**405
   Wills, Harry, **2:**408–9
   See also Boxing Hall of Fame
International League of Baseball Clubs in America and Cuba, **1:**167–68
International Olympic Committee (IOC), **1:**81–82
International Tennis Hall of Fame, **1:**13
International Track Association, **1:**60; **2:**236, 339, 375
Interscholastic Athletic Association of Middle Atlantic States, **1:**168
Irish, Ned, **1:**71, 138
Irvin, Monte, **1:**169; **2:**219, 395
Isaacs, John, **1:**24; **2:**258
Islam
   Abdul-Jabbar, Kareem, **1:**3–4
   Ali, Muhammad, **1:**8–9
   Rashad, Ahmad, **2:**293–95
It's Good to Be Alive (television film), **1:**101

Jack, Beau, **1:**45; **2:**405
Jack Johnson (documentary), **1:**100, 176
Jack, "Rajo," **1:**171
Jackie Robinson Story, The (film), **1:**101; **2:**310
Jackson, Bo, **1:**171–72
Jackson, Henry. *See* Armstrong, Henry
Jackson, Inman, **1:**138
Jackson, Jesse, **2:**293
Jackson, Jimmy, **2:**419
Jackson, Levi, **1:**172
Jackson, Mannie, **1:**173
Jackson, Melody. *See* Armstrong, Henry
Jackson, Morris, **2:**353
Jackson, Nell, **2:**373
Jackson, Peter, **1:**43, 173–75; **2:**289
Jackson, Reggie, **1:**38, 175
Jackson, Rufus "Sonnyman" and "See," **2:**286
Jackson, Wayne, **1:**199
Jacobs, Mike, **1:**210
Jamaica Kid, **1:**104
James, Clyde, **2:**354
James, Craig, **1:**83
Jarvis, Mike, **1:**71
Jeannette, Joe, **1:**44, 176; **2:**234, 408
Jefferson, Bernie, **1:**176–77
Jeffries, James, **1:**100
Jeffries, Jim, **1:**44, 174, 178
Jenkins, "Fats," **1:**24
Jenner, Bruce, **2:**263
Jensen, Arthur R., **2:**291
Jesse Owens Story, The (television film), **1:**102
Jet (magazine), **1:**54; **2:**421
Jeter, Emily, **2:**353
Jockeys. *See* Horse racing
Joe Louis Story, The (film), **1:**100
Joe Palooka, Champ (film), **1:**100
Johansson, Ingemar, **1:**45; **2:**276
Johnson, Battling Jim, **1:**176
Johnson, Ben, **1:**133

Johnson, C. Howard, **1:**203
Johnson C. Smith University, **1:**63, 150, 151
Johnson, Cornelius, **1:**7, 177–78; **2:**265, 372
Johnson, Earvin "Magic." *See* Johnson, Magic
Johnson, Fred, **2:**363
Johnson, George, **1:**63
Johnson, Jack, **1:**16, 44, 100, 176, 178–79; **2:**234, 289, 408
Johnson, John Henry, **1:**179
Johnson, John Lester, **1:**176
Johnson, Judy. *See* Johnson, William "Judy"
Johnson, Magic, **1:**16, 26, 180; **2:**266
Johnson, Michael, **1:**181–82
Johnson, Oscar, **1:**10; **2:**363
Johnson Publishing Company, **1:**54
Johnson, Rafer, **1:**59, 182–83; **2:**266, 372
Johnson, Robert L., **1:**183–84
Johnson, Robert W., **1:**120
Johnson, Walter, **1:**12; **2:**363, 405
Johnson, William, **2:**414
Johnson, William "Judy," **1:**67, 129, 184
Joiner, William A., **1:**168
Jones, Barbara, **1:**161, 185–86; **2:**228
Jones, Bill, **1:**24
Jones, David "Deacon," **1:**132, 186
Jones, Doug, **1:**110
Jones, Hayes, **1:**186–87
Jones, James Earl, **1:**100, 101
Jones, K. C., **1:**187
Jones, Laura, **1:**42
Jones, Lucious, **2:**303
Jones, Marion, **1:**188
Jones, "Piano Man," **2:**241
Jones, Robert Tyre "Bobby," **2:**397
Jones, Roy, **2:**266
Jones, Sam, **1:**188–89
Jones, Uriah, **1:**99
Jones, Wali, **1:**189–90
Jones, Wally, **1:**153
Jordan, Michael, **1:**26, 102, 120, 190–91; **2:**266
Journalists. *See* Sportswriters
Joyner, Al, Jr., **1:**133, 192
Joyner-Kersee, Jackie, **1:**133, 191–93; **2:**265, 372

Kalule, Ayub, **1:**206
Kane, Martin, **2:**290–91
Kansas City Call (newspaper), **2:**422
Karolyi, Bela, **1:**135
Keep Fighting (film), **1:**100
Keith, Floyd, **1:**34
Kelly, Fred "Bud," **1:**165
Kelly, Leroy, **1:**195
Kemp, Lee, **2:**418
Kemp, Ray, **1:**107, 195–96
Kennedy, Robert F., **1:**132
Kerr, Johnny, **1:**120
Kersee, Bob, **1:**47, 133, 192
Keyes, Leroy, **1:**196
King, Don, **1:**196–97
King, Henry, **1:**160

GENERAL INDEX

King Solomon's Mines (film), **1:**101
King, William "Dolly," **1:**25, 197–98
Knight, Bob, **2:**366
Knight, David, **2:**287
Kram, Mark, **1:**112
Ku Klux Klan, **1:**25, 160
Kuhn, Bowie, **1:**103
Kuznetsov, Vasily, **1:**183

La Guardia, Fiorello, **1:**202
Labor issues
  in baseball, **1:**103–4
  in football, **2:**220, 379
Lacayo, Richard, **2:**312
Lacy, Sam, **1:**22, 199–200; **2:**345
Ladies Professional Golf Association, **1:**121
Lakes, Charles, **1:**135
Lalonde, Donny, **1:**207
Lamar, Ed, **2:**251
LaMotta, Jake, **1:**45; **2:**311–12
Lanctot, Neil, **1:**154
Landis, Kenesaw Mountain, **1:**69; **2:** 261, 304
Lane, Betty Jean, **1:**200
Lane, Dick, **1:**201
Lane, Floyd, **1:**25
Langford, Sam, **1:**44, 104, 176, 201–2; **2:**408
Lanier, Bob, **1:**202–3
Lansbury, Jennifer, **1:**156
Lapchick, Joe, **2:**258
Lapchick, Richard, **1:**155; **2:**291
Larkin, Tippy, **2:**405
Lasker, Terrence, **1:**99
Lautier, Lewis, **1:**200
League of Colored Base Ball Players, **1:**203
LeDroit Park, **1:**168
Lee, Canada, **1:**100
Lee, Jimmy, **1:**160
Lee, Spike, **1:**100
Lees, Tom, **1:**174
LeFlore, Ron, **1:**101
Lemon, Meadowlark, **1:**102, 138, 203–5
Lenglen, Suzanne, **1:**6
Leonard, Buck, **1:**205–6
Leonard, Sugar Ray, **1:**46, 137, 144, 206–7; **2:**266, 312
Leslie, Lisa, **1:**207–8
Lester, Jack, **2:**234
LeVias, Jerry, **1:**208–9
Lew, Harry "Bucky," **1:**23
Lewis, Carl, **1:**209–10; **2:**372–73
Lewis, "Country," **1:**200
Lewis, John Henry, **1:**44–45, 129, 210–11
Lewis, Oliver, **1:**211
Lewis, Steve, **2:**339
Lewis, William Henry, **1:**211–12
Lewison, Peter, **1:**99
Liberti, Rita, **1:**154
Lifeboat (film), **1:**100
Lightfoot, Charlie, **1:**165
Lilliard, Joe, **1:**107, 195, 212
Lincoln University, **1:**63, 150; **2:**296, 363

Lipscomb, Gene "Big Daddy," **1:**213
Liston, Sonny, **1:**45, 213–14; **2:**266, 277
Little, Floyd, **1:**214
Livingstone University, **1:**63, 150
Lloyd, Earl, **1:**25, 214–15
Lloyd, John Henry, **1:**215–16
Lofton, Michael, **1:**99
Lomax, Michael E., **1:**154
Lombardi, Vince, **1:**51, 201; **2:**374
Long, Bingo, **1:**101
Los Angeles Mirror-News (newspaper), **2:**389
Los Angeles Sentinel (newspaper), **2:**389, 421
Lott, Ronnie, **1:**216
Louis, Joe, **1:**16, 44, 45, 54, 66, 76, 100, 124, 167, 202, 210–11, 217–18; **2:**261, 299, 348–49, 384, 389
Love and Basketball (film), **1:**102
Love, Nat, **2:**312
Lucas, Jerry, **1:**39
Lundy, Lamar, **1:**132
LuValle, James, **1:**218; **2:**372
Lyght, Trent, **2:**354
Lyman, Hazel, **1:**42

M. C. Hammer (Stanley Burrell), **1:**160
M Street High School, **1:**168
Macci, Rick, **2:**406, 407
MacCracken, Henry, **1:**106
Mackey, Biz, **2:**219
Mackey, John, **2:**220–21
Magers-Powell, Rose, **2:**381
Maher, Charles, **2:**290
Malcolm X, **1:**8
Malina, Robert, **2:**291
Malone, Karl, **2:**221–22
Malone, Moses, **2:**222–23
Managers. *See* Coaches and managers
Manley, Abe, **2:**223
Manley, Effa, **2:**223
Manning, Danny, **2:**224
Manning-Mims, Madeline, **2:**224–25, 362, 373
Manuel, Jerry, **1:**72
Mapledale Country Club, **2:**377
Maravich, Pete, **2:**403
Marble, Alice, **1:**121; **2:**363
Marcello, Ronald, **1:**155
Marciano, Rocky, **1:**45, 66, 217; **2:**241, 384
Marshall, Bob, **2:**225–26
Marshall, Jim, **2:**226
Marson, Mike, **1:**166
Martin, Charles, **1:**155
Martin, Clyde, **1:**125
Marvin, Lee, **1:**50
Mary, Queen of England, **2:**312–13
Mashiani, Jan, **2:**264
Mathewson, Alfred Dennis, **1:**156
Mathias, Bob, **1:**59; **2:**372
Mathis, Buster, **1:**112
Matson, Ollie, **2:**227
Matthews, Margaret, **1:**77; **2:**227–28
Matthews, Vincent, **1:**17; **2:**266

GENERAL INDEX

Matthews, William Clarence, **2:**228–29
Mattingly, R. N., **1:**168
Maxim, Joey, **2:**241, 384
May, George S., **1:**130
Mays, Willie, **1:**16, 38; **2:**229–30
McAuliffe, Jack, **1:**85
McCard, H. S., **1:**10
McCauley, Ed, **2:**318
McCovey, Willie, **2:**230
McDaniel, Jimmy, **2:**363
McDaniel, Mildred, **2:**231, 373
McDaniel, Pete, **1:**155
McElhenny, Hugh, **1:**179
McGall, Albert, **2:**289
McGee, Pam, **2:**231–32
McGowan, Alex, **2:**364–65
McGrath, H. Price, **1:**211
McGuire, Dick, **2:**400
McGuire, Edith, **2:**232–33, 362, 373, 375
McIntyre, Manny, **1:**165
McKegney, Tony, **1:**166
McLendon, John, **1:**71; **2:**233–34
McMahon, Roderick and Edward, **2:**251
McNeil, Lori, **1:**118; **2:**364
McVey, Sam, **1:**44; **2:**234, 408
Mead, Chris, **1:**153
Mee, Bob, **1:**176
Meehan, Chuck, **1:**68
Meehan, Willie, **2:**408
Meriweather, Willie, **1:**120
Metcalfe, Ralph, **1:**7; **2:**235, 289, 369–70, 371
Miceli, Joe, **2:**405
Michigan Chronicle (newspaper), **1:**76
Mid-Eastern Athletic Conference, **1:**151
Mikan, George, **1:**24, 143
Milburn, Rod, **2:**235–36
Miller, Cheryl, **2:**236, 267
Miller, John, **2:**244
Miller, Patrick B., **1:**154, 156; **2:**292
Miller, Walk, **1:**104
Minter, Alan, **1:**137
Mitchell, Bobby, **1:**79; **2:**237
Molinas, Jack, **1:**51
Molineaux, Tom, **1:**43, 45, 210; **2:**237–38, 303, 334
Monday, Kenny, **2:**418
Monday Night Football (television show), **1:**107
Monk, Art, **2:**238–39
Monplaiser, Sharon, **1:**99
Monroe, Earl, **1:**115; **2:**239–40
Monroe, Willie, **1:**137
Montgomery, Bob, **2:**405
Montgomery, Eleanor, **2:**240
Moon, Warren, **2:**240–41
Moore, Archie, **1:**45, 66, 100; **2:**241–42, 276
Moore, Bobby. *See* Rashad, Ahmad
Moore, Davey, **1:**45
Moore, Lenny, **2:**242–43
Moorer, Michael, **1:**109
Morehouse College, **1:**150
Morgan, Joe, **2:**243–44

Morgan, Marion, **2:**227
Morgan State University, **1:**151, 162; **2:**354
Morris Brown College, **1:**150
Morris, Cecil, **2:**315–16
Morris, James, **2:**393
Moses, Edwin, **2:**244, 372
Moss, Simeon, **1:**199
Most Valuable Player (American Basketball
        Association)
    Gilmore, Artis, **1:**123
    Haywood, Spencer, **1:**143–44
Most Valuable Player (major league baseball)
    Aaron, Hank, **1:**1
    Banks, Ernie, **1:**19
    Baylor, Don, **1:**27
    Bonds, Barry, **1:**38–39
    Campanella, Roy, **1:**57–58
    Griffey, Ken, Jr., **1:**132–33
    Henderson, Rickey, **1:**146
    Mays, Willie, **2:**229–30
    McCovey, Willie, **2:**230
    Morgan, Joe, **2:**243–44
    Newcombe, Don, **2:**258–59
    Robinson, Frank, **2:**308–9
    Robinson, Jackie, **2:**309–10
    Thomas, Frank, **2:**365
Most Valuable Player (National Basketball
        Association)
    Abdul-Jabbar, Kareem, **1:**3
    Johnson, Magic, **1:**180
    Jordan, Michael, **1:**190–91
    Malone, Karl, **2:**221–22
    Malone, Moses, **2:**222–23
    Olajuwon, Hakeem, **2:**263
    Reed, Willis, **2:**297
    Robertson, Oscar, **2:**303–4
    Robinson, David, **2:**306
    Unseld, Wes, **2:**378
Most Valuable Player (National Football League)
    Allen, Marcus, **1:**9–10
    Brown, Larry, **1:**50–51
    Campbell, Earl, **1:**58–59
    Payton, Walter, **2:**278–79
    Rice, Jerry, **2:**301
Most Valuable Player (Women's National Basketball
        Association)
    Leslie, Lisa, **1:**207–8
    Motley, Marion, **2:**245–46
Motown Records, **1:**42
Mr. America, **2:**392–93
Mr. Olympia, **2:**393
Mr. T, **1:**100
Ms. Olympia, **2:**393
Mugabi, John, **1:**137
Muhammad, Eddie Mustaffa, **2:**344
Munger, George, **2:**361
Murphy, Calvin, **2:**246–47
Murphy, Isaac, **1:**68, 159; **2:**247–48, 289
Murray, Bob, **2:**354
Murray, Eddie, **2:**248

Murray, Jim, **1**:204
Murray, Lenda, **2**:394
Murray, Rich, **2**:248
Myer, Billy, **1**:85
Myers, Dave, **1**:68

NAACP. *See* National Association for the Advancement of Colored People
Naismith, James, **1**:71; **2**:233
Naismith Memorial Basketball Hall of Fame
   Abdul-Jabbar, Kareem, **1**:3–4
   Archibald, Nate, **1**:11
   Baylor, Elgin, **1**:28
   Bellamy, Walter, **1**:32–33
   Chamberlain, Wilt, **1**:64–65
   Chaney, John, **1**:65–66
   Frazier, Walter, Jr., **1**:112–13
   Gaines, Clarence "Bighouse," **1**:115
   Gervin, George, **1**:119–20
   Greer, Hal, **1**:130
   Hawkins, Connie, **1**:140–41
   Haynes, Marques, **1**:142–43
   Johnson, Magic, **1**:180
   Jones, K. C., **1**:187
   Jones, Sam, **1**:188–89
   Lanier, Bob, **1**:202–3
   Malone, Moses, **2**:222–23
   McLendon, John, **2**:233–34
   Monroe, Earl, **2**:239–40
   New York Renaissance Five, **1**:24
   Robertson, Oscar, **2**:303–4
   Russell, Bill, **2**:318
   Thompson, David, **2**:367–68
   Unseld, Wes, **2**:378
Naked Gun (film), **1**:101
Nathaniel, Clifton. *See* Clifton, Nat "Sweetwater"
National Association for the Advancement of Colored People (NAACP), **1**:68, 74, 145, 197; **2**:261, 394
National Association of Colored Base Ball Clubs of the United States and Cuba, **2**:251
National Association of Colored Professional Base Ball Clubs, **1**:168; **2**:255
National Association of Intercollegiate Athletics (NAIA), **2**:233–34
National Baseball Hall of Fame
   Aaron, Hank, **1**:2
   Banks, Ernie, **1**:19
   Bell, James "Cool Papa," **1**:31–32
   Brock, Louis, **1**:48
   Campanella, Roy, **1**:57–58
   Charleston, Oscar, **1**:67
   Doby, Larry, **1**:86
   Foster, Rube, **1**:110–11
   Gibson, Bob, **1**:121–22
   Gibson, Josh, **1**:122
   Irvin, Monte, **1**:169
   Jackson, Reggie, **1**:175
   Johnson, William "Judy," **1**:184
   Lacy, Sam, **1**:200
   Leonard, Buck, **1**:205–6

National Baseball Hall of Fame *(continued)*
   Lloyd, John Henry, **1**:215–16
   Mays, Willie, **2**:229–30
   McCovey, Willie, **2**:230
   Morgan, Joe, **2**:243
   Paige, Satchel, **2**:275
   Puckett, Kirby, **2**:286–87
   Robinson, Frank, **2**:308–9
   Robinson, Jackie, **2**:309–10
   Smith, Wendell, **2**:341
   Stargell, Willie, **2**:346–47
   Stearnes, Norman "Turkey," **2**:347
   Wells, Willie, **2**:395
   Williams, Joseph "Smokey," **2**:405
   Winfield, Dave, **2**:410–11
National Bowling Association, **1**:42; **2**:252
National Collegiate Athletic Association (NCAA)
   AAU and, **2**:371
   African-American coaches in, **1**:71–72
   beginning of, **1**:106
   Black Coaches Association and, **1**:34
   Central Intercollegiate Athletic Association and, **1**:63
   football and television contracts, **1**:107
   and historically black colleges and universities, **1**:151; **2**:234
   minority hiring in, **2**:293
National Colored League, **2**:401
National Football League, **1**:105, 106–7
National Junior Tennis League, **2**:364
National Negro Bowling Association. *See* National Bowling Association
National Track and Field Hall of Fame
   Albritton, David, **1**:7
   Beamon, Bob, **1**:29
   Borican, John, **1**:40
   Boston, Ralph, **1**:41–42
   Calhoun, Lee, **1**:57
   Campbell, Milt, **1**:59
   Dillard, Harrison, **1**:84–85
   Evans, Lee, **1**:97
   Johnson, Rafer, **1**:182–83
   Manning-Mims, Madeline, **2**:224–25
   McGuire, Edith, **2**:233
   Metcalfe, Ralph, **2**:235
   Milburn, Rod, **2**:236
   Owens, Jesse, **2**:271–72
   Temple, Ed, **2**:362
   Tolan, Eddie, **2**:370
   Tyus, Wyomia, **2**:375
   Woodruff, John, **2**:416
NBC (National Broadcasting Company), **1**:107; **2**:291–92, 295
NCAA. *See* National Collegiate Athletic Association
Negro American League, **1**:22; **2**:252–53, 255
Negro in Sports, The (Henderson), **1**:145, 153
Negro League Baseball Museum, **2**:253
Negro leagues, **1**:110–11, 153–54; **2**:275, 347, 348–49
   See also individual leagues; Negro League Baseball Museum

GENERAL INDEX

Negro National League, **1:**22, 37, 41, 54, 67, 91, 111, 129, 169; **2:**223, 252, 253, 254, 255, 261, 422
Negro Southern Intercollegiate Athletic Conference, **1:**151
Negro Southern League, **2:**253, 254, 255
Negro World Series, **1:**38
Nehemiah, Renaldo, **2:**256
Nelson, "Battling," **1:**117
Nelson, Ben, **1:**40
Nelson, Byron, **2:**417
New York Age (newspaper), **1:**54
New York Amsterdam News (newspaper), **1:**41, 54
New York Herald (newspaper), **1:**159
New York Olympic Club. *See* New York Pioneer Club
New York People's Voice (newspaper), **1:**41
New York Pioneer Club, **1:**76; **2:**256–57
New York Renaissance Five, **1:**24; **2:**257–58, 328
Newcombe, Don, **2:**219, 258–59, 395
Newell, Pete, **1:**39
Newsome, Ozzie, **2:**259
Nicklaus, Jack, **1:**93–94
Nike, **1:**20, 191; **2:**355
Nixon, Richard, **2:**421
Norfolk, Kid, **1:**104
Norman, Gerald, Jr., **2:**394
Norman, Peter, **2:**340
Norris, James, **1:**217
Norris, Terry, **1:**207
North Carolina Central University, **1:**63
Norton, Gerald, Jr., **2:**363
Norton, Ken, **1:**100, 158, 197; **2:**260
Norwood, Stephen, **1:**154
Nunn, William, Jr., **2:**260–61
Nunn, William, Sr., **2:**261

Oberlin Athletic Club, **1:**168
O'Brien, Dan, **2:**263
Okino, Betty, **1:**135
Olajuwon, Hakeem, **2:**263–64, 321
Oldfield, Barney, **1:**171
O'Leary, Daniel, **1:**139–40
Olin, Bob, **1:**210
Oliva, Sergio, **2:**393
Olsen, Merlin, **1:**132
Olympia (film), **1:**102
Olympic Games, **2:**264–67
　AAU and, **2:**371
　Adams, Lucinda, **1:**4
　African-American reporters at, **1:**76
　Africans in, **2:**265, 373
　Albritton, David, **1:**7
　Ali, Muhammad, **1:**8–9; **2:**266
　Ashford, Evelyn, **1:**15
　Barkley, Charles, **1:**20
　Barksdale, Don, **1:**20–21
　basketball, **2:**266
　Beamon, Bob, **1:**28–29
　Bellamy, Walter, **1:**32–33
　Berlin Games (1936), **1:**102

Olympic Games *(continued)*
　black-power protests (Mexico City, 1968), **1:**17, 29, 60, 69–70, 91–92, 97; **2:**265, 266, 340, 372
　Boozer, Bob, **1:**39–40
　Boston, Ralph, **1:**41–42
　boxing, **2:**266
　Brisco-Hooks, Valerie, **1:**46–48
　Butler, Sol, **1:**55
　Calhoun, Lee, **1:**57
　Campbell, Milt, **1:**59
　Carlos, John, **1:**60, 70, 97; **2:**265, 266, 372
　Coachman, Alice, **1:**72–74
　Collett, Wayne, **2:**266
　Corbitt, Ted, **1:**75–76
　Daniels, Isabelle, **1:**77
　Dantley, Adrian, **1:**77–78
　Davis, John Henry, **1:**79
　Dawes, Dominique, **1:**80
　De Frantz, Anita, **1:**81–82; **2:**267
　Devers, Gail, **1:**82–83
　Dillard, Harrison, **1:**84–85
　Drew, Howard, **1:**88
　Edwards, Teresa, **1:**92–93
　Evans, Lee, **1:**97
　Faggs, Mae, **1:**99
　Ford, Phil, **1:**108
　Foreman, George, **1:**109
　Frazier, Joe, **1:**112
　Gaines, Clarence "Bighouse," **1:**115
　Garrison, Zina, **1:**118
　Gault, Willie, **1:**119
　Gordon, Ed, Jr., **1:**125–26
　Gourdin, Ned, **1:**126–27
　Griffith-Joyner, Florence, **1:**133
　gymnastics, **2:**267
　Hayes, Bob, **1:**141–42
　Haywood, Spencer, **1:**143–44
　Hightower, Stephanie, **1:**146–47
　Hill, Grant, **1:**148–49
　Hines, Jim, **1:**149
　Holman, Steve, **1:**157–58
　Hubbard, William DeHart, **1:**161
　Hudson, Martha, **1:**161
　Hurt, Eddie, **1:**162
　Johnson, Cornelius, **1:**177–78; **2:**265
　Johnson, Magic, **1:**180
　Johnson, Michael, **1:**181–82
　Johnson, Rafer, **1:**182–83; **2:**266
　Jones, Eleanor, **2:**240
　Moses, Edwin, **2:**244
　O'Brien, Dan, **2:**263
　Olajuwon, Hakeem, **2:**263–64
　Owens, Jesse, **2:**265, 271–72
　Patterson, Floyd, **2:**276–77
　Patterson, Mickey, **2:**277–78
　Pickett, Tidye, **2:**282–83
　Poage, George, **2:**283
　Pollard, Fritz, Jr., **2:**284–85
　Raveling, George, **2:**295–96
　Reed, Vivian Brown, **1:**49

Olympic Games *(continued)*
   Reynolds, Butch, **2:**298
   Robertson, Oscar, **2:**303–4
   Robinson, David, **2:**306
   Robinson, Mack, **2:**310–11
   Rudolph, Wilma, **2:**317
   Russell, Bill, **2:**318–19
   Scott, Charlie, **2:**324
   Smith, John, **2:**338–39
   Smith, Tommie, **1:**60, 70, 97; **2:**265, 266, 340, 372
   Spinks, Leon, **2:**343
   Spinks, Michael, **2:**343–44
   Stokes, Louise, **2:**348
   swimming, **2:**267
   Swoopes, Sheryl, **2:**354–55
   Taylor, John Baxter, **2:**359–60
   Temple, Ed, **2:**362
   Thomas, Debra, **2:**364–65
   Thomas, John, **2:**367
   Tolan, Eddie, **2:**369–70
   Torrence, Gwen, **2:**370
   track and field, **2:**264–66
   Tyus, Wyomia, **2:**375–76
   volleyball in, **2:**381–82
   Walker, Herschel, **2:**384–85
   Walker, Leroy, **2:**385–86
   Watts, Quincy, **2:**391–92
   weightlifting in, **2:**392
   Westbrook, Peter, **1:**99
   White, Jo Jo, **2:**398–99
   White, Willye, **2:**401–2
   Whitfield, Mal, **2:**402
   Williams, Archie, **2:**403
   Williams, Serena, **2:**406, 407
   Williams, Venus, **2:**406, 407
   winter sports, **2:**267, 364–65, 385
   Woodruff, John, **1:**7; **2:**416
   Woodward, Lynette, **2:**415–16
100 Percent Wrong Club, **2:**303
One In a Million: The Ron LeFlore Story (television film), **1:**101
O'Neal, Shaquille, **1:**102; **2:**268–69
O'Neil, Buck, **2:**269–70
O'Ree, Willie, **1:**166; **2:**270
Orr, Jack, **1:**153
Our Home Colony (Walker), **2:**387
Owens, Jesse, **1:**7, 16, 41, 74, 102; **2:**235, 265, 271–72, 277, 289, 290, 310, 371, 372, 386
Owens, R. C., **2:**272–73
Owl, The (newspaper), **1:**54

Pacino, Al, **1:**101
Paddock, Charlie, **1:**55
Paige, Satchel, **1:**16, 22, 41, 67, 101, 205; **2:**275, 315, 349, 405
Paine, George, **2:**393
Palace, Fred, **2:**315
Palermo, Blinky, **1:**213; **2:**404, 405
Palmer, Arnold, **2:**417
Pardon the Interruption (television show), **2:**345

Paris, John, **1:**166
Parker, Eugene, **1:**7
Parker, Jim, **2:**276
Parrish, Bernie, **1:**17
Patterson, Floyd, **1:**16, 45, 95, 213; **2:**241, 266, 276–77
Patterson, Inez, **2:**353
Patterson, Mickey, **2:**277–78
Paul, Joan, **1:**155
Payton, Edward, **2:**278
Payton, Walter, **2:**278–79, 337
Peacock, Eulace, **2:**289
Pearson, Drew, **2:**279–80
Peete, Calvin, **1:**125; **2:**280–81
Pele, **1:**35
Penneyman, Martha. *See* Hudson, Martha
Pennington, Richard, **1:**155
People's Voice (newspaper), **2:**345
Pep, Willie, **1:**45
Percy, Lord (British commander), **2:**302
Perenchio, Jerry, **1:**112
Perez, Tony, **2:**243
Perkins, Don, **1:**148; **2:**281
Perry, Joe, **2:**282
Perry, Leila, **2:**414
Peters, Brock, **1:**100
Peters, Roumania and Margaret, **2:**363
Peterson, Horace M., III, **2:**253
Peterson, Robert, **1:**154
Pettingill, C. H., **2:**330
Petway, Bruce, **2:**347
Phal, Louis, **1:**44
Philadelphia American (newspaper), **2:**410
Philadelphia Tribune (newspaper), **2:**345, 410
Phillips, Bum, **2:**316
Phipps, Prikeba (Keba), **2:**381–82
Piccolo, Brian, **1:**101
Pickett, Bill, **2:**312–13
Pickett, Tidye, **2:**282–83, 348
Pierce, J. W., **1:**63
Pierce, Richard, **1:**154
Pingatore, Gene, **2:**366
Pinto Jim, **2:**312
Pittsburgh American (newspaper), **2:**410
Pittsburgh Courier (newspaper), **1:**68–69, 116; **2:**260–61, 286, 303, 341, 345, 389, 410
Pittsburgh Kid (film), **1:**100
Poage, George, **1:**151; **2:**264, 283, 371
Police Academy films, **2:**337
Pollack, Syd, **2:**348–49
Pollard, Fritz, **2:**283–84, 304
Pollard, Fritz, Jr., **1:**7, 106; **2:**284–85
Poole, Harold, **2:**393
Posey, Cum, **1:**23–24; **2:**219, 285–86
Powell, Michael, **1:**29
Powels, George, **1:**103; **2:**308
Prairie View A & M, **1:**150
Predominantly white colleges and universities (PWCU), **1:**152, 154
Price, Bernie, **1:**24

GENERAL INDEX

Primer on College Football, A (Lewis), **1:**211
Professional Bowlers Association, **1:**42
Professional Football Hall of Fame
   Adderley, Herb, **1:**5
   Bell, Bobby, **1:**30–31
   Blount, Mel, **1:**36–37
   Brown, Jim, **1:**49–50
   Brown, Roosevelt, **1:**52
   Campbell, Earl, **1:**58–59
   Dickerson, Eric, **1:**83–84
   Greene, Joe, **1:**128–29
   Harris, Franco, **1:**139
   Johnson, John Henry, **1:**179
   Jones, David "Deacon," **1:**186
   Kelly, Leroy, **1:**195
   Lane, Dick, **1:**201
   Lott, Ronnie, **1:**216
   Mackey, John, **2:**220–21
   Matson, Ollie, **2:**227
   Mitchell, Bobby, **2:**237
   Moore, Lenny, **2:**243
   Motley, Marion, **2:**245–46
   Newsome, Ozzie, **2:**259
   Parker, Jim, **2:**276
   Payton, Walter, **2:**278–79
   Perry, Joe, **2:**282
   Renfro, Mel, **2:**297–98
   Sayers, Gale, **2:**323
   Shell, Art, **2:**326–27
   Simpson, O. J., **2:**331
   Singletary, Mike, **2:**332
   Swann, Lynn, **2:**352–53
   Tunnell, Emlen, **2:**374
   Upshaw, Gene, **2:**378–79
   Warfield, Paul, **2:**388–89
   Willis, Bill, **2:**407–8
   Winslow, Kellen, **2:**413
Professional Golfers Association, **1:**93, 124–25; **2:**342, 377, 397
Proposition 42 (NCAA), **2:**295
Proposition 48 (NCAA), **1:**66, 152; **2:**295
Protests. *See* Boycotts and protests
Pruett, Scott, **2:**300
Pryor, Aaron, **1:**46
Pryor, Richard, **1:**101; **2:**325
Puckett, Kirby, **2:**286–87
Purnell, J. Whipper, **2:**287
Pyle, Charles C. "Cash and Carry," **1:**6
Pythian Base Ball Club, **2:**287–88

Qawi, Dwight Muhammad, **2:**344
Quarry, Jerry, **1:**95

Racial theories, **2:**289–92
   Berlin Olympic Games and Nazi, **2:**265, 372
   Cobb on, **1:**74; **2:**290
   Louis-Schmeling fight and Nazi, **1:**217
   scholars on, **1:**156

Racism. *See* Apartheid; Boycotts and protests; Civil rights; Ku Klux Klan; Segregation and integration; Stereotypes
Radcliff, Alec, **2:**292
Radcliffe, Ted, **2:**292–93
Rainbow Coalition for Fairness in Athletics, **2:**293
Rampersad, Arnold, **1:**17, 155
Ramsey, Charles, **2:**392
Ransom, Samuel, **1:**23
Rashad, Ahmad, **2:**293–95
Raveling, George, **2:**295–96
Ray, Albert, **1:**199
Ray, Shawn, **2:**393
Reach Sporting Goods, **1:**203
Reed, Dwight, **2:**296
Reed, Vivian Brown, **1:**49
Reed, Willis, **2:**297
Reed-Smith, Andre, **2:**335
Reese, Sara Lomax, **1:**35
Remember the Titans (film), **1:**101
Remnick, David, **1:**153
Renfro, Mel, **2:**297–98
Retton, Mary Lou, **1:**135
Reynolds, Butch, **2:**298
Rhetta, B. M., **1:**10
Rhoden, William, **2:**345
Rhodes, Ray, **2:**298–99
Rhodes, Ted, **1:**125; **2:**299, 328, 342, 377, 397
Rhodesia, **1:**69
Ribbs, Willy T., **2:**300
Rice, Jerry, **1:**62; **2:**301
Richardson, Nolan, **1:**71; **2:**301–2, 369
Richmond, Bill, **1:**43; **2:**238, 302–3
Rickard, Tex, **1:**117
Rickey, Branch, **1:**69, 105; **2:**309
Ricks, "Pappy," **1:**24
Riefenstahl, Leni, **1:**102
Riskiev, Rufat, **2:**343, 344
Ritchie, Andrew, **1:**153
Rizzuto, Phil, **2:**398
Roberts, Eric, **2:**261
Roberts, Randy, **1:**153
Roberts, Ric, **2:**303
Roberts, Robin, **2:**230
Robertson, Oscar, **1:**25, 35, 39, 40; **2:**266, 303–4
Robeson, Paul, **1:**24, 101, 106, 167; **2:**304–5, 396
Robinson, Bill A. "Bojangles," **2:**370
Robinson, David, **2:**306
Robinson, Eddie, **1:**71, 152; **2:**307, 404, 423
Robinson, Frank, **2:**308–9, 409
Robinson, Jackie, **1:**16, 17, 22, 24–25, 57, 69, 100–101, 154–55, 167; **2:**243, 309–10, 311, 341, 349
Robinson, Mack, **1:**7; **2:**310–11, 372
Robinson, Sugar Ray, **1:**16, 45, 100; **2:**311–12
Rockefeller, Nelson, **2:**421
Rocky films, **1:**100
Rodgers, Johnny, **2:**313–14
Rogan, Wilbur, **2:**315
Rogers, George, **2:**315–16

GENERAL INDEX

Rogosin, Donn, **1:**154
Roosevelt, Franklin D., **1:**69, 126
Roosevelt, Theodore, **1:**106
Rose, Pete, **2:**243
Rosenbloom, Carroll, **2:**273
Ross, Barney, **1:**11
Roxborough, John, **1:**217
Rozelle, Pete, **1:**107
Rozier, Mike, **2:**316
Ruck, Rob, **1:**154
Rudolph, Wilma, **1:**16, 47, 49, 77, 102, 152, 161, 167; **2:**233, 265, 317, 362, 372, 373, 414
Runyan, Damon, **2:**292
Russell, Bill, **1:**16, 17, 25, 69, 96, 187; **2:**266, 318–19, 368
Russell, Cazzie, **2:**297, 319–20
Ruth, Babe, **1:**1, 6, 175; **2:**229, 230
Rutigliano, Sam, **1:**148

Saddler, Sandy, **1:**45
Saitch, "Bruiser," **1:**24
Salow, Morris, **1:**110
Salzberg, Charles, **1:**155
Sampson, Charles, **2:**313
Sampson, Ralph, **2:**321
Samuel, Tony, **1:**72
Sanders, Barry, **2:**321
Sanders, Deion, **2:**322
Sanders of the River (film), **1:**101
Sanford, G. Foster, **2:**304
Saperstein, Abe, **1:**24, 71, 138, 143; **2:**358
Sarron, Petey, **1:**11
Sayers, Gale, **1:**101; **2:**279, 323
Schiffer, Frank, **1:**105
Schlichter, H. Walter "Slick," **2:**251, 401
Schmeling, Max, **1:**44, 217
Schorling, John, **1:**110–11
Schroeder, Joyce Tanac, **1:**135
Schwartzwalder, Ben, **1:**49
Schwarzenegger, Arnold, **2:**393
Schwikert, Tasha, **1:**135
Scotch Hills Country Club. *See* Shady Rest Golf and Country Club
Scott, Charlie, **2:**324
Scott, Wendell, **2:**300, 324–25
Scott, William L., **2:**330
See-Saw Circle, **2:**361
Segregation and integration, **2:**289
  auto racing, **1:**171; **2:**325
  baseball, **1:**22–23, 69, 100–101, 154–55, 200; **2:**229, 255, 287–88, 303, 304, 309–10, 341, 387, 401, 422
  basketball, **1:**69, 75, 138, 198, 214–15; **2:**258, 318
  bodybuilding, **2:**392–94
  bowling, **1:**42, 69; **2:**252
  boxing, **1:**43–44, 85, 174, 176, 178, 202; **2:**234, 408
  coaching, **2:**301–2
  at Coachman celebration, **1:**73
  college athletics, **1:**68, 103, 107, 130, 142, 151, 195, 208–9; **2:**229, 328, 396

Segregation and integration *(continued)*
  fencing, **1:**99
  football, **1:**107, 195, 212; **2:**237, 328, 330, 351, 374, 390
  golf, **1:**123–25, 130–31; **2:**299, 342
  Henderson and, **1:**145
  high school athletics, **1:**121
  historians on, **1:**154–55
  hockey, **1:**69, 165–66
  horse racing, **1:**159–60
  McLendon's efforts at integration, **2:**233–34
  Nunn and *Pittsburgh Courier*, **2:**261
  rodeo, **2:**312–13
  sportswriters and, **2:**344–45
  swimming, **2:**353–54
  tennis, **1:**10, 69; **2:**363–64, 391, 394
  track and field, **1:**76; **2:**256–57
Selke, Frank, **1:**165
Sepia (magazine), **1:**54
Sergeant Joe Louis on Tour (film), **1:**100
Shady Rest Golf and Country Club, **1:**124; **2:**325–26
Shanahan, Mike, **2:**326
Sharkey, Jack, **2:**409
Sharman, Bill, **1:**187; **2:**318
Shavers, Ernie, **1:**158
Shavlakadze, Robert, **2:**367
Shaw University, **1:**63, 150, 151
Sheffield, John, **1:**199
Shell, Art, **2:**326–27
Shell, Donnie, **2:**261
Shelton, Bryan, **2:**364
Shippen, John, Jr., **1:**124; **2:**326, 327
Shockley, William B., **2:**291
Showboat (film), **1:**101
Shriver, Pam, **1:**118
Shula, Don, **2:**412
Sidat-Singh, Wilmeth, **1:**24; **2:**327–28
Sifford, Charlie, **1:**125; **2:**328–29, 377, 397
Silas, Paul, **1:**72; **2:**329–30
Silhouettes (newsletter), **2:**253
Silva, Chris, **2:**354
Simmons, Ozzie, **2:**330
Simmons, Ron, **2:**419
Simms, Willie, **2:**330–31
Simons, William, **1:**155
Simpson, O. J., **1:**101, 147; **2:**331
Sims, Billy, **2:**321
Singletary, Mike, **2:**332
Sinnette, Calvin, **1:**155
Sirhan, Sirhan, **1:**132
Skelly, Jack, **1:**43, 85
Slaight, Allan, **2:**367
Slater, "Duke," **2:**332–33
Slaughter, Fred, **1:**6–7
Slavery, **2:**333–34
Slavin, Frank, **1:**174
Sloan, Ted, **2:**331
Slocum, Hilton, **1:**24
Slowe, Lucy Diggs, **2:**334–35, 363

★ I-15 ★

GENERAL INDEX

Smith, Bruce, **2**:335–36
Smith, "Bubba," **1**:101; **2**:336–37
Smith, C. Lamont, **1**:7
Smith, Calvin, **1**:149
Smith, Charles. *See* Smith, "Bubba"
Smith, Emmitt, **2**:337–38
Smith, John, **2**:338–39, 391
Smith, Marshall, **2**:290
Smith, Ozzie, **2**:339
Smith, Ronald, **1**:155
Smith, Thomas, **1**:155
Smith, Tommie, **1**:29, 60, 70, 97; **2**:265, 266, 340, 372
Smith, Walker, Jr. *See* Robinson, Sugar Ray
Smith, "Wee Willie," **1**:24
Smith, Wendell, **1**:22, 69, 76; **2**:261, 341, 345
Smith, Will, **1**:100
Smith, Yvonne, **1**:156
Smythe, Conn, **1**:165
Snowden, Fred, **2**:341–42
Snyder, Jimmy "The Greek," **2**:291
Sol White's History of Colored Base Ball, **2**:401
Soldier's Story, A (film), **1**:101
Soria, Sixto, **2**:343, 344
Soul Train (television show), **2**:278–79
South Africa, **1**:69, 92
Southern Negro League. *See* Negro Southern League
Southwestern Athletic Conference, **1**:151
Southwestern Colored Cowboys Association, **2**:312–13
Sowell, Rick, **1**:199
Space Jam (film), **1**:102
Speedy, Walter, **1**:124
Spelman College, **1**:151
Spiller, Bill, **2**:328, 342, 397
Spinks, Leon, **1**:46, 158; **2**:260, 343
Spinks, Michael, **1**:46, 158; **2**:343–44
Spirit of the Times (newspaper), **1**:159
Spirit of Youth (film), **1**:100
Spivey, Donald, **1**:154, 155
Sports Illustrated (magazine), **1**:59; **2**:290–91
Sports Illustrated Women/Sport (magazine), **2**:355
Sportswriters, **2**:344–45
  Bostic, Joseph, **1**:41; **2**:345
  Cowans, Russ, **1**:76
  Lacy, Sam, **1**:199–200; **2**:345
  Nunn, William, Jr., **2**:260–61
  Nunn, William, Sr., **2**:261
  Roberts, Ric, **2**:303
  Smith, Wendell, **2**:341, 345
  Washington, Chester, **2**:389
  Wilson, Rollo, **2**:410
  Young, Andrew S. "Doc," **2**:421
  Young, Fay (Frank A.), **2**:422–23
Square Joe (film), **1**:176
St. Augustine's College, **1**:63
St. Julien, Marlon, **1**:160
St. Paul's College, **1**:63
Stadler, Joseph, **2**:264, 283
Stagg, Amos Alonzo, **2**:307
Stallone, Sylvester, **1**:100

Stallworth, Dave, **2**:346
Stallworth, John, **2**:261
Stanley, Marianne, **2**:236
Stargell, Willie, **2**:346–47
Starr, Bart, **1**:5, 201
Stearnes, Norman "Turkey," **2**:347, 395
Steinbrenner, George, **2**:411
Stent, Sophronia Pierce, **1**:99
Stereotypes
  in basketball films, **1**:102
  about black quarterbacks, **2**:241
  in boxing films, **1**:100
Stewart, Bobby, **2**:374
Stewart, Emanuel, **1**:144
Stewart, George, **2**:394
Stingley, Darryl, **2**:358
Stokes, Louise, **2**:282, 348
Stone, Oliver, **1**:101
Stone, Toni, **2**:348–49
Stovey, George, **2**:349–50
Strickland, Bill, **1**:7
Stringer, Vivian, **1**:71; **2**:350–51
Strode, Woody, **1**:101; **2**:351, 390
Strong, Nat, **1**:167, 168; **2**:251
Sullivan, James, **1**:88
Sullivan, John L., **1**:43, 85, 174
Super Bowl
  Adderley touchdown interception in, **1**:5
  establishment of, **1**:107
  Williams as first winning African-American quarterback, **2**:404
Supreme Court
  baseball's reserve clause challenge, **1**:103–4
  football and television contracts, **1**:107
Suttles, George "Mule," **2**:405
Swann, John, **2**:354
Swann, Lynn, **2**:352–53
Swoopes, Sheryl, **2**:267, 354–55

Taggert, Tomas D., Jr., **1**:200
Taliaferro, George, **2**:357
Tanner, James M., **2**:290
Tarkanian, Jerry, **1**:120
Tatum, Jack, **2**:357–58
Tatum, Reece "Goose," **1**:138, 143, 204; **2**:358
Taw, Len, **2**:264
Taylor, Charles, **2**:359
Taylor, John Baxter, **1**:151; **2**:264–65, 289, 359–60
Taylor, Lawrence, **2**:360–61
Taylor, Marshall "Major," **1**:16, 68; **2**:289, 360–61
Television. *See* Films and television
Temple, Ed, **1**:4, 71, 77, 161; **2**:233, 362, 373, 375, 414
Temple University, **1**:35
Tennessee A & I, **1**:151
Tennessee State University, **1**:152; **2**:354, 362, 414
Terrell, Kim, **1**:42
Terry, John, **2**:392
Theismann, Joe, **2**:280
Thomas, Debra, **2**:267, 364–65

★ I-16 ★

GENERAL INDEX

Thomas, Frank, **2:**365
Thomas, Isiah, **2:**366–67
Thomas, John, **2:**367
Thomas, Thurman, **2:**335
Thomas, Wendell, **1:**199
Thompson, David, **2:**367–68
Thompson, John, **1:**98; **2:**368–69
Thomson, John, **1:**146
Thorpe, Jim, **1:**125; **2:**284
Tick Tick Tick (film), **1:**101
Tidye Pickett, **2:**265
Tiger, Dick, **1:**110
Title IX, **2:**414
Tittle, Y. A., **2:**273
Tolan, Eddie, **1:**126; **2:**289, 369–70, 371
Tomas, Enrico, **2:**393
Tomlinson, Nikki, **1:**99
Torrence, Gwen, **2:**370
Towering Inferno, The (film), **1:**101
Traveling All-Stars & Motor Kings (film), **1:**101
Tribune Independent (newspaper), **1:**76
Tricard, Louis Mead, **2:**362
Troye, Edward, **1:**159
Truman, Harry S., **1:**73
Tunnell, Emlen, **1:**16; **2:**374
Tunney, Gene, **1:**104; **2:**408, 409
Turner, Ted, **1:**2
Tuskegee Institute, **1:**2, 124, 150, 151, 152; **2:**363, 414
Tygiel, Jules, **1:**153, 155; **2:**345
Tyler, Dorothy, **1:**73
Tyson, Cicely, **1:**102
Tyson, Mike, **1:**46; **2:**344, 374–75
Tyus, Wyomia, **2:**362, 372, 373, 375–76

Ueberroth, Peter, **1:**92
Unitas, Johnny, **2:**243
United Golfer (magazine), **2:**377
United Golfers Association, **1:**93, 124, 131; **2:**299, 326, 328, 377, 397
United States Colored Golfers Association. *See* United Golfers Association
United States Golf Association (USGA), **1:**125, 130–31; **2:**377
United States Lawn Tennis Association (USLTA), **1:**10, 121; **2:**363, 394
United States League (Negro baseball), **1:**129
United States Tennis Association, **2:**364
Unseld, Wes, **2:**378
Upshaw, Gene, **2:**326, 378–79
U.S. Golf Association, **2:**327
USA Track and Field, **2:**371
Uzcudun, Paolino, **2:**409

Vandenberg, Wayne, **1:**28
Vann, Robert L., **2:**261, 389
Vaughn, Govoner, **1:**173
Veeck, Bill, **1:**86, 205
Venable, Charlie, **1:**42
Vertinsky, Patricia, **1:**156
Virginia State University, **1:**63, 151

Virginia Union University, **1:**63, 150
Vitale, John, **1:**213

Wake-Robin Golf Club, **1:**124; **2:**383
Walcott, "Jersey Joe," **1:**45, 66
Walcott, Joe, **2:**383–84
Waldorf, Lyn, **1:**176–77
Walker, Herschel, **2:**267, 384–85
Walker, Leroy, **2:**373, 385–86
Walker, Mel, **2:**386
Walker, Moses Fleetwood, **1:**22, 68; **2:**350, 386–87
Walker, Weldy, **2:**387
Wallace, Coley, **1:**100
Wallace, Nunc, **1:**85
Walsh, Christy, **1:**6, 16
Walsh, Stella, **1:**200
Walter, Mickey, **1:**104
Ward, Charlie, **2:**387–88
Warfield, Paul, **2:**388–89
Warmund, Joram, **1:**155
Warner, Ed, **1:**25
Warner, Pop, **2:**307
Washington, Allen, **1:**63
Washington, Benjamin, **1:**168
Washington, Booker T., **1:**2
Washington, Chester, **2:**389
Washington, Denzel, **1:**100, 101, 102
Washington, Gene, **2:**389–90
Washington, Jim, **1:**153
Washington, Kenny, **2:**351, 390
Washington, MaliVai, **2:**364
Washington, Marian, **2:**415
Washington, Ora, **2:**363, 391
Washington, Rudy, **1:**34
Washington Tribune (newspaper), **1:**200
Watkins, Fenwich, **1:**24
Watts, Bobby, **1:**137
Watts, Quincy, **2:**339, 391–92
Wave Community Newspapers, **2:**389
WCBM, **1:**41
Weathers, Carl, **1:**100, 101
Weider, Joe, **2:**393
Weir, Reginald, **2:**363, 394
Wells, Melvin, **2:**393
Wells, Willie, **2:**395
Wepner, Chuck, **1:**214
Wertz, Vic, **2:**229
West, Charlie, **2:**396
West, Jerry, **1:**39; **2:**297, 304
West, Mae, **1:**179
Westbrook, Peter, **1:**99; **2:**267
Wheeler, Flex, **2:**393
Wheeler, Howard, **1:**125; **2:**328, 377, 397
Wheeler, John N., **1:**16
When We Were Kings (documentary), **1:**100
Whitaker, Pernell, **2:**266
White, Bill, **2:**397–98
White, Charles, **1:**9–10
White, Jacob, **2:**287
White, Jo Jo, **2:**398–99

★ I-17 ★

GENERAL INDEX

White Men Can't Jump (film), **1**:102
White, Morgan, **1**:135
White, Reggie, **2**:399–400
White, Sherman, **2**:400
White, Sol, **1**:168; **2**:400–401
White, Willye, **2**:228, 401–2
Whitfield, Fred, **2**:313
Whitfield, Mal, **2**:402
Wicks, Sidney, **2**:403
Wiggins, David, **1**:154, 155–56
Wilberforce University, **1**:124, 150
Wilbon, Michael, **2**:345
Wiley College, **1**:150
Wilkerson, John, **1**:118
Wilkes, Keith, **1**:102
Wilkie, Wendell, **1**:202
Wilkins, Lenny, **1**:72
Wilkinson, G. C., **1**:168
Wilkinson, J. L., **2**:252, 254
Wilkinson, John F. N., **1**:10
Willard, Jess, **1**:44, 100
William Morris Agency, **1**:6
Williams, Archie, **1**:7; **2**:372, 403
Williams, Billy Dee, **1**:101
Williams, Bobby, **1**:72
Williams, Charles H., **1**:63
Williams, Doug, **2**:307, 404
Williams, Hank, **1**:24
Williams, Henry L., **2**:225
Williams, Ike, **1**:45; **2**:404–5
Williams, Joseph "Smokey", **2**:405
Williams, Linda, **1**:156
Williams, Lucinda, **1**:161; **2**:228
Williams, Serena, **1**:102; **2**:364, 406, 407
Williams, Venus, **1**:102; **2**:364, 406, 407
Williamson, Fred, **1**:101
Willingham, Tyrone, **1**:72
Willis, Bill, **2**:246, 407–8
Willis, Willie, **1**:42
Wills, Harry, **1**:44, 176; **2**:408–9
Wills, Maury, **2**:409
Wills Moody, Helen, **2**:363, 391
Wilma (television film), **1**:102
Wilson, Clyde, **1**:42
Wilson, Rollo, **2**:410
Wilson, Tome, **2**:255
Winfield, Dave, **2**:410–11
Winkfield, Jimmy, **1**:160; **2**:411–12
Winkfield, Robert, **1**:160
Winslow, Kellen, **2**:412–13
Winston-Salem University, **1**:63
Winter, Tex, **1**:39
Witt, Katarina, **2**:267, 365
Womble, Warren, **1**:39
Women, **2**:413–14
  Adams, Lucinda, **1**:4–5
  Ashford, Evelyn, **1**:15
  biographies of, **1**:153
  Black Women in Sports Foundation, **1**:35
  Brisco-Hooks, Valerie, **1**:46–48

Women *(continued)*
  Coachman, Alice, **1**:72–74
  Daniels, Isabelle, **1**:77
  Dawes, Dominique, **1**:80
  De Frantz, Anita, **1**:81–82
  Devers, Gail, **1**:82–83
  Edwards, Teresa, **1**:92–93
  Faggs, Mae, **1**:99
  Garrison, Zina, **1**:118
  Gibson, Althea, **1**:120–21
  Green, Tina Sloan, **1**:199
  Gregory, Ann, **1**:130–31
  Hightower, Stephanie, **1**:146–47
  historians on, **1**:156
  historically black colleges and universities, **1**:152
  Hudson, Martha, **1**:161
  Hymes, Lula Mae, **1**:162–63
  Jones, Barbara, **1**:185–86
  Jones, Marion, **1**:188
  Joyner-Kersee, Jackie, **1**:191–93
  Lane, Betty Jean, **1**:200
  Leslie, Lisa, **1**:207–8
  Manley, Effa, **2**:223
  Manning-Mims, Madeline, **2**:224–25
  Matthews, Margaret, **2**:227–28
  McDaniel, Mildred, **2**:231
  McGee, Pam, **2**:231–32
  McGuire, Edith, **2**:232–33
  Miller, Cheryl, **2**:236
  Montgomery, Eleanor, **2**:240
  Patterson, Mickey, **2**:277–78
  Pickett, Tidye, **2**:282–83
  Reed, Vivian Brown, **1**:49
  Rudolph, Wilma, **2**:317
  Slowe, Lucy Diggs, **2**:334–35
  Stokes, Louise, **2**:348
  Torrence, Gwen, **2**:370
  Tyus, Wyomia, **2**:375–76
  Washington, Ora, **2**:391
  White, Willye, **2**:401–2
Women's Basketball Hall of Fame
  Stringer, Vivian, **2**:350–51
Women's International Bowling Congress, **1**:42; **2**:252
Wood, Wilbur, **1**:23
Woodard, Lynette, **2**:267
Wooden, John, **1**:3, 123, 183; **2**:258
Woodman, Joe, **1**:201
Woodruff, John, **1**:7; **2**:371–72, 416
Woods, Eldrick "Tiger," **1**:102, 125; **2**:416–17
Woodson, Carter G., **1**:153
Woodward, Lynette, **2**:415–16
World Boxing Council, **1**:46
Worthy, James, **2**:418
Wright, Archibald Lee. *See* Moore, Archie
Wright, Ernie, **2**:252
Wright, Stan, **2**:373
Wright, William H., **1**:10

Xavier University, **1**:151

Yancey, Bill, **1**:24
Yancey, Joseph J., **2**:256
Yang, C. K., **1**:183
YMCA (Young Men's Christian Associations), **1**:99
Yoshida, Toshiaki, **2**:382
Young, Andrew S. "Doc," **1**:153; **2**:421
Young, Buddy, **2**:421–22
Young, Fay (Frank A.), **1**:76; **2**:345, 422–23
Young, Kevin, **2**:339
Young, Monroe, **2**:255

Young, Whitney, **1**:144
Younger, Paul "Tank," **2**:423
YWCA (Young Women's Christian Associations), **1**:99

Zang, David W., **1**:153
Zouski, Steve, **1**:109
Zuk, Bob, **2**:347
Zurita, Juan, **2**:405

SPORTS INDEX

Auto racing, **2:**324–25
  Jack, "Rajo," **1:**171
  Ribbs, Willy T., **2:**300
  segregation and integration, **1:**171; **2:**325

Baseball, **1:**21–23
  Aaron, Hank, **1:**1–2
  American Negro League, **2:**253
  Ashford, Emmett, **1:**13–14
  Banks, Ernie, **1:**19
  Baylor, Don, **1:**27, 72
  Bell, James "Cool Papa," **1:**22, 31–32
  Bolden, Edward, **1:**37–38
  Bonds, Barry, **1:**38–39
  Brock, Louis, **1:**48
  Campanella, Roy, **1:**57–58
  Charleston, Oscar, **1:**22, 67
  coaching and managerial positions, **1:**23, 72
  Doby, Larry, **1:**86
  East-West All-Star Game, **1:**22, 129; **2:**252
  East-West League, **2:**253, 254
  Eastern Colored League, **1:**91; **2:**253, 254
  films about, **1:**100–101
  Flood, Curt, **1:**103–4
  Foster, Rube, **1:**22, 110–11
  Gibson, Bob, **1:**121–22
  Gibson, Josh, **1:**22, 122
  Grant, Frank, **1:**127
  Greenlee, Gus, **1:**22, 129
  Griffey, Ken, Jr., **1:**132–33
  Gwynn, Tony, **1:**134
  Henderson, Rickey, **1:**146
  historically black colleges and universities, **1:**150, 151–52
  Irvin, Monte, **1:**169
  Jackson, Bo, **1:**171–72
  Jackson, Reggie, **1:**175
  Johnson, William "Judy," **1:**184
  League of Colored Base Ball Players, **1:**203
  Leonard, Buck, **1:**205–6
  Lloyd, John Henry, **1:**215–16
  Mackey, Biz, **2:**219
  Manley, Effa, **2:**223
  Matthews, William Clarence, **2:**228–29
  Mays, Willie, **2:**229–30
  McCovey, Willie, **2:**230
  Morgan, Joe, **2:**243–44
  Murray, Eddie, **2:**248
  National Association of Colored Base Ball Clubs of the United States and Cuba, **2:**251
  Negro American League, **1:**22; **2:**252–53, 255

Baseball *(continued)*
  Negro leagues, **1:**110–11, 153–54
  Negro National League, **1:**22, 37, 41, 54, 67, 91, 111, 129, 169; **2:**223, 252, 253, 254, 255, 261, 422
  Negro Southern League, **2:**253, 254, 255
  Negro World Series, **1:**38
  O'Neil, Buck, **2:**269–70
  Paige, Satchel, **2:**275
  Posey, Cum, **2:**285–86
  Puckett, Kirby, **2:**286–87
  Radcliffe, Ted, **2:**292–93
  reserve clause challenge of Curt Flood, **1:**103–4
  Robinson, Frank, **2:**308–9
  Robinson, Jackie, **1:**17, 22, 57, 69, 100–101
  Rogan, Wilbur, **2:**315
  Sanders, Deion, **2:**322
  segregation and integration, **1:**22–23, 69, 100–101, 154–55, 200; **2:**229, 255, 287–88, 303, 304, 309–10, 341, 387, 401, 422
  Smith, Ozzie, **2:**339
  sportswriters and, **2:**345
  Stargell, Willie, **2:**346–47
  Stearnes, Norman "Turkey," **2:**347
  Stone, Toni, **2:**348–49
  Stovey, George, **2:**349–50
  Thomas, Frank, **2:**365
  Walker, Moses Fleetwood, **1:**22; **2:**386–87
  Wells, Willie, **2:**395
  White, Bill, **2:**397–98
  White, Sol, **2:**400–401
  Williams, Joseph "Smokey," **2:**405
  Wills, Maury, **2:**409
  Winfield, Dave, **2:**410–11
  See also Most Valuable Player (major league baseball); National Baseball Hall of Fame

Basketball, **1:**23–26
  Abdul-Jabbar, Kareem, **1:**3–4
  Archibald, Nate, **1:**11
  Barkley, Charles, **1:**19–20
  Barksdale, Don, **1:**20–21
  Baylor, Elgin, **1:**28
  Bellamy, Walter, **1:**32–33
  Bing, Dave, **1:**33
  Boozer, Bob, **1:**39–40
  Brown, Roger, **1:**51
  Bryant, Kobe, **1:**52–53
  Chamberlain, Wilt, **1:**64–65
  Chaney, John, **1:**65–66
  Clifton, Nat "Sweetwater," **1:**71
  coaching and managerial positions, **1:**72
  Cooper, Chuck, **1:**25, 69, 75

SPORTS INDEX

Basketball (continued)
   Dantley, Adrian, **1**:77–78
   Dukes, Walter, **1**:89
   Edwards, Teresa, **1**:92–93
   Embry, Wayne, **1**:95–96
   Erving, Julius, **1**:96
   Ewing, Patrick, **1**:97–98
   films about, **1**:101–2
   Ford, Phil, **1**:108
   Gaines, Clarence "Bighouse," **1**:115
   Gervin, George, **1**:119–20
   Gibson, Bob, **1**:121–22
   Gilmore, Artis, **1**:122–23
   Greer, Hal, **1**:130
   Gregory, George, Jr., **1**:131
   Harlem Globetrotters, **1**:24, 25, 64, 71, 89, 121, 137–38, 143, 173, 204–5; **2**:358, 415
   Harlem Magicians, **1**:75, 143
   Hawkins, Connie, **1**:140–41
   Hayes, Elvin, **1**:142
   Haynes, Marques, **1**:142–43
   Haywood, Spencer, **1**:143–44
   Henderson, Edwin Bancroft, **1**:23
   Hill, Grant, **1**:148–49
   historically black colleges and universities, **1**:151
   Jackson, Mannie, **1**:173
   Johnson, Magic, **1**:16, 26
   Johnson, Robert L., **1**:183–84
   Jones, K. C., **1**:107
   Jones, Sam, **1**:188–89
   Jones, Wali, **1**:189–90
   Jordan, Michael, **1**:26, 190–91
   King, William "Dolly," **1**:197–98
   Lanier, Bob, **1**:202–3
   Lemon, Meadowlark, **1**:203–5
   Leslie, Lisa, **1**:207–8
   Lloyd, Earl, **1**:214–15
   Malone, Moses, **2**:222–23
   Manning, Danny, **2**:224
   McGee, Pam, **2**:231–32
   McLendon, John, **2**:233–34
   Miller, Cheryl, **2**:236
   Monroe, Earl, **2**:239–40
   Murphy, Calvin, **2**:246–47
   New York Renaissance Five, **1**:24; **2**:257–58
   Olajuwon, Hakeem, **2**:263–64
   Olympic Games, **2**:266
   O'Neal, Shaquille, **2**:268–69
   Posey, Cum, **2**:285–86
   Raveling, George, **2**:295–96
   Reed, Willis, **2**:297
   Richardson, Nolan, **2**:301–2
   Robertson, Oscar, **2**:303–4
   Robinson, David, **2**:306
   Russell, Bill, **2**:318–19
   Russell, Cazzie, **2**:319–20
   Scott, Charlie, **2**:324
   segregation and integration, **1**:69, 75, 138, 198, 214–15; **2**:258, 318
   Sidat-Singh, Wilmeth, **2**:327–28

Basketball (continued)
   Silas, Paul, **2**:329–30
   slam dunk, **1**:141
   Snowden, Fred, **2**:341–42
   Stallworth, Dave, **2**:346
   Stringer, Vivian, **2**:350–51
   Swoopes, Sheryl, **2**:354–55
   Tatum, Reece "Goose," **2**:358
   Thompson, David, **2**:367–68
   Thompson, John, **2**:368–69
   Unseld, Wes, **2**:378
   Ward, Charlie, **2**:387–88
   Washington, Ora, **2**:391
   White, Jo Jo, **2**:398–99
   White, Sherman, **2**:400
   Wicks, Sidney, **2**:403
   Woodward, Lynette, **2**:415–16
   Worthy, James, **2**:418
   See also All-Americans (college basketball); Most Valuable Player (American Basketball Association); Most Valuable Player (National Basketball Association); Most Valuable Player (Women's National Basketball Association); Naismith Memorial Basketball Hall of Fame
Bobsled, **1**:119; **2**:385
Bodybuilding, **2**:392–94
Bowling, **1**:42
   National Bowling Association, **2**:252
   segregation and integration, **1**:42, 69; **2**:252
Boxing, **1**:43–46
   Ali, Muhammad, **1**:8–9, 45–46
   Armstrong, Henry, **1**:11–12, 45
   Charles, Ezzard, **1**:45, 66
   Dixon, George, **1**:43, 85–86
   Ellis, Jimmy, **1**:95
   films about, **1**:100
   Flowers, Tiger, **1**:44, 104
   Foreman, George, **1**:46, 109
   Foster, Bob, **1**:46, 110
   Frazier, Joe, **1**:46, 112
   Gans, Joe, **1**:44, 117
   Golden Gloves, **1**:44, 45
   Hagler, "Marvelous" Marvin, **1**:46, 137
   Hearns, Thomas, **1**:46, 144
   Holmes, Larry, **1**:46, 158
   Jackson, Peter, **1**:173–75
   Jeannette, Joe, **1**:176
   Johnson, Jack, **1**:44, 178–79
   King, Don, **1**:196–97
   Langford, Sam, **1**:201–2
   Leonard, Sugar Ray, **1**:46, 206–7
   Lewis, John Henry, **1**:210–11
   Liston, Sonny, **1**:45, 213–14
   Louis, Joe, **1**:44, 45, 217
   McVey, Sam, **2**:234
   Molineaux, Tom, **2**:237–38
   Moore, Archie, **1**:45; **2**:241–42
   Norton, Ken, **2**:260
   Olympic Games, **2**:266
   Patterson, Floyd, **1**:45; **2**:276–77

Boxing *(continued)*
    Richmond, Bill, **2:**302–3
    Robinson, Sugar Ray, **1:**45; **2:**311–12
    segregation and integration, **1:**43–44, 85, 174, 176, 178, 202; **2:**234, 408
    slavery and, **2:**334
    Spinks, Leon, **1:**46; **2:**343
    Spinks, Michael, **2:**343–44
    Tyson, Mike, **1:**46; **2:**374–75
    Walcott, Joe, **2:**383
    Williams, Ike, **2:**404–5
    Wills, Harry, **2:**408–9
    See also Boxing Hall of Fame; International Boxing Hall of Fame

Cycling, **2:**361–62

Fencing, **1:**99
Figure skating, **2:**364–65
Football, **1:**105–8
    Abbott, Cleveland, **1:**2
    Adderley, Herb, **1:**5
    Allen, Marcus, **1:**9–10
    Alley-Oop pass, **2:**273
    Bass, Dick, **1:**26–27
    Bell, Bill, **1:**29–30
    Bell, Bobby, **1:**30–31
    Blount, Mel, **1:**36–37
    Brown, Jim, **1:**49–50
    Brown, Larry, **1:**50–51
    Brown, Roosevelt, **1:**52
    Bullock, Matthew, **1:**53–54
    Campbell, Earl, **1:**58–59
    Carmichael, Harold, **1:**61
    Caroline, J. C., **1:**61–62
    Carter, Cris, **1:**62–63
    Davis, Ernie, **1:**78–79
    Dickerson, Eric, **1:**83–84
    Drew, Charles, **1:**87–88
    Eller, Carl, **1:**94–95
    films about, **1:**101
    Flippin, George, **1:**102–3
    Follis, Charles, **1:**105
    free agent compensation, **2:**273
    Gaither, Jake, **1:**115–16
    Galimore, Willie, **1:**116
    Garrett, Mike, **1:**117–18
    Gault, Willie, **1:**119
    Gray, Edward, **1:**128
    Greene, Joe, **1:**128–29
    Grier, Rosey, **1:**132
    Harris, Franco, **1:**139
    Hayes, Bob, **1:**141–42
    Hill, Calvin, **1:**147–48
    Hines, Jim, **1:**149
    historically black colleges and universities, **1:**150, 152
    Holland, Jerome Brud, **1:**157
    Jackson, Bo, **1:**171–72
    Jackson, Levi, **1:**172

Football *(continued)*
    Jefferson, Bernie, **1:**176–77
    Johnson, John Henry, **1:**179
    Jones, David "Deacon," **1:**186
    Kelly, Leroy, **1:**195
    Kemp, Ray, **1:**195–96
    Keyes, Leroy, **1:**196
    Lane, Dick, **1:**201
    LeVias, Jerry, **1:**208–9
    Lewis, William Henry, **1:**211–12
    Lipscomb, Gene "Big Daddy," **1:**213
    Little, Floyd, **1:**214
    Lott, Ronnie, **1:**216
    Mackey, John, **2:**220–21
    Marshall, Bob, **2:**225–26
    Marshall, Jim, **2:**226
    Matson, Ollie, **2:**227
    Mitchell, Bobby, **2:**237
    Monk, Art, **2:**238–39
    Moon, Warren, **2:**240–41
    Moore, Lenny, **2:**242–43
    Motley, Marion, **2:**245–46
    Nehemiah, Renaldo, **2:**256
    Newsome, Ozzie, **2:**259
    origins of, **1:**105–6
    Owens, R. C., **2:**272–73
    Parker, Jim, **2:**276
    Payton, Walter, **2:**278–79
    Pearson, Drew, **2:**279–80
    Perkins, Don, **2:**281
    Perry, Joe, **2:**282
    Pollard, Fritz, **2:**283–84
    Rashad, Ahmad, **2:**293–95
    Reed, Dwight, **2:**296
    Renfro, Mel, **2:**297–98
    reserve clause challenge of John Mackey, **2:**220
    Rhodes, Ray, **2:**298–99
    Rice, Jerry, **2:**301
    Robinson, Eddie, **2:**307
    Rodgers, Johnny, **2:**313–14
    Rozier, Mike, **2:**316
    Sanders, Barry, **2:**321
    Sanders, Deion, **2:**322
    Sayers, Gale, **1:**101; **2:**323
    segregation and integration, **1:**107, 195, 212; **2:**237, 328, 330, 351, 374, 390
    semiprofessional, **1:**106
    Shell, Art, **2:**326–27
    Sidat-Singh, Wilmeth, **2:**327–28
    Simmons, Ozzie, **2:**330
    Simpson, O. J., **2:**331
    Singletary, Mike, **2:**332
    Slater, "Duke," **2:**332–33
    Smith, Bruce, **2:**335–36
    Smith, Emmitt, **2:**337–38
    Strode, Woody, **2:**351
    Swann, Lynn, **2:**352–53
    Taliaferro, George, **2:**357
    Tatum, Jack, **2:**357–58
    Taylor, Charles, **2:**359

SPORTS INDEX

Football *(continued)*
   Taylor, Lawrence, **2**:360–61
   Tunnell, Emlen, **2**:374
   Upshaw, Gene, **2**:378–79
   Walker, Herschel, **2**:384–85
   Warfield, Paul, **2**:388–89
   Washington, Gene, **2**:389–90
   Washington, Kenny, **2**:390
   West, Charlie, **2**:396
   White, Reggie, **2**:399–400
   Williams, Doug, **2**:404
   Willis, Bill, **2**:407–8
   Winslow, Kellen, **2**:412–13
   Young, Buddy, **2**:421–22
   Younger, Paul "Tank," **2**:423
   See also All-Americans (college football); Heisman Trophy; Most Valuable Player (National Football League); Professional Football Hall of Fame; Super Bowl

Golf, **1**:123–25
   caddies, **1**:93, 123–24
   Elder, Lee, **1**:93–94
   films about, **1**:102
   Gregory, Ann, **1**:130–31
   Mapledale Country Club, **2**:377
   Peete, Calvin, **2**:280–81
   Rhodes, Ted, **2**:299
   segregation and integration, **1**:123–25, 130–31; **2**:299, 342
   Shady Rest Golf and Country Club, **1**:124; **2**:325–26
   Shippen, John, Jr., **1**:124; **2**:327
   Sifford, Charlie, **2**:328–29
   Spiller, Bill, **2**:342
   tee invention for, **1**:124
   Wake-Robin Golf Club, **1**:124, 383
   Wheeler, Howard, **2**:397
   Woods, Eldrick "Tiger," **1**:125; **2**:416–17
Gymnastics, **1**:134–35
   Dawes, Dominique, **1**:80, 135
   Olympic Games, **2**:267

Handball, **2**:263
Hockey. *See* Ice hockey
Horse racing, **1**:159–60
   American style of, **2**:331
   Lewis, Oliver, **1**:211
   Murphy, Isaac, **2**:247–48
   race result form development, **1**:211
   segregation and integration, **1**:159–60
   Simms, Willie, **2**:330–31
   slavery and, **2**:334
   Winkfield, Jimmy, **2**:411–12

Ice hockey, **1**:165–66
   Dorrington, Arthur, **1**:69, 87
   O'Ree, Willie, **2**:270
   segregation and integration, **1**:69, 165–66

Lacrosse, **1**:199

Pedestrian racing, **1**:139–40

Race car driving. *See* Auto racing
Rodeo, **1**:36; **2**:312–13
Rowing, **2**:333–34
   De Frantz, Anita, **1**:81–82
Rugby, **1**:105

Swimming, **2**:267, 353–54

Tennis, **2**:363–64
   American Tennis Association, **1**:10
   Ashe, Arthur, Jr., **1**:12–13, 16, 17, 102; **2**:363, 364
   films about, **1**:102
   Garrison, Zina, **1**:118
   Gibson, Althea, **1**:10, 12, 16, 69, 118, 120–21; **2**:363–64
   segregation and integration, **1**:10, 69; **2**:363–64, 391, 394
   Slowe, Lucy Diggs, **2**:334–35
   Washington, Ora, **2**:391
   Weir, Reginald, **2**:394
   Williams, Serena, **1**:102; **2**:406
   Williams, Venus, **1**:102; **2**:407
   See also International Tennis Hall of Fame
Track and Field, **2**:371–73
   Abbott, Cleveland, **1**:2
   Adams, Lucinda, **1**:4–5
   Albritton, David, **1**:7–8
   amateurism rules challenged by Nehemiah, **2**:256
   Ashford, Evelyn, **1**:15
   Beamon, Bob, **1**:28–29
   Borican, John, **1**:40
   Boston, Ralph, **1**:41–42
   Brisco-Hooks, Valerie, **1**:46–48
   Butler, Sol, **1**:55
   Calhoun, Lee, **1**:57
   Campbell, Milt, **1**:59
   Carlos, John, **1**:60
   coaches in, **2**:373
   Coachman, Alice, **1**:72–74
   Corbitt, Ted, **1**:75–76
   Daniels, Isabelle, **1**:77
   Devers, Gail, **1**:82–83
   Dillard, Harrison, **1**:84–85
   Drew, Howard, **1**:88
   drug-testing challenge of Butch Reynolds, **2**:298
   Faggs, Mae, **1**:99
   films about, **1**:102
   Gault, Willie, **1**:119
   Gordon, Ed, Jr., **1**:125–26
   Gourdin, Ned, **1**:126–27
   Griffith-Joyner, Florence, **1**:133
   Hayes, Bob, **1**:141–42
   Hightower, Stephanie, **1**:146–47
   Hines, Jim, **1**:149
   historically black colleges and universities, **1**:151, 152

Track and Field *(continued)*
    Holman, Steve, **1:**157–58
    Hubbard, William Dehart, **1:**161
    Hudson, Martha, **1:**161
    Hymes, Lula Mae, **1:**162–63
    Johnson, Cornelius, **1:**177–78
    Johnson, Michael, **1:**181–82
    Johnson, Rafer, **1:**182–83
    Jones, Barbara, **1:**185–86
    Jones, Hayes, **1:**186–87
    Jones, Marion, **1:**188
    Joyner-Kersee, Jackie, **1:**191–93
    Lane, Betty Jean, **1:**200
    Lewis, Carl, **1:**209–10
    LuValle, James, **1:**218
    Manning-Mims, Madeline, **2:**224–25
    Matson, Ollie, **2:**227
    Matthews, Margaret, **2:**227–28
    McDaniel, Mildred, **2:**231
    McGuire, Edith, **2:**232–33
    Metcalfe, Ralph, **2:**235
    Milburn, Rod, **2:**235–36
    Montgomery, Eleanor, **2:**240
    Moses, Edwin, **2:**244
    Nehemiah, Renaldo, **2:**256
    New York Pioneer Club, **1:**76
    O'Brien, Dan, **2:**263
    Olympic, **2:**264–66, 371–73
    Owens, Jesse, **2:**271–72
    Patterson, Mickey, **2:**277–78
    Pickett, Tidye, **2:**282–83
    Poage, George, **2:**283
    Pollard, Fritz, Jr., **2:**284–85

Track and Field *(continued)*
    Reed, Vivian Brown, **1:**49
    Reynolds, Butch, **2:**298
    Robinson, Mack, **2:**310–11
    Rudolph, Wilma, **2:**317
    segregation and integration, **1:**76; **2:**256–57
    slavery and, **2:**334
    Smith, John, **2:**338–39
    Smith, Tommie, **2:**340
    Stokes, Louise, **2:**348
    Taylor, John Baxter, **2:**359–60
    Temple, Ed, **2:**362
    Thomas, John, **2:**367
    Tolan, Eddie, **2:**369–70
    Torrence, Gwen, **2:**370
    Tyus, Wyomia, **2:**375–76
    Walker, Leroy, **2:**385–86
    Walker, Mel, **2:**386
    Watts, Quincy, **2:**391–92
    White, Willye, **2:**401–2
    Whitfield, Mal, **2:**402
    Williams, Archie, **2:**403
    Woodruff, John, **2:**416
    See also National Track and Field Hall of Fame

Ultramarathon running, **1:**75–76
    See also Pedestrian racing

Volleyball, **1:**65; **2:**381–82

Weightlifting, **2:**392, 394
    Davis, John Henry, **1:**79
Wrestling, **2:**418–19

Ref.
GV
583
.A567

2004
v.1